GNVQ3

John Ellison   Jim Bedingfield   Tom Harrison

The authors are all Senior Lecturers in Law at New College Durham

Business Education Publishers Ltd

1993 M

ISBN 0 907679 55 2

First published in 1993

Cover Design by Caroline White
Illustrations by Gerard Callaghan

Published in Great Britain by Business Education Publishers Ltd.

Sales Office
Leighton House 10 Grange Crescent Stockton Road
Sunderland Tyne & Wear SR2 7BN
Telephone 091 567 4963 Fax 091 514 3277

British Cataloguing-in-Publications Data
A catalogue record for this book is available from the British Library

Printed in Great Britain by BPCC Wheatons Ltd Hennock Road Marsh Barton Exeter EX2 8RP

Preface

This book has been written to meet the requirements of the GNVQ option unit Business Law. Its comprehensive and up to date text provides full coverage of the option syllabus. Activities, unit test questions and assignments in each of its chapters provide the opportunity for students to confirm their achievements of learning and understanding and can be used as a complete assessment framework.

For ease of expression the book adopts the practice of using 'he' for 'he or she' and 'his' for 'his or hers'.

Emphasis has been placed upon setting business law in its broader commercial context. An introductory chapter examining the idea of law and certain key aspects of the English legal system is included to assist students studying law for the first time.

JE
JB
TH

Acknowledgements

We would like to thank Caroline, Moira, Gerard and Paul at Business Education Publishers for all the assistance they have provided in the production of this book. Most especially we must record our thanks to our tolerant and long suffering wives and children.

All errors and omissions remain the responsibility of the authors.

The law is stated as at 1st September 1993

JE JB TH

Durham
September 1993

Table of Contents

Chapter 4
Contractual Agreements in Business
The Nature and Scope of

Chapter 5
Rights of Business Customers and Consumers

Table of Cases

Chapter 1

An Introduction to Business Law

The Nature and Purpose of Law

The principal objective of a legal system is the establishment of rules which in the broadest sense are designed to regulate relationships. Human societies are highly complex social structures. Without systems of rules or codes of conduct to control them, such societies would find it difficult to maintain their cohesion, and would gradually break up. The interdependence of each member of the community with its other members brings people into constant contact and this contact sometimes leads to disagreement and conflict. It is unrealistic to expect in a Western culture like ours which recognises that people should have the freedom to express their individualism, there will never be occasions when the activities of one person interfere with those of another. Someone operating a commercial enterprise by selling second hand cars in the street outside his house, or building an extension, or holding regular all night parties may regard these activities as the exercise of his personal freedoms. They may however give rise to conflict if his neighbours resent the street being turned into a used vehicle lot, or find the light to their windows and gardens cut out by the new building, or that they cannot sleep at night for the noise. What the law seeks to do in circumstances where interests conflict in this way is to attempt to reconcile differences by referring their solution to established principles and rules which have been developed to clarify individual rights and obligations. The relationships between neighbours are of course but a small part of the complex pattern of relationships most people are involved in and which the law attempts to regulate. A book devoted to the study of business law focuses specifically on the particular legal relationships that are a product of business activity.

The task of defining what is meant by business activity is dealt with in some detail later in Chapter 2, but we can note at this initial stage that essentially businesses are provider organisations, selling goods and services to anyone who requires them. The customers of a business are usually referred to as consumers. They may be other businesses themselves, but they also include of course individuals, ultimate consumers, who use the goods and services for their own private benefit. Once we begin to examine the business world in any detail we encounter far more complex legal relationships than the simple neighbour example given above. We find an environment in which an enormously diverse range of transactions are constantly taking place, resources of labour, capital, and land are being acquired and disposed of, all kinds of property are being bought and sold, information and advice is being given and sought, and decisions are regularly being made which have an impact on the owners, managers and customers of the organisations with which they are associated. In short we are seeing a sophisticated market economy conducting its operations.

The business environment is not however an area of commercial activity of importance to the business community alone. All of us are involved in it in one way or another. The most obvious illustration of how this occurs comes from when we look at ourselves in our role as consumers, that is as users of products and services. Whether we are buying clothes, household goods, holidays, shares, having the car repaired, opening a bank account, taking a job or renting a flat we will be engaging in a business relationship. It does not always have to be a formal matter, and usually will not be. But all these activities are carried on within a legal framework which, as we shall see in this book, attempts to set out the responsibilities of the participants.

A useful starting point for our study is to simplify the types of relationship that most business organisations are likely to be engaged in by setting them out diagrammatically. In this way it is possible to obtain an overview of the business environment (Figure 1.2). As well as the external dimension of a business organisation's relationships, it will also have an internal dimension to its activities which is equally important to it. Figure 1.1 provides a simple illustration of the internal shape of a business organisation, indicating the relationships which exist inside a business. The example used is that of a registered company.

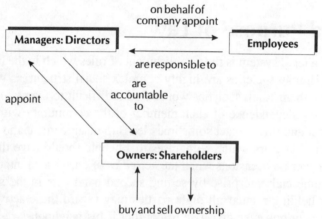

Figure 1.1 *The Internal Dimensions of a Business Organisation – the Limited Company*

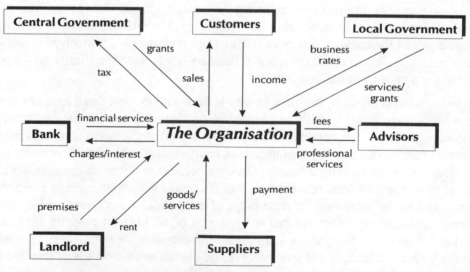

Figure 1.2 *The External Dimensions of a Business Organisation*

Even at the superficial level of analysis provided by these models, they enable us to see that business organisations are at the centre of a web of relationships all of which have a strong legal dimension to them. For instance, a business may take decisions on the basis of expert advice provided by a professional advisor in return for payment of a fee or charge. Inaccurate or incomplete advice relied upon by the business may cause it to suffer commercial damage. If this occurs the business may have a legal remedy against the advisor, and will seek to recover any losses it has sustained. Similarly, within the organisation legal relationships exist between managers, owners and staff, thus for example, directors of a limited company are accountable to the shareholders in general meeting, and can be dismissed from their office by a company resolution in circumstances where they have been guilty of commercial incompetence or malpractice. Chapter 3 is devoted to examining the nature of legal relationships that exist in business. An exploration of the law as it applies to business thus involves examining the legal framework within which all businesses, from the multinational corporations to the one man businesses, pursue their commercial objectives. We have noted that this framework has to do with the relationships their business activity creates. What we must next do is to ascertain more precisely the purposes which underpin the legal regulation of business affairs.

The Purpose of a System of Business Law

Complex, affluent, property owning societies develop detailed and sophisticated rules to regulate themselves, and in the United Kingdom as in most modern states almost every aspect of human activity is either directly or indirectly affected by law. These laws seek to achieve different purposes. One major classification in any legal system involves distinguishing between those legal rules which are concerned with private rights and obligations, a branch of law referred to as *civil* law, and those whose primary purpose is the welfare of society generally, and its protection by means of rules that seek to prevent anti-social forms of behaviour, supported by the power to punish those who break them. This is the *criminal* law.

Legal rules in the field of business are designed to fulfil certain primary purposes. These include the remedying of private grievances, the control of anti-social activities and the regulation of harmful activities.

The remedying of private grievances

Various branches of law are concerned with recognising personal rights which can be enforced by means of legal proceedings if they are infringed, or even where there is simply a threat to infringe them. One of these branches is the law of tort. It is based upon the existence of a set of obligations referred to as torts, or civil wrongs, which have been evolved by the courts as a response to the need for established codes of conduct to protect people from certain types of harm. Tortious obligations are imposed by law, rather than arising by agreement between the parties as is the case with contractual obligations. In effect the law of tort recognises legal rights, which entitle anyone whose rights have been infringed to sue the wrongdoer for compensation. Examples of torts include those of trespass, nuisance and defamation. The tort of negligence, which is considered in detail further on in the book is probably the most important of all the torts which affect business operations.

The law of contract is a further example of a branch of law dealing in private rights and obligations. Contractual agreements involve the making of promises which are legally enforceable. A party to a contract therefore has the right to take legal action against the other party to the agreement in the event of that person being in breach of his contractual obligations.

Both the law of contract and the law of tort are crucial to the effective functioning of the business environment. Without the ability to enter into binding agreements businesses would be left fully exposed to the risk of their transactions being unilaterally terminated by the other contracting party. Such vulnerability would seriously undermine business confidence and would hamper economic activity generally, and without the ability to seek compensation and redress for wrongs committed against them businesses could suffer significant economic harm. Consider for instance, a situation where a small under-insured business could obtain no compensation following the total destruction of its stock and premises due to negligent repair work carried out to an adjoining gas main by the gas company.

The control of anti-social activities

This is essentially the task of the criminal law. Whilst it is not possible to prevent crimes from being committed, the presence of penal sanctions, such as imprisonment and fines, which are used to support the criminal code, can act as a deterrent to the commission of an offence.

There is no adequate definition of a crime. Lord Diplock in *Knuller v. Director of Public Prosecutions* 1972 attempted to pinpoint the essential differences between civil and criminal law when he said, *"Civil liability is concerned with the relationship of one citizen to another; criminal liability is concerned with the relationship of a citizen to society organised as a state."*

Businesses, like individuals, are subject to the criminal law. Of the wide range of offences that an organisation might commit in the course of its business, the following provide some illustrations:

(a)   offences in the field of consumer protection. These are many and varied. They include offences connected with false trade descriptions applied to goods and services, consumer credit arrangements such as engaging in activities requiring a licence but where no licence has been granted, and safety obligations for certain manufactured items, for instance oil heaters and electric blankets, which must meet standards laid down under government regulations;

(b)   offences in the field of employment, such as a contravention of the obligations owed to employees under health and safety legislation;

(c)   offences connected with the operation of registered companies, such as failure to file accounts or the insertion of untrue statements in a prospectus;

(d)   offences in relation to tax liability, such as the making of false returns.

The regulation of harmful activities

Methods of legal regulation include licensing, registration and inspection. These are useful mechanisms for exercising effective control over a range of activities, which, if uncontrolled, could be physically, economically and socially harmful. Thus powers of inspection, supported by enforcement mechanisms, are granted to factory inspectors working for the Health and Safety Executive. The inspection of work places such as factories and building sites enables inspectors to ascertain whether safety legislation is being complied with, and that employees' physical requirements are thus being met. Certain types of trading practices which are potentially anti-competitive can only be pursued legitimately if the agreements in which they are contained are registered with the Director General of Fair Trading, under the Restrictive Trade Practices Act 1976. Even then they are only legally permissible if they are approved by the Restrictive Trade Practices Court. Additionally anyone in the business of providing credit facilities is obliged to register under the Consumer Credit Act 1974 with the Director General of Fair Trading before being legally permitted to lend money. The aim is to eliminate unscrupulous finance dealers from the credit market, overcoming the social problems which arise when poorer members of society borrow at high rates of interest which they are unable to afford, often in an effort to extricate themselves from other debts. And in cases of alleged malpractice in the management of registered companies the Department of Trade and Industry has the power to carry out investigations into the affairs of companies, for instance to establish the true ownership of shares in a company.

The Importance of Law to Business

The legal system affects businesses just as it does individuals. Every aspect of business life, from formation and operation to dissolution is conducted within an environment of legal regulation. As we have seen above, many purposes are being served in applying legal regulation to business activity. In broad terms the underlying characteristics of business law may be seen as the dual aims of:

(a) providing a practical and comprehensive framework of legal rules and principles to assist the organisation in its commercial affairs; whilst at the same time

(b) ensuring a sufficient level of protection for the legitimate interests of those who come into direct contact with it. This includes not only members of the public in their capacity as consumers, but also business creditors and the employees and owners of business enterprises.

There appears to be one fundamental and compelling reason why business organisations are likely to seek to comply with the law. If they fail to do so it will cost them money, either directly or indirectly. A business which is in breach of law, whether the civil law or the criminal law, will in most cases suffer from the breach commercially.

The commercial consequences to an organisation which has been found to have broken or otherwise failed to comply with the law includes the possibility of:

- an action for damages against the business, brought by someone seeking financial compensation from it. Such an action may be the result of a breach of contract committed by the business, or be in respect of some form of tortious liability it has incurred. An alternative claim brought against it could be for an injunction restraining it from pursuing a particular course of action;

- a claim that the action of the business is devoid of legal effect because it has failed to follow procedures which bind it. For instance, a limited company cannot act unless it has correctly followed the registration procedures laid down by statute, and has received a certificate of incorporation. Nor can it alter its own constitution, its memorandum and articles of association, unless this is done in accordance with relevant statutory procedures regarding notice periods, the holding of a meeting and the need to secure an appropriate majority of votes cast;

- the loss of an opportunity to take some form of legal action, because the time limit for doing so has passed, for instance bringing a late appeal against an unfavourable planning decision;

- a prosecution brought against it alleging breach of the criminal law, resulting in a fine, or in certain circumstances the seizure of assets;

- the exercise of enforcement action against it for its failure to comply with some legal requirement, for example to take steps to remedy a serious hazard to health, as a result of which its business operations are suspended;

- the bringing of a petition to have the organisation brought to an end. A registered company can for example be wound up compulsorily by its unpaid creditors.

Thus there are sound commercial reasons for keeping properly informed about the law and complying with it as it affects business, quite apart from any moral or social responsibility for doing so. Moreover, legal proceedings often attract public attention and result in adverse publicity to the organisations involved, whilst at a personal level individuals engaged in managing a business may find themselves dismissed and facing civil and/or criminal liability if they are responsible for serious errors of judgment which carry legal consequences, such as negligent or dishonest performance in handling a company's financial affairs.

Developing Legal Knowledge and Skills

Usually it is not possible for people in business to find the time or develop the skills to cope with all the legal demands of operating a business, however there will remain strong reasons for acquiring at least a basic level of legal knowledge and skills and devoting some time to legal issues as and when they arise. This is because:

(a)   many straightforward legal problems can be resolved simply by means of a letter or a telephone call to the other party involved. Legal advice has to be paid for, and in some situations will be both an unnecessary expense, and a time consuming activity;

(b)   certain legal problems require immediate action, for example, what rights the employer has to dismiss an employee against whom an allegation of sexual misconduct has been made; or what rights a buyer has to reject goods delivered late by the seller;

(c)   the daily routine of a business involves frequent encounters with matters of a legal nature, such as examining contracts, signing cheques, negotiating deals and organising the workforce. It would be impractical to seek professional advice regularly in these routine areas;

(d)   many business activities are closely legally regulated, and a working knowledge of them is essential if the business is to function effectively. For example a business providing credit facilities needs to employ staff who are fully aware of the strict legal requirements regulating such transactions;

(e)   when expert advice and assistance is being sought the effectiveness of the process of consultation is assisted if the precise issues can be identified from the outset, and relevant records and materials can be presented at the time. In addition, when the advice is given it will be of little value in the possession of someone who can make no real sense of it;

(f)   managing a business effectively demands a working knowledge of the legal implications not only of what is being decided, but also of the processes by which it is decided. For instance company directors ought to be familiar with the basic principles of the law of company meetings, since it is by means of such meetings that important decision making is achieved.

Obtaining and Using Legal Information

Having established the importance of legal rules and procedures in the running of a business, the next question which emerges is how to obtain and apply relevant legal principles, so that the process of business decision making and practical operation is informed and guided by the legal environment in which it functions. Large organisations employ their own professional advisors. Public companies and local authorities will have departments specialising in legal, financial and other areas of professional work. In such organisations it will be the role of staff in the legal department to deal with the routine legal aspects of the work of the business, and it may be expected of them to produce and distribute to relevant personnel details of legal changes which are likely to have an effect on the way in which the business works. For example, following the introduction of the Health and Safety at Work Act 1974, employers were required to fulfil a number of general duties set out by the Act to ensure the health, safety and welfare of their employees whilst at work. The Act specifically stated that these duties were to include providing staff with any necessary information, instruction, training and supervision. Smaller organisations, whose scale of business operations is insufficient to make the employment of a full time lawyer financially viable will instead rely for their legal needs on the services of a law firm, which will probably be locally based, to deal with legal matters as and when they arise. The nature of such an arrangement makes it unlikely that legal changes affecting the business will always be picked up by their legal advisers and fed into the business in advance of the change. Most of the legal work performed will be as a response to matters which are routinely passed on to the firm, such as the renewal of the business lease, actions for the recovery of debts and financial borrowing by means of the use of a security such as a mortgage or debenture.

In the smallest organisations, such as one man businesses, there may be reluctance to seek legal services at all, unless it is absolutely necessary for the business to do so. Professional advice costs money, and time is taken up in meetings with professional advisors. Whilst this may be a short-sighted view, and one which can result in the organisation getting itself into greater difficulty in the long term, it is nevertheless the case that such organisations will occasionally try to 'go it alone'.

It is clear that the nature of advice and assistance that organisations have need of to operate satisfactorily, is often of a detailed and technical kind which only accountants, lawyers and other professionals are capable of providing. However, it would be quite wrong to assume that in consequence there is little value to be gained from employing staff who have a basic knowledge and appreciation of principles of bookkeeping, or how the Sale of Goods Act 1979 works. Daily, practical business operations raise a range of issues, many of which, whilst broadly located in areas of technical expertise of which staff have no deep knowledge, can be easily dealt with by people with only a general level of knowledge. There is no reason why a small trading organisation should not be able to cope with most of the contractual disagreements that will arise from time to time between it and its suppliers and customers in the ordinary course of business.

Whatever method a business uses to obtain legal support, it is obvious that business managers are not doing their jobs properly if they are ignorant of the legal implications inherent in the daily activities carried out by their organisations. How they manage their premises, their staff, their financial affairs and their trading operations should be guided by their business ability, and part of this ability involves recognising the legal implications inherent in pursuing different courses of action. Certainly the failure of management to identify and respond to changes in the law which directly affects the business will prevent it from adapting its operations to accommodate and comply with these changes. How significant such a failure might be can be usefully illustrated by referring to many modern statutes, for example the Consumer Protection Act 1987. This legislative enactment is of considerable importance to any business which is a producer of goods that will ultimately be purchased by consumers. The Act significantly alters the basis of a producer's liability for defective products, and as is the case in respect of many contemporary legal changes, the failure of the organisation to recognise the change and reassess its operational activity in the light of it, can result in the payment of large sums by way of compensation. Legal changes can produce immediate alterations to the extent of an organisation's liabilities, affecting the very heart of its commercial activities. In these circumstances it is essential that information is fed into the organisation to enable appropriate action to be taken. Given the dynamic nature of modern business, the capacity of an organisation to respond to change, of whatever kind it might be, is often crucial to its continued commercial survival. In the case of law essentially there are two stages involved in reacting to a legal change; obtaining the relevant information, and applying it.

Obtaining legal information and being able to understand and apply it effectively requires us to examine the various sources of English law.

Sources of English Law

The expression 'source of law' carries with it a number of different meanings, but we only need to concentrate on two of them. They are:

- source of law as a way of describing where the law is located, that is where one can obtain legal source materials; and

- source of law in the sense of where the law comes from, in other words who makes it.

As we shall see these two apparently separate ideas are very closely linked.

Legal source materials

To operate a detailed system of law it is essential that the law be recorded. The effective development of English law as a coherent and uniform body of established rules and principles dates back to the thirteenth century, by which time it was already possible to find comprehensive written accounts of the law. The recording of the law in a written form means that, as far as possible, the ambiguity, inconsistency and lack of precision that comes about when rules are merely passed on by word of mouth is eliminated. In practice, as we shall see, expressing the law by means of the written word is no guarantee of achieving absolute certainty as to meaning, although it does usually seem to achieve a satisfactory and workable framework within which individuals and organisations can conduct their affairs in confidence.

There are two forms of written law:

- the reports of court proceedings in which the judgments delivered by the court contain the statements of principle which express the relevant law; and

- the publication of UK and EC legislation. This includes subordinate legislation, and the various forms of EC legislation.

Both these legal sources are publicly available. Major academic libraries usually hold an extensive range of law reports covering the decisions of all the superior courts, as well as keeping volumes of statutes. In such libraries the statutes are usually held in bound volumes chronologically, the main series being published under the title *Current Law Statutes Annotated*, but also by subject title. Statutes published in this format are under the title *Halsburys Statutes*, and both these series include annotations, notes, to assist the reader in understanding and applying the law concerned. Individual Acts of Parliament can also be purchased from branches of HMSO.

Law Making Institutions

Until the 1st January 1973 English law was created by two separate law making institutions, the courts and Parliament. However in 1973 the United Kingdom became a member of the European Economic Community (the EEC, but usually referred to more simply now as the EC), the effect of which in legal terms was to introduce a new, third, law making source. The impact of this fundamental change has been considerable, although there are many areas of activity which remain outside the jurisdiction of the law making bodies of the EC. Business operations however fall within the remit of the work of the Community. It is appropriate to look at our own domestic law makers, and examine the methods by which they create the laws which we will be encountering throughout this book. In an historical context it was the courts which originally developed our law, and so we shall consider the courts first.

The law making function of parliament and the EC are examined in the mandatory unit Business in the Economy, here we will consider the role of the courts in resolving conflict and law making.

The Courts of England and Wales

For the purpose of the administration of justice in England and Wales two separate court structures exist, one dealing with civil law matters and the other criminal matters. Some courts exercise both a civil and criminal jurisdiction. An example is provided by the Magistrates courts, which are primarily criminal courts but which also exercise a limited but nevertheless important civil jurisdiction in family matters.

An appeals structure gives the parties involved in any form of legal proceedings the opportunity to appeal against the trial court on points of law or fact. The trial court is the court in which the case is first tried, and in which evidence is given on oath to the court by witnesses appearing for the parties involved, in an attempt at enabling the court to establish for the purposes of the case the relevant material facts. The court in which a case is first tried is known as a court of *first instance*. Usually *leave to appeal* must be granted either by the trial court or the appellate court although certain appeals are available as of right.

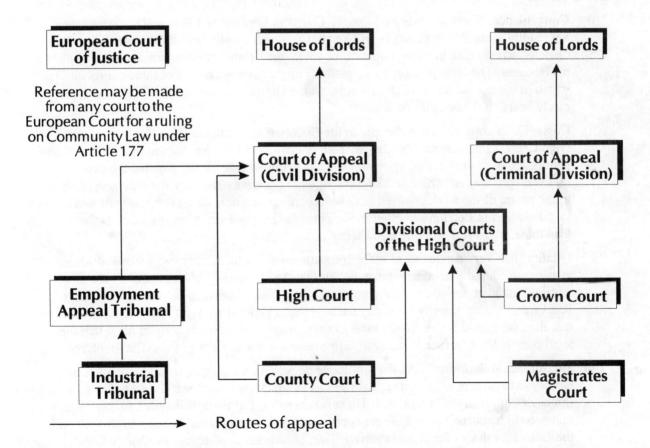

Figure 1.3 *Civil and Criminal Courts Structure in England and Wales, including Employment Tribunals*

The civil courts

In a civil court an action is commenced by a *plaintiff* who sues the other party, called the *defendant*. If either party takes the case before a higher court on appeal that party is known as the *appellant* and the other as the *respondent*.

Before commencing proceedings the plaintiff must decide whether the case is worth bringing. This is likely to involve a number of considerations including costs, time, the complexity of the action, and the resources of the defendant. We will return to look at these considerations in more detail later in the chapter.

A diagram of the structure of the civil courts is shown in Figure 1.3. Each court has a particular *jurisdiction*, a word which signifies the court's competence to hear a particular action. Civil cases are tried at first instance either before the County Court or before the High Court of Justice. Appeals from either of these courts are heard before the Court of Appeal (Civil Division). The highest appellate court is the House of Lords. A litigant, that is a person bringing legal proceedings, is thus faced with the choice of whether to bring the claim in the County Court or the High Court.

County Court or High Court?

The decision as to whether to bring proceedings in the County Court or the High Court will be based upon a number of factors.

(i)   **Convenience.** There are over 400 County Courts in England and Wales. This means they are readily accessible to plaintiffs. A County Court can usually hear those cases where the cause of action arose in its own district, or where the defendant either resides or carries on his business. Thus it is possible that a plaintiff might have the choice of three courts in which to commence proceedings. By contrast the High Court sits in London, and only rarely hears civil cases outside London.

(ii)   **Costs**. Court costs are much cheaper in the County Court than the High Court. Bringing a High Court action may involve the payment of additional lawyers, for instance a firm of solicitors acting as the London agents for the local firm who originally handled the case. Lawyers' professional charges, like those of other professionals, vary not only according to the nature of the work involved but also according to where they carry out their work. Legal charges in London and other major cities for example are generally much higher than those of lawyers working elsewhere.

(iii) **Quality**. It is very dangerous to make comparisons about the quality or standard of justice as between courts. Sometimes it may be felt that the complexity of a case makes it a more suitable candidate for consideration before a High Court judge than before a circuit judge in a County Court. Equally it may be the case that a plaintiff's lawyer is entirely confident that the case should go before the local County Court. It is worth bearing in mind that the legal complexity of a case is not necessarily related to the amount of the claim involved.

(iv)   **Jurisdictional limitations**. As we saw above because of the geographical distribution of County Courts there are jurisdictional rules as to which court can hear the case. No such limitations apply to the High Court. However there are further jurisdictional considerations that need to be borne in mind. These concern the type of action that is being dealt with and the financial value of the claim involved. Over certain kinds of action the County Court has exclusive jurisdiction, such as applications for the renewal of a business lease and in consumer credit cases such as the repossession of goods subject to a hire purchase agreement. With respect to the financial value of a claim, regulations introduced under the Courts and Legal Services Act 1990 have made it possible for the County Courts to deal with many more actions than was previously the case. To cope with the increased workload there are now 72 continuous trial centres. In general, cases with a value of below £25,000 will be heard in the County Court, and with a value of more than £50,000 in the High Court. For those between £25,000 and £50,000 the case will be allocated to either the County Court or the High Court on the basis of financial substance, complexity, importance and the need for the matter to be dealt with as quickly as possible. When a legal claim is brought it is, of course, not always possible to quantify in advance the amount the plaintiff is claiming. A claim for compensation for personal injuries will be for an unspecified sum, or in legal terminology an unliquidated amount, it being left to the court to decide on the evidence the figure which should be awarded. A claim for loss of profits on the other hand can be expressed in a quantified or liquidated form. In the past plaintiffs would often seek to overcome financial allocation requirements by overvaluation of claims. The value to be attached to such claims is now to be the amount in money which the plaintiff could reasonably state the case to be worth to him.

For the purpose of determining small claims, that is those claims not exceeding £1,000, rules made under the County Courts Act 1984 require that the matter must be referred to the arbitration procedure operated by the County Courts. In brief this provides for a relatively informal method for considering the claim, which will usually be heard before a district judge (previously known as a Registrar) rather than a circuit judge, the title given to the senior judge attached to the Court. Although the parties may be legally represented they must normally pay for their own lawyers' fees themselves, whatever the outcome of the case. Thus a successful plaintiff cannot recover from the defendant the costs of being legally represented. County court procedures and arbitration are considered in more depth in Chapter 5.

The organisation and work of the supreme court of judicature

The Supreme Court of judicature is the collective title given to two superior civil courts, the High Court of Justice and the Court of Appeal (Civil Division). These courts sit in London at the Royal Courts of Justice.

The High Court of Justice

The High Court of Justice is for administrative convenience separated into three divisions, each with its own particular jurisdiction. These are the Queen's Bench Division, the Chancery Division and the Family Division. In addition to the cases which are heard in London, High Court cases are also heard at certain centres outside London. These centres are known as High Court and Crown Court Centres, and they include Birmingham, Bristol, Manchester, Leeds and Cardiff.

The Queen's Bench Division hears contractual and tortious actions and any claim not specifically allocated to the other divisions. This makes it the busiest division of the High Court. There is no financial upper limit on its jurisdiction, so it is competent to deal with claims for any amount, though it does not normally try matters which the county court is competent to hear. Two specialised courts within the Queen's Bench Division are the Admiralty Court, which has jurisdiction over shipping matters, and the Commercial Court, which hears only commercial actions and has the advantage for businesses of using a simplified form of procedure. The Queen's Bench Division is headed by the Lord Chief Justice, abbreviated to LCJ.

The Chancery Division has as its nominal head the Lord Chancellor (who is also the head of the Judiciary); however, in practice, the organisation of the work of the court is carried out by the Vice-Chancellor. The jurisdiction of the division includes company law and partnership matters, mortgages, trusts and revenue disputes.

When the High Court deals with a case at first instance exercising what is known as its *'original jurisdiction'* a single judge is competent to try the case. Such a judge is known by the title 'Mr. Justice' or 'Mrs. Justice' in the case of a woman judge, married or unmarried, so a reference to Smith J is a reference to Justice Smith, a High Court judge.

Each division possesses an appellate jurisdiction which is exercised by three judges (sometimes only two) sitting together, and when it is being exercised the court is known, rather confusingly, as a Divisional Court. The work of the Divisional Courts of the Queen's Bench Division is of considerable importance, and covers the following matters.

(i)   Hearing criminal appeals from Magistrates Courts and the Crown Court by means of a *case stated*. This is a statement of the lower courts' findings of fact which is used by the Divisional Court for redetermining a disputed point of law.

(ii)   Hearing civil appeals from certain tribunals.

(iii)   Exercising a supervisory jurisdiction over inferior courts and tribunals. This is carried out by means of applications made to the court for the issue of the prerogative orders. These orders provide remedies to protect people and organisations from various forms of injustice. There are three of them; certiorari, prohibition and mandamus.
Certiorari brings before the court cases from inferior courts and tribunals that have already been decided, or are still being heard, to determine whether the inferior body has exceeded its jurisdiction or denied the rules of natural justice. (An example of these rules is one which provides that both parties in a case must be given the opportunity to be heard.) If such an injustice has occurred the earlier decision will be quashed.
Prohibition is used to prevent inferior courts, tribunals and other judicial and quasi-judicial bodies from exceeding their jurisdiction.
Mandamus is a command used to compel performance of a legal duty owed by some person or body. It may be used against a government department, a local authority, or a tribunal which is unlawfully refusing to hear a case.

The Divisional Courts of Chancery hear appeals on bankruptcy matters from County Courts with bankruptcy jurisdiction.

The Court of Appeal (Civil Division)

Acting in its civil capacity this court has the Master of the Rolls as its president (referred to in written form as MR). Its judges are called Lord Justices of Appeal (referred to as LJ or LJJ in plural), and the quorum of the court is three.

The court can hear appeals from all three divisions of the High Court and appeals from the County Courts. It also deals with appeals from certain tribunals, such as the Employment Appeal Tribunal.

The appeal is dealt with by way of a rehearing, which involves reviewing the case from the transcript of the trial and of the judges' notes. The court may uphold or reverse the whole or any part of the decision of the lower court, alter the damages awarded, or make a different order concerning costs.

The House of Lords

The House of Lords fulfils two functions, for it is not only the upper chamber of Parliament, but also the final appellate court within the United Kingdom. When it sits as a court its judges are those peers who hold or have held high judicial office. By convention lay peers do not sit. The judges are known as Lords of Appeal in Ordinary or, more commonly, Law Lords, and they are presided over by the Lord Chancellor. Although the quorum of the court is three, usually five judges sit. Majority decisions prevail in cases of disagreement.

The House of Lords hears appeals from the Court of Appeal, but only if that court or the Appeals Committee of the House has granted leave.

The Administration of Justice Act 1969 enables certain appeals from the High Court to be heard by the House of Lords without first passing through the Court of Appeal. This is known as the *leapfrog* procedure, and it is available only where the appeal involves a point of general public importance, for example on a question of the interpretation of a statutory provision, and then only if the parties consent, and if the House of Lords grants leave for the appeal. It has been used only rarely.

The Criminal Courts

The structure of the criminal courts under the criminal justice system within England and Wales is shown in Figure 1.3. Business organisations are less likely to find themselves involved in legal proceedings within the criminal courts than in the civil courts, and the following account provides merely a brief outline of the way in which criminal cases are dealt with.

In the criminal court proceedings are normally brought in the name of the Crown against the accused (commonly called the defendant). The proceedings are known as prosecutions and if the defendant is found guilty of the offence for which a charge or charges have been brought against him, the defendant is said to be convicted. The court will then determine the appropriate punishment. Most prosecutions are brought by the Crown Prosecution Service, although there are many other agencies involved in the enforcement of the criminal code, including local authorities under trading standards and public health legislation, the Inland Revenue, Customs and Excise, the Health and Safety Executive and the Equal Opportunities Commission and the Commission for Racial Equality. The range of agencies involved provides a clear illustration of the extent to which the criminal law infiltrates all aspects of life.

Organisations, just as they may sue or be sued, may institute criminal proceedings, such as a theft charge brought by a department store against an alleged shoplifter, or be prosecuted themselves. Corporate bodies, such as registered companies, which are regarded as legal persons in their own right, usually incur criminal liability through the acts of their human agents, normally their employees. It is important to appreciate that a corporation will not be responsible for the acts of every employee, but only for the acts of a person, *"...who is in actual control of the operations of a company or part of them and who is not responsible to another person in the company for the manner in which he discharges his duties in the sense of being under his orders."* Lord Reid, in *Tesco Supermarkets Ltd. v. Natrass* 1972.

Corporate liability arising through the misconduct of an employee is said to be vicarious, or substituted liability, and such liability is considered thoroughly in Chapter 3. In the case of criminal liability, a corporation is generally only vicariously liable if the offence is one of strict liability, meaning an offence where liability can arise without fault on the part of the wrongdoer. A corporation can also be *directly* liable under the criminal law for any offence except murder. It could not be convicted of murder since this offence carries a mandatory life sentence, and a corporation cannot be imprisoned. Direct or primary liability for criminal acts has only been recognised by the courts in more modern times.

> In *Lennard's Carrying Company Co. Ltd. v. Asiatic Petroleum Co. Ltd.* 1915, Viscount Haldane remarked that, *"A corporation is an abstraction. It has no mind of its own any more than it has a body of its own; its active and directing will must consequently be sought in the person of somebody who...is really the directing mind and will of the personality of the corporation."* This suggests someone at the very top of the organisation, someone who, in Viscount Haldane's words is in effect the corporation itself since, *"his action is the very action of the company itself."*

It was upon this basis of legal reasoning that the charge of manslaughter was brought against P&O in respect of the deaths resulting from the Zeebrugge disaster in 1987. Although the company was not convicted it is apparent that there is no technical bar to the bringing of a prosecution for 'corporate crimes' of this kind.

The classification of criminal offences

There are various ways in which it is possible to classify criminal offences. Here we shall note two of them.

Firstly the distinction which is drawn between offences of strict liability and those requiring a mental element. Traditionally a crime consists of two elements, both of which must be proved before a conviction is possible. These elements are the *actus reus* of the offence, and the *mens rea* of the offence. The actus reus consists of the definition of the particular prohibited conduct, which may be either an action or a failure to act. The mens rea, or guilty mind, is the accompanying state of mind which is required for the offence. Thus such words as *wilfully*, *knowingly*, *with intent*, and *permitting* are all concerned with defining particular states of mind. As an illustration the Theft Act 1968 defines theft by stating that, *"A person is guilty of theft if he dishonestly appropriates property belonging to another with the intention of permanently depriving the other of it."*. Here the words "dishonestly" and "intention" provide the *mens rea* of the offence.

For reasons of policy some offences do not require a *mens rea*. They are referred to as absolute offences or offences of strict liability and cover cases where the offence is contained in a statute and where effective enforcement would be difficult if *mens rea* were required, for instance in cases of environmental pollution. Even in these cases however the courts will usually imply the existence of a *mens rea* requirement on the grounds that this is what Parliament intended, since, in Lord Reid's words in *Sweet v. Parsley* 1969 *"... there has for centuries been a presumption that Parliament did not intend to make criminals of persons who were in no way blameworthy in what they did."*.

Secondly the distinction which is drawn between serious and less serious offences. *Indictable* offences, the most serious, can only be tried before a judge and jury, whilst *summary* offences, the less serious, are dealt with in the Magistrates Courts. Jury trials are conducted in Crown Courts. The seriousness of an offence is obviously associated with its potential threat to society; in crude terms this is measurable by looking at the level of punishment that can be meted out to a person convicted of the offence. Some offences for instance are only punishable by a fine, and these are dealt with by Magistrates Courts. Others will carry the possibility of a prison sentence up to a specified maximum. Magistrates' powers are limited to imposing fines of up to £2,000 and/or sentences of up to 6 months' imprisonment. In many cases where a custodial sentence can be imposed by a Magistrates Court the accused is given the choice of being tried summarily before the Magistrates, or on indictment before the Crown Court. Magistrates Courts hear 98% of all criminal cases.

Law Making by the Courts

As we have already seen the two major domestic sources of lawmaking are the courts and the legislature. Whilst the legislature creates law through the introduction of statutes, the law making role of the courts is very different. Parliament enjoys a virtually unlimited lawmaking capacity. The courts on the other hand are subject to very significant restrictions in their role as lawmakers. This is entirely proper since the courts are manned by members of the judiciary, the judges, who are neither elected by the public to this office nor are accountable to the public for the way in which they discharge their responsibilities.

The primary role of the courts, and the various tribunals which supplement the courts system, is the resolution of legal disputes which are brought before them. This process has a history dating back to Norman times.

In order to resolve a dispute it is necessary to have a reference point; some identifiable rule or principle which can be applied in order to solve the problem. One approach is simply to treat each case on its own merits, but such a system would hardly be just for decisions would turn on the character of the individual judge, whose values, prejudices, qualities of analysis and reasoning power would dominate the decision making process. Such a system would be unpredictable and capricious. English law, in common with other law making systems, adopted an approach that sought to achieve a level of certainty and consistency. It did this by means of a process referred to as *stare decisis*, literally 'standing by the decision'. Today we talk of the doctrine of judicial precedent. Under the doctrine of judicial precedent, the successor to the stare decisis system, judges when deciding cases must take into account relevant precedents, that is earlier cases based upon materially similar sets of facts. Whether a court is bound to follow an earlier case of a similar kind can be a matter of considerable complexity, however the general rule is that the decisions of higher courts are binding on lower courts within the hierarchical courts structure that can be seen in diagram in Figure 1.3.

English law became enshrined in the precedent system, and much of our modern law is still found in the decisions of the courts arrived at by resolving the cases brought before them. Not surprisingly this body of law is often referred to as case law. It is these cases, or precedents, which make up the contents of the law reports which were considered earlier in the chapter. The bulk of the law of contract and the law of tort is judge made law, or as it is more usually known, the common law.

In addition to developing and refining the common law, the judges in modern times have played an increasingly important role in the task of interpreting and applying statutory provisions, and we need to consider in outline the way in which they have fulfilled this responsibility.

Statutory Interpretation

When a dispute comes before a court it is the task of the court to hear the evidence, identify the relevant law and apply it. The legal principles which the court has to apply may be common law principles. Often however they will be principles, or rules, which are contained in statutes. Where this is so, the court has to ascertain the meaning of the statute in order to apply it, and sometimes this can cause problems for a court because it discovers that the language of the statute is not entirely clear. The courts take the view that their responsibility is to discern Parliament's will or intention from the legislation under consideration, and in cases of difficulty the courts apply certain principles of construction or interpretation to aid them in this task These are usually referred to as the rules of statutory interpretation, although it seems doubtful that the courts regard them as rules in the ordinary sense. There are three main rules.

(a) *The literal rule.* Applying this approach a court will give the words of a statute their ordinary natural grammatical meaning, that is they will be applied literally provided there is no ambiguity.

In *R. v. Hinchy* 1960 the House of Lords used this approach in a tax case. The defendant had incorrectly completed a tax return for which the penalty under statute was *"treble the tax that ought to be charged"*. This presumably meant three times the excess owed. However the Court construed "tax" to mean the whole tax bill for the year, the difference between £42 and £418.

(b) *The golden rule.* This is used to overcome the problems which occur when the application of the literal rule produces so absurd a result that Parliament could not be taken as having intended it. It simply provides that an interpretation be given which best overcomes the absurdity.

(c) *The mischief or purposive rule.* This rule involves the court in interpreting the statute in accordance with the apparent purpose for which it has been passed, so that its purpose is as far as possible fulfilled. By emphasising the purpose for which the rule was made the courts can look beyond the words used and so give the rule a broader interpretation.

Recently in *Knowles v. Liverpool City Council* 1993 a council flagger sued his employer for damages in negligence when he was injured by a flagstone he was handling which broke because it had not been properly cured by the supplier. Under the Employers' Liability (Defective Equipment) Act 1969 an employer may be deemed to be liable in negligence if an employee is injured as a result of defective equipment supplied by a third party. Equipment is defined in the Act as including plant and machinery, vehicles, aircraft and clothing. The issue before the Court of Appeal was whether the definition would cover flagstones which were work materials. The court thought that the term equipment should be interpreted broadly to include the *"materials which an employee is given by his employer to use to do his job. Such a broad approach reflects the general purpose of the legislation and is consistent with the ordinary meaning of the word in the context of an employee carrying out his job"*. As consequence the employer was liable under the Act for the injuries sustained to the employee by defective equipment used in the course of employment.

Other aids to interpretation include certain sub-rules, the most important of which is the *ejusdem generis* rule which requires that if in a statute, general words are preceded by two or more specific words, the general words should be treated as being of the same kind *(ejusdem generis)* as the specific words. For instance in *Lane v. London Electricity Board* 1955, the words *"shock, burn or other injury"* were used in statutory regulations regarding safety in electrical installations. The plaintiff, who broke his leg as a result of inadequate lighting in an electricity sub-station had not, in the court's opinion, suffered an " other injury" since the specific words, if properly construed, suggested injuries arising from direct contact with electricity.

Most statutes also contain an interpretation section which provides specific definitions for words and phrases which are contained in the statute and in addition the Interpretation Act 1978, which is incorporated into many statutes, gives presumptive interpretations to common words and phrases, for instance that the expression 'man' when used in a statute should include 'woman', and vice versa, unless some contrary intention appears. Recently in *Pepper v. Hart* 1993 the House of Lords held that to assist the courts in discovering Parliament's intention in any statute it is permissible to examine statements made in Parliament during the bill's passage. This was done in *R v. Warwickshire County Council* 1993 dealt with in Chapter 3.

The meaning of 'common law'

In its modern day usage the expression *common law* has come to mean law other than that contained in statutory provisions. Thus common law in this sense means judge made law embodied in case decisions. The expression common law is also sometimes used to describe, in a broader sense, the *type* of legal system that operates in

England and Wales, and indeed has been adopted by countries all over the world and particularly in the Commonwealth.

The common law of England dates back as far as the Norman Conquest and has its origins in the decisions of the royal judges who attempted to develop and apply principles of law 'common' to the whole country. This they did by modifying and adapting rules of Norman law, and rules contained in Saxon local custom. The development of the common law was a long process evolving over hundreds of years. When the process had been completed England and Wales was in possession of a unified and coherent body of law which remains even today the foundation upon which larger and significant areas of our law, such as the law of contract and torts are based.

The judgment of the court

Whatever the nature of a case coming before a court the most vital legal aspect of the legal proceedings comes at the end of the case when judgment is delivered. Certain parts of the judgment will be binding for the future, whilst the remainder of the judgment will have merely persuasive authority whenever it is considered by a court in the future. These ideas need further explanation.

The binding element of a judgment

When a decision is reached on a dispute before a superior court, the judges will make their decision known by making speeches known as judgments. Within a judgment, the judges will refer to numerous matters, such as the relevant legal principles which are drawn from existing cases or statutes, a review of the facts of the case, their opinion on the relevant law, their actual decision and the reasons for it. As far as the parties to a dispute are concerned, the matter they are most concerned with is the actual decision, that is who has won the case. The main matter of relevance to the law, however, is the reason for the decision. This is known as the *ratio decidendi* of the case (the reason for deciding). The *ratio* expresses the underlying legal principle relied on in reaching the decision and it is this which constitutes the binding precedent. As we have seen this means that if a lower court in a later case is faced with a similar dispute it will in general be bound to apply the earlier *ratio decidendi*.

The persuasive element of a judgment

All other matters referred to in a judgment are termed *obiter dicta* (things said by the way). The *obiter* forms persuasive precedent and is likely to be taken into account by a lower court in a later similar case, although a lower court is not bound to follow it.

To illustrate the distinction between *ratio* and *obiter* we will examine the decision of the House of Lords in *Smith v. Stages and Another* 1989. In this case it was necessary to determine the extent to which an employer may be made liable for the actions of his employee, in particular when an employee is in the course of employment. Vicarious or "substituted" liability is explored in Chapter 3. In this case an action was brought on behalf of an employee, who as a passenger in the defendant's car, suffered personal injuries as a result of the negligent driving of the defendant, a fellow employee. Despite the fact that the employers neither required nor authorised the journey by car to and from their particular workplace they were joined as second defendants on a claim that they were vicarously liable for the driver's negligence. The House of Lords held that here the employers were vicariously liable for the employee's negligent driving. The court decided that employees who are required to travel to and from non regular workplaces, and in receipt of wages for doing so, remain within the course of their employment, even if they have a choice as to the mode and time of travel. This statement forms the *ratio* of the judgment and is binding on a lower court if faced with a similar factual situation.

In the course of the judgment however a number of suggestions were made by the House of Lords in relation to the question as to when an employee is acting in the course of his employment during travelling time. The receipt of wages would indicate that an employee was travelling in his employer's time, and acting in the course of his employment. Equally so would an employee travelling in the employer's time between different workplaces. An employee travelling in his employer's time from his ordinary residence to a workplace, other than his regular workplace, to the scene of an emergency such as a fire, accident or mechanical breakdown of plant, would also be acting in the course of his employment. Deviations or interruptions of a journey undertaken in the course of employment unless merely incidental would normally take an employee outside the course of his employment. All of these suggestions are *obiter dicta* which is persuasive authority which may or may not be followed by a lower court dealing with a similar case.

Activity

Elderflower champagne is the name given to a non-alcoholic drink made from elderflowers, sugar, citric acid and lemons to which carbonated water is added. It is produced in Britain and sold at about £2.45 in green bottles, the same size and shape of bottles of French champagne. In 1992 French champagne producers brought a legal action against the British producers of the elderflower drink. The case was heard in 1993 and widely reported in the national press.

Conduct some research into this case by referring to back copies of quality national newspapers for their reports of the decisions in the early spring and summer of 1993, and answer the following questions.

1. Name the plaintiff and the defendant in the court action.

2. Why did the plaintiff sue the defendant and how did they claim that the law had been infringed.

3. Which court heard the case and what was the decision?

4. What do you consider to be the reason or reasons for the decision?

5. To which court did the unsuccessful party appeal and which judges heard the appeal.

6. What was the decision of the appeal court and what do you consider to be the reason or reasons for it?

Change and the Law

Legal rules are not made simply for their own sake. They are made because there is a need for them. It may not always be easy to recognise why particular areas of law, or specific legal rules have become necessary. Nor will people always agree that a particular need has been properly established, or that legal rule making is the best way to respond to an identified problem or issue. However it remains true that all laws originate out of some sense of need for formal regulation or control of a particular situation. We have already seen the variety of purposes these legal rules are designed to fulfil, each purpose being an area of need for rule creation. One way of expressing these ideas is to say that legal rules are an effect rather than a cause.

Although certain fundamental needs are constant, such as food and shelter, others are more variable. Whilst our need for law to regulate human conduct is always present, the form and content of the law varies over time, altering and adapting to take account of the dynamic nature of modern society. We have always had a need for laws to provide for order in society, and the criminal law is the outcome. Crimes have been recognised since earliest times as offences against the well-being of society, which if allowed to pass unchecked would undermine the fabric of society. Criminal laws have thus been created to protect the individual and property. However whilst crimes such as murder and theft have always been regarded as an essential part of the criminal code, the means by which we define these crimes today, and the legal penalties that are attached to them are not exactly as they were a hundred years ago, or even thirty years ago. Law evolves as society evolves, and this is entirely appropriate for law is the servant of society rather than its master.

It is possible to identify certain general causes of legal change, and the following list indicates what these may be.

(a) *Social Causes*

For example to provide tenants with legal protection from unscrupulous landlords who threaten eviction if the tenant refuses to pay unjustifiable rent increases.

(b) *Economic Causes*

Within a free market economy trading practices often develop which may be harmful to general economic needs. For example, dominant suppliers who use their market dominance to restrict competition in the supply of such goods are distorting market conditions. Governments may find it necessary to intervene by means of legislation to curb the growth of dominant market suppliers.

(c) *Political Causes*

For instance a government may feel it appropriate to introduce legislation to penalise councils who overspend.

(d) *Technological and Scientific Developments*

Technological change has from time to time created problems which require legal regulations to control. The growth in the use of computers over the past twenty years as a means of storing personal data, has given rise to concern over the apparent loss of rights of individuals whose lives are recorded in this way and who may have little or no control over the use to which such information is put. Legislation now seeks to provide a measure of security for individuals in this situation.

In reality the change factors we have listed here overlap to a considerable extent. For example, the decision to join the European Economic Community was both political and economic. Legally it was achieved by passing the European Communities Act 1972. Potentially it also had social implications, since for example, the Community was pledged to move towards enabling a free movement of labour between the member states. A more specific example of the overlap is provided by various aspects of modern employment legislation. The creation of the right of employees not to be unfairly dismissed by their employers, which is at present contained in the Employment Protection (Consolidation) Act 1978 (as amended), illustrates the use of a legal device (statute) to achieve a social objective (job security), which has political implications (electorally popular) and includes an economic dimension (restriction on employers' freedom to reduce the size of the workforce).

The protection of the interests of the buying public has produced a spate of legal change over the past two decades. It is a recognition by Parliament that consumers' rights are a matter of national interest and debate, making them a part of the political agenda. Increases in the spending power of the nation, together with great technological advances in the production of consumer durables from compact discs to microwave ovens have led to an enormous growth in the demand for goods from consumers, and producers have responded accordingly. As 'consumerism' has expanded, and the demand for consumer rights has increased, so the law has been invoked as the means of achieving an appropriate level of consumer protection. Statutory changes have sought to regulate this particular market.

An illuminating illustration of the change process in operation is provided by one facet of modern consumer law. Back in 1893, the Sale of Goods Act was passed as a means of codifying the law of sale. Codification involves bringing all the law in a specific field together in a single statute. It is a way of clarifying the law, and it assists the task of discovering the law on a particular subject if it is primarily contained in a single statute. The rules that were expressed in the Act were based upon the need for a clear legal framework within which trade could be effectively conducted between businesses. At that time the interests of private consumers of goods were given little consideration. One of the provisions of the Act stipulated that in any sale of goods transaction between a buyer and a business seller, the seller would be treated as impliedly promising the buyer that the goods were of a certain standard, known technically as the standard of 'merchantable quality'. The seller was however at liberty to exclude this implied promise if he did so clearly, a right eagerly grasped by most sellers, who had no desire to increase their liabilities unnecessarily. At this time the predominant business philosophy was *caveat emptor*, let the buyer beware. It was essentially the buyer's task to satisfy himself that what he was buying was suitable and fit.

By the 1970s it was felt that the interests of private consumers were being largely overridden by the majority of sellers, who simply avoided their legal obligations to provide merchantable goods by the use of contractual clauses excluding liability. This, of course, they were perfectly legally entitled to do, but it was felt that consumers were being treated harshly by being denied the opportunity to reject defective goods, from whose sale the seller had made a profit. In 1973 legislation was introduced which invalidated any attempt by a seller to exclude liability for breach of the merchantable quality provisions in such transactions.

Sellers however continued to exclude, confident that private consumers were largely unaware of their rights, and that in any event attempting to exclude was not unlawful, simply invalid. This subsequently lead to further statutory intervention, so that since 1978 an attempt to exclude liability has constituted a criminal offence, under the Consumer Transactions (Restrictions on Statements) Order. The order has proved an effective deterrent to most traders, and consumer rights have been fully secured in this field.

One other cause of legal change requires brief mention, that of legal clarity. Legislation is introduced from time to time as an attempt at simply clarifying legal rules, rather than creating new ones. The codified Sale of Goods Act mentioned above provides an example.

As you consider the various aspects of business law covered in this book it will soon become apparent to you through an examination of legislative and case law developments just how dynamic our legal system is. This in turn is simply a reflection of a way in which as a society we evolve through change.

Unit Test Questions

1. How would you define business activity?

2. Distinguish between the law of contract and the law of tort.

3. What is the purpose of the criminal law in relation to business?

4. What are the commercial consequences to an organisation which has failed to comply with the law?

5. Give four reasons why individuals involved in business should have at least a basic knowledge of business law.

6. Define the following: plaintiff; defendant; jurisdiction; appellant; respondent; first instance.

7. What factors would be considered in deciding whether to sue in the County Court or High Court?

8. Name the divisions of the High Court of Justice.

9. Which judges sit in the House of Lords?

10. How are criminal offences classified?

11. Where would you find the 'common law'?

12. State the rules of statutory interpretation.

13. Define and distinguish between ratio decidendi and obiter dicta.

14. What are the causes of legal change?

15. What is the purpose of codifying the law?

Element 9.1

Investigate the legal forms of business organisations

Performance Criteria

1. Legal characteristics of business organisations are compared
2. Legal process of formation and dissolution is outlined
3. Reasons for choice of legal status by a business organisation are explained

Range

Legal characteristics:

Legal personality; liability of stakeholders; name; size

Formation:

Partnership Document, Company Registration Documents

Dissolution:

Voluntary/Involuntary, Bankruptcy/Insolvency

Choice of Status:

Liability; capacity; administrative burden; tax position; rights of membership and withdrawal

Evidence Indicators

A case study of business organisations which compares the legal characteristics of types of business organisations, identifies the legal structures and suggests reasons for the choice of that structure

The Legal Forms of Business Organisations

The logical starting point in a study of business law is to examine the business organisations which are involved in conducting business activity. To do so we need to be clear about what the expression *business organisations* means. The problem this raises is that business is an economic concept rather than a legal one. The law does on occasion find it necessary to define the meaning of business, but only in specific situations limited to the context of a particular problem. For instance tax liability may depend upon deciding whether a person who has bought and sold a certain number of cars during the year is trading, and is thus in business as a car dealer. But the answer to such a question would tell us very little about the nature and quality of businesses in general, even though it would provide a solution to the particular tax problem.

In order then to appreciate fully the law as it applies to business organisations it is helpful to draw briefly from economics, and summarise what an economist sees as making up a business organisation. It should be remembered that the decision to form a business is a commercial rather than a legal one, and that those who set up businesses will treat the legal form the business is to take as a secondary rather than a primary consideration. First you decide your business aims and objectives. Then you decide on the form of business appropriate to achieve them. As we shall see, examining the general economic background to business organisations is also useful because it helps to explain why substantial parts of business law have evolved, either as an aid to the business community in achieving commercial aims, or as a means of regulating business activities and curbing undesirable practices.

Common Characteristics of Business Organisations

Most business organisations will display the following characteristics.

(a) *They will establish their business aims*. In general organisations are set up for a specific purpose; selling particular products, providing a service, and so on. Of course businesses are also likely to evolve as the commercial environment changes and new commercial opportunities present themselves;

(b) *The identity of the organisations will be distinct*. It will, for example, be possible to establish who owns the organisation, and who is employed by it;

(c) *There will be some form of leadership in the organisation*. Leadership will be provided in the form of a system of management within it;

(d) *There will be accountability within the organisation.* The organisation itself will possess accountability. It will be accountable to those who own it, those whom it employs, and those with whom it trades. Similarly those people it employs are legally accountable to the organisation to fulfil their obligations towards it. We shall see that this idea of legal accountability is fundamental to the principles and practice of English business law.

Business is a broad and loosely defined term. Perhaps most people understand it to mean a commercial enterprise which aims to make as much money as possible for its owners. There are, however, many other kinds of business. For instance some organisations have scientific, educational, or social goals, and are not primarily concerned with the profit motive in the same way as commercial businesses; examples include charitable organisations such as Oxfam and the National Trust, educational bodies like the GCSE and A level examining boards and BTEC, and a broad spectrum of other bodies such as local chambers of trade, and sports and social clubs. Local authorities are not commercial organisations either although as incidental activities they may operate profit making ventures such as sports and leisure centres. The expression 'business' is however a wide one, and used in some senses would certainly apply to the organisations just mentioned even though they are non-commercial. The expression is often used in a general sense to describe the way in which an organisation is run, a 'business-like operation', meaning it is run efficiently. It is also used to characterise the type of organisational activity being carried out, thus someone may loosely describe Greenpeace as being 'in the environment business'. For our purposes we will be using business in its commercial sense, looking at organisations which aim to make a profit for their owners, and which are owned privately, rather than by the state.

The Classification of Business Organisations

It is easy to get bogged down in charts and diagrams which classify business organisations in different ways, but as a starting point it is helpful to take a birds-eye view of how these organisations relate to each other. The figure below provides a broad classification, which distinguishes organisations according to ownership and then breaks down private sector business organisations which form the subject matter of this chapter, into their specific legal categories.

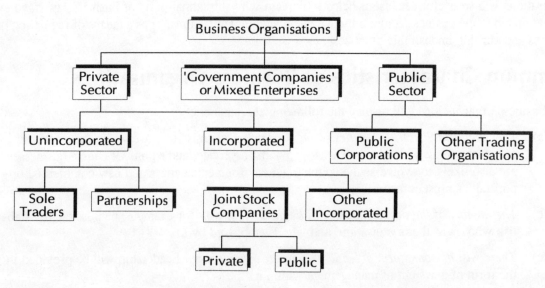

Figure 2.1 *Classification of business organisations*

Two features of the figure above require special attention. These are the distinctions between:

(a)   corporate and unincorporated bodies; and

(b)   private and public sector organisations.

It is outside the scope of this unit to examine the differences between public and private sector organisations in any detail, however it is important to be clear as to the significance of the distinction. Essentially what distinguishes a public sector from a private sector organisation is who owns, and therefore controls it. In the case of the public sector this will be the state; in the private sector it will be private individuals and organisations. Most of the work carried out by organisations in the public sector is not principally concerned with commercial trading, but rather with the provision of public services such as health, education and housing, and the management of a wide range of social welfare benefits such as pensions. The state does however engage in commercial trading in certain areas. British Rail is a state trading organisation; so too is Her Majesty's Stationery Office (HMSO). Much of the law contained in this book is as applicable to these state organisations as to those trading in the private sector.

A further distinguishing feature is the method used to create a public sector organisation. Usually they are created by a specific Act of Parliament, thus British Coal, which is state owned, was created by the Coal Industry Nationalisation Act, 1946. The use of an Act of Parliament to create a *private* sector organisation, whilst not unknown, is most unusual nowadays.

Corporate and Unincorporated Bodies

Under English Law all business enterprises can be classified into two basic legal forms. They are either *corporate* bodies or *unincorporated* bodies. An unincorporated body is either an individual or more usually a group of individuals, who have joined together to pursue a common business purpose. The body and the individuals who compose it are not separate from each other under the law, even though they may trade under a business name, rather than using their own names, thereby creating the appearance that the business is a separate entity. A corporate body, or *corporation*, is also made up of a group of individuals who have joined together for a common purpose, but by the process of legal incorporation they have created an artificial legal person which has a separate legal identity from the members who compose it. The distinction between corporate and non-corporate bodies is thus fundamental to an understanding of the law as it applies to organisations.

Corporate Bodies

The corporation has proved itself to be the most significant business for the pursuit of commercial activity in the United Kingdom, for reasons that are explained below. Two basic types of corporation exist, the corporation sole and the corporation aggregate.

Corporations sole

These consist of a single person and all the successors of that person. The bishops are corporations sole and so is the Crown. The Bishop of Durham is not only an individual but an office, and the office itself continues to exist despite one bishop being replaced by another. This is known as perpetual succession and can be a useful legal device because it can mean, for example, that property held by the office of the Bishop of Durham does not have to be transferred from one holder of the office to the next. Corporations sole are not primarily commercial organisations.

Corporations aggregate

These are by far the most numerous type of corporation, and they consist of a number of people who combine to form or constitute the corporation, such as the elected members of a county or district council or the shareholders of a limited company.

Corporations may be created in the following ways:

(a) *by Royal Charter*. Charter, or common law corporations, are rarely created today, although many of the early trading organisations such as the Hudson's Bay Company were created in this way. The charter is granted by the Monarch acting under the royal prerogative upon the advice of the Privy Council. Examples of twentieth century charter corporations include the BBC and the older universities, and professional bodies such as the Institute of Housing;

(b) *by a particular statute*. Here an Act of Parliament creates and grants powers to the corporation. Public corporations such as the Independent Broadcasting Authority have been created in this way, and outside London, the corporate status and powers of all local authorities in England and Wales are contained in the Local Government Act 1972;

(c) *by registration under the Companies Act 1985*. The 1985 Act recognises two basic forms of registered company, public limited companies and private limited companies. The distinction between public and private companies is examined later in the chapter.

The liability of the members of a registered company may be limited either by shares or guarantee, or in rare cases be unlimited. This is provided for by s.1(2) of the Companies Act 1985 which states that a company may be:

(i) limited by *shares*, where the liability of the company members, the shareholders, is limited to any amount as yet unpaid on their shares; or

(ii) limited by *guarantee*, where the members' liability is limited to an amount they have guaranteed to contribute in the event of the company being brought to an end, a process known technically as winding up; or

(iii) *unlimited*, where the members are fully liable for the debts of the company, in the event of it being wound up.

Unlimited companies can only operate as private companies. They operate primarily as service and investment companies. Although the number of public limited companies is relatively small (whilst they are numbered in thousands, private companies are numbered in hundreds of thousands), they are certainly of great commercial importance. They include the major banks, and multinational organisations such as ICI, British Airways and Lloyds Bank. It is usual to find that public companies have begun life as private companies which have become sufficiently successful commercially to warrant *going public*, that is offering their shares to the general public.

The classification of companies registerable under the Companies Act 1985 is contained in the following figure.

Public Limited Companies	Private Companies
limited by shares	limited by shares
limited by guarantee (with a share capital)	limited by guarantee
	unlimited

Figure 2.2 *Classification of Registered Companies under the Companies Act 1985*

Certain other statutes allow for incorporation by registration, for example working mens' clubs and organisations such as workers' co-operatives, can incorporate by registration under the Industrial and Provident Society Acts 1965-1975. The latter group, which have grown in number over recent years can also be registered as companies limited by guarantee, or may operate as partnerships (see later).

Statutory registration was first introduced under the Companies Act 1844, to provide a method of forming corporations which was less expensive and cumbersome than obtaining a charter or sponsoring legislation through Parliament. The system of statutory registration proved immediately popular and helped to provide the capital which the growth of business activity at that time urgently needed. Capital was provided by investors attracted not only by the investment prospects offered by newly formed registered companies but also by the financial protection available through limited liability. The registered company remains just as popular with investors today, and has been further stimulated by the privatisation programme of the Thatcher and Major Governments, under which many previously state owned businesses have been sold off to the public, for example Jaguar Cars, British Telecom, British Airways, and the Electricity Companies.

Later we will consider in more detail the legal implications of trading as a corporate body, but before so doing, it is helpful to look first at business organisations which function as unincorporated bodies, and examine their legal status. As we shall see, the legal status of a business is a matter of considerable importance to its members, not least because it is largely responsible for describing what their rights and responsibilities are, and hence their relationship to the organisation and to each other.

Unincorporated Bodies

The two types of unincorporated businesses we need to consider are the sole trader and the partnership.

Sole Traders

The term 'sole trader' is an expression used to describe an individual who is self employed operating a business alone and who has sole responsibility for its management. In practice, of course, sole traders rarely work alone and will usually employ staff to assist them in the operation of the business. There are no specific legal formalities relating to the creation of such businesses. However operating as a sole trader will necessarily involve the owner in buying and selling, employing staff and acquiring business premises. As an employer, a sole trader is subject to the law relating to employment contained in the common law, (that is law defined by the courts) and numerous statutes, (law determined by Parliament), the most important of which is the Employment Protection (Consolidation) Act 1978 (as amended). In addition, as a supplier of goods or services, a sole trader must comply with the law relating to consumer protection, for example the Sale of Goods Act 1979, the Trade Descriptions Act 1968 and the Supply of Goods and Services Act 1982 (see Chapter 5). Some types of business enterprise must also acquire a licence to permit them to operate. For example a publican requires a licence to sell intoxicating drinks and a turf accountant a betting and gaming licence.

A sole trader's business will normally be financed by the owner himself, which means that the opportunities for raising business capital are necessarily restricted. Whilst the sole owner is entitled to all the profits of the business, he has unlimited liability in relation to its losses and so must bear them personally. The sole trader form of business is therefore most suitable for an individual who wishes to retain absolute control of the sort of business enterprise which requires only a modest amount of financial investment. Obvious examples include retail shops and service trades such as plumbing and hairdressing. Collectively, sole traders provide a valuable service to the community by making a wide range of goods and services available in a personal way, meeting needs which might otherwise be unfulfilled.

The responsibility for decision making in such a business rests with the owner, and there is no individual or group to which he is made directly accountable. This is very attractive to those who wish to 'be their own boss'. Of course there are groups who will be affected by the owner's actions such as the customers or clients, the creditors to whom the business owes money, and especially the employees of the business. Such groups have a valid interest in the decisions made by the sole trader and may ultimately seek to hold him accountable for his actions. For instance an employee may complain that employment rights have been infringed, or a customer that consumer rights have been abused. Accountability is perhaps at its most extreme level in the event of the sole trader becoming insolvent, that is being unable to meet the debts of the business.

Over recent years there has been a substantial increase in the number of one-man businesses being established and this trend has been encouraged by the government by giving grants and offering tax advantages to small businesses. The present climate of unemployment has resulted in large numbers of skilled and unskilled workers losing their jobs and many receive lump sum payments as compensation. There is evidence that increasing numbers of such individuals have been willing to use their redundancy payments as initial capital to set up a business in which they will be their own employer.

Partnerships

The other major form of unincorporated business organisation is the partnership. Partnerships are commonly referred to as 'firms' and the Partnership Act 1890 states under s.4 that: *"Persons who have entered into a partnership with one another for the purposes of this Act are called collectively 'a firm', and the name under which their business is carried on is called the firm-name"*. There are no detailed legal formalities required when individuals agree to operate a business together and thus form a partnership, and the advantages to a business enterprise of forming a partnership are somewhat similar to those enjoyed by the sole trader. The partners are capable of managing their own firm as they see fit, of sharing the profits and being able to deal directly with their customers or clients.

The partnership provides the compromise of allowing an extension of skill and expertise and the possible influx of additional capital by the introduction of extra partners. This extra potential for capital allows many partnerships to grow to become substantial business enterprises.

Although it has always tended to be overshadowed by the limited company, the partnership remains a significant form of business organisation in the United Kingdom, and is the choice of many people either setting up a new business or modifying an existing one. There are in fact over two million businesses operated either as partnerships or under sole trader arrangements, a clear indication of their popularity as a business form.

An agreement between two or more persons to form a partnership will constitute a contract but there is no legal requirement as to its specific form. It may be oral, in writing, contained in a deed, or even implied by the law from the surrounding circumstances. The Partnership Act 1890, which contains most of the legal rules relating to partnerships, defines a partnership under s.1 simply as the *"relation which subsists between persons carrying on business in common with a view of profit"*. It follows from this definition that it is quite possible for a business to be run as a joint venture without the participants ever being aware that their business is in law a partnership. Whilst this may be of no consequence to them for as long as they are able to work together in harmony, in the event of a dispute it is important to them to ascertain whether their relationship constitutes a partnership. If it does the provisions of the 1890 Act will apply, and as we shall see the effect of this statute on the partnership business in terms of the rights and obligations it lays down is substantial.

The main risk in operating a business as a firm is that if the business should get into financial difficulties, the liability of the partners is not limited in any way. The individual members are liable to the extent of their personal wealth to pay off partnership debts, which may result in them losing their house and car and most of their other personal possessions.

Partnership formalities

As noted earlier, a partnership agreement can be created in many ways. The 1890 Act lays down no formalities. It is of course commercially desirable, and common practice, for partners to execute a deed of partnership, in which they provide for matters such as the capital contribution required from each member of the firm, and how profits and losses are to be divided. If the partners do not agree such details then the rights and duties laid down under the Act will apply to the partnership.

By s.716 Companies Act 1985, a partnership cannot validly consist of more than twenty members. An exception is made however for certain professions, such as accountants and solicitors, who are prevented by statute from practising as limited companies. No restriction is placed upon the size of such firms. Some of the largest firms of lawyers and accountants have in excess of a hundred partners.

The partners may choose any name they please for the firm provided it is not similar to an existing name and therefore not likely to mislead others. Also, there is a legal restriction that the last name must not be the word 'limited' or any abbreviation of it, for this would indicate that the organisation is a company having limited liability. The words 'and Co' at the end of the partnership name refers to the fact that there are partners in the firm whose names do not appear in the firm name. Under the Business Names Act 1985 when a firm carries on business using a trading name which does not consist of the surnames of all the partners then their names must appear on their business stationery, and their true names and addresses must be prominently displayed at their business premises in a place to which the public have access. Non-compliance with these statutory provisions is a criminal offence.

The definition of partnership

It will be recalled that the definition of a partnership under s.1 requires there to be:

- a business;
- carried on in common by its members;
- with a view to making a profit.

Under the Act *"business"* includes every trade, occupation or profession. Although business is a broad term it does seem that it involves the carrying on of some form of commercial activity. This may be for a single purpose.

> In *Spicer (Keith) Ltd. v. Mansell* 1970 the Court of Appeal held that two persons who were working together for the purpose of forming a limited company, and had opened a bank account and ordered goods in this connection were not in partnership prior to the

incorporation of the company (which in fact was never formed). The reason was that at that time, they were preparing for business, rather than operating an existing one.

Further examples of how the courts have approached the question of determining whether a business exists are provided by the following two cases. They in fact involve individuals rather than firms, but they provide a useful illustration of the thin line that often exists between a mere hobby and a business.

> In *Eiman v. London Borough of Waltham Forest* 1982 the issue was whether the defendant had been rightly convicted in the Crown Court of the offence of making a demand for unsolicited goods *"in the course of a trade or business"*, contrary to the Unsolicited Goods and Services Act 1971. As a full time employee of the local authority the accused had, as a hobby, composed and published a book of verse. He had then sent out copies of the book to local libraries and made a demand for payment. The High Court held that the Crown Court was entitled to convict the defendant as what had started as a hobby, had become a *"business"* as defined by the Act and therefore the Unsolicited Goods and Services Act did apply. The court found it possible to reach such a conclusion despite the fact that this was an isolated incident without any intention to make a profit.

> In *Blakemore v. Bellamy* 1983 the question was whether the accused's spare time activity of buying and selling motor cars through advertisements, contravened the Fair Trading Act 1973, and the Business Advertisements (Disclosure) Order 1977. This is because in the course of a business it is an offence to *"advertise goods for sale"* without making it clear that the goods were sold in the course of a business. Offences under the Trade Descriptions Act, 1968 were also alleged which involved applying false trade descriptions to two of the vehicles in the course of a business. Despite the number of transactions involved, eight in all, the High Court agreed with the Magistrates' finding that the defendant's activity was merely a hobby rather than a business. Accordingly the statutory provisions had not been infringed, for the sales were merely private bargains. This was despite the fact that the defendant's objective in making the sales was to achieve gain or reward and as a seller he had clearly demonstrated skill and expertise in the business of buying and selling cars.

The business must be a joint venture, which implies mutual rights and obligations existing between the members of it. There may still be a joint venture even though one (or more) of its members is a *sleeping partner* who does not take an active part in the management of the business but simply contributes capital.

There must be a profit motive underlying the business. It will be a question of fact whether the partners aim to make a profit.

Help in determining when a business may be treated as a partnership is provided by s.2. It states that where a person receives a share in the profits of a business, this will be prima facie evidence that he is a partner, although the presumption can be shifted by other conflicting evidence. The section goes on to state a list of situations which do not, of themselves, make a person a partner, namely where a person:

(i)   receives a debt or other liquidated amount out of the profits of a business, whether or not by instalments;

(ii)   being a servant or agent is paid out of a share of the profits of the business;

(iii) being the widow or child of a deceased partner receives an annuity (an annual set payment) out of a portion of the profits of the business in which the deceased was a partner;

(iv) lends money to a person engaged or about to engage in business, on a written contract signed by, or on behalf of the parties to it that the lender shall be repaid either at a rate of interest varying with the profits, or as a share of the profits;

(v) receives by way of annuity or otherwise a portion of the profits of a business in consideration of the sale by that person of the goodwill of the business.

In *Pratt v. Strick* 1932 a situation of the kind described in (v) above occurred. A doctor sold his medical practice together with its goodwill, on terms that for the following three months he would remain living at the practice, introducing patients, and sharing profits and losses equally with the purchaser. It was held that the practice was the purchaser's as soon as he bought it.

Two further situations are specified by s.2 which it indicates do not automatically give rise to a partnership. Firstly co-ownership of land, even where profits are shared from the use of the land. Secondly the sharing of gross returns even if the people sharing the returns have a common right or interest in the property which is yielding the income. This draws a distinction between returns and profit. A return is the revenue obtained by some business activity, such as the receipts obtained from the sale of a book over a fixed period, whilst the profit is the sum left after deducting costs from revenue. In the example these would include printing and transport costs.

Registered Companies

As we have already seen the registered company limited by shares is a corporate body, an artificial person recognised by the law, which has an identity separate and distinct from the members which compose it. The members of such an organisation are referred to as its shareholders. The limited company is the most common type of business enterprise operated as a corporation, although there are of course many other types of corporation in existence. These were considered earlier in the chapter.

Many thousands of registered limited companies operate in this country and between them they employ the majority of the nation's workforce and comprise about two thirds of the income made by the private sector. Companies can be formed which have only two members. They can also develop into massive multi-national UK registered enterprises which have thousands of shareholders. Such is the diversity of these organisations that it is difficult to generalise on their structure and behaviour but most have been formed with the expectation of future expansion financed by the raising of capital through the issue of shares. As separate legal entities they also give the owners the protection of limited liability and it is this feature more than any other that has contributed to their popularity. Another appealing feature is that ownership can be divorced from management, thus an investor can stake capital in a company without having to be involved in the actual running of it whilst maintaining control over the managers by means of their accountability in the general meeting.

Limited liability means that in the event of the company facing financial difficulty the shareholders' legal liability to contribute to the payment of debts is limited to the amount, if any, unpaid on their shares. For instance, if an individual purchases twenty £1 shares in the company and pays 25p on each share (these are called partly paid shares) he is only liable to contribute the amount of the share value remaining unpaid, in this case 20 x 75p, a total of £15.

It is of course only the shareholders whose liability is limited. The company itself is fully liable for its debts, and may be brought to an end through the process of winding-up if it cannot meet them.

Companies can expand and diversify by raising additional capital when it is needed, through the issue of more shares, and hence large scale commercial organisations have evolved with thousands of shareholders holding between them millions of shares. The growth of this form of business enterprise and the recognition of the company as a separate legal entity has however posed many problems and led to many abuses. The law has recognised these difficulties. Various Companies Acts, now consolidated in the Companies Act 1985, have attempted to regulate corporate behaviour, bearing in mind not only the interests of the shareholders themselves but also the interests of outsiders who trade with them.

The concept of corporate personality

As we have seen the limited company is an artificial legal person, and has some although not all the powers and responsibilities of a natural person. It is capable therefore of owning property, entering into contracts such as trading contracts and contracts of employment, and of suing or being sued in its own name. But its artificial nature imposes some obvious limitations upon its legal capacity. It cannot generally be held liable for criminal acts, since most crimes involve proving a mental element such as intention or recklessness and a corporation has as such no mind. Nevertheless there may occur circumstances in which the collective intention of the Board of Directors can be regarded as expressing the will of the corporation. Lord Denning has spoken of the company as having a human body, the employees being the hands that carry out its work while *"others are directors and managers who represent the directing mind and will of the company and control what it does"*.

Since the membership of a company is distinct from the corporate body this means that the company shareholders are separate from the company which has a legal personality of its own. Changes in its membership, including the death or bankruptcy of members, will have no effect upon the company, which may have an almost perpetual life span if there remain investors willing to become or to remain members of it.

The separation of a company from its members was confirmed in the leading case of *Salomon v. Salomon & Co.* 1897. Salomon owned a boot and shoe business. His sons worked in the business and they were anxious to have a stake in it so Salomon formed a registered company with himself as managing director, in which his wife, daughter and each son held a share. The company's nominal capital was £40,000 consisting of 40,000 £1 shares.

The company resolved to purchase the business at a price of £39,000. Salomon had arrived at this figure himself. It was an honest but optimistic valuation of its real worth. The company paid him by allotting him 20,000 £1 shares treated as fully paid, £10,000 worth of debentures (a secured loan repayable before unsecured loans) and the balance in cash. Within a year of trading the company went into insolvent liquidation owing £8,000 to ordinary creditors and having only £6,000 worth of assets. The plaintiff, Mr. Salomon, claimed that as a debenture holder with £10,000 worth of debentures he was a secured creditor and entitled to repayment before the ordinary unsecured creditors. The unsecured creditors did not agree. The House of Lords held that despite the fact that following the company's formation, Salomon had continued to run the business in the same manner and with the same control as he had done when it was unincorporated, the company formed was a separate person from Salomon himself. When the company was liquidated therefore, and in the absence of any fraud on the creditors and shareholders, Salomon, like any other debenture holder, was a secured creditor and entitled to repayment before ordinary creditors. The Court thus upheld the principle that a company has a separate legal existence from its membership even where one individual holds the majority of shares and effectively runs the company as his own.

A company is also the owner of its own property in which its members have no legal interest, although clearly they have a financial interest.

> In *Macaura v. Northern Assurance Co. Ltd.* 1925 it was held that a majority shareholder has no insurable interest in the company's property. A fire insurance policy over the company's timber estate was therefore invalid as it had been issued in the plaintiff shareholder's name and not the company's name.

Both the Courts and Parliament have accepted that situations may arise in which it is right and proper to prevent the members from escaping liability by hiding behind the company. The result has been the creation of a number of exceptions to the principle of limited liability. These exceptions seem to be based broadly upon public policy considerations, and many of them are associated with fraudulent practices.

So for example if a company is wound up and the court is satisfied that the directors have carried on the business with an intention to defraud the creditors, they may be made personally liable for all the company's debts. This would cover trading and incurring debts, where they knew that there was no reasonable prospect that the creditors would be paid.

In special cases, the courts will disregard the separate legal personality of a company because it was formed or used to facilitate the evasion of legal obligations. This is sometimes referred to as 'lifting the veil of incorporation', meaning that the court is able to look behind the corporate, formal identity of the organisation to the shareholders which make it up. Clearly this is a very significant step, since it is effectively denying the protection which the members have sought to obtain by incorporation.

> In *Gilford Motor Co. Ltd. v. Horne* 1933 the defendant had been employed by the plaintiff motor company and had entered into a valid agreement not to solicit the plaintiff's customers or to compete with it for a certain time after leaving the company's employment. Shortly after leaving the employment of the motor company, the defendant formed a new company to carry on a similar business to that of his former employers and sent out circulars to the customers he had previously dealt with whilst working for the old business. In an action to enforce the restraint clause against the new company the court held that as the defendant in fact controlled the new company, its formation was a mere *"cloak or sham"* to enable him to break the restraint clause. Accordingly an injunction was granted against the defendant and against the company he had formed, to enforce the restraint clause.

The courts are also prepared to lift the veil in order to discover the relationship within groups of companies. It is a common commercial practice for one company to acquire shares in another, often holding sufficient shares to give it total control over the other. In these circumstances the controlling company is referred to as a *holding* company, and the other company its *subsidiary*. In appropriate cases a holding company can be regarded as an agent of its subsidiary, although it is more usual to find the subsidiary acting as an agent for the holding company.

> In *DHN Food Distributors Ltd. v. Tower Hamlets LBC.* 1976 an arrangement under which two subsidiaries of the holding company were wholly owned by it and had no separate business operations from it, was held by the court to constitute a single corporate body rather than three separate ones.

> In *Re: Bugle Press Ltd.* 1961 the company consisted of three shareholders. Two of them, who together had controlling interest, wanted to buy the shares of the third, but he was not willing to sell so the two of them formed a new company which then made a 'take-over

bid' for the shares of the first company. Not surprisingly the two shareholders who had formed the new company accepted the bid. The third did not. However since he only held 1/10 of the total shareholding, under what is now s.428 Companies Act 1985, the new company was able to compulsorily acquire the shares. The Court of Appeal however held that this represented an abuse of the section. The minority shareholder was in effect being evicted from the company. The veil of the new company was lifted and, in the words of Harman LJ: this revealed a *"hollow sham"*, for it was *"nothing but a little hut built round"* the majority shareholders.

In addition there are a number of provisions contained in the Companies Act 1985 which have the effect of lifting the veil. They include the following:

(a)   a fall in the membership of a company to below 2, under s.24. In these circumstances if the condition continues for more than six months, the sole shareholder becomes personally liable for the company's debts incurred after that time. Note that to be a member of a company it is only necessary to hold a single share.

(b)   Under s.349(4) if an officer of a company or any person on its behalf:

(i)   uses the company seal and the company name is not engraved on it;

(ii)   issues or authorises the issue of a business letter or signs a negotiable instrument and the company name is not mentioned;

(iii) issues or authorises the issue of any invoice, receipt or letter of credit of the company and again the company name is not mentioned;

that person shall be personally liable for debts incurred unless they are paid by the company.

In *Penrose v. Martyr* 1858 a bill of exchange was drawn up with the word 'limited' omitted after the company's name and the company secretary who had signed the bill on the company's behalf was held to be personally liable for it.

(c)   Under powers granted to the Department of Trade and Industry to investigate the affairs of any company within the same group as one primarily under investigation by a DTI Inspector. S442(1) provides that where there appears to be good reason to do so, the Department may appoint inspectors to investigate and report on the membership of any company in order to determine the true identity of the persons financially interested in its success or failure, or able to control or materially influence its policy.

(d)   Under sections 213 and 214 Insolvency Act 1986. These important provisions, which need to be carefully considered, are invoked in the course of the winding up of a company. We shall be looking closely at the winding up process at the end of the chapter. In cases where sections 213 and 214 apply they have the effect of lifting the corporate veil, exposing those who have been engaged in the running of the company to personal liability, and they therefore represent a significant inroad to the principle of limited liability and the separation of the company from its members. Indeed s.214 has been described as one of the most important modifications to the principle of limited liability this century. S.213 deals with cases of fraudulent trading, and s.214 with cases of wrongful trading and are considered in more depth in the discussion of winding up procedures.

Classification of Companies

S1 Companies Act 1985 provides that a registered company limited by shares may be either a *public* or a *private* one. The most significant distinction between them is that a public limited company is permitted to advertise publicly to invite investors to take shares in it. A private company cannot advertise its shares in this way. Once purchased, shares in a public company can then be freely disposed of by the shareholder to anyone else who is willing to buy them. By contrast private companies commonly issue shares on terms that if the member wishes to dispose of them they must first be offered to the existing members. Where such rights are available to members they are known as *pre-emption* rights.

Before 1980 all companies were treated as being public ones, unless the company's articles of association contained specific provisions which enabled it to acquire private company status. Legislation passed in 1980, and now contained in the Companies Act 1985, completely reversed this situation, making private companies the residual class. Thus all companies are now treated as though they are private ones, unless certain requirements have been met which allow the company to be registered as a public limited company. This change was introduced to make it easier to define public companies for the purpose of complying with EC company law directives applicable to public companies.

Registration as a public limited company

This can be achieved by satisfying the following requirements:

(i) stating both in the company name, and in its memorandum that it is a public company. Thus its name must end in the words *"public limited company"* or the more convenient form *"plc."* The name of a private company will end with the word *"limited"* or *"Ltd."*;

(ii) registering a memorandum of association which is in the form contained in Table F of the Companies (Tables A to F) Regulations 1985;

(iii) meeting the requirements of s.11 of the 1985 Act, which states that the company must have an authorised share capital figure of at least £50,000. The memorandum of association always contains a capital clause stating the amount of capital a company can raise by issuing shares, and it is in this clause that the authorised share capital amount appears. At least one quarter of this amount must be paid up before the company can commence trading, or exercise its borrowing powers, and the company must have allotted shares up to the authorised minimum (ss.101 and 107). Consequently a plc. must have at least £12,500 paid up share capital before it starts trading, and be able to call for an additional £37,500 from its members.

It may be useful here to explain these terms regarding company capital.

The *nominal share capital* is the amount that the company is legally authorised to raise by the issue of shares, the *paid-up share capital* is the amount the company has received from the shares it has issued, and the *uncalled capital* is the amount remaining unpaid by shareholders for the shares they hold; e.g. a company may issue £1 shares but require those to whom they are allotted to pay only 50p per share for the present.

The expression *allotment of shares* describes the notification by the company, usually in the form of a letter, that it has accepted an offer for the shares, and that the new shareholders name will be entered on the register of shareholders.

A registered company which does not meet the three requirements listed above will be treated as a private company. Private companies differ from public companies in a number of respects, and an examination of these differences is a way of gaining an appreciation of the nature of these two forms of registered company.

We can carry out the examination by considering the advantages and disadvantages of a private company over a public one.

The advantages of a private company

In contrast to a public company a private company enjoys the following advantages:

- it does not require a minimum level of share capital either to register or to commence trading. Its share capital could legitimately comprise of £1 made up of two 50 pence shares, the members holding a share each;

- it can avoid s.89 Companies Act 1985, which provides that ordinary shares issued for cash by the company must first be offered to existing ordinary shareholders in proportion to the nominal value of their existing holdings – a *rights issue*. S.91 provides that s.89 can be excluded by a private company in its articles;

- it has a much greater freedom to issue shares in return for assets other than cash than a public company has; (e.g. where it purchases property which it pays for by transferring fully paid shares to the vendor);

- the directors have more freedom in their financial dealings with the company and need not disclose as much information about such dealings in the company accounts as is the case for directors of public companies;

- subject to its size it may be excluded from publication of some or all of its accounts;

- no special qualifications are required of the company secretary;

- it has power to purchase its own shares, and may do so out of capital;

- it can use procedures to avoid the need to hold meetings and satisfy various other statutory obligations. These procedures were introduced by provisions contained in the Companies Act 1989, designed to make it easier for private companies to comply with the substantial level of statutory regulation imposed upon registered companies. The objective has been to further deregulate the private company, thereby assisting it in the conduct of its business affairs. What the Act does is to permit private companies to *deregulate* themselves by means of the use of two types of resolution, the written resolution and the elective resolution. By using the *written* resolution procedure a private company is able to do anything which would otherwise require a resolution of the members in a general meeting of the company. An *elective* resolution can be used by a private company as a means of avoiding a number of formalities that it would otherwise have to observe under company legislation such as the need to obtain the authority of the members before the company issues shares, the need to lay accounts and reports before the general meeting, the need to hold an annual general meeting, and to reappoint auditors annually. Like the written resolution, the elective resolution requires the unanimous approval of all the company members entitled to attend and vote at a general meeting.

The disadvantages of a private company

The only major disadvantage it suffers is that it cannot advertise its securities to the public through the issue of a prospectus or other advertising device. S.170 Financial Services Act 1986 however does enable the Secretary of State to make regulations allowing for purely private advertisements between the issuer and the recipient. This lack of capacity to raise capital through the public issue of shares can really only be regarded as a disadvantage if the growth of the business needs to be financed in this way, when the company faces a choice between remaining privately owned and seeking finance by other means, or of going public and reducing the level of control exercisable by the original members over the new business as new members are brought in. It is worth bearing in mind that in general, company survival is achieved by growth. Such growth may be through the expansion of its core business. Alternatively it may occur through mergers with other companies, or, most commonly, where one company acquires another. But however growth occurs it must always be financed.

The meaning of the expression 'public company'

As we have seen a public limited company is one which satisfies certain statutory criteria. However the expression public company is sometimes used in a commercial rather than a legal sense to denote companies whose shares are dealt with on the Stock Exchange; major United Kingdom organisations such as ICI and Marks and Spencer are examples. Technically such companies are 'listed' or 'market' companies. Not all public limited companies are quoted i.e. listed on the Stock Exchange, but only the largest ones which are able to meet the stringent entry requirements the Stock Exchange demands. Those public limited companies which are not quoted on the Stock Exchange will offer their securities in one of the intermediate securities markets, such as the Unlisted Securities Market (the USM) a 'junior league' of the Stock Exchange set up in 1980. The other intermediate securities markets are the Over the Counter Market and the Third Market. Thus public and private companies can be classified by reference to the method by which their shares can be issued.

Activity

Carry out some simple research in your local community to establish as far as possible the legal nature of the businesses operating within it. Which are corporate bodies and which are not? Have a look inside business premises you visit to see if you can find registration of business name certificates publicly displayed there.

Formation of a Registered Company

A company is incorporated and so comes into being when the Registrar of Companies issues it with a document called the certificate of incorporation. This certificate is issued following an application by the persons who wish to form the company. They are known as the company's *promoters*. The two main documents which must be included in the application are the memorandum of association and the articles of association. Once the certificate of incorporation has been granted a private company can commence trading immediately. However a public company must be issued with a further document, a trading certificate, before it is authorised to start trading.

The Memorandum of Association

The memorandum of association and the articles of association set out the constitution of a registered company. They are the two major documents within a group of documents to be sent to the Registrar of Companies prior to incorporation. A memorandum is required by the Companies Act 1985 which specifies that it must include the following matters:

(i)   the name of the company with 'limited' as the last word in the case of a private company, or 'public limited company' in the case of a public company;

(ii)   the situation of the registered office identifying whether the company is situated in England or Scotland;

(iii)   the objects of the company;

(iv)   the liability of the members;

(v)   the nominal capital of the company and its division into numbers of shares and denominations.

The Registrar of Companies maintains a file for all registered companies, which is open to public inspection on payment of a fee. The file for each company includes the company memorandum. The contents of the memorandum are of importance to the members of the company itself (the shareholders), and especially to those who deal with the company commercially. The indication that the company has limited liability shown by the inclusion of the word 'limited', serves as a warning to outsiders that in the event of the company being unable to meet its financial liabilities at any time, its shareholders, as we have previously seen, can only be called upon to make good any loss up to the value which remains unpaid to the company on their shares. Once however the shares have been fully paid the shareholders' financial liability ceases. Of course the liability of the company, as opposed to its members, is not limited in any way and if it is wound up all its assets will be used to meet the claims of the creditors.

Stating the country in which the company is situated determines whether it is an English or Scottish company. Usually a Notice of Situation of Registered Office, giving the company's full address is sent to the Registrar together with the Memorandum. It must, in any event, be sent to him within fourteen days of incorporation of the company. The registered office is important since documents are effectively served on the company by posting or delivering them to this address. Thus a writ (a document used to commence legal proceedings) served on the company will be effectively served if delivered to the registered office.

The *objects clause* sets the contractual limits within which the company can validly operate. The need to state the company's objects may be seen as a protection to shareholders by giving them some reassurance as to the ways in which their capital may be used by the directors. A company, can, however, resolve to alter its objects, and in any event it is usual to draft the objects clause very widely. Furthermore even if a company acts outside its objects clause the transaction will in most cases be binding on it, although the members may seek to censure the authorising directors. This matter is considered in more detail below.

The *liability clause* is a formality which merely states the nature of the shareholders' liability, that is whether it is limited by shares, by guarantee, or unlimited.

The *capital clause* sets out the amount of capital the company is authorised to raise by the issue of shares, and the way in which the shares are to be divided. This amount can be raised by the agreement of the shareholders without difficulty, although a reduction in the share capital, whilst possible, is more of a problem to achieve. It is a basic principle of company law that share capital should be maintained to protect the interests of the company's creditors.

The memorandum concludes with the names and addresses of those people agreeing to take shares in the company on its formation and indicating how many shares each will take. These people are called *subscribers*. The subscribers for the shares in the memorandum will often be appointed as directors. As the statutory minimum membership of a company is two, two subscribers to the memorandum will suffice to form the company. Each subscriber will agree to take a certain number of shares on incorporation of the company, and the subscribers are therefore the first members of the company. Subsequently new members will join the company when it allots shares to them and their names are entered on the register of members which every company must maintain, and which is open to public inspection. Usually the subscribers will have been the promoters – the people engaged in setting up the company.

Company name

Generally a company is free to choose the name it wishes to adopt, although as we have seen the word 'limited' for a private company or 'plc' for a public company must be inserted at the end of the company name. This is required by s.26 Companies Act 1985. The section also provides that the name cannot be the same as one already held on the index of company names kept by the Registrar. Nor can a name be used which would in the opinion of the Secretary of State constitute a criminal offence or be offensive.

It is a tort for a person to represent his business as that of another and thereby obtain profit from that other's business goodwill. In such circumstances the injured business can claim under the tort of passing off against the business guilty of the deception and recover damages and obtain an injunction, by way of a remedy.

> In *Ewing v. Buttercup Margarine Co. Ltd.* 1917 the plaintiff, who carried on business using the name Buttercup Dairy Co. obtained an injunction against the defendant company on the grounds that the public might be confused as to the identity of the two organisations.

It makes no difference whether the name is real or invented.

> In *Exxon Corporation v. Exxon Insurance Consultants International Ltd.* 1981 the plaintiffs obtained an injunction to prevent the defendants from passing off its goods as the defendant's by the use of the word 'Exxon'. The plaintiffs, formerly the Esso Company, had invented the word *Exxon* as a replacement name. They were however unsuccessful in seeking an injunction for breach of copyright. The court held that the word 'Exxon' was not an *"original literary work"* under the Copyright Act 1956, since, in the words of Stephenson LJ a *"literary work is something intended to afford either information and instruction or pleasure in the form of literary enjoyment"*.

The objects clause and the ultra vires doctrine

Being a corporate body the registered company can only lawfully do those things which its constitution allows it to do. This is a feature of corporate status which we have already considered. It is a direct consequence of the artificiality of corporations which, being purely creations of the law, only possess a restricted capacity. As a condition of incorporation every registered company must include a statement in its memorandum which sets out what the company has been formed to do. The scope or extent of this statement, known as the company's *objects clause*, is initially decided by the people setting up the company, its promoters. They will often become the company's first directors following its incorporation.

The details contained in the objects clause provide shareholders with a description of the range of activities their company can legitimately undertake. It is right that as investors, a company's shareholders should know the purpose for which their financial contribution can be used. A rational investor will want to establish how well the board of directors manages the company, something which can be achieved by looking at the company's trading performance in its particular line of business. An investor may be less willing to put money into an enterprise where the board has a wide freedom under the company's objects clause to pursue diverse commercial activities, some of which may fall well outside their experience as managers. This is particularly likely in the smaller private companies, for whereas the boards handling the affairs of public companies will include executive directors having wide commercial experience, in small private limited companies directors will sometimes have at best only a rudimentary knowledge of business management, and at worst none at all.

If a company acts outside the limits of its permissible activities as expressed in the objects clause it is said to be acting *ultra vires*, that is beyond its powers. At common law an ultra vires transaction has always been treated as a nullity, consequently an ultra vires contract entered into by a company was neither enforceable by it or against it. Even if the other contracting party was unaware that the company was exceeding its powers as expressed in the memorandum this would provide no relief, for under the doctrine of *constructive notice* a person dealing with a company was deemed to be aware of its public documents and hence of any restrictions on the company's capacity contained in them. Nor could the company subsequently ratify in general meeting an ultra vires transaction made on its behalf by the directors. Ratification has the effect of retrospectively validating a transaction, but in the case of an ultra vires contract this is not possible since the contract is a nullity.

> The application of these principles is seen in *Ashbury Railway Carriage Co. Ltd. v. Riche* 1875. The company's objects included the power to manufacture or sell rail rolling stock and carry on business as mechanical engineers and general contractors. The company purchased a concession to finance the building of a railway in Belgium, but later the directors repudiated the contract. In an action for breach of contract against the company, the House of Lords held that the contract was ultra vires and void from the outset. Lord Cairns expressed the law when he said, *"This contract was entirely beyond the objects in the memorandum ... If it was a contract void at its beginning, it was void because the company could not make the contract".*

When the United Kingdom became a member of the European Community on 1st January, 1973, the European Communities Act 1972, by which entry was effected, in a hurried attempt at providing for some measure of harmonisation between English company law and company law as it applied in the other member states, introduced an important statutory modification to the ultra vires doctrine. This modification which was contained in s.9(1), and was subsequently incorporated unchanged into the Companies Act 1985 as s.35, provided that in favour of a person acting in good faith with a company, any transaction decided on by its directors was deemed to be within the capacity of the company to make. Whilst not eliminating the doctrine of ultra vires s.35 went some way towards reducing its impact. The Companies Act 1989, which implements more fully the first EC directive on company law, has introduced a new s.35 which goes much further towards eliminating ultra vires as it affects the registered company. As we shall see however the doctrine is still not completely dead.

The present law

The new s.35 states that, *"The validity of an act done by a company shall not be called into question on the ground of lack of capacity by reason on anything in the company's memorandum."* In other words it validates transactions which would otherwise be void on the grounds of breaching the company's constitution as expressed in the memorandum. The section goes on to say that anyone making a transaction with the company is not obliged to check the memorandum to ascertain whether it authorises the transaction. A further provision, s.711A, abolishes the doctrine of constructive notice of matters which would be disclosed by a company search. Previously, as we have seen, a person dealing with a company was in some circumstances deemed to have knowledge of information contained in the public file of the company held at the Companies Registry. This principle no longer applies.

The changes introduced under the Companies Act 1989 do not however completely eliminate the application of ultra vires to registered companies. In this context three matters need to be noted:

(i)   a shareholder still retains the power to seek an injunction to restrain the company from entering into an ultra vires transaction, although this opportunity is lost once the transaction has been made, whether or not it has been carried out;

(ii)   directors are still obliged to act within their company's constitution. S.35(3) says, *"it remains the duty of the directors to observe any limitations on their powers flowing from the company's memorandum"*. The company can now ratify action taken by directors in excess of their powers by means of a special resolution, thus reversing the position in the Ashbury Railway Carriage case, and an additional special resolution may be passed to relieve the directors of any liability they may have incurred for breach of duty as a result of exceeding the company's powers;

(iii) as a result of s.109 Companies Act 1989 if a director exceeds his powers and the other party to the contract is a director of the company or the holding company, the company can if it chooses avoid the contract. The section is an attempt at preventing directors defrauding the company using the provisions of the new s.35.

Whilst the powers of a company are found in its memorandum, the rules regulating the way in which these powers should be exercised are usually contained in the articles of association. Articles may, for example, cut down on the general powers enjoyed by directors to make contracts within the company's authorised areas of business, by requiring that transactions involving more than a certain amount of money be approved by the members through an ordinary resolution passed at a meeting of the company. This can give rise to circumstances where an outsider enters into a transaction with a company which its memorandum authorises, but where the company's internal rules have not been complied with. Internal rules contained in a company's articles of association, being contained in its public file, came within the doctrine of constructive notice: the outsider was deemed to be aware of them. What he could not know was whether they had in fact been complied with when a company decision was made.

For instance, he would have no way of discovering whether a resolution required to be passed by the company under the articles had been passed. As a response to this difficulty the rule in *Royal British Bank v. Turquand* 1856 provided that an outsider was entitled to assume that the necessary rules of internal management had been complied with.

The rule in *Turquands Case* is affected by the Companies Act 1989. It provides that a third party dealing in good faith with a company can treat the company's constitution as imposing no restrictions on the power of the board of directors or persons authorised by them to bind the company. This provision thus supersedes the rule in *Turquands Case*. A third party is assumed to be acting in good faith, unless the contrary can be shown. Knowledge that the directors are acting beyond their powers does not, in itself, amount to bad faith.

Alteration of the objects clause

By virtue of s.4 Companies Act 1985, a company may by means of a special resolution alter its object clause at any time and for any reason. The alteration is effective so long as no application is made to the court to cancel it within 21 days of the special resolution, and the company sends the Registrar within a further 15 days a copy of the altered memorandum. An application to cancel can be made by the holders of at least 15% of the issued share capital of any class, and the alteration is only effective in these circumstances where the court confirms it. It is relevant to point out in connection with the alteration of objects that a company can now adopt a single object to carry on business as a general commercial company (s.3A). A company formed with such an object will be able to carry on any business or trade, and do anything incidental or conducive to such a business or trade.

The Articles of Association

The articles of association of a registered company must be supplied to the Registrar of Companies prior to incorporation. Like the memorandum of association the articles will then be included in the company's file kept at Companies House in Cardiff.

The articles are concerned with the internal administration of the company, and it is for those setting up the company (its promoters) to determine the rules they consider appropriate for inclusion within the articles. The Companies Act 1985 does however provide a set of model articles which a company can adopt in whole or in part if it wishes. If a company fails to provide a set of articles then the model articles contained in the 1985 Act automatically apply to the company. They are known as *Table A* Articles. Matters which are normally dealt with in the Articles include the appointment and powers of the board of directors, the rules in relation to members' meetings and voting and the types of shares and rights attaching to the share categories.

Other registration documents

In addition to the memorandum and articles of association there are certain other documents which must be supplied to the Registrar prior to incorporation. These include a Statutory Declaration that all the requirements of the Act have been complied with. Fees must also be paid.

Having examined all the documents filed and ensured that they are in order, the Registrar then issues a certificate under official seal which certifies that the company is incorporated. The certificate is conclusive evidence that all the requirements of the Companies Act 1985 have been complied with and that the company is a company authorised to be registered and duly registered under the Act. A private company can enter into contracts, borrow money, and carry on business immediately on incorporation. However a public limited company registered under the 1985 Act cannot commence business until a certificate is issued by the Registrar that the share capital of the company is not less than the authorised minimum (i.e. £50,000 with at least one-quarter paid up). If more than a year after the incorporation of a public company it has not been issued with such a certificate the Secretary of State may petition the court for the company to be wound up.

Financing a Limited Company

There are various methods used by companies to raise capital, the issue of shares and debentures being two of the most significant methods. Before considering them in more detail, it will be helpful to recap and expand upon the meaning of the expression 'capital' which we encountered earlier in the chapter whilst examining the contents of the memorandum of association. Capital is unfortunately a broad expression carrying a number of meanings, however in relation to limited companies the following are the most common uses of the expression:

(i) *Nominal (or authorised) capital*
     This expression refers to the value of shares that a company is authorised to issue, and is included in the capital clause of its memorandum of association.

(ii) *Issued capital*
     This refers to the value of capital in the form of shares which have been actually issued to the shareholders.

(iii) *Paid-up capital*

This is the amount of capital which has actually been paid up on the shares issued, or the amount of capital that the company has actually raised and received. Under s.351 Companies Act 1985 if a company makes a reference to share capital on its business stationery or order forms, it must refer to its paid-up capital.

(iv) *Unpaid capital*

If shares which have been issued are not fully paid for, the amount outstanding is referred to as unpaid capital, e.g. if 5,000 shares issued have a nominal value of £1 each and only 50p has been paid up on them, then the paid up capital is £2,500 and the unpaid capital is £2,500. Shareholders may be required to pay up the unpaid amount on their shares by the company making a 'call' on them to do so.

(v) *Reserve capital*

A company, by special resolution (75% majority vote) may declare that any portion of its unpaid capital shall not be called up except if the company is being brought to an end by a winding up. This is called reserve capital and cannot be converted into ordinary capital for use in the operation of the company without the court's permission.

It is important to remember that the references to capital being made here are to share capital. The law regards capital as something positive, a financial contribution to the company which it can use for the purpose of its business. For instance it purchases business premises, which are then regarded as fixed capital, and stock, which becomes circulating capital. Accountants see capital in a different way. They regard it as something the company owes: the members are owed the company's share capital; the debenture holders are owed the loan capital. To the economist capital again has a different meaning. In the context of any discussion concerning capital it is clearly important to establish in which sense the term is being used. Here we are using the term in the legal sense.

Classes of shares

In Chapter 3 we shall be considering the definition of a share but for the present we may simply note that a shareholder is a stakeholder in the organisation - a company member. There is nothing to prevent a registered company limited by shares from issuing one class of shares with equal rights. Usually, however, different classes of shares are issued with varying rights attaching to them relating to such matters as voting, payment of dividends and return of capital on liquidation. The three main types of shares are:

(a) *Preference shares*

The main characteristic of a preference share is that it will have the right to a preferred fixed dividend. This means that the holder of a preference share is entitled to a fixed amount of dividend, e.g. 6% on the value of each share, before other shareholders are paid any dividend. They are presumed to be cumulative which means that if in any year the company fails to declare a dividend, the shortfall must be made up out of profits of subsequent years. A preference share is therefore a safe investment with fixed interest, no matter how small or large is the company's profit. As far as return of capital on a winding up is concerned, the preference shareholder will rank equally with ordinary shareholders for any payment due, unless the preference shares are made 'preferential as to capital'. Normally, preference shares do not carry voting rights and therefore the preference shareholder has little influence over the company's activities.

(b) *Ordinary shares*

Ordinary shares are often referred to as the *equity share capital* of a company. When a company declares a dividend and the preference shareholders have been paid, the holders of ordinary shares are entitled to the remainder. It follows therefore that an ordinary share-holder in a well-managed company making high profits will receive a good return on his investment and consequently the value of his shares will rise, e.g. a £1 ordinary share could have a market value of £1.25. Unfortunately, the reverse is also true and they may fall in market value so that ordinary shares inevitably involve a certain risk. This risk is re-flected in the amount of control that an ordinary shareholder has over the company's business. While voting rights are not normally attached to preference shares, they are at-tached to ordinary shares enabling the ordinary shareholder to voice an opinion in a general meeting and vote on major issues involving the running of the company. Ordinary shareholders will thus have the capacity to remove directors who have mismanaged the business of the company. An ordinary resolution is required in order to do so.

A private company, it will be recalled, is unable to issue its shares publicly. If it does so it loses its status as a private company. A public limited company can publicly advertise its shares which it may do either to acquire initial capital or more commonly to increase its existing capital. The methods used by a public limited company to raise capital from the public are:

(i)   through direct invitation to the public, through the issue of a *prospectus*;

(ii) by an *offer for sale*. This involves the company selling the total number of shares it hopes to issue to an organisation which specialises in financial transactions of this kind. Such or-ganisations are known, not surprisingly, as 'issuing houses'. They resell to the public at a higher price, by publishing a document called an 'offer for sale', which contains an appli-cation form for the prospective shareholder to complete and return to the issuing house; and

(iii) by *placing*. Again an issuing house is involved. It may subscribe for the share issued itself, reselling as in (ii) usually inviting its own clients to purchase the shares, or it may simply seek persons interested in purchasing the shares acting merely as an agent for the com-pany, which will pay a fee for the service provided. This is called 'brokerage'. The most common method used is (ii) above.

There are detailed legal provisions dealing with the public sale of shares. They are designed to protect the investing public, and are contained in the Financial Services Act 1986. One of the most important features of this statutory protection relates to the obligation on the company to disclose specific information of relevance to investors in reaching a decision as to whether to buy.

Debentures

A trading company may, as an alternative to a share issue, raise money by means of issuing a debenture or series of debentures. These may be secured by a charge or be unsecured. The definition of 'debenture' is very wide and includes all forms of securities (undertakings to repay money borrowed) which may or may not be secured by a charge on the company's assets. Indeed a mortgage of the company's property to a single individual may be regarded as a debenture within the definition. Debentures are usually made by means of a trust deed which will create a *fixed* charge over specific company property by mortgage and/or a *floating* charge over the rest of the company assets. The distinction between a fixed and floating charge is essentially that a company is not free to deal with assets subject to a fixed charge, i.e. by selling or mortgaging, but is free to deal with any of its assets covered by a floating charge. However, on the occurrence of a particular event, a floating charge is said to crystallise and is then converted into a fixed charge. Such an event occurs when money becomes payable under a condition in the debenture such as repayment of interest, and the debenture holder takes some steps to enforce his security because the interest due is unpaid.

The principal rights of a debenture holder are contained in the debenture deed. They will include:

(i)   the date of repayment of the loan and the rate of interest;

(ii) a statement of the assets of the company which are subject to fixed or floating charges;

(iii) the rights of the company to redeem the whole or part of the monies owing;

(iv) the circumstances in which the loan becomes immediately repayable, i.e. if the company defaults in repayment of interest;

(v)   the powers of the debenture holder to appoint a receiver and manager of the assets charged.

Other Forms of Financing

These include loans, which may be short term, such as overdraft arrangements and longer term loans which will normally be secured. Additionally through the use of factoring a company may raise money by selling its debts.

The acquisition of assets

It may be briefly noted here that a limited company is able to acquire property and property rights in the same way as an individual. As well as purchasing property outright, companies frequently take leased property such as vehicles and land under which they acquire limited rights of ownership. They also obtain goods on credit terms, for example by hiring equipment. The legal considerations applying to such arrangements are examined in detail later in the book.

Activity

Using your school, college or local library, see if you can find out how many public and private companies are at present incorporated. See if you can also find out how many of them have been wound up during the year.

The Termination of Business Organisations

The life of a business organisation can come to an end for many reasons. It may have achieved what its members required of it, so that it no longer has any useful value. It is not, for instance, unknown for a group of people to form a limited company for the purpose of carrying out a specific business venture, and insert a provision in the company's articles of association making it clear that the business is to last for a fixed period, or that it will expire on the happening of a certain event. A group of businessmen may contribute capital to a company they have formed, with the aim that the company will purchase, renovate and then sell certain industrial premises, or buy and then resell some other substantial asset. The company will end when the sale takes place if its sole purpose was the making of the sale.

A business may also come to an end because the commercial foundations upon which it was based have ceased to exist, or it has become no longer commercially viable to continue. If this occurs there is nothing to prevent the organisation from diversifying if this is acceptable to the members, thus prolonging the life of the business.

Most businesses which are terminated however, do not end their own lives out of choice, but because such action has been forced on them by their creditors. This occurs when the creditors lose confidence in the capacity of the organisation to repay them. It is a common feature of commercial life that when a business develops financial ill-health, its creditors will seek to reduce their losses by dissolving the business whilst there are still assets remaining in it.

Thus in considering the law as it affects the dissolution of businesses it is helpful to bear in mind the health of the organisation at the time it is being dissolved. The law, quite understandably, exerts far greater control over businesses which are terminated in circumstances of financial failure, than in cases where they are brought to an end fit and healthy, and nobody will lose money. Dissolution is important to the members of the business, who will be concerned as to what share of the assets they are entitled to, and for much the same reason it will be of concern to the creditors; they will want to know what the assets of the business are, and how they are to be distributed.

The process of dissolution

The process laid down for terminating or dissolving a business depends upon two factors:

- what the type of business is; and
- what its financial condition is.

We have previously seen that business organisations can be classified according to their legal status. Some are corporate bodies, some are unincorporated associations, whilst others are simple one man businesses. By now it should be clear that there are significant differences between these alternative business forms. This is reflected in the procedures for dissolving them. In the case of a limited company the procedure by which it is dissolved is referred to as a winding-up. Bankruptcy is the term used to describe the process by which an insolvent individual's assets are collected in, converted into money and distributed between his creditors. There is no technical term to describe the process for terminating a partnership. It is simply referred to as dissolution.

Dissolution of a Partnership

When the commercial activity of a partnership ceases so does the business itself, for it is no longer being *"carried on"* as required under the Partnership Act 1890. In such circumstances the partnership will be dissolved, and its assets disposed of to those legally entitled to them. Alternatively a partnership which is still in operation, may be dissolved on any one of a number of different grounds.

Dissolution can occur either with or without the intervention of the court. Under the Partnership Act 1890 a partnership is dissolved *without* the intervention of the court, in any of the following circumstances:

(a)   if it was entered into for a fixed term, when that term expires;

(b)   if it was entered into for a single venture, when that venture has been completed, for example, where the aim of the business is to acquire a single piece of property and resell it;

(c)   if entered into for an undefined time, by any partner giving notice to the other or others of his intention to dissolve the partnership. If such a notice is served then the partnership is dissolved from the date mentioned in the notice as the date of dissolution. If no date has been given, dissolution operates from the time the notice was received, subject to its articles providing for some other date;

(d) by the death or bankruptcy of any partner. Partnership articles will often provide that in such an event the partnership will continue to be run by the remaining partners. In the case of the death of a partner the articles may provide that the surviving partners will continue to run the business in partnership with the personal representative of the deceased;

(e) if a partner's share of the business is charged to secure a separate judgment debt, the other partners may dissolve the business;

(f) by the happening of an event which makes it unlawful for the business of the firm to be carried on, or for the members of the firm to carry it on in partnership. This may occur, for example, where there is a partnership between a British partner and a foreign partner, the business is carried on in the United Kingdom, and war breaks out between the countries of the respective partners.

Dissolution can be granted by *the court* on an application to dissolve, made by a partner, in any of the following cases:

(a) where a partner is suffering from a mental disorder;

(b) where a partner other than the partner petitioning:

(i) becomes in any way permanently incapable of performing their part of the partnership contract, e.g. through physical illness, or

(ii) has been guilty of misconduct in business or private life, as in the opinion of the court, bearing in mind the nature of the partnership business, is calculated to be prejudicial to the carrying on of the business, or

(iii) wilfully or persistently commits a breach of the partnership agreement, or otherwise behaves in a way in matters relating to the partnership business that it is impractical for the other partners to carry on in business with that partner.

Cases on dissolution on these grounds have included a refusal to meet for discussions on business matters, the keeping of erroneous accounts, persistent disagreement between the parties, and in *Anderson v. Anderson* 1857 where a father and son were in partnership together, by the opening by the father of all his son's correspondence;

(iv) where the business of the partnership can only be carried on at a loss;

(v) if circumstances have arisen which, in the opinion of the court, render it just and equitable that the partnership be dissolved.

In *Re: Yenidje Tobacco Co. Ltd.* 1916 although the company was trading profitably the court held that it was just and equitable to wind it up, on the basis that its two directors had become so hostile towards each other that they would only communicate by means of messages passed to each other via the Secretary, and that this amounted to a position of deadlock. It was pointed out that a private limited company is similar to a partnership, and that had the directors been partners in a partnership, there would have been sufficient grounds for dissolution. Lord Justice Warrington stated:

"... I am prepared to say that in a case like the present, where there are only two persons interested, and there are no shareholders other than those two, where there are no means of over-ruling by the action of a general meeting of shareholders the trouble which is occasioned by the quarrels of the two directors and shareholders, the company ought to be wound up if there exists such a ground as would be sufficient for the dissolution of a private partnership at the suit of one of the partners against the other. Such grounds exist in the present case."

The partnership and bankruptcy

Two distinct insolvency situations may arise which affect the partnership:

- one of the partners is declared personally bankrupt, whilst the remaining partners are personally solvent. This automatically brings the partnership to an end, although a new one may well be formed, without the bankrupt partner. The reason the firm automatically dissolves in such circumstances is because the bankrupt party's share passes to his trustee in bankruptcy, and thus in effect he is withdrawing his contribution and his stake in the business;

- the partnership itself is insolvent. If this is so, all the partners will normally have bankruptcy proceedings brought against them. It should be remembered that since a partnership does not grant limited liability to its members, they become personally liable for the debts which cannot be met by the assets of the firm.

The administration and distribution of assets

If the partnership is dissolved its property is gathered in, and used to pay all debts and liabilities. If after this is done a surplus is left it is distributed between the partners. What they receive will depend upon what their partnership agreement says. If it makes no provision for such a situation, the following rules are laid down by the 1890 Act:

(a) If there is no loss suffered by the firm, the surplus is used firstly to repay the capital contribution of the partners, and then to the partners in equal shares. Thus if the firm has three partners, A, B, and C, whose respective capital contributions were £2,000, £1,000 and £500, and on dissolution the firm has debts of £3,000 and assets of £8,000, the distribution to the partners will be as follows:

		£
Assets available for distribution		8,000
Firm's debts		3,000
Surplus assets available for distribution		5,000
Repayment of capital contributions:	A	2,000
	B	1,000
	C	500
		3,500
Remaining surplus to be equally distributed		1,500

The share of net assets taken by each partner will be:

A £2,500   B £1,500   C £1,000

(b) If there are losses these are met in the following order:

    (i) out of profits;

    (ii) out of capital;

    (iii) by the partners individually according to the proportions by which they shared profits.

Using the example of A, B and C above, if the partnership assets on dissolution were £5,000 and the debts £3,000, then assuming profits were shared equally, the distribution to each partner would be as follows:

	£
Assets available for distribution	5,000
Firm's debts	3,000
Surplus assets available for distribution	2,000
Repayment of total capital contributions	3,500
Shortfall	1,500
Losses shared equally	500

A receives £2,000 – £500   =   £1,500
B receives £1,000 – £500   =   £500
C receives £500 – £500   =   £0

Where there has been a bankruptcy situation with either a partner or the firm itself being adjudicated bankrupt, there will be two groups of creditors; those of the partners personally, and those of the firm itself. It is important therefore that the personal debts and property of the partners can be kept separate from those of the partnership itself.

Dissolution of a Registered Company

We have already seen that the process by which a registered company can be brought to an end is known as a winding up or a liquidation. The process is a detailed and complex one. It is regulated by the Insolvency Act 1986, a statute based upon the report of Sir Kenneth Cork. Shortly before the Royal Assent was granted, the Insolvency Bill as it then was, came back to the House of Lords for approval, where Lord Denning remarked, *"In 1977 Sir Kenneth Cork and his committee entered upon a review of the insolvency law. They sat for five years and heard the most expert evidence. It is the most technical subject you can imagine. Both lawyers and accountants hate it. Most of them know nothing about it."*

The main aspects of it will be examined shortly, but before doing so two further points need to be made regarding dissolution. The first is that there are other methods by which a company can be dissolved that do not involve winding up procedures. The second is that where the threat of dissolution is based upon company insolvency, alternatives to the drastic step of terminating the company by winding it up and realising its assets are available to creditors. A creditors composition may be entered into, or an administration order may be made by the court. These points are considered below.

Methods of dissolution

A company is created by incorporation through registration. It can therefore only come to an end when the registration is discharged. Once this happens the contractual relationship between the company and its members, based upon the memorandum and articles of the company, also comes to an end.

A company can be dissolved:

(a)   by proceedings brought by the Attorney-General for cancellation of the registration, on the grounds that the company's objects are illegal.

In *Attorney-General v. Lindi St. Claire (Personal Services) Ltd.* 1980 a lady, Miss St. Claire, formed the defendant company for the purposes of prostitution. The Registrar had granted it a certificate of incorporation, after refusing to register it under various names submitted by Miss St. Claire, including Hookers Ltd., Prostitutes Ltd. and even Lindi St. Claire French Lessons Ltd. The Court however granted the cancellation on the grounds that the objects of the company were illegal;

(b)   by an order of the court where the company is transferring its undertaking to another company under a scheme of reconstruction or reorganisation;

(c)   by the Registrar, who under s.652 Companies Act 1985, may strike off the register a company that is defunct. A defunct company is one which is no longer carrying on business. The section lays down a procedure to be followed by the Registrar before he can validly exercise the power to remove the company from the register. This has become a very common method of dissolution, for it is cheap and easy;

(d)   by being wound-up, which may be either voluntary or compulsory. The legal provisions relating to company liquidations are contained in the Insolvency Act 1986. The title of this statute is perhaps rather misleading, since it contains provisions which regulate not only companies which are being dissolved on the basis of their insolvency, but also companies which, for a variety of reasons, are being wound up fully able to meet their liabilities.

The process of winding up

Like a partnership, a limited company can be wound up as mentioned above either *voluntarily*, or *compulsorily* by order of the court. The grounds for winding up, whether on a voluntary or compulsory basis, are set out in the Insolvency Act 1986. They recognise that winding up is a step which may become necessary not only in cases of financial instability, but also because the company, which is of course a creature of statute, has failed to comply with the statutory provisions which bind it, or simply because the members no longer wish to trade together. When examining the operation of the limited company it is common to draw an analogy with natural persons. Thus the company is said to be born when its certificate of incorporation is granted, and henceforth its brain, the board of directors, guides its actions and formulates its decisions, which are executed through those it employs. Following this analogy through to its conclusion the process of winding up is akin to the process of administering the estate of a deceased person. Assets are collected and used to satisfy debts owing, after which any property remaining can be distributed to those lawfully entitled to them. In the case of a company this will be to its members. However the process of administering the estate of a deceased person commences with death, whereas winding up is a process which culminates in the dissolution of the company, the administration being completed before the life of the company ends.

Terminology

A number of technical expressions are used in liquidation and it is helpful to briefly identify and describe them before proceeding further.

A *petition* is an application to the court requesting the court to exercise its jurisdiction over company liquidations. A petition is presented where the liquidation is compulsory. In such cases the court has a major role to play. This is not so however in voluntary liquidations, where the liquidation is under the control of either the members or the creditors of the company.

A *contributory* is a person liable to contribute to the assets of a company if it is wound up. Existing members whose shares have not been fully paid fall within the definition of a contributory, and so do similarly placed past members, whose shareholding ceased within the year preceding the winding up. However a past member is not liable in respect of any debt contracted after his membership ceased. Nor is he required to make a contribution if the existing members are able to satisfy the contributions required of them.

A *liquidator* is a person appointed to take control of the company, collect its assets, pay its debts, and distribute any surplus to the members according to their rights as shareholders. The liquidator therefore holds a position of great responsibility, and it is important to ensure that only individuals of integrity are qualified to hold such a post. In recent years some disquiet has been felt as a result of company liquidations in which the liquidator has been found to be conducting the winding up for the benefit of directors, rather than the company's creditors. The Insolvency Act 1986 copes with this by requiring that only an *insolvency practitioner*, a term covering liquidators, can act in a winding up. He must be authorised to do so by his own professional body (these include accountancy bodies and the Law Society), or by the Department of Trade and Industry. Certain people are completely excluded. An applicant must be shown to be a fit and proper person, and must provide security, to become an insolvency practitioner.

The *Official Receiver* is appointed by the Department of Trade, and is concerned both with personal insolvency and with corporate insolvency. Official receivers are attached to courts with insolvency jurisdiction, and they act in the capacity of liquidators in the case of compulsory liquidations, being appointed automatically when a *winding up order* is made, that is when the court issues an order that the company be wound up. The Official Receiver (OR) remains in this office until another liquidator is appointed.

Finally the *London Gazette* is an official publication used to satisfy the requirement of providing public notice of certain legal events, for example, in the case of a liquidation notice of a creditors' meeting.

The Basic Aspects of a Company Liquidation

We have already seen that when the process of winding-up has been completed the company will be struck off the register of companies and will cease to exist. Of course no further claims can then be made against it. Consequently for anyone who is connected with the company, whether as an investor, creditor or employee, winding-up is of great significance.

Although statutory winding up provisions are detailed, and sometimes complex, there are basically three aspects to a liquidation:

(a)   who has the ability to institute and control the winding up, and on what grounds;

(b)   what are the legal provisions to be fulfilled during the procedure; and

(c)   in what order are claims made against the company for payment met?

Methods of Winding Up

Under s.73 Insolvency Act 1986 two methods of winding up are recognised. These are:

(a)   a *voluntary* winding up, which according to s.90 may be either:

(i)   a members' voluntary winding up, or

(ii)   a creditors' voluntary winding up, and

(b)   a winding up by the court, usually referred to as a *compulsory* winding up.

Voluntary winding up is more common than compulsory liquidation. It is a less formal procedure, and is therefore quicker and cheaper.

Voluntary winding up

Shareholders can at any time resolve to end the company. They initiate the procedure by passing a resolution to wind up, either a special resolution if the company is solvent, or, in the case of insolvency, an extraordinary resolution that it cannot continue in business by reason of its liabilities. An ordinary resolution is sufficient where the time period fixed in the articles for the life of the company has passed, or an event stipulated in the articles as giving rise to dissolution has taken place.

Under s.86 when the resolution is passed the liquidation procedure begins. The consequences are that:

- the company ceases to carry on business, other than to enable it to wind up;

- the company's corporate status remains intact until dissolution;

- transfers of shares, and changes in members' rights are void unless sanctioned by the liquidator;

- the directors' powers cease when the liquidator is appointed, although he, or in a creditors' voluntary winding up, they themselves, may permit the directors to continue; and

- if the liquidation is due to insolvency, company employees, who may include directors, will be dismissed. The liquidator may however employ them under a new contract.

Notice of the resolution must be advertised in the *London Gazette* within fourteen days of it being passed. If a majority of the directors within five weeks of the passing of the resolution make a statutory declaration that the company is solvent, then the company members manage the winding up. This includes the appointment of their own liquidator. This is a valuable power for the person appointed will be under their control, rather than the control of the creditors or the court. The court can nevertheless remove a liquidator on the basis of unfitness for office. The declaration of solvency states that the directors have examined the company's affairs and formed the opinion that within a stated period (up to a maximum of twelve months) the company will be able to pay its debts in full. If a declaration of solvency is not made, the winding up is creditors' winding up. A creditors' meeting must be summoned by the company. Details of this meeting must be posted to creditors and members giving them at least seven days notice, and be advertised in the London Gazette and two local newspapers.

The business of the creditors' meeting is to receive from the directors a full statement of the company's affairs, to draw up a list of creditors with estimates of their claims, to appoint a liquidator who will insert a notice in the *London Gazette* notifying other creditors to send in claims and if considered necessary, appoint a liquidation committee.

The liquidation committee cannot consist of more than five people. It is designed to work in conjunction with the liquidator.

The liquidators' powers in a voluntary winding up

The liquidator has wide powers to act for and in the name of the company, without the need to consult anyone or obtain the sanction of the court.

The liquidator can:

- bring or defend legal proceedings on behalf of the company;
- continue to operate the company's business to the extent necessary to wind it up beneficially;
- issue company documents and use the company seal;
- claim in insolvency proceedings brought by the company against an insolvent estate in which the company has an interest;
- deal with any negotiable instrument issued by or received by the company;
- raise money needed by the company on security of its assets;
- collect in monies due from contributories;
- appoint an agent to carry out work on behalf of the liquidator.

In addition to these powers the liquidator may, in a members' voluntary winding up with the sanction of an extraordinary resolution of the company, or in a creditors' voluntary winding up with the sanction of the Court, the liquidation committee or the creditors:

- pay off in full any class of creditors;
- enter into any compromise or arrangement with creditors.

It is possible for a voluntary winding up to be converted into a compulsory winding up, on a petition to the Court by a creditor or contributory. This will only be successful if the Court is satisfied that it is inappropriate for the winding up to proceed as a voluntary one, for instance where the liquidator is found to have some personal interest in the company he is winding up.

Fraudulent and Wrongful Trading

The concept of fraudulent trading is a well known one in company law. It is a crime under the Companies Act 1985, and gives rise to civil liability under the Insolvency Act 1986. Civil liability can only occur when the company is being wound up. If in the course of the liquidation it appears to the liquidator that the company's business has been carried on with intent to defraud creditors or for any fraudulent purpose, the liquidator may apply to the court for an order that any person who has knowingly been a party to such conduct be liable to contribute to the assets of the company. The court can order such a contribution as it thinks proper in the circumstances. In this way the creditors as a whole are compensated in the winding up for any serious wrongdoing committed by the directors, or any other party, in their management of or dealings with the company. The expression *fraudulent* is not defined by statute, however the courts have provided some indication of what must be established.

> In *Re William C. Leitch Brass Ltd.* 1932 it was said that a company will be acting fraudulently by incurring debts either knowing it will be unable to meet them when they fall due, or reckless as to whether it will be able to pay them at such time. An important qualification to liability was given in *Re Patrick & Lyon Ltd.* 1933 where it was said that the behaviour of the directors had to demonstrate real moral blame, and it is this feature of fraudulent trading which presents the major limitation upon its effectiveness as a civil remedy. So long as the directors can satisfy the court that, even when the company was in an insolvent situation, they genuinely and honestly believed that the company would be able to meet its debts when they fell due, then it is unlikely that they will be held personally accountable. Clearly the less business competence and experience they possess the easier it will be for them to avoid liability.

It was because of this difficulty in establishing fraudulent trading that the Cork Committee, in the course of examining the reform of the insolvency laws in the early 1980s, recommended the introduction of an additional head of civil liability, which could be established by proving negligence. This recommendation was implemented by the wrongful trading provisions contained in s.214 Insolvency Act 1986. Only a director can incur liability for wrongful trading, and as with s.213 action can only be taken by the liquidator of the company. The liquidator needs to establish that the person was at the time a director, that the company had gone into insolvent liquidation, and that at some time before the proceedings to wind up commenced, the person against whom they were being brought knew or ought to have concluded that there was no reasonable prospect that the company would avoid going into insolvent liquidation. If these criteria are met the court may declare the person concerned liable to contribute to the assets of the company. The section is particularly harsh on directors in a number of aspects. Insolvent liquidation means, in the context of s.214, that the assets as realised in the liquidation are insufficient to meet not only the company's debts and other liabilities, but also the costs of the winding up itself, which are generally substantial. The standard of skill expected of the director is based upon two sets of criteria, that is not only the general knowledge, skill and experience which that particular director holds, but also the skill and experience that can be reasonably expected from a reasonably diligent director. The test is an objective rather than a subjective one. Even the defence available under the section operates in a harsh fashion towards directors. It provides that no order may be made by the court if it is satisfied that the person in question took every step with a view to minimising the potential loss to the company's creditors as he ought to have taken. The expression 'every step' is clearly very stringent.

> The wrongful trading provisions were applied in *Re Produce Marketing Consortium Ltd.* 1989 where two directors had continued to trade when the accounts showed their company to be insolvent, in the honest but unrealistically optimistic belief that the company's fortunes would change. They were ordered by the court to contribute £75,000 plus interest to the assets of the company.

It seems that s.214 is a more potent weapon in the hands of liquidators than s.213. Establishing fraud is more difficult than establishing negligence, and this together with the rigorous standards demanded by s.214 suggests that wrongful trading is likely to be regarded increasingly by liquidators as a more attractive remedy than fraudulent trading. Even so there may still be reasons why a claim under s.213 may be brought by a liquidator. Perhaps the most significant is where a contribution is being sought from someone other than a director, for unlike s.214, s.213 catches anyone 'knowingly' a party to the fraud.

In *Re Gerald Cooper Chemicals Ltd.* 1978 the court held that a creditor who accepts money from the company knowing it has been procured by carrying on business with the intent to defraud other creditors by the act of paying him, will be liable under s.213. Templeman, J. stated *"A man who warms himself with the fire of fraud cannot complain if he is singed"*.

Compulsory winding up

A compulsory winding up is carried out by the Court. This is either the High Court or, if the company's paid up share capital does not exceed £120,000, the County Court in whose district the company has its registered office. Not all County Courts however, possess the necessary insolvency jurisdiction.

Proceedings are commenced by a person presenting a petition to the appropriate court. The petitioner may be the company itself, by resolution, the Secretary of State following an investigation or, in most cases, a creditor.

> In *Re Othery Construction Ltd.* 1966 Lord Buckley stated that if a fully paid up shareholder is to successfully petition to wind up:

"... he must show either that there will be a surplus available for distribution amongst the shareholders or that the affairs of the company require investigation in respects which are likely to produce such a surplus".

Under s.122 a company may be wound up by the court if:

(a) the company has passed a special resolution requesting it; or

(b) in the case of a company registered as a public company, the company has been registered for more than a year, but as yet no certificate of ability to commence business has been issued. This certificate, which is issued by the Registrar, can only be obtained when certain financial details have been given to him. The company cannot commence business until the certificate, which is required under s.117 Companies Act 1985, has been issued. Private companies do not require such a certificate and can commence business immediately on incorporation; or

(c) the company does not commence business in the first year of its incorporation, or suspends business at any time for a whole year. An order will only be granted on this ground if the company has no intention of carrying on business again.

In *Re Middlesbrough Assembly Rooms Co.* 1880 a shareholder petitioned for winding up where the company had suspended trading for over three years, because of a trade depression. The majority shareholders opposed the petition on the basis that the company intended to recommence trading when the economic situation improved. It was held that in the circumstances the petition should be dismissed;

(d) if the membership has fallen below two; or

(e) if the company is unable to pay its debts. This is the ground most commonly relied upon. The company is deemed to be unable to pay its debts if a creditor who is owed a sum exceeding £750 by the company has left a written demand for it at the company's registered office, and the demand has remained unpaid for a period of three clear weeks. The company is not however regarded as neglecting the debt if it bona fide disputes the payment of it. Alternatively the company is deemed unable to pay its debts if:

   (i) execution has been issued on a judgment in favour of a creditor which is returned either wholly or partially unsatisfied; or

   (ii) it is proved to the satisfaction of the court that the company is unable to pay its debts as they fall due.

In *Re A Company* 1986 it was held that a company can be regarded as unable to pay its debts under this ground, where it has funds but persistently fails or neglects to pay its debts unless it is forced to do so. Many companies have a deliberate policy of holding back payment for as long as possible, and for some this may be their means of survival; or

   (iii) where the court is satisfied that taking into account the company's present and future liabilities, the value of its assets is less than the amount of its liabilities; or

(f) the court is of the opinion that it is just and equitable that the company should be wound up. This ground covers a number of situations. For instance it covers cases where the substratum of the company has been destroyed.

In *Re German Date Coffee Co.* 1882 the company was wound up on the basis that it had become impossible to carry out the main object in the memorandum of association, namely the acquisition and working of a German patent to make coffee from dates, because the patent could not be obtained.

It also extends to circumstances in which the company has been formed for a fraudulent purpose; where the company is a sham, having no business or property; or where the rights of members are being flouted.

In *Loch v. John Blackwood Ltd.* 1924 a director with voting control refused to hold meetings, produce accounts or pay dividends. The court held that the company could be wound up.

In *Ebrahami v. Westbourne Galleries* 1972 two individuals E and N had operated successfully in partnership together for many years. Later they converted the business to a company, with themselves as sole shareholders and directors, and after a time N's son was allowed into the business. This was granted as a favour by the plaintiff, who transferred some of his shares to the son. Unfortunately his generosity was met by N and his son combining their interests to force the plaintiff out of the business. The court granted the plaintiff's application to wind up. Commenting on the expression "just and equitable" Lord Wilberforce said:

"The words are a recognition of the fact that a limited company is more than a mere legal entity, with a personality in law of its own; that there is room in company law for the recognition of the fact that behind it, or amongst it, there are individuals, with rights, expectations and obligations ... which are not necessarily submerged in the company structure".

The petition to wind up is presented to the district judge of the court who fixes a time and place for the hearing. The petition must be advertised in the *London Gazette* at least seven clear days (excluding Saturday and Sunday) before the hearing. Rules of Court set out the form in which this advertised information must be provided; if they are not complied with the petitioner may have to meet all the court costs. The aim of the advertisement is to invite interested parties, the company's creditors and contributories, to oppose or support the petition. A person intending to appear at the hearing must give notice of this to the petitioner. After presentation of the petition a provisional liquidator may be appointed who is generally the Official Receiver. In any event when the hearing takes place, and the court makes a winding-up order, the Official Receiver becomes provisional liquidator by statute, and continues as liquidator unless the meeting of the creditors and contributories agree to the appointment of some other liquidator. This person must be an insolvency practitioner. The 1986 Act sets out the liquidator's powers. Essentially his task is to collect and realise the company's assets, including unpaid sums due to the company from contributories for their shares, to settle the lists of creditors and contributories, pay the company's debts in a fixed order, and finally to adjust the rights of the contributories distributing any surplus assets among them. At meetings of creditors and contributories it may be decided to apply to the court to form a committee of inspection. Having fulfilled these responsibilities the liquidator applies to the court for an order that the company be dissolved, and is then released from his or her role. The court, it should be noted, has a complete and unfettered discretion as to whether to make an order for winding up. It may as an alternative conditionally or unconditionally adjourn the hearing, make an interim order, or dismiss the petition altogether.

The order of priorities

On dissolution there are likely to be many claims against the assets of the company. Provided the company is solvent this does not create any problems, but if it is insolvent the question which arises is how the shortfall is dealt with. Do all the company's creditors absorb the loss according to the proportion of credit they have provided, or do some creditors rank before others, so that whilst those at the top of the list may be repaid in full, those at the bottom could find themselves with nothing?

The answer is that the Insolvency Act 1986 lays down an order of priorities for the distribution of assets. The relevant provisions are contained in ss.175 and 176, which lays down the following order:

(a)   the costs of winding up (for example the liquidator's fees);

(b)   preferential debts. These include: income tax deducted from the pay of company employees under the PAYE system over the past year; VAT payments owed by the company that have accrued over the past six months; wages and salaries of employees outstanding for the previous four months, up to a present maximum figure of £800 per employee. A director may be a salaried employee, and thus qualify under this head, however a director's fee rather than a salary will not rank as a preferential debt. If assets are sufficient, preferential debts are paid in full. If not, the available assets are distributed rateably between the preferential creditors, and in these circumstances property subject to a floating charge must be applied first in the payment of preferential debts, the holder being entitled only to the balance. Creditors who have the security of a fixed charge over assets of the company are, of course, able to realise the assets charged to meet the company's liability towards them;

(c)   ordinary unsecured debts, such as sums owing to trade creditors. If these cannot be paid in full they are paid rateably amongst the creditors;

(d)   the members according to their rights under the memorandum and articles. It may be that one class of shareholders is entitled to repayment of a certain amount of the surplus before the others, thus preference shareholders may receive repayment of their paid up capital in priority to ordinary shareholders.

Advantages and disadvantages of compulsory winding up

The main advantages of a compulsory winding up over a voluntary winding up are:

(a)   Under s.129 Insolvency Act 1986 a compulsory winding up is deemed to commence when the petition is presented, whilst in a voluntary winding up it commences when the resolution is passed (s.86). The effect is that a compulsory winding up will commence earlier. This can be important since as part of the task of collecting in assets the liquidator can apply to the court to recover assets disposed of by the company within a fixed period before the insolvency, and can seek to have certain transactions set aside where these transactions occurred within a certain date of the insolvency. Going back further into the recent past of the company may mean the recovery of a larger quantity of assets. Examples include:

(i)   the setting aside of a transaction made by the company at undervalue within the two years before the winding up has commenced. A transaction at undervalue would cover a gift made by the company at a time it was unable to pay its debts;

(ii)   the setting aside of a preference made by the company to a connected person (e.g. a director) within two years of the winding up commencing, or to any other person (e.g. a trade creditor) within six months of the winding up commencing. Again this must have occurred at a time when the company was unable to pay its debts. A preference would occur where the directors, in the knowledge that the company is completely insolvent, settle the debts of just one of the company's creditors, in the expectation that if they subsequently set up a new company the trade creditor will continue to supply them;

(iii) the avoidance of floating charges created by the company within the two years prior to the insolvency if the chargee is a connected person, and one year if the chargee is anyone else.

(b) Wider powers of investigation into the management of the company's affairs, for example where the directors have been acting wrongfully.

The main disadvantages are that a compulsory liquidation will be slower and more expensive. The company will always be the respondent under a compulsory winding up order, and as the 'loser' in the action it will meet both sides' costs, thus reducing the money available for the creditors when the realised assets are finally distributed.

Alternatives to Winding Up

Whilst as we have seen, a company may be dissolved for reasons other than financial difficulty, many dissolutions are the result of a financial crisis. Directors faced with this situation may have the future affairs of the company taken out of their hands in a compulsory or creditors' liquidation, the result of which will be that the life of the company will come to an end, and some creditors at least will be left with their debts unsatisfied. One of the aims of the Insolvency Act 1986 was to provide alternatives to this drastic outcome, which would act as financial rescue packages for companies in difficulty.

(a)   Corporate voluntary arrangements – compositions with creditors

These are provided for by ss1–7 Insolvency Act 1986. They enable a company which is insolvent or partially insolvent to follow a procedure which will result in a legally binding arrangement with its creditors. In outline the following stages have to be followed. The directors, or the liquidator if a winding up is in progress, choose an insolvency practitioner to act as a 'nominee', and help them produce proposals to put to the creditors. These may be a composition or a scheme of arrangement for the company i.e. the revision of its financial affairs in some way, such as alterations to class rights, or the extension of time for payment given by debenture notices.

The proposals are reported to the court and a meeting of creditors and shareholders is called both of which must approve them. The outcome is reported to the court. If approved, the proposals bind all the creditors and shareholders having notice of them, under s.5.

(b)   Administration orders

One of the problems with a voluntary arrangement is of course the difficulty of obtaining the agreement of large creditors, such as banks. They will want greater control over the organisation of the company's affairs. In such circumstances an administration order may be a useful device. Such an order can be made by the court once it is satisfied that the company is, or is likely to become, unable to pay its debts, and that an administration order would be likely to achieve:

(i) the survival of the company, and the whole or any part of its undertaking as a going concern; or

(ii)   the approval of a voluntary arrangement (i.e. because of the appointment of an administrator); or

(iii) a more advantageous realisation of the company's assets than in a winding up.

The company itself, its directors, a creditor or creditors may petition the court for such an order, and if granted the court will appoint the receiver who will be responsible for the management of the affairs, business and property of the company for the duration of the order. This can include the calling of meetings and the appointment and removal of directors. Any winding up petition previously presented must be dismissed on the grant of an administration order. The administrator is empowered to carry on the business of the company generally, including dealing with and disposing of its assets, borrowing, employing agents and so on. He can establish subsidiary companies and transfer the whole or some part of the existing business to them. He can remove directors, and appoint new directors, and call meetings of the members and the creditors. His duties are to control and manage the company's assets and business operations, initially in accordance with directions from the court given in the order, and subsequently in accordance with the proposals he has put forward as to how the purposes stated in the order are to be achieved. The administrator's proposals must be sent to the Registrar of Companies and all the creditors within three months of the administration order being made. A creditors' meeting must then be held to approve the proposals before they can be implemented.

> It remains to be seen how much use will be made of the administration order as an alternative to liquidation, however a useful illustration of an order in operation occurred in *Re Consumer & Industrial Press* 1987. The company involved, a small printing and publishing organisation, had only one major asset when it became insolvent, a magazine which it published. An application was made for the appointment of an administrator, so that he could exercise the statutory power to borrow in the company's name in order to continue publishing the magazine. In this way it could be sold as a going concern, rather than it going out of publication and having far less value. The Court held that in the interests of the creditors the order should be granted.

Individual Insolvency

Personal insolvency occurs when an individual finds himself in serious financial difficulties and is unable to pay his creditors when debts fall due. If the creditors are unwilling or unable to wait for payment, the debtor may face bankruptcy proceedings under the Insolvency Act 1986. Broadly the purpose of bankruptcy is to ensure a fair distribution of assets to creditors and to allow the debtor to make a fresh start after his discharge.

The law relating to individual insolvency has undergone substantial change in recent years. The procedures under the Bankruptcy Act 1914 have been abolished and replaced with simpler procedures first introduced by the Insolvency Act 1985 and now contained in the Insolvency Act 1986. The new legislation was introduced with two main aims:

(a)   to encourage voluntary arrangements between debtors and creditors; and

(b)   to simplify and update bankruptcy procedures and bring them into line with the procedures applicable to company liquidations.

Under the 1986 Act there are two possible outcomes of individual insolvency: a *voluntary arrangement* or a *bankruptcy order*.

Voluntary arrangements

Where an individual is facing insolvency, he may try to avoid a bankruptcy order by proposing a voluntary arrangement with his creditors. The advantages from the debtor's point of view of such an arrangement are that he avoids the stigma, loss of status and adverse publicity associated with a bankruptcy order, and avoids the disabilities to which an undischarged bankrupt is subject. The benefit of a voluntary arrangement for the creditor is that it should be less expensive, leaving more assets available for payment to him; and it will usually be quicker than bankruptcy procedure, which means that he will be paid sooner. The disadvantage from the creditors point of view is that the supervisor of a voluntary arrangement will not have as many powers as a trustee in bankruptcy, for example to set aside transactions at an undervalue or preferences.

The option of making a voluntary arrangement existed under the old bankruptcy law. Such an arrangement could be made under the Deeds of Arrangement Act 1914. In practice, however, deeds of arrangement are not used to any great extent, mainly because any one creditor, no matter how small the sum owed to him, could petition for bankruptcy if he did not accept the debtor's proposals. He could do this even though all of the other creditors were prepared to accept them. Under the 1986 Act, as we shall see, a dissenting creditor must accept a voluntary arrangement if more than 75% by value of creditors agree to it.

Procedure for making a voluntary arrangement under Part VIII of the Insolvency Act 1986

If a debtor wishes to make a voluntary arrangement he must choose an insolvency practitioner to help him draw up a proposal which can be presented to his creditors. An insolvency practitioner, usually an accountant or a solicitor, must be qualified in relation to insolvency and must be authorised by the Department of Trade to act in that capacity. The insolvency practitioner will have an important role to play in the voluntary arrangement, first as a "nominee" preparing and presenting the proposal; and later as supervisor, implementing the proposal if it is accepted by the creditors.

When the proposal is prepared, and an insolvency practitioner has agreed to act nominee, the debtor must apply to the court for an interim order. Once this application is made, the court has power to suspend any legal proceedings against the debtor or his property.

The court will make an interim order if it is satisfied that it would be appropriate to do so, in order to allow the debtor to go ahead and make his proposal. If the court believes that the debtor is not acting in good faith or that the proposal is wholly unrealistic it may refuse to make the order. If an interim order is made, it will last for 14 days unless it is extended by the court. The effect of the order is that no bankruptcy petition can be presented against the debtor and no other legal proceedings may be commenced or continued against him without the court's permission.

Before the interim order expires, the nominee must report to the court stating whether he thinks that a meeting of creditors ought to be summoned to consider the debtor's proposal. To enable the nominee to make his report, the debtor has a duty to deliver a statement of affairs to him, together with the details of his proposal.

After receiving the nominee's report, the court will extend the interim order to allow the creditors to consider the debtor's proposal. The nominee must call a meeting of creditors. He must inform every creditor of whom he is aware about the meeting.

The purpose of the creditors' meeting is to decide whether or not to accept the debtor's proposals for a voluntary arrangement, either in the form put forward by the debtor or in a modified form.

If the creditors are unable to agree to the proposal, the court can discharge the interim order and normal bankruptcy proceedings will probably follow. If a scheme is approved by over 75% in value of creditors voting at the meeting, the voluntary arrangement will be binding upon all creditors who had notice of the meeting and were entitled to vote.

The voluntary arrangement may be challenged by a dissatisfied creditor who must apply to the court to set it aside within 28 days. His application can be made on the grounds that there was a material irregularity in the calling or conduct of the creditors' meeting; or that the voluntary arrangements unfairly prejudice his interests as a creditor.

The procedure described here is presented diagramatically in Figure 2.3.

If the proposal is approved at the creditors meeting, the nominee becomes its supervisor. The debtor must hand over his property to the supervisor, who will then carry out the arrangements. During the implementation of the voluntary arrangement by the supervisor, any of the parties, including the debtor, any creditors or the supervisor himself may apply to the court for directions to resolve any problems that may arise. When the task of supervision has been completed, the supervisor must notify all creditors and the debtor.

Bankruptcy Orders

A petition for a bankruptcy order may be presented by a creditor, the debtor himself, or by the supervisor or a creditor bound by a voluntary arrangement where the debtor has defaulted under the arrangement.

Petition by a creditor

A petition by a creditor must be based on an unpaid debt or debts owed to him by the debtor. The amount owing must be at least £750. In order to commence bankruptcy proceedings, a creditor either must obtain a judgment debt for at least £750 and be unable to enforce it; or he must serve on the debtor a *statutory demand* for payment of the debt (see Figure 2.4). Where a statutory demand is served and the debtor fails to pay within three weeks, the creditor can petition the court for a bankruptcy order. The court can dismiss the creditor's petition if it is satisfied that the debtor is able to pay all of his debts or that he has made an offer to provide security for the payment of the debt or to enter into a voluntary arrangement and the creditor has unreasonably refused to accept his offer.

Petition by the debtor

The sole ground on which a debtor may petition for his own bankruptcy is that he is unable to pay his debts. His petition must be accompanied by a *statement of affairs* setting out details of his assets and liabilities.

Where the debtor's unsecured debts are less than £20,000, his assets are £2,000 or more and he has not been bankrupt or made a voluntary arrangement within the last five years, the court will appoint an insolvency practitioner to investigate the possibility of a voluntary arrangement and prepare a report. If the report is favourable the court will make an interim order with a view to a creditors' meeting and a voluntary arrangement. If the report of the insolvency practitioner indicates that a voluntary arrangement would be unlikely to succeed, the court, if it agrees, will make a bankruptcy order. In these circumstances the order will be by way of a summary administration of the bankrupt's estate.

The advantages of a summary administration are that the procedures are simple and, from the debtor's point of view, he will be discharged from the bankruptcy after two years.

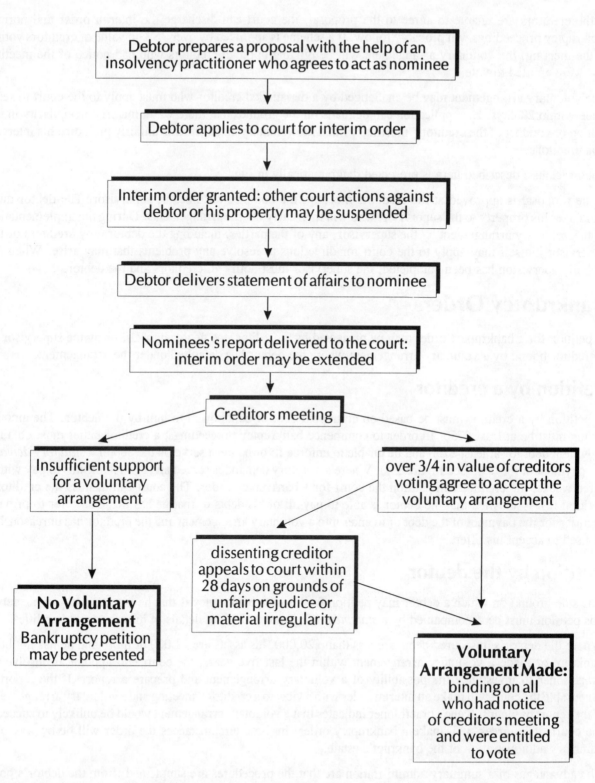

Figure 2.3 *Procedure for making a voluntary arrangement*

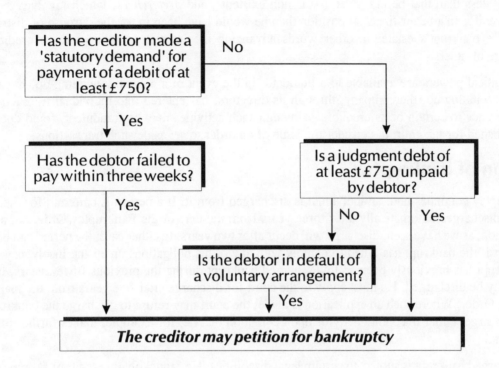

Figure 2.4 *Bankruptcy petition by a creditor*

The trustee in bankruptcy

The function of the trustee in bankruptcy is to collect in the assets of the bankrupt and distribute them in accordance with the rules in the Insolvency Act. The order of priority for repayment of debts is similar to that described for the winding-up of companies. All of the bankrupt's property vests in the trustee in bankruptcy, with the exception of tools, vehicles and equipment for use by the bankrupt in his employment or business; and such clothing, bedding, furniture and household equipment as are necessary to satisfy the basic domestic needs of the bankrupt and his family.

Any property which is acquired by the bankrupt before he is discharged can be claimed by the trustee. The trustee may also apply to the court for an *income payments order*. Under the terms of such an order part of any income to which the bankrupt is entitled whilst undischarged will be transferred to the trustee for the benefit of the creditors.

Creditors must submit proof of any debts to the trustee in bankruptcy. When the trustee has collected in all the bankrupts property he can declare and distribute a final dividend to creditors. After this has been done he will call a final general meeting of creditors and report on the administration of the estate.

Two further powers of the trustee enable him to apply to the court for an order to overcome certain types of transaction entered into by the bankrupt prior to the presentation of the bankruptcy petition. These are transactions at *an undervalue*, meaning a transaction in which the consideration received by the bankrupt is significantly less than that he has given (or is non existent), and *preferences*, which involves the bankrupt putting a creditor in a better financial position than he would have been in for the purpose of distributing the assets of the bankrupt's estate; in other words advancing the interests of one or more creditors to the disadvantage of others.

Almost identical powers are available to a liquidator in the event of a company winding-up, in cases where prior to the winding up, the company, through its directors, has entered into individual transactions or has given preference to certain of its creditors. Although such activities may be fraudulent, fraud does not need to be established for the court to consider the issue of an order to set aside such transactions.

Duration of bankruptcy

The bankruptcy continues until an individual is discharged from it. If a person is bankrupt for the first time, he will be discharged automatically after three years from the date of the Bankruptcy Order. In a summary administration, as we have seen, discharge will occur after two years. In either case, the period can be extended by the court if the bankrupt has failed to comply with any of his obligations under the Insolvency Act 1986. If the bankrupt has previously been an undischarged bankrupt during the previous fifteen years, he will not automatically be discharged. He must apply to the court for discharge after five years from the making of the Bankruptcy Order. Where such an application is made, the court may refuse to discharge the bankrupt. It may grant a discharge, either unconditionally or upon condition that he, for example, makes further payments to his creditors.

An undischarged bankrupt is subject to certain legal disabilities. He cannot obtain credit; or become a member of Parliament, a justice of the peace or a councillor.

Discharge from bankruptcy releases the bankrupt from the debts which existed at the commencement of his bankruptcy. A discharge from bankruptcy, however, does not affect his liability for fines imposed by a court for any criminal offence, or the enforcement of any security by a secured creditor.

Choosing the Legal Form for a Business

This chapter has examined in detail the legal characteristics of the two principal forms of private sector business organisation, the partnership and the registered company. It will by now be clear that the differences between them are significant, not only from a legal standpoint but from a commercial one also. We can conclude our examination of business organisations by examining the basis upon which the decision may be taken whether to operate in partnership or form a registered company, that is whether or not to incorporate.

Partnership or registered company?

There are two circumstances in which the opportunity for choosing the legal form of the business is illusory.

(i)   Sometimes people drift into business relationships rather than discuss and plan them in advance. Perhaps what began as a mere hobby pursued by two friends develops into a money making venture, and they find themselves in a business relationship without any conscious decision on their part. If their relationship satisfies the definition of a partnership contained in s.1 Partnership Act 1890, then the law will regard them as partners. They do not need to have entered into a written agreement. They many not even be aware of their legal status. In law however they are now operating as a firm.

(ii)   If professional people, such as accountants, architects, doctors or lawyers seek to carry out their work in combination with co-professionals, the law prevents them from incorporating their business. It is only permissible for them to carry out their work collectively in partnership so the opportunity of incorporating is denied them.

Assuming however that like-minded people are anxious to establish a joint business venture, what factors are likely to influence them in deciding whether or not to incorporate? The following checklist of points covers all the major factors, and illustrates the essential legal and commercial differences between the partnership and the registered company.

Registered companies and partnerships compared

(i)   *Legal status*

A registered company is a corporate body once its certificate of incorporation is granted to it. It is an artificial entity and is required to establish its nationality, a registered office where it can be served with formal notices, and provide itself with a name which it must use for the purpose of conducting business. It is legally separate from its members, who may make contracts with it, for example by selling to it a business previously operated as a partnership or on a sole trader basis.

A partnership is not a corporate body. It is no more than the sum total of the individuals who make it up. Although it must register under the Business Names Act 1985 any name it uses to trade under which does not consist of the surnames of all the partners, this name (e.g. Smith and Co.) does not give it any special persona, although for practical convenience Rules of the Supreme Court enable proceedings by and against the firm to be brought in the firms name.

(ii)   *Members' liability*

In a company, the financial liability of the members for any legal liabilities of the business such as trading debts ends when they have fully paid for their shares. There are however particular circumstances where members may still face personal liability, although these are restricted. An example is the potential personal liability of directors who continue to run the company in circumstances where they know or ought to realise the company is unlikely to avoid an insolvent liquidation, and it subsequently goes into an insolvent liquidation (wrongful trading). Essentially however a shareholder has limited liability.

The liability of partners for the debts of a firm is unlimited. If the assets of the firm are insufficient to meet the liability the creditor can look to the personal property of the individual partners. They may have bankruptcy proceedings brought against them. Limited liability is however available in a limited partnership, a special form of partnership which may be established under the provisions of the Limited Partnership Act 1907. There are however very few limited partnerships in operation.

(iii)   *Agency*

In a company, mere membership does not of itself invest the shareholder with the power to act as an agent for and on behalf of the company. Agency powers are contained in the articles of association of the company and these powers are the principal agency source.

Articles normally grant full powers as agents to the board of directors. In a firm however each partner is an agent of the other partners and of the partnership as a whole (s.5 Partnership Act 1890).

(iv) *Management*

Whereas companies are managed by those granted the power to do so under the articles – the directors of the company, in a firm all the members have the full right to take part in its management. Denial of this right would entitle the aggrieved partner to petition to have the firm dissolved. Thus whilst ownership and management are often in separate hands in the case of a registered company, this is never the position in a firm. Consequently the means available to company members to require directors to account for their actions are of crucial importance, and company law provides that certain decisions, such as alterations to the articles, can only legitimately be carried out at a general meeting of the company where all the membership is entitled to be present.

(v) *Membership*

There is no limit placed on the number of members a registered company may have. New members can join the company with little restriction, although the directors may have the power to refuse a share transfer in some cases. In a firm however a new partner can only join with the consent of all the existing members, emphasising the close commercial relationship of the partners. Moreover normal trading partnerships are restricted to a maximum of twenty partners. There is no limit however placed on the size of a professional partnership.

(vi) *Taxation*

A company pays corporation tax on a flat rate basis on its profits. Shareholders are taxed on the dividends the company pays them.

In a partnership partners pay tax on the apportioned profits they receive from the business under Schedule D. This covers earnings from a trade, profession or occupation and enables them to pay tax on a preceding year basis and claim allowances against their tax liability for expenses incurred in their work for the business, e.g. costs of running a car. Tax paid on a preceding year basis means that tax liability for one fiscal year is met by making two equal payments of tax on the 1st January of the following fiscal year, and the 1st July of the next fiscal year, i.e. tax liability of £10,000 for fiscal year 1992/93 paid by instalments of £5,000 on 1st January 1994 and 1st July 1994.

(vii) *Borrowing*

Companies, particularly larger ones, have much greater borrowing capability than partnerships. They can raise loan capital by issuing debentures and provide security by way of floating charges, neither of which partnerships can do.

(viii) *Formalities and public inspection*

Whereas a firm can maintain complete secrecy over its affairs (other than providing details of its proprietors where the Business Names Act 1985 applies) a registered company must provide the Registrar of Companies with a wealth of detail about itself on a regular basis. All of this information is held on its file and is available for public inspection. Thus its membership, its annual accounts, and details of the property it has charged, are amongst the long list of details which the Registrar must be provided with. There are also fees to be paid when such documents are delivered e.g. £25 on filing a copy of the annual return, and also of course a considerable internal administration burden for the company in satisfying the extensive information demands of company legislation. Financial penalties can be exacted against companies in default. Moreover company legislation in general is highly prescriptive, demanding particular procedures to be followed, and forms to be used, if a company is to lawfully conduct its affairs.

(ix) *Contractual scope*

Despite the dilution of the ultra vires principle as it applies to registered companies some limited aspects of it remain. A firm on the other hand is not subject to ultra vires.

(x) *Capital*

There are stringent rules controlling the way in which registered companies use capital. In particular it is a general principle of company law that capital investment be maintained and not reduced. A firm however has complete freedom over the way in which it uses its capital.

Activity

Form a group of three or four. Assume that the members of the group have come up with a business idea which you would all like to develop. This could be any kind of business activity you choose. Further assume a fixed amount of initial capital available to the prospective business, made up of contributions of £1,500 from each member of your group. These sums of money represent the hard earned savings of each person. Discuss within the group which form of organisation, partnership or company, is most appropriate for your business, bearing in mind the factors referred to above.

Unit Test Questions

1. Name three characteristics common to all business organisations.

2. What is the distinction between a public sector and a private sector organisation?

3. What is the distinction between a corporate body and an unincorporated body?

4. What is the difference between a registered company limited by shares and a company limited by guarantee?

5. State the main features of a sole trader business.

6. How does the Partnership Act 1890 define a partnership?

7. State the legal formalities relating to the creation of a partnership business.

8. What do the words 'and Co' signify at the end of a partnership name?

9. Why might it be necessary to distinguish between a hobby and a business?

10. What is meant by the expression 'limited liability'?

11. Describe a case decision which illustrates the concept of corporate personality.

12 When can the veil of incorporation be lifted?

13. What is the most significant distinction between a public and a private company?

14. Define the expressions 'nominal share capital' and 'paid up share capital'.

15. State five advantages that a private company has over a public company.

16. State the matters that must be included in the Memorandum of Association.

17. What is the purpose of the 'objects clause'?

18. State the effect of s.35 of the Companies Act 1989 in relation to ultra vires.

19. How can a company change its objects clause?

20. What are the differences between ordinary shares and preference shares?

21. Give the definition of a debenture.

22. What is the distinction between fixed and floating charges?

23. What is the difference between bankruptcy, dissolution and winding up?

24. On what grounds can a partner apply to the court to dissolve a partnership business?

25. State the various ways that a company can be dissolved.

26. Explain the following technical expressions relating to the winding up of a company

    petition; contributory; liquidator; official receiver.

27. State the two methods of winding up under the Insolvency Act 1986.

28. What are the consequences of initiating a voluntary liquidation procedure?

Assignment *The Rise and Fall of John Russell*

During the summer of 1992 the further success of John Russell Ltd as a commercial enterprise seemed assured. The company had been incorporated at the beginning of 1990 out of an existing partnership business, for the purposes, to quote its objects clause of "carrying on the business of motor vehicle dealers and ancillary activities". The new company quickly established a name for itself, and by the winter of 1991 it felt itself in a strong enough commercial position to proceed with arrangements for the design and construction of expensive and prestigious new sales and office premises on the outskirts of Birmingham. Architects Van Mildert, Clarke, Foster were contracted to carry out the design work, the builders appointed were Western Construction plc, and the office equipment and the computer system was purchased from Zenith Office Supplies Ltd. The downfall of the company was if anything more dramatic than its rapid growth. It came with the loss of the most lucrative business, fleet car sales. During the first five months of 1993 its three principal fleet customers failed to place new orders as a result of recessionary pressures. John Russell Ltd's three directors, Paul O'Grady, Jim Morgan, and John Russell himself, the managing director, struggled to keep the company afloat. Still owing large sums on the new premises and advised by their accountants that the business "would be unlikely to survive beyond the end of the year" they decided to keep trading in the hope the fleet market would return. In the meantime, with insufficient funds to pay all the creditors, the directors decided to pay their architects charges of £75,000 in full, and to ask the architects to use their influence with the builders, Western Construction, to allow Russells more time to pay the final instalment of the building work, a sum of £400,000, now four months overdue. The strategy did not work. The builders lost patience and petitioned the court at the end of July 1993 to have the company compulsorily wound up. The petition was granted and Simon Scott was subsequently appointed as liquidator.

You have recently joined the firm of accountants, in which Simon Scott is a partner, as an administrative assistant. In order to give you some experience of company liquidations, and also because he has a heavy workload at present, Simon Scott has asked you to consider a number of aspects of the John Russell liquidation. In particular he would like you to report back to him on the following matters.

1. Whether the payment made to the architects can be recovered for the company's creditors.

2. If any form of personal liability is likely to have been incurred by the directors in their conduct of the operations of John Russell Ltd.

3. Whether the contract the company made to purchase the computer system from Zenith Office Supplies can be avoided. The system purchased is more sophisticated than John Russell Ltd needs, and perhaps falls outside its objects clause. Paul O'Grady is also a director of Zenith, although he has never disclosed the fact to the John Russell board.

Task Advise Simon Scott in writing as to the legal position on the three points referred to above.

Element 9.2

Investigate the legal relationships in business

Performance Criteria

1. Rights and duties of key parties are identified

2. The interrelationship between stakeholders is explained

3. The nature of liability to others for wrongful acts is described

Range

Key Parties:

Shareholders; directors; employees; customers; suppliers; creditors

Inter-relationships:

Employer/employee; Board of Directors/shareholders; partners/other partners; stakeholders/providers of finance;business/community; business/customers

Liability:

Vicarious; tortious; criminal; contractual

Evidence Indicators

An investigation and explanation of the implications for those involved, of a range of wrongful acts carried out by a business

Chapter 3

The Legal Relationships in Business

In this chapter we will explore the rights and duties of people who are involved in or affected by the activities of different types of business organisation. For this purpose it is necessary to identify the inter relationships that an individual can have with a business in its various roles, for instance as employer, supplier of goods and services, business occupier and member of the community. In Chapter 2 we examined the two main legal forms of business, the company and partnership. We shall begin therefore by considering the inter relationship between a registered company, its membership and its board of directors, and then go on to consider the legal relationship between partners and the partnership business, in particular in relation to the power of individual partners to bind the firm legally by their actions.

Almost all businesses, whether corporate or unincorporated will employ staff, supply and purchase goods or services, occupy premises, participate as members of the community (paying business rates and providing work for example) and so engage in numerous legal relationships as a supplier, customer, creditor, debtor, employer, community member and business occupier. We shall be looking at the nature of many of these important relationships, concluding with an examination of legal liability as it affects businesses. You may find it useful to refer back to the diagrams at the beginning of Chapter 1 which provide a simplified picture of the types of relationship we shall be considering.

The Nature of Legal Relationships

A legal relationship is one where the parties involved, whether as individuals or organisations, are connected to each other by way of legal rights or legal obligations. Because the relationship is a legally recognised one, rather than say one based upon a moral foundation, it is possible to take appropriate measures such as court proceedings if the relationship is upset or damaged. By way of an illustration, if a business organisation sells a defective product to a customer the customer will normally have enforceable rights enabling him to obtain a remedy against the supplier.

The nature of a particular relationship is determined by the way the law regards the connection between the parties to it. Different kinds of relationship generate different sets of rights and obligations (or duties). This is only to be expected for the purposes underlying legal relationships vary enormously. Consider for instance the different purposes which bring together in the form of legal relationships employers and employees, directors and shareholders, sellers and buyers of goods and services, and the partners in a partnership. It is essential for anyone engaged in business activity to recognise and understand the legal consequences which flow from specific types of business relationship. We can approach the task by considering the legal rights and obligations which attach to the key parties involved in business.

The Key Parties in Business

The key parties in a registered company

We saw in the last chapter that a registered company is a corporate body. It is a person in law. A registered company is composed of those people who at any given time hold shares in it, its members or shareholders. They exercise ultimate control over the company through decisions arrived at in a general meeting. It is however impractical for a variety of reasons for shareholders to run a company on a day to day basis. There may be too many of them, for instance, to achieve any kind of sensible control over how the company conducts all its business activities, and in any case they may lack the necessary commercial experience. Thus companies place their management in the hands of directors, in effect creating two sources of control over the company, the shareholders in general meeting and the board of directors through board meetings. The complexity of company management, together with potential for abuse of power by directors has led to detailed regulation of the position of directors.

The Directors of a Company

The management of a registered company is carried on by the directors who are responsible for policy making, contract making and supervising the company property. Company directors are normally appointed in a manner prescribed in the articles of association, for example by the company in general meeting or by the existing directors. The Companies Act 1985 (s.303) specifically provides, however, that despite anything in the articles to the contrary, a director may be removed by an ordinary resolution, that is by simple majority of the members in a vote. There is nothing to prevent the articles conferring special voting rights on certain occasions.

> In *Bushell v. Faith* 1970 the company had an issued share capital of £300 equally divided between three members. Each share carried one vote. The articles provided, however, that on a resolution to remove a director, the directors' individual shares should carry three votes per share. Two of the members voted to remove the third from his position as director but were defeated because their 200 votes were cancelled by the individual director's 300 votes. The Court held this to be in order.

Directors' powers and duties

The specific powers of directors are stated in the articles but in addition to this actual authority to carry out functions, the directors will also have an authority to act which is implied under the law. This is because the director is an agent of the company and can bind it whether he acts within his actual or apparent authority.

It is important to be aware of the two issues which emerge here:

(a)   what the contractual capacity of the company is; and

(b)   what the agency powers of the directors are.

As we have previously seen, at one time there was no question in law of a director, or indeed the full board, being able legitimately to make a contract outside the objects of the company, even if the company itself had attempted to authorise such action. It was ultra vires and beyond the company's, and therefore the directors', powers. Since the Companies Act 1989, other than in special circumstances, a company will be held bound by an ultra vires contract. It is within the capacity of directors to bind the company to an outsider in this way. However in such circumstances the directors will be responsible to the company for such action. They should know the limitations imposed upon their own company's contractual capacity by its constitution. Indeed the 1989 Act specifically states that it is the duty of directors to observe such limitations. Thus the company may seek a remedy against a director for a breach of such a duty, and perhaps seek to remove the director from the board.

In addition the rule in *Royal British Bank v. Turquand* 1856 which was discussed in the last chapter, established that where a company acting through its board has failed to comply with its own internal rules, this will not invalidate the transaction. Here a company conferred power on the directors to borrow such sums as were authorised by an ordinary resolution of the general meeting. The directors borrowed money without such a resolution being passed. The Court held that the company was bound by the loan and laid down the following basic principles:

(i)   An outsider who is dealing with a company is not bound to inquire whether the internal regulations of the company have been complied with, such as passing resolutions to authorise specific acts. Basically, therefore, an outsider is entitled to assume that the directors have acted properly.

(ii)   An outsider is not entitled to rely on this presumption if he is aware of the irregularity or ought in the circumstances to have made inquiries.

Turquand is now replaced by the provisions of the 1989 Act which indicate that an outsider is deemed to be acting in good faith. It appears that as an agent a director will not be capable of binding the company where he acts outside his actual or apparent authority and the outsider is or ought reasonably to be aware that he has exceeded his authority.

This aspect of the principle can be seen operating in the following cases.

In *Howard v. Patent Ivory Manufacturing Co.* 1888 the directors of the company had power to borrow up to £1,000, with larger amounts having to be authorised by the general meeting. The company borrowed £3,500 from the directors without a resolution being passed. The court held that as the directors were aware of the procedural irregularity the borrowing was only valid up to £1,000.

In *Underwood Ltd. v. Bank of Liverpool* 1924 the director of a company paid cheques, made payable to the company, into his personal account. An action was brought against the bank to recover the sums paid. The court held that the bank was not entitled to assume that the director was acting properly, as the circumstances were so unusual that the bank ought to have been suspicious.

Even if an individual has not been actually appointed as director or managing director, should the company, through the directors, expressly or impliedly represent him as such, then as far as the outsider is concerned the individual will have all the apparent authority of a director.

In *Freeman Lockyer v. Buckhurst Properties* 1964 an individual director, with the consent of his fellow directors, employed the plaintiff architects to do some work. The director had been held out as managing director although he had not been appointed to this post, and the contract of employment was held to be binding. To enter into such a contract was within the apparent scope of a managing director's power.

Since it is the directors who are responsible for managing the company, it is of great concern to establish what they are legally capable of carrying out in the company's name, and to what extent they are accountable to the company for their actions.

Their powers are conferred on them by the articles, and in general these powers cannot be removed from them by resolution in a general meeting. Alteration of the articles themselves will be necessary.

The Companies Act 1985 does not define the term 'director' in a way which is very helpful. It says simply, a director is *"any person occupying the position of director, by whatever name called"*. This is contained in s.741. The courts however have provided some useful indications as to the nature of the director, variously describing such a person as a trustee, agent and managing partner.

> However Lord Jessel stated in *Re Forest of Dean Coal Mining Co.* 1878, *"It does not matter much what you call them, so long as you understand what their true position is which is that they are merely commercial men, managing a trading concern for the benefit of themselves and all other shareholders in it"*.

It is clear that a director stands in a fiduciary capacity to the company, and like an agent for a principal, must act in good faith (bona fide) and not make personal use of his position. The nature of a director's fiduciary duty can be broken down into the following components.

1. A director must act bona fide in what he considers is the interest of the company.

> The powers that are invested in directors are to be used for the benefit of the company as a whole, that is all the shareholders, rather than some sectional interest such as a class of shareholders, the company employees, the directors, a holding or subsidiary company. Thus a breach of duty will occur where the directors:
>
> - *issue new shares to themselves, not because the company needs more capital but merely to increase their voting power;*
>
>   In *Piercy v. S. Mills & Co. Ltd.* 1920 the directors used their powers to issue new voting shares to themselves, solely to acquire majority voting power. The Court held that the directors had abused their powers and the allotment was declared void.
>
> - *approve a transfer of their own partly-paid shares to escape liability for a call they intend to make;*
>
>   In *Alexander v. Automatic Telephone Co.* 1900 the directors used their position to require all shareholders to pay 3s 6d on each share excluding themselves. The Court held that his was a clear abuse of power and the directors were required to pay to the company the same amounts.
>
> - *negotiate a new service agreement between the company and its managing director simply in order to confer additional benefits on him or his dependents;*
>
>   In *Re W and M Roith* 1967 it was held that a new service contract negotiated between a managing director and his company was unlawful as it was solely to make a pension provision for his widow and that no regard had been taken as to whether this was for the benefit of the company.

- *abdicate responsibility for the running of the company and appoint a manager with full powers not under the control of the board of directors, or obey the majority shareholder without exercising their own judgment or discretion.*

2. A director must not place himself in a position where there is likely to be conflict between personal interests and duty to the company.

Directors act as agents on behalf of the company they represent and in such a capacity they must not enter into engagements where there is, or is likely to be, a conflict between the interests of the company and their own personal interests. The Companies Act 1985 therefore requires a director to give notice at the board meeting of a personal interest, direct or indirect, in any contracts or proposed contracts in which the company is involved. Failure to disclose such an interest is also a criminal offence and can result in fines being imposed. In addition any director who uses position to make personal profit may be made to account for such a profit to the company.

In *Cook v. Deeks* 1916 the directors of a railway company having negotiated a contract on behalf of the company decided to make the contract in their own names. The Court held that the benefit of the contract belonged to the company and the directors should account to the company for any profit made.

If a director uses his position to make a secret profit for himself, he will be in breach of his contract of employment, and may also be made to hand over such profit to the company.

In *Boston Deep Sea Fishing & Ice Co. v. Ansell* 1888 the managing director of a trawling business received a secret commission on placing an order for the construction of fishing boats. The Court held that the company was entitled to the commission.

It seems that a director will remain accountable even where the company has not sustained a loss.

In *Industrial Development Consultants v. Cooley* 1972 the defendant acted as the managing director of a design company. In this capacity he tried to obtain some design work for the company from the Eastern Gas Board. The Board indicated to him that they were not prepared to give his company the work. Realising he might gain a contract for himself he left his company on the pretence of being close to a nervous breakdown. He set up his own company and secured the gas board contract. It was held that he must account to his former company for the profit he had made, despite the fact that it was most unlikely the company would ever have obtained the work for itself.

The Financial Services Act 1986 makes it a criminal offence for an *insider*, that is an individual connected with a company as a director, officer, employee or someone having a professional or business relationship with it, to deal on a recognised stock exchange in the company's shares in prescribed circumstances. These are that the insider has information obtained through his connection with the company which it would be reasonable to expect him not to disclose and which he knows to be price sensitive unpublished information. Obviously many people who deal with and work in companies are ideally placed to either purchase or dispose of shares having obtained confidential information about such matters as possible takeovers, trading difficulties and so on. A person who receives information from an insider, a *tippee*, may also commit an offence if it has been knowingly obtained.

In *Re Attorney General's Reference (No 1 of 1988)* 1989 the Court decided that a person can be said to have 'obtained' insider information regarding a company even where it has been volunteered to him, without him seeking it out. If such a person goes on to deal an offence is committed under the 1986 Act.

The Criminal Justice Act 1988 provides for a maximum penalty of seven years and/or an unlimited fine.

A further duty imposed upon a director is the common law obligation to exercise care and skill in performing his work. This duty is variable one. In *Re City Equitable Fire Insurance Co. Ltd.* 1925 Romer J commented:

> *"The position of a director of a company carrying on a small retail business is very different from that of a director of a railway company. The duties of a bank director may differ widely from those of an insurance director, and the duties of a director of one insurance company may differ from those of another ... The larger the business carried on by the Company the more numerous, and the more important the matters that must of necessity be left to the managers, the accountants and the rest of the staff".*

Provided the directors act honestly this will normally be sufficient to fulfil the duty.

> In *Re New Marshonaland Exploration Co.* 1892 the directors approved a loan of £1,250 and failed to ensure that security was given. The Court held that in the absence of fraud the directors were not liable for this *"error of judgment"*.

Clearly however there are circumstances in which a director can fall short of what the law expects. The standard of care is a subjective one that is of a variable standard based upon the skill and knowledge of the individual in question. A highly paid professional director of a public limited company is expected to demonstrate a high level of business acumen.

Even non executive directors with experience or qualifications in areas of relevance to the work of their company may find high objective standards appropriate to their specialism being expected of them in law.

> In *Dorchester Finance Co. Ltd. v. Stebbing* 1989 the company lost money as the result of gross negligence committed by the company's sole executive director. He had failed to take out adequate securities on loans made by the company, as a result of which it found itself unable to recover the money advanced. The two non executive directors, who had little to do with the company, had signed cheques in blank at the executive directors request. All three men had considerable financial experience. The Court held the two non executive directors equally liable with the executive director to the company in damages.

Persons who may not be appointed

Table A which we considered in Chapter 2, contains no restrictions on who may be appointed as a director, although articles may be drafted to include such restrictions. For instance the company may seek to exclude minors from acting as directors, or perhaps another company.

Under statute, a person cannot be a company's sole director and secretary at the same time, nor its sole director and auditor. In addition statute provides that no person shall be appointed as a director of a public company, or of a private company which is the subsidiary of a public company, if at the time of his appointment he has reached the age of 70. This provision may be varied or excluded altogether under the articles.

Under the Company Directors Disqualification Act 1986 it is an offence for an undischarged bankrupt to act as a director without permission of the court. Articles may provide that anyone who has been bankrupt shall not be appointed as a director, and Table A more specifically states that a directors office becomes vacant on his bankruptcy. The 1986 Act also empowers the court to make a *disqualification order* against a named person, preventing him for the duration of the order, without leave of the court, from being a director of a company, or being concerned with or taking part in, directly or indirectly, the promotion, formation or management of a company.

Grounds for a disqualification order

Under the 1986 Act a number of grounds are identified under which the court may grant a disqualification order. Breach of an order renders the disqualified person liable to criminal proceedings carrying a maximum penalty of six months imprisonment, and it also renders the person personally liable for the company's debts. These are formidable penalties, and certainly the imposition of personal liability, with its effect of lifting the corporate veil, is seen as an appropriate way to deal with someone who has had a disqualification order made against him, because he has shown himself not fit to be a director, yet has continued in breach of the order to manage a company.

The grounds are:

- *conviction of an indictable offence;* An indictable offence is one which can be tried before a Crown Court, however such an offence may be dealt with summarily before Magistrates. The Crown Court can on conviction disqualify for up to fifteen years, the Magistrates Court up to five years. There is no minimum disqualification period. One of the most common offences associated with company affairs is fraud.

In *R v. Corbin* 1984 the defendant ran a business selling yachts through companies he owned. He was convicted of various fraudulent practices including borrowing from finance companies to buy yachts, falsely stating he had paid a deposit on them. He received two a half years imprisonment and a disqualification order for five years.

- *persistent breaches of company law;*
  Here the breaches in question involve the failure to provide any return account or documents required to be filed with the Registrar of Companies. There is a presumption that a person has been persistently in default if he has been convicted of a default three times in the past five years. The maximum period for disqualification is five years.

- *fraud, fraudulent trading or breach of duty revealed in a winding up;*
  The Court may make an order following the offence of fraudulent trading under s.458 Companies Act 1985, or where the person has otherwise been guilty of any fraud in relation to the company or in breach of duty, in his capacity as an officer, liquidator, receiver or manager. The maximum period for disqualification is fifteen years.

- *unfitness;*
  When a company becomes insolvent the person involved in administering the insolvency such as the liquidator or administrative receiver must make a return to the Secretary of State regarding the conduct of the company's directors. On the basis of this information the Secretary of State may apply to the Court for a disqualification order against an individual director on the grounds of his unfitness as evidenced in the return. The Court must then satisfy itself as to the unfitness before it can make an order. The 1986 Act lists the factors to be considered by the Court in reaching its decision. In broad terms these factors share a common feature, namely the way the directors have managed the company. The list is a long one, and it includes any breach of duty by the director in relation to the company; any misapplication or retention of company money or property by the director;

the directors failure to keep proper company records, or prepare or file annual company accounts; and the directors responsibility for the company becoming insolvent.

Removal of directors

If the directors have voting control of the company they cannot be removed. Where this does not occur s.303 of the 1985 Act provides that a company may by means of an ordinary resolution remove a director before his term of office expires, despite anything in the articles or in any agreement made between the company and the director. The section does not deprive the director of his right to sue for breach of contract on removal, if he has this right.

A common provision in articles is that directors hold office for three years, after which time they must either retire or offer themselves for re-election. Any changes in the directors must be notified to the Registrar of Company's. The company must keep a register at its office, available for public inspection, containing a list of the directors and the company secretary. Directors are also required by statute to disclose to the company and its members matters such as their financial interests in the company and connected companies.

Auditors

The auditing of company accounts is a process by which the company auditors carry out an annual investigation into the financial affairs of the company, so that they can confirm, primarily for the shareholders benefit, that the companies books reflect the actual position of the company's finances.

The relationship between the auditors, shareholders and directors of a company was summarised by Bingham L.J. in *Caparo Industries v. Dickman* 1990:

> *"The members, or shareholders, of the company are its owners. But they are too numerous, and in most cases too unskilled, to undertake the day-to-day management of that which they own. So responsibility for day-to-day management of the company is delegated to directors, The shareholders, despite their overall powers of control, are in most companies for most of the time investors and little more. But it would, of course, be unsatisfactory and open to abuse if the shareholders received no report on the financial stewardship of their investment save from those to who the stewardship had been entrusted. So provision is made for the company in general meeting to appoint an auditor (Companies Act 1985, s.384) whose duty is to investigate and form an opinion on the adequacy of the company's accounting records and returns and the correspondence between the company's accounting records and returns and its accounts (s.237). The auditor has then to report to the company's members (among other things) whether in his opinion the company's accounts give a true and fair view of the company's financial position (s.236). In carrying out his investigation and in forming his opinion the auditor necessarily works very closely with the directors and officers of the company. He receives his remuneration from the company. He naturally, and rightly, regards the company as his client. But he is employed by the company to exercise his professional skills and judgment for the purpose of giving the shareholders an independent report on the reliability of the company's accounts and thus on their investment."*

All registered companies must appoint auditors, unless the company is a dormant one, that is a *"small"* company which has had no *"significant accounting transaction"* since the end of the previous financial year. Appointment is made at each general meeting at which accounts in respect of an accounting reference period are laid. It is thus the members who make the appointment. The first auditors may be appointed by the directors, and casual vacancies may be filled either by the directors, or by the company in general meeting. A private company may now, by means of an elective resolution, opt out of annual appointment arrangements, so that the appointed auditors will continue in office until either side choose to terminate the appointment.

It is clearly important that auditors be both independent from the company, and suitably qualified to perform their functions. Only a registered auditor can carry out company auditing work, and a registered auditor is someone who is regarded as qualified by the Chartered Institutes of Accountants, or the Chartered Association of Certified Accountants, or the Department of Trade and Industry as having the appropriate overseas or other professional qualifications. Education, training and other matters affecting the work of auditors has now been brought under general statutory control. Certain persons are not permitted to act as auditors. These include an officer or servant of the company, a person employed by them, officers and servants of the company's holding or subsidiary companies or persons who have a *connection* with the company. A body corporate may act as an auditor.

A company may remove an auditor by means of an ordinary resolution under s.391. The provisions relating to such a removal are identical to those contained in s.303 for the removal of directors. An auditor may also resign from office, by depositing a notice to that effect at the company's registered office. The resignation is ineffective unless it either states that there are no circumstances connected with the resignation that should be brought to the attention of the members or creditors or alternatively it contains a statement outlining what those circumstances are. If such a statement is made a copy of it must be sent within fourteen days to all members, debenture holders, and every person entitled to receive notices of general meetings of the company. In such cases the auditor may also require the directors to convene an extraordinary general meeting of the company for the purpose of considering the resignation, a very powerful if rarely used threat.

Payment of auditors is determined by the company in general meeting.

Liability of auditors

In *Caparo Industries plc v. Dickman* 1990 the House of Lords was required to consider the extent of an auditor's liability for negligently audited accounts. The auditors in question had verified accounts which showed a pre-tax profit of £1.2m, when the company had in fact sustained a loss of over £400,000. Caparo Industries, who already held shares in the audited company, took more of its shares and later made a take-over bid for it on the strength of the inaccurate accounts. Caparo sued the auditors when the true position was discovered. The action was unsuccessful. The Court took the view that auditors of a public limited company owe no duty of care either to a potential investor or to an existing member who takes more shares in the company. To allow otherwise would be to create an unlimited liability on the part of auditors. On the facts there was not a sufficient relationship of proximity between the parties. The audited accounts went into general circulation and might foreseeably have been relied on by strangers for many different purposes. The duty of the auditors was a statutory duty owed to the company as a whole, to enable the members as a body to exercise proper control over it. A duty of care could however arise in cases when auditors have provided accounts with the intention or knowledge that they would be supplied by the company to a particular person or class of people, for example a specific bank, or banks generally, even though the precise purpose for which the accounts will be used is not known by the auditors.

The Shareholders in a Company

The shareholders who make up the membership of public and private companies include both individual investors and institutional investors. The latter include organisations such as pension funds. Investors will usually be seeking a return on their investment in the form of dividend payments from the company to them. They will also be looking for the market value of their shares to increase.

Whilst the principal obligation of shareholders is to pay for their shares, the rights they enjoy and general position they hold within the company is more complex, and we shall now examine it. To begin with it will be useful to consider what holding a share actually means.

Shares

The nature of shares has been considered both by Parliament and the courts. Thus s.182 Companies Act 1985 provides that shares are personal property and that they are transferable in accordance with the provisions in the articles, whilst in *Borland's Trustee v. Steel Bros. & Co. Ltd.* 1901 Farwell J stated that; *"A share is the interest of a shareholder in the company measured by a sum of money, for the purpose of liability in the first place, and of interest in the second"*. This is a helpful definition. It indicates that a member:

(i)   has a liability to pay the company, which arises when he applies for the shares, or when they are allotted to him, or when having received them he is called upon to pay for them; and

(ii)   has an interest in the company and certain rights which flow from this. These rights are determined by the class or type of shares he acquires and what the articles identify as the rights attached to the class, such as voting rights, and rights to dividends. Whatever these rights may be the shareholder is a part owner of the company. It is of course impossible to say which part is owned. The shareholders collectively own the undertaking of the company, and the company is a single person, thus the company is in effect the agent of the shareholders. It is they who ultimately determine the actions of the company through shareholders' meetings. Invariably the company will appoint directors to carry out the management of the company. The directors will be responsible to the shareholders for their actions, and in carrying out the business of the company will themselves be agents of it (see Figure 3.1).

A shareholder can transfer his shares by selling them or giving them away, for instance as a gift during his lifetime or under his will after his death. S.183 Companies Act 1985 requires a *"proper instrument of transfer"* to be delivered to the company for a valid assignment of ownership to occur. All this means is that a written document is necessary. It does not need to be a deed unless the articles require one. The shareholders' document of title to the shares is a share certificate, issued by the company. The shareholder obtains legal title to the shares when his name is entered by the company onto its register of shareholders. The share certificate is a document of considerable importance. Although physically transferring it from one person to another does not pass legal ownership in the shares (registration is required), s.186 of the 1985 Act states that the certificate is prima facie evidence of the shareholder's ownership in the shares. It is in other words a statement by the company that at the time it was issued the person named on it was the owner, and had paid for the shares to the extent stated. The company is bound by this statement in respect of those who have relied upon its accuracy.

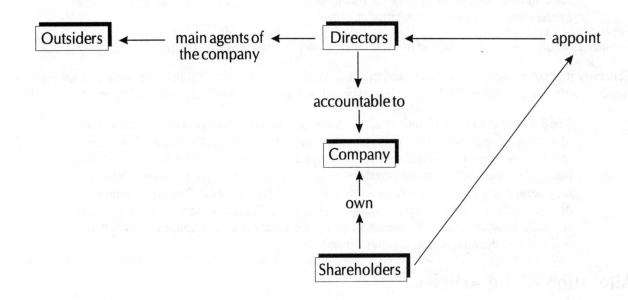

Figure 3.1 *Shareholders and Company Controllers*

The Statutory Contract

An important provision for shareholders is s.14 of the Companies Act 1985 which provides that the articles and the memorandum of a company constitute a binding contract between the company and its members. The section has caused some difficulty for the courts in the past, in their attempts at precisely identifying its effects. It states that the company and its members are bound to each other as though each shareholder has covenanted to observe the provisions of the memorandum and articles, the *statutory contract*. It also provides that any money owed by a member to the company is a speciality debt. This means the company has twelve years in which to recover the debt. In the case of debts arising from a simple contract the period would otherwise be six years.

The effect of the articles on shareholders can be summarised as follows:

The company is bound to the members in their capacity as members, and they are bound to it in the same way.

> An illustration of this principle is provided by *Salmon v. Quin & Axtens Ltd.* 1909. Here the articles gave directors full management powers, but prevented the directors from purchasing or letting any premises if the managing director dissented. The directors however resolved to deal in premises, despite the dissent of the managing director, and an extraordinary meeting of shareholders affirmed this action by a simple majority. The managing director sought an order from the court that the resolutions were invalid. The Court of Appeal agreed. The resolutions conflicted with the articles, and the company was bound by the articles. It could be restrained from its proposed action.

In *Hickman v. Kent or Romney Marsh Sheepbreeders Association* 1915 the articles of
the association stipulated that disputes between itself and its members should be referred
to arbitration. The plaintiff, a member, brought court action against the association in
relation to a number of matters. It was held that in accordance with the articles these
matters must be referred to arbitration.

The members are contractually bound to each other, under the terms of the articles.

Generally it is not possible for an individual member to enforce the contract in his own name against another
member, although exceptionally this may be possible if the articles grant him a personal right.

The position is illustrated in the case of *Rayfield v. Hands* 1960. A clause in the articles
of a private company stated, *"Every member who intends to transfer shares shall inform
the directors who will take the said shares equally between them at a fair value."* The
plaintiff notified the defendant directors of his intention to transfer his shares, however
they denied any liability to take and pay for them. The court held they were obliged to
do so, firstly because of their binding obligation indicated by the word "will" and
secondly because the clause was a term of the contractual relationship between the
plaintiff and the directors as company members.

Alteration of the Articles

Although the constitutional documents of a company make up the terms of the contract between itself and its
members, the memorandum and articles are not tablets of stone. The company does have the opportunity to
amend them provided it does so lawfully. In the case of the articles they may be altered or added to by means
of a special resolution which requires a 75% majority of the members voting in favour of it. No such resolution
is necessary if there is unanimous agreement of the members to the proposed alteration. Alterations must
however be made *bona fide*, that is in good faith, and for the benefit of the company as a whole. This is an
important aspect of the law regulating companies, for as we have just seen articles constitute a contract between
the company and its members and identify members' rights, such as the right to vote. Clearly the ability of
the company to change the terms of this contract at some future time may have the effect of placing individual
members who might be harmed by such changes, in a disadvantageous position. Thus the courts reserve the
power to refuse an alteration to the articles which has such an effect, unless there is a benefit to the company
as a whole and the alteration has been made in good faith. This principle is best appreciated by looking at
some of the caselaw on the subject.

In the leading case, *Allen v. Gold Reefs of West Africa* 1900 the articles of the company
which already granted it a lien on partly paid shares to cover any liabilities owed to it
by a member, were altered by extending the lien to holders of fully paid shares as well.
A lien is simply a charge on shares, enabling the company to sell the shares in order to
meet the debts owed to it by the members. Here a shareholder who at the time of his
death held both fully and partly paid shares in the company and owed the company money
for the partly paid shares, was also the only holder of fully paid shares. His executors
challenged the alteration on the grounds of bad faith, but the court upheld the alteration.
There was no evidence that the company was attempting to discriminate against the
deceased personally; it was simply chance that he was the only holder of fully paid
shares. In the words of Lord Lindley, *"The altered articles applied to all holders of fully
paid shares and made no distinction between them."*

It seems that the test which should be applied is whether the proposal is in the honest opinion of those voting for it, for the benefit of the members. An alteration may be challenged if it is, *"so oppressive as to cast suspicion on the honesty of the persons responsible for it, or so extravagant that no reasonable men could really consider it for the benefit of the company."* (Bankes L.J. in *Shuttleworth v. Cox Bros. & Co. (Maidenhead) Ltd.* 1927). If it can be established that the alteration has the effect of discriminating between members, granting advantages to the majority which are denied to the minority then a challenge will normally be successful, although an alteration may be upheld as bona fide even though the members voting for it are improving their own personal prospects.

> In *Greenhalgh v. Arderne Cinemas Ltd.* 1951 the articles of company, which prohibited the transfer of shares to a non member as long as an existing member was willing to pay a fair price for them, were altered to enable a transfer of shares to anyone by means of an ordinary resolution passed in a general meeting. The alteration was made because the majority shareholder wished to transfer his shares to a non member. This was held to be a valid alteration.

The courts will also uphold alterations which cause direct prejudice to individual members, as long as they are shown to be alterations made in good faith, and in the company's interest.

> In *Sidebottom v. Kershaw Leese & Co.* 1920 an alteration was made enabling the directors, who were the majority shareholders, to request the transfer to their nominees at a fair value the shares of any member competing with the company's business. The court found this to be a valid and proper alteration for, in the words of Lord Sterndale M R, *"it is for the benefit of the company that they should not be obliged to have amongst them as members, persons who are competing with them in business and who may get knowledge from their membership which would enable them to compete better."*

> By way of contrast in *Brown v. British Abrasive Wheel Co.* 1919 a majority of the shareholders (98%) were willing to provide the company with much needed extra capital if they could buy the 2% minority interest. As the minority were unwilling to sell, the majority proposed to alter the articles so as to enable nine-tenths of the shareholders to buy out any other shareholders. The plaintiff, representing the minority, brought an action to restrain the majority. It was held by the Court that the alteration would be restrained as it was not for the benefit of the company as a whole but rather for the benefit of the majority shareholding, and was in any case too wide a power and was therefore unlawful as constituting a potential fraud on the members.

In addition the following common law and statutory conditions apply to an alteration:

- *it must be lawful*, that is not be in conflict with the Act or with the general law;

- *it must not create a conflict between the memorandum and the articles*. If this does occur the provisions of the memorandum will prevail for it is the superior document;

- *it will require the leave of the court in certain circumstances*. These are where a minority of members have applied to the court for the cancellation of an alteration to the objects clause (s.5), where there has been an application for the cancellation of a resolution of a public company to re-register as a private company (s.54), or where a petition has been presented to the court on the ground that the affairs of the company are being conducted in a manner unfairly prejudicial to some part of the membership (s.461);

- *if it involves an increase in a member's liability it will only be valid if the member has given a written consent (s.16);*

- *if it affects the rights attached to a particular class of shareholders it is subject to the capacity of those disagreeing with the change who may apply to the court for a cancellation.* This power is available to 15% or more of the holders of the shares who did not give their consent, and it must be exercised within 21 days.

Controlling the company – the power of the members

A company has two principal sources of control over its affairs. These are the shareholders in general meeting and the directors. The most important matters affecting the company, for example changes in its constitution, rest with the shareholders in general meeting. Decisions reached at such meetings are arrived at through the putting of resolutions, which are then voted on. Generally a simple majority vote is sufficient to carry them, although some matters of special significance require a 75% majority. Since voting power plays such an important role in company matters the type of shares the company has issued is of considerable significance. Some shares, for example ordinary shares, usually carry full voting rights.

However other classes of share, such as preference shares, may carry no voting rights at all and therefore exclude shareholders of that class from effectively influencing the company in its decision making.

Since all public companies and many private companies consist of numerous members it is impractical to operate the company on a daily basis by means of general meetings. The articles will therefore provide for directors to be responsible for the daily running of the company and usually grant them the right to exercise all the powers of the company. They will remain answerable to the members in a general meeting although acts carried out by the directors within the powers delegated to them under the articles cannot be affected by decisions of a general meeting. So, if the directors have acted contrary to the wishes of the members, the ultimate sanction is to dismiss them or to change the articles and so bring in provisions that restrict the powers of the directors. In small companies the directors will often be the principal or only shareholders, so that such considerations will not be relevant.

Meetings

The fundamental principle of accountability of the directors to the members necessarily involves strict regulation of the company's operation. The Companies Act 1985 provides therefore that every company must, in each year, hold an annual general meeting and that every member is entitled to notice of this meeting. In addition, the holders of one-tenth or more of paid-up shares with voting rights may at any time compel the directors to call an extra-ordinary general meeting. The articles usually regulate the procedures to be adopted at these meetings, but in any case the minutes of all meetings must be strictly recorded.

Decisions at general meetings are usually taken by ordinary resolution, that is a simple majority of voting members present. For some types of business, usually related to the company's constitution such as the alteration of the articles or objects of the company, a special resolution is necessary which requires a three-quarter majority of voting members.

Types	Business	When called	Notice
Annual General Meeting	Declaring dividends Directors' and Auditors' reports, Appointment of Directors	Within 18 months of incorporation then once a year with no more than 15 months between each	At least 21 days Items of ordinary business need not be mentioned in notice
Extraordinary General Meeting	All business is 'special' e.g. alteration to articles, memorandum removal of Directors	Whenever Directors think fit, or if demanded by holders of one tenth or more of paid up shares	At least 14 days If called by members they must state why they want it

Shareholders' rights – majority rule, minority protection

As we have already noted the rights enjoyed by a member of a company are primarily contractual, arising from the class of shares acquired and the rights attached to them as specified in the articles. Unlike a partner, who will always possess the right to take part in the management of the firm, a shareholder will not always be involved in the daily management of the company, unless the organisation has a very small membership and its shareholders are also its directors. Companies' articles usually confer power on directors to operate the business, which they will perform on behalf of the members. The effect of such an arrangement is that ownership and management are separated. Nevertheless, ultimate control of the business is in the hands of the shareholders by the exercise of voting power in the general meeting. Where appropriate they can vote to remove a director.

In any vote which does not produce a unanimous outcome there will be two groups, the majority shareholders and the minority shareholders. In effect it is the majority that make the company decisions. If the minority have a grievance, legally there is little they can do to redress it. The courts have been reluctant to assist minority shareholders who are claiming they have been oppressed or have had their interests prejudiced by the majority. Since it is the majority who rule the company it is not for the court to thwart their actions. If the minority are arguing that the majority have acted in breach of the memorandum or the articles, then it is a wrong which has been done to the company. The proper plaintiff is the company itself, not the minority shareholders. Of course they will find it impossible to pass a resolution that the company sue the majority, for the voting strength of the majority will be sufficient to block such a move. This leaves the minority in a very vulnerable position.

> The case of *Foss v. Harbottle* 1843 laid down as a general principle that the courts will not interfere in the internal management of a company at the insistence of the minority shareholders. Here an action had been brought by the minority alleging that the directors were responsible for losses that had occurred when they sold some of their own land to the company, at what was alleged to be an over valuation. The Court held that the action must fail as the proper plaintiff in such circumstances was the company itself. As the action to which the minority shareholders objected could have been ratified by the majority then it was the majority shareholders who should decide whether an action should be brought in the company name. The Court saw no merit in interfering in the internal management of a company by passing judgment on its commercial decisions.

In *Pavlides v. Jenson and others* 1956, a company sold an asbestos mine for £182,000 when its real value was close to £1,000,000. A minority shareholder brought an action for damages against three directors who were responsible for the sale and against the company, alleging gross negligence. The Court held that the action could not be brought by a minority shareholder because it was the company itself which should decide whether to redress the wrong that had been committed.

Thus the process of incorporation, having invested a company with a separate legal personality, dictates that the company and individual members are separate. If a wrong is committed against the company it is the company, by virtue of a decision made by the Board of Directors that should seek redress for it.

The rule in *Foss v. Harbottle* does not however apply to every type of action taken by the majority. In certain situations the court will hear a claim brought by minority shareholders, even though the majority do not wish it. Thus:

- proposed ultra vires activities can be restrained, even by a member holding a single share;

- where directors attempt to do something requiring a special resolution which they do not obtain, then action cannot be ratified by an ordinary resolution. Were this to be otherwise, the protection for minorities granted in circumstances where a three quarter majority is needed would be avoided;

- where a wrong is suffered to a member in his personal capacity, through the action of the directors.

   For instance in *Pender v. Lushington* 1877 the company chairman wrongfully refused to accept the votes cast by certain shareholders. The resolution they opposed was in consequence able to be carried. The Court held that the company could be restrained from carrying out the proposed resolution;

- when a fraud has been committed against the minority. This does not mean fraud in the criminal sense, rather conduct which is grossly unfair.

   An example is provided by *Daniels v. Daniels* 1978. Here two company directors, in 1970, instructed the company to sell land to one of them for £4,250. In 1974 the land was resold for £120,000 and a minority shareholder brought an action claiming that damages should be payable to the company. The Court held that despite no allegation of fraud the action by the individual shareholders should be allowed to proceed.

In addition to the common law, the Companies Act 1985 confers certain statutory rights on minority shareholders.

An important example of this is s.459 which gives a member the right to apply to the court for an order on the ground that the affairs of the company are being or have been conducted in a manner which is unfairly prejudicial to some members (including at least himself), or that any actual or proposed act or omission of the company is or would be prejudicial.

If the case is proved the court may issue an order to:

- regulate the company's affairs for the future;

- require the company to act or refrain from acting in a particular way;

- authorise civil proceedings in the name and on behalf of the company by a person; or

- require the purchase of any member's shares by the company or by other members.

An example of a court order regulating a company's future affairs is seen in *Re H R Harmer Limited* 1959. The company was run by an elderly father acting as chairman and his two sons as directors. The father had voting control. He largely ignored the wishes of the board of directors and ran the business as his own. On an application by the sons as minority shareholders, alleging oppression, the Court held that relief should be granted. The father was appointed life president of the company without rights, duties or powers and was ordered not to interfere with the company's affairs.

The Partners of a Firm

The background to the relationship of the partners

There are obvious problems inherent in attempting to reach the sort of joint decisions which are necessary to successfully manage a partnership and it is not uncommon for partners to disagree. There are also risks involved, both in having unlimited liability and in the fact that individual partners may be responsible for the acts and defaults of their co-partners. Each partner is an agent of the co-partners and as such has an agent's power to bind the partnership by his acts undertaken within the ordinary course of the business. It is crucial therefore that each partner has trust and confidence in his co-partners, the relationship being one of the utmost good faith. This is sometimes given its Latin name and is known as a relationship of *uberrimae fidei*. Each partner is therefore under a duty to make a full and frank disclosure to the firm of any matters affecting it that come to the partner's attention.

The power of a partner to bind the other members of the firm by his actions illustrates how important it is that each partner should trust and have confidence in his co-partners, not only in regard to their business ability but also as to their business ethics. In *Helmore v Smith* 1886 Bacon V-C remarked that, *"mutual confidence is the life-blood"* of the firm, whilst in *Baird's Case* 1870 James LJ stated:

> *"Ordinary partnerships are by the law assumed and presumed to be based upon the mutual trust and confidence of each partner in the skill, knowledge and integrity of every other partner. As between the partners and the outside world (whatever may be their private arrangements between themselves), each partner is the unlimited agent of every other in every matter connected with the partnership business, or which he represents as the partnership business, and not being in its nature beyond the scope of the partnership".*

In the course of business, partnerships enter into transactions with other organisations and individuals and inevitably such transactions are negotiated and executed for the partnership by individual partners, rather than by the firm as a whole. It has already been noted that each partner is an agent of his co-partners. *"In English law a firm as such has no existence; partners carry on business both as principals and as agents for each other within the scope of the partnership business; the firm-name is a mere expression, not a legal entity"*, stated Lord Justice Farwell in *Sadler v. Whiteman* 1910.

Under the law of agency, the person who appoints the agent is called the principal. The principal is bound by contracts made within the agent's actual and apparent authority. If the agent acts within either of these two spheres the contract concluded between the agent and the third party becomes the principal's contract, and hence it is the principal and the third party who become bound to each other. The *actual* authority of an agent is the express power given by the principal. A firm may for instance expressly resolve in a partnership meeting that each partner shall have the power to employ staff. Authority may also arise where the agent's power to make a particular contract or class of contracts can be implied from the conduct of the parties or the circumstances of the case. The *apparent*, or *ostensible* authority of an agent is the power which the agent appears to others to hold. Of a partner's apparent authority s.5 Partnership Act, 1890, says:

> *"Every partner is an agent of the firm and his other partners for the purpose of the business of the partnership; and the acts of every partner who does any act for the carrying on in the usual way business of the kind carried on by the firm of which he is a member bind the firm and his partners, unless the partner so acting has in fact no authority to act for the firm in the particular matter, and the person with whom he is dealing either knows that he has not authority, or does not know or believe him to be a partner".*

Whether a particular contract is one carrying on in the usual way business of the kind carried on by the firm is a question of fact.

> In *Mercantile Credit Co. Ltd. v. Garrod* 1962 the court had to decide what would be considered as an act of a *"like kind"* to the business of persons who ran a garage. It was held that the sale of a car to a third party by one of the partners bound the other partners. This was despite an agreement between them that provided for the carrying out of repair work, and the letting of garages, but expressly excluded car sales.

A private limitation of the powers of an agent is not an effective way to bring the restriction to the notice of an outsider dealing with the agent, and the law recognises this. But if, for example, partner has acted as an agent for his firm in the past with a particular third party, and he carries out a further transaction of a similar kind with the third party after the firm has taken away his express authority, the third party can nevertheless hold the firm bound unless he knew at the time of contracting of the partner's lack of authority.

The exact scope of an agent's apparent authority under s.5 has been the subject of much litigation, and the following powers will usually fall within the agent's apparent authority:

1.   *in the case of all types of partnership the power to:*

   - sell the goods or personal property of the firm;

   - purchase in the firm's name goods usually or necessarily used in the firm's business;

   - receive payments due to the firm;

   - employ staff to work for the firm.

2.   *in the case of a partnership whose business is the buying and selling of goods (a trading partnership), the following additional powers are within the partner's authority:*

   - to borrow money for a purpose connected with the business of the firm;

   - to deal with payments to and from the firm.

A partnership has no separate legal identity so it is the individual partners who are ultimately accountable for all the firm's debts. Under the Partnership Act every partner is jointly liable with the other partners for all the debts and obligations of the firm incurred whilst being a partner. A legal action by a creditor seeking to recover money owed to him may be brought against any one or more of the firm's partners. However if the judgment obtained in the court does not satisfy the creditor he cannot then sue the remaining partners for, having sued one partner, he is precluded from suing the others for the same debt. Nevertheless the creditor, if he had chosen to do so, could have sued the firm in its own name rather than suing an individual partner of the firm. This has the effect of automatically joining all the partners in the action, and means that the judgment will be met out of assets of the firm as a whole and, if necessary, out of the property of the individual partners.

The Act goes on to provide that the firm is liable for the *"wrongful act or omission of any partner"* committed within the ordinary course of the firm's business. The term "wrongful" certainly embraces tortious acts although it appears that it does not extend to criminal acts.

An exception however occurs in relation to fraudulent acts carried out within the scope of the firm's business.

> In *Hamlyn v. Houston & Co.* 1903 the defendant firm was run by two partners as a grain merchants. One of the partners bribed the clerk of a rival grain merchant, and obtained information from him which enabled the firm to compete at greater advantage. The Court of Appeal held that both partners were liable for this tortious act. Obtaining information about rivals was within the general scope of the partners' authority, and therefore it did not matter that the method used to obtain it was unlawful. In the words of Lord Collins, M.R: *"It is too well established by the authorities to be now disputed that a principal may be liable for the fraud or other illegal act committed by his agent within the general scope of the authority given to him, and even the fact that the act of the agent is criminal does not necessarily take it out of the scope of his authority"*.

It is no defence for a firm to show that it did not benefit from the unlawful act of its agent.

> The House of Lords in *Lloyd v. Grace, Smith & Co.* 1912 held a solicitor's firm liable for the fraud of its managing clerk who induced one of the firm's clients to transfer certain properties into his name. In advising the client the clerk was acting within the scope of his authority, and that alone made the firm liable for his acts.

Although the Act does not apply to criminal matters two points should be noted. Firstly, there may be occasions when one partner may be held vicariously liable for an offence committed by another. Vicarious liability is considered later in the chapter. Secondly, a partner may be a party to an offence committed by another simply because it is in the nature of that partnership that they work together.

> In *Parsons v. Barnes* 1973 where two partners worked together in a roof-repairing business, one of them was convicted of an offence under the Trade Descriptions Act 1968, by being present when his co-partner made a false statement to a customer.

If a partner acting within the scope of his apparent authority receives and misapplies the property of a third person while it is in the firm's custody the firm is liable to meet the third person's loss. Similarly when the firm has received property of a third person in the course of its business, and the property has been misapplied by a partner while in the firm's custody, it must make good the loss. The liability of partners for misapplications of property, or wrongs of the firm, is stated by the Act to be joint and several. This means that if a judgment is obtained by a plaintiff against one partner, this does not operate as bar to bringing a further action against all or any of the others if the judgment remains unsatisfied. Where liability is merely joint this is not possible.

> In *Plumer v. Gregory* 1874 two of the partners in a firm consisting of three solicitors accepted on the firm's behalf and subsequently misappropriated money entrusted to them by the plaintiff, a client of the firm. The third member of the firm was unaware of these events, which only came to light after the other partners had died. The plaintiff's action against the remaining partner succeeded, for the firm was liable to make good the loss, and liability of the members was joint and several.

Changes in membership

The membership of a firm will normally alter from time to time. It may wish to expand its business by bringing in new partners to provide the benefit of additional capital or fresh expertise. Existing partners may leave the partnership to join a new business, or to retire. A changing membership poses the question of the extent to which incoming and outgoing partners are responsible for the debts and liabilities of the firm. Although partners are responsible for any matters arising during their membership of the firm, incoming partners are not liable for the debts incurred before they joined, nor outgoing partners for those incurred after they leave, provided the retiring partner advertises the fact that he is no longer a member of the firm. This involves sending notice to all customers of the firm while that person was a partner, and advertising the retirement in a publication known as the *London Gazette*. If this is not done a person dealing with the firm after a change in its membership can treat all apparent members of the old firm as still being members of the firm. With regard to existing liabilities the partner may be discharged from them when he retires through the agreement of the new firm and the creditors.

Rights and duties of the partners

Ideally the partnership relationship should be regulated by a comprehensive partnership agreement. If it is not, the provisions of the Partnership Act will apply when the parties are in dispute as to the nature of their duties and are unable to reach agreement amongst themselves, but in a business enterprise of this sort, where a member's entire wealth lies at stake, it is clearly of great value to execute a detailed agreement setting out in precise form the powers and responsibilities of the members. For instance it would be prudent for the agreement to provide grounds for the removal of partners, since the Act makes no such provision. Because the members of the firm have the freedom to make their own agreement, without the statutory controls imposed upon other forms of business organisation, such as the registered company, the partnership stands out as a most flexible form of organisation.

The duties that the Act sets out are based upon a single foundation of fundamental importance to all partnerships, namely that the relationship between the parties is of the utmost good faith.

> This principle can be seen in *Law v. Law* 1905. A partner sold his share in the business to another partner for £21,000, but the purchasing partner failed to disclose to his co-partner certain facts about the partnership assets, of which he alone was aware. When the vendor realised that he had sold his share at below its true value he sought to have the sale set aside. The Court of Appeal held that in such circumstances the sale was voidable, and could be set aside.

A partner is under a duty to his co-partners to render true accounts and full information of all things affecting the partnership. Personal benefits can only be retained with the consent of the other partners.

> In *Bentley v. Craven* 1853 one of the partners in a firm of sugar refiners, who acted as the firm's buyer, was able to purchase a large quantity of sugar at below market price. He resold it to the firm at the true market price. His co-partners were unaware that he was selling on his own account. When they discovered this they sued him for the profit he had made, and were held to be entitled to it. It was a 'secret profit' and belonged to the firm.

A partner is under a duty not to compete with his firm by carrying on another business of the same nature unless the other partners have consented. If a partner is in breach of this duty he must account to the firm for all the profits made and pay them over. If the partnership agreement prohibits the carrying on of a competing business, the court may grant an injunction to stop a partner who disregards the limitation.

Further rights and duties are set out in the Act which states that, in the absence of a contrary agreement:

- all partners are entitled to take part in the management of the partnership business;

- any differences arising as to ordinary matters connected with the partnership business are to be decided by a majority of the partners, but no change can be made in the nature of the partnership business without the consent of all the partners;

- no person may be introduced as a partner without the consent of all existing partners;

- all partners are entitled to share equally in the profits of the business irrespective of the amount of time they have given to it, and must contribute equally towards any losses. The Act does not require the firm to keep books of account, although this will normally be provided for in the partnership agreement, together with specific reference to the proportions of the profit each partner is entitled to. If however there are partnership books they have to be kept at the principal place of business, where every partner is entitled to have access to them for the purpose of inspection and copying;

- if a partner makes a payment or advance beyond the agreed capital contribution he is entitled to interest at 5% p.a.;

- a partner is not entitled to payment of interest on his capital until profits have been ascertained;

- the firm must indemnify a partner in respect of payments made and personal liabilities incurred in the ordinary and proper conduct of the business of the firm, or in or about anything necessarily done for the preservation of the business or property of the firm (e.g. paying an insurance premium);

- a partner is not entitled to remuneration for acting in the partnership business.

In cases where the firm consists of active and sleeping partners the partnership agreement will often provide that as well as taking a share of the profits the active partners shall be entitled to the payment of a salary.

If any of the terms of the partnership agreement are broken, damages will be available as a remedy, and where appropriate an injunction may be granted.

Partnership property

It can be of importance, particularly to the partners themselves, to establish which assets used by the partnership actually belong to the firm itself, rather than to an individual partner. Mere use of property for partnership purposes does not automatically transfer ownership in it to the business.

> In *Miles v. Clarke* 1953 the defendant started up a photography business which involved him in acquiring a lease and photographic equipment. After trading unsuccessfully he was joined by the plaintiff, a free-lance photographer, who brought into the firm his business connection which was of considerable value. The partners traded profitably for some time, on the basis of equal profit sharing. Later, as a result of personal difficulties, it became necessary to wind up the firm. The plaintiff claimed a share in all the assets of the business. The Court held that the assets of the business other than the stock-in-trade

which had become partnership property, belonged to the particular partner who had brought them in.

The Act provides that all property and rights and interests in property originally brought into the partnership or subsequently acquired by purchase or otherwise on account of the firm, must be held and applied by the partners exclusively for the purpose of the partnership and in accordance with the partnership agreement. Such property is called 'partnership property' and will normally be jointly owned by the partners. Because a partner is a co-owner of partnership property, rather than a sole owner of any particular part of the partnership's assets, he may be guilty of theft of partnership property if it can be established that his intention was to permanently deprive the other partners of their share.

Under the Act property bought with money belonging to the firm is deemed to have been bought on account of the firm, unless a contrary intention appears.

The Rights and Duties of Business and Private Consumers

A commercial business, whatever its size or legal status, will be concerned with trading activities which are designed to provide it with a profit. These activities will involve it in two distinct sets of operations:

- as a *purchaser* of goods and services, probably though not necessarily obtained from other businesses; and

- as a *supplier* of goods or services to other business and to private consumers.

Particular legal rights and duties are associated with both these sets of operations, and we need to establish precisely what rights and duties attach to each of them. In this context there are two important points which must be borne in mind. Firstly the legal rights available to the consumer depend upon whether the consumer is a business or a private individual; generally a greater degree of legal protection is available to the latter. Secondly the type of transaction being carried out determines the rights and duties that are associated with it, hence a contract to *supply a service* such as dry cleaning or hairdressing does not contain exactly the same kind of protection for the consumer as does a contract to *sell goods* such as compact disk player of a pair of jeans.

In summary therefore, we can only establish the rights and duties of buyers and sellers of goods and services by determining whether the parties are dealing as businesses or private consumers, and having done so by identifying the kind of transaction they have entered into.

Dealing as a consumer

In a broad sense anyone to whom goods or services are supplied can be regarded as a consumer and, as we shall see in Chapter 5, the law gives protection to all consumers. However, the protection available is greater in the case of the private consumer. The Fair Trading Act 1973 defines a private consumer in s.137 as:

"the person to or for whom goods or services are, or are sought to be, supplied in the course of a business carried on by the supplier, and who does not receive or seek to receive the goods or services in the course of a business carried on by him".

The Unfair Contract Terms Act 1977 also provides a statutory definition of a private consumer. The Act states in s.12 that:

"a party to a contract deals as a consumer in relation to another party if:

(a) *he neither makes the contract in the course of a business nor holds himself out as doing so; and*

(b) *the other party does make the contract in the course of a business; and*

(c) *where the contract involves the supply of goods, the goods are of a type ordinarily supplied for private use or consumption".*

This definition is examined in Chapter 5.

Supplying in the course of a trade or business

Many of the legal rules which govern consumer protection apply only where goods or services are supplied in the course of a trade or business. There is no generally applicable precise definition of the expression 'business', although there are a number of decided cases which give some guidance.

> In *Havering London Borough v. Stevenson* 1970 a car hire firm regularly sold its cars after a period of use in the business. A sale in these circumstances was held to be in the course of its trade or business as a car hire firm.
>
> On the other hand, in *Davies v. Sumner* 1984 the defendant was a self employed courier, who had a contract with a TV company to transport films and video tapes. He purchased a new car in June 1980, and travelled 118,000 miles in it before trading it in for another in July 1981. The mileometer had gone around the clock, and showed only 18,000 miles. The defendant did not disclose the true mileage, and was later charged with having applied a false trade description "in the course of a trade or business". The House of Lords held that he was not guilty, as this was a one-off sale which could not be regarded as an integral part of his business.
>
> In *Blakemore v. Bellamy* 1983 the defendant's spare time activity of buying, refurbishing and selling cars was held to be a hobby rather than a business. This was so even though he had sold eight different cars over a period of fifteen months and he had not driven them all himself or had them insured.

Business sellers may sometimes masquerade as private sellers for example by advertising in the small ad's in a newspaper. The purchaser may be misled by this and think that his legal remedies are limited because he has purchased from a private seller. In order to prevent such disguised business sales the Business Advertisements (Disclosure) Order 1977 makes it a criminal offence for a trader or a businessman to advertise goods for sale without making it reasonably clear that the goods are being sold in the course of a business.

The nature of the transaction

We noted earlier that different types of consumer transactions attract different rights and obligations. These rights and obligations are considered in Chapter 5, and for the moment we need only to record that the principal transactions both business and private consumers are likely to be engaged in will be:

- contracts of sale – where the buying/selling of goods is the objective of the contract;

- contracts of hire – where the hirer obtains possession and use of goods;

- contracts for the supply of services;

- contracts for work done and materials supplied; and

- contracts for the sale or supply of goods on credit.

Civil and criminal liability

Although transactions of the kind listed above usually give rise to civil liability if the contract is broken in some way, there are also numerous circumstances in which breach of consumer protection legislation will result in criminal liability for the business. Perhaps the best known use of the criminal code to support consumers' rights is the Trade Descriptions Act 1968. This important provision is examined later in this chapter.

The Rights and Duties of Employees in a Business

All business organisations, whether operating as corporate bodies or unincorporated associations will recruit a workforce to enable them to carry on business activity. Despite the growth in recent years of the use of self employed contractors, particularly in the service industries, the predominant method of recruiting staff is still by entering into a contract of employment, also called a contract of service. The relationship of employer and employee is governed by the contract of employment which, in its express terms will identify the rights and duties of the parties. In addition there are numerous rights and duties which are implied into an employment contract through the operation of the common law and to a lesser extent statutes.

The law relating to the recruitment of staff and statutory rights and duties in employment such as equal rights and unfair dismissal is covered in the mandatory unit, human resources. Here we will briefly identify the main express and implied terms of employment which regulate the relationship between the employer and employee.

Express terms

Employers are required by statute to provide their employees with a written statement of the main terms and conditions of employment. Such terms must cover matters including:

- the names of the parties to the contract and the commencement date;
- the scale of remuneration, the method of calculation and the intervals of payment;
- the hours, holidays, sickness and sickness pay;
- the job title, length of notice and pension rights;
- the grievance and disciplinary procedure.

A well drafted contract of employment should also identify the place of work and the extent to which this could be subject to change.

In addition it is also a useful exercise to provide the employee with a comprehensive job description which identifies responsibilities and indicates the work that the employee will be required to perform. It should be stressed however that to fully appreciate the relationship of employer and employee you should be aware of the terms that are implied into the contract of employment by the common law.

Implied terms

In every contract of employment, certain terms are implied by the courts and tribunals through the operation of the common law. These terms are the source of many of the rights and duties of both the employer and employee, and are an integral part of the contract of employment.

Terms are implied into a contract of employment by the common law imposing duties on both the employer and employee. Duties are imposed on the employer to maintain a relationship of trust and confidence to pay wages, to provide the opportunity for the employee to earn the expected wage, to indemnify, and to provide a safe system of work. Duties of the employee include to act in good faith, to account for money received, to respect trade secrets, and to obey lawful instructions.

To pay wages

The common law implies a term into the contract of employment imposing a duty on the employer to pay a reasonable wage for the work done. In the majority of cases, of course, the parties to the contract of employment will have expressly agreed a rate of pay or referred to a rate of pay contained in a collective agreement. However, in the unlikely event that no wage is expressly agreed and in the case of a dispute, the courts will value the service provided and imply a reasonable wage.

To provide work and indemnify

Generally there is no duty on an employer to provide work for his employees as long as their contractual remuneration is paid. If, however, an employee's pay depends upon the performance of work (piece-work), then the employer is under an obligation to provide sufficient work to enable a reasonable wage to be earned. A further exception is where the employee's occupation is such that the opportunity to work is an essential part of the contract because of the possibility of loss of reputation, as for example in the case of an actor, entertainer or journalist.

Under the common law, an employee is entitled to be indemnified for loss or expense incurred in the course of employment. In most cases, of course, expenses are provided for expressly in the contract of employment.

To provide a safe system of work

The present law relating to an employer's duties in relation to the safety of his work-force is embodied within the common law and statute. The common law duty arises under the tort of negligence and involves providing employees with a safe system of work.

To maintain trust and confidence

The Employment Appeal Tribunal has stated that *"there is an implied term in a contract of employment that the employers will not, without reasonable and proper cause, conduct themselves in a manner calculated or likely to destroy or seriously damage the relationship of confidence and trust between the parties"*. It has been held to be a breach of this term by an employer who failed to treat an allegation of sexual harassment with due seriousness and gravity, to unjustly criticise an employee, to abuse an employee publicly and to fail to treat an employee fairly in relation to a disciplinary matter.

To provide information

The House of Lords has held that there is an implied term in a contract of employment imposing a duty on the employer to take reasonable steps to provide an employee with certain information. Here the information in question related to pension rights which had been negotiated on the employee's behalf but they had not been informed of the benefits they conferred.

The duty of good faith

This duty is the most fundamental obligation of an employee and involves serving his employer faithfully. Faithful service involves working competently, respecting the employer's property, and not taking industrial action such as strikes, go-slows, working to rule etc., which would disrupt the employer's business.

The relationship of trust and confidence which is said to exist between employer and employee may also demand that an employee reports matters of interest to his employer.

> In *Sybros Corporation and Another v. Rochem Ltd.* and others 1983, the Court of Appeal held that, while there is no general duty to report a fellow employee's misconduct or breach of contract, an employee might be so placed in the hierarchy of an organisation as to have a duty to report either his 'superiors' or 'inferiors'' misconduct.

To account for money received

There is an implied duty on an employee not to accept any bribes, commissions or fees in respect of his work other than from his employer.

> In *Boston Deep Sea Fishing & Ice Co. v. Ansell* 1888, an employee who received a secret commission from other companies for placing orders with them was treated as having been in breach of his duty and his dismissal was justified.

To respect trade secrets

An employee would be in breach of this duty by working for a competitor in his spare time.

> In *Hivac v. Park Royal Scientific Instruments Co.* 1946, an employee was restrained from working for a competitor engaged in work of a similar nature.

Certainly, there would be a flagrant breach of contract if an employee were to disclose trade secrets or other confidential information during the course of his employment. Even an ex-employee may be restrained.

> In *Printer & Finishers Ltd. v. Holloway* 1965, an ex-employee was restrained from showing secret documents to a competitor and disclosing confidential information he had obtained during his employment.

To obey reasonable orders

This duty could be included within the general obligation to render faithful service. To be reasonable an order must be lawful, for there is no duty to obey an unlawful order, for instance to falsify records. In determining the reasonableness of an order, all the circumstances must be considered and a close examination made of the contract of employment.

> In *UK Atomic Energy Authority v. Claydon* 1974, the defendant's contract of employment required him to work anywhere in the UK Accordingly, it was held to be a reasonable order to require him to transfer to another base within the UK

> Also, in *Pepper v. Webb* 1969, when a head gardener, asked to plant some flowers, replied "I couldn't care less about your bloody greenhouse or your sodding garden" and walked away, the court held that the refusal to obey the instructions, rather than the language which accompanied the refusal, amounted to a breach of contract.

Having considered the legal position of the key parties in business, directors, shareholders, partners, customers and employees we can now explore the extent to which legal liability may be imposed upon a business organisation both under civil and criminal law.

Legal Liability in Business

The expression legal liability has been used in various places throughout this chapter, and occurs throughout the book. This is hardly surprising for legal liability is one of the most fundamental of all legal concepts, and we now need to consider the impact it has upon business.

A legal liability arises when someone is under a legal obligation to do or refrain from doing something, and is answerable if they act in breach of such an obligation. Businesses are subject to an extensive range of actual and potential legal liabilities resulting from the performance of their business operations. There are different ways these liabilities can be categorised. If we look at them from the standpoint of the purposes they are designed to meet we come across one of the most well known of all legal categorisations, the division of the law into civil and criminal branches. The distinction between civil and criminal law was discussed in Chapter 1. Essentially, civil law is concerned with private rights and obligations and the remedying of private grievances whereas the criminal law is concerned with the welfare of society generally. Civil law is concerned with compensating victims, criminal law with, amongst other things, the punishment of offenders. Both civil liability and criminal liability arise from the existence of legal rules. In civil law the legal rules which have the greatest impact upon business operations are those involved with contractual and tortious liability.

Contractual liability in business

A contractual liability arises when two or more parties enter into a contractual relationship with each other. A contract is a legally enforceable agreement. Contract-making is the life blood of business. It is the way businesses trade. Because contract-making is so significant in business operations we need to examine it in some detail, and the next chapter is devoted entirely to the subject of the negotiation and completion of business contracts.

Tortious liability in business

A tort is a civil wrong, and a person or organisation committing a tort is someone who incurs tortious liability. Unlike a contract, where liability depends upon the making of an agreement, in tort liability arises without the need for any agreement between the parties but simply through the operation of the general law.

The civil law recognises a number of distinct areas of tortious liability, each of them resulting from the development of specific torts. Torts are designed to protect people from certain recognised kinds of harm, and to grant them legal remedies if they actually sustain harm as a consequence of a tort being committed against them. Tortious harm covers such areas as:

- the protection of business and personal reputations – the tort of *defamation*;

- the unlawful interference with another's land or personal property – the tort of *trespass*; and

- the unlawful interference with a person's use and enjoyment of and – the tort of *private nuisance*.

The basis upon which liability arises depends upon the specific rules governing each tort. Some torts for instance, require no proof of fault on the part of the wrongdoer. The tort of trespass to land is an example.

Another is the tort of *Rylands v. Fletcher*, where strict liability is imposed upon a landowner in respect of any damage caused by the escape of non-natural things brought onto the land. Relying on this tort, strict liability has been imposed for damage caused by escaping water, gas, electricity, germs and even people.

Tortious liability however is normally associated with fault, which involves establishing that the defendant failed to act as a reasonable person would have acted in a particular set of circumstances. Thus in the tort of negligence, a defendant who is not shown to be at fault will not incur liability.

> In *Dixon v. London Fire and Civil Defence* 1993 water had leaked from a fire appliance onto the floor of the fire station. The court heard that such leaks were endemic in the fire service and appeared to be insoluble. As a consequence the court held that the fire authority was not in breach of the legal duty of care that it owed to a fire officer who had slipped and fell as a result of the wet floor.

We need to consider the tort of negligence in some detail.

The Tort of Negligence

Liability in the tort of negligence arises where foreseeable damage to the plaintiff is caused by the defendant's breach of a legal duty to take care. The tort has wide application and includes liability for losses or injuries suffered at work, on the roads, in dangerous premises, or as a result of medical accidents, professional malpractice or defective products.

A central feature of liability in negligence is that liability is fault-based. A defendant will be liable only if the court is satisfied that he failed to take reasonable care. It can be argued that a fault-based system is far from ideal as a means of ensuring fair treatment and proper financial assistance to those who are injured or disabled through no fault of their own. Indeed it has often been said that the law of negligence is like a lottery in which a few successful litigants are handsomely rewarded. Many other claimants are unable to obtain compensation due to lack of evidence of fault, lack of a substantial defendant to pursue or the refusal of the court to impose liability in the circumstances of the case.

One alternative to a system of fault-based liability is the introduction of strict liability for injuries sustained either generally or in particular categories of situation. Under a system of strict liability the injured party should find it much easier to obtain compensation because he will not need to prove a failure to take care on the part of the defendant. Such a system could be financed centrally through taxation, for example an additional tax on petrol to finance a scheme for road accidents. Alternatively it could be funded by compulsory insurance for those who would be exposed to liability. A further alternative is to have a combination of both methods of funding. However the likelihood of the widespread introduction of strict liability for these and other categories of personal injuries in the foreseeable future is remote. A notable exception is the introduction of strict liability for injuries caused by defective products to the customer in the Consumer Protection Act 1987. This is examined in Chapter 5.

The significance of negligence liability for the business

A business is exposed to potential claims in negligence from a number of diverse sources. It is especially vulnerable because, under the rules of vicarious liability examined later it is liable as an employer for wrongful acts committed by its employees in the course of their work. The prudent business will wish to take steps to minimise the liabilities to which it is potentially exposed. There are two things it can do. Firstly ensure that business practices and the systems under which its employees operate are tightly structured and controlled so as to reduce the risk of injury and thereby prevent claims arising. Secondly maintain an appropriate range of insurance policies to cover those risks which are most likely to affect the particular type of business.

Types of insurance cover available

Insurance companies usually offer a wide range of policies and will arrange cover to meet the requirements of the individual business. Some types of cover are compulsory and therefore all businesses affected must have them. Others, although not compulsory, are such that no prudent businessman would consider it worthwhile to operate without them. Most businesses would be covered by all or most of the following types of policy:

(a) *employers liability* – employers have a duty of care at common law to provide a safe system of work, safe equipment and premises and safe fellow employees. Under the Employers Liability (Compulsory Insurance) Act 1969 all employers other than Local Authorities and nationalised industries are required to insure against the risk of personal injury to their employees. The insurance must be contained in an approved policy which has prescribed contents. The policy must be issued by an authorised insurer.

(b) *motor vehicles* – under the Road Traffic Act 1988 the driver of a motor vehicle is required to be insured against third party personal injury and property risks. Most businesses running motor vehicles, and indeed most other motorists, obtain insurance cover well beyond the minimum laid down by the Act. Additional cover beyond the statutory minimum could include the risks of fire, theft of the vehicle, or full comprehensive cover which would include losses of the insured person's vehicle or property caused by his own fault.

(c) *product liability* – a policy of this type is designed to cover liability for injury or losses caused by defective products manufactured or supplied by the insured in the course of his business. It should cover liabilities arising in contract, negligence or under the Consumer Protection Act 1987.

(d) *public liability* – product liability cover is often included in this type of policy. The policy generally includes loss or injury sustained by a member of the public as a result of the activities of the business, for example liability under the Occupiers Liability Act 1957 for injury to a customer caused by the unsafe state of the business premises, or the organisation's liability in negligence resulting from an accident caused by an employee in failing safely to carry out his duties.

(e) *premises and stock* – this provides insurance against loss of or damage to business property caused by fire, theft or negligence.

(f) *professional indemnity* – a policy of this type covers the insured for claims made against him in respect of professional negligence, for example a claim against an architect for miscalculating the depth of the foundations of a multi-storey building or specifying inadequate reinforcements for the structure. In some professions, for example, solicitors, professional indemnity insurance is in effect compulsory because the professional body will refuse to issue a Practising Certificate without evidence of premium payment on an appropriate policy.

(g) *legal expenses insurance* – this is a relative newcomer to the UK insurance market and provides the insured with a full indemnity for legal costs incurred in engaging in legal action in the civil or criminal courts.

Having identified some of the major types of insurance cover available to protect the businessman from losses which could otherwise be incurred by the business, it is worth pointing out that the levels of cover, in terms of the financial limits on the claims that the insurer would satisfy, are a matter of commercial judgment which will depend on the nature of the business concerned.

Additionally, the businessman entering into a contract of insurance must disclose all material facts which could affect the insurer's assessment of the risk. He would also be well advised to examine carefully the detailed wording of the policy in order to be certain that he is actually getting the cover which he wants.

It is interesting to notice that, because of the universal use of insurance by businesses, many of the commercial cases litigated before the courts are in reality disputes between insurance companies standing in the shoes of the named plaintiffs and defendants who have often already been paid out by the insurance companies.

Liability in Negligence

In order to succeed in a claim in negligence the plaintiff will have to prove three things:

- that the defendant owed him a legal duty of care,

- that the duty was broken, and

- that the defendant's breach of duty resulted in foreseeable loss or damage to the plaintiff.

Once the plaintiff has established these elements there are a number of defences available to the defendant. He may try to establish:

- that the plaintiff contributed to his injury by his own negligence – the defence of contributory negligence.

- that the plaintiff had voluntarily assumed the risk of injury – a defence based on consent known technically as a volenti non fit injuria, or

- that the plaintiff's claim is out of time and therefore statute-barred under the Limitation Act 1980 (as amended).

We shall now examine in more detail the elements of liability and the defences available in a negligence claim.

The tort of negligence is an area of legal liability which has been developed by the common law through the decisions of judges in individual cases over the centuries. The process is a continuing one and significant developments have taken place in recent years particularly in relation to the question of when a duty of care is owed by a defendant to the plaintiff.

The major milestone in the evolution of the law of negligence is the decision of the House of Lords in *Donoghue v. Stevenson* 1932 in which Lord Atkin laid down general principles which could be applied to any situation in order to determine whether a duty of care is owed. Prior to 1932 there were no legal principles of general application which defined the circumstances in which a person could be liable for loss or injury caused by his carelessness to another.

The facts of *Donoghue v. Stevenson* 1932 are that the plaintiff's friend bought her a bottle of ginger beer in a cafe. The ginger beer was in an opaque bottle and, after pouring some of it and drinking from her glass, the remainder was poured from the bottle into the glass. This was found to contain the remains of a decomposed snail, the sight of which caused the plaintiff to suffer shock and become ill. As the drink was a gift from her friend, the plaintiff had no contract with the seller. She therefore sued the manufacturer claiming that he owed a duty of care to her to ensure that his product was not contaminated during the process of manufacture. The defendant argued that he owed no legal duty to the plaintiff because there was no contract between them and the case fell outside the existing recognised categories of duty. The House of Lords rejected the defendant's arguments and, by a slim majority of three judges to two, found for the plaintiff.

This case is important for two reasons. First, in the field of product liability, because Lord Atkin's judgment defines the duty of a manufacturer of a product towards a person injured by a defect in the product.

Second, in the context of the development of the law of negligence as a whole, because Lord Atkin in formulating the neighbour principle, laid down a general principle of liability for harm caused unintentionally by the defendant. For this reason the decision in *Donoghue* is often regarded as marking the birth of negligence as a tort. In the celebrated passage from his judgment Lord Atkin said:

> *"The rule that you are to love your neighbour becomes in law, you must not injure your neighbour; and the lawyers' question, Who is my neighbour? receives a restricted reply. You must take reasonable care to avoid acts or omissions which you can reasonably foresee would be likely to injure your neighbour. Who, then, in law is my neighbour? The answer seems to be – persons who are so closely and directly affected by my act that I ought reasonably to have them in contemplation as being so affected when I am directing my mind to the acts or omissions which are called in question."*

The defendant's duty is a duty to take reasonable care to avoid causing foreseeable harm and it is owed to anyone closely and directly affected by the defendant's conduct. The close relationship necessary between the defendant and plaintiff in order for a duty to exist is often referred to as a relationship of proximity between the parties.

> The status of the neighbour principle as a rule of general applicability was underlined by the House of Lords in *Home Office v. Dorset Yacht Co.* 1970. Here the plaintiff's yacht was damaged by borstal trainees who had escaped while on a training exercise on an island. They had been carelessly left unsupervised by their guards. Applying the neighbour principle, it was held that the defendant owed a duty of care to the plaintiff whose yacht had been moored between the island and the mainland, as it was reasonably foreseeable that the trainees might use the yacht as a means of escape. The defendant was vicariously liable for the failure of its employees to supervise the trainees. This breach of duty caused the plaintiff's loss for which the Home Office was liable.

There may be cases in which a straight application of the neighbour principle will suggest the existence of a duty of care, but nevertheless the court would refuse to recognise a duty because there are valid justifications for failing to impose liability. The justifications which are used in these circumstances are often referred to as considerations of *public policy*. We can interpret this expression as meaning reasons based on judicial perceptions of what may or may not be in the best interests of the community at large.

It should be appreciated that in the majority of claims for personal injuries or damage to property, for example in the field of product liability, there will not be any policy considerations restricting the application of the neighbour principle in order to establish that a duty of care exists. It is in relation to claims for financial loss, for example in the area of professional negligence, that policy considerations – such as the fear of creating open-ended liability – may be taken in to account.

Breach of Duty

Once it has been established that the defendant in a given situation owes a duty of care to avoid injury to the plaintiff, the next question which falls to be decided is whether the defendant was in breach of that duty. It should be stressed that these are two separate issues and only after the court is satisfied that a duty exists will it go on to consider the question of breach. A breach of duty is a failure to take reasonable care. This involves a finding of fault on the part of the defendant.

In the words of Alderson B. in *Blyth v. Birmingham Waterworks Co.* 1856:

> *"Negligence (in the sense of a breach of duty) is the omission to do something which a reasonable man, guided upon those considerations which ordinarily regulate the conduct of human affairs, would do, or something which a reasonable and prudent man would not do."*

The duty of care is broken when a person fails to do what a reasonable man would do in the same circumstances. The standard of care required of the defendant in a particular case will vary according to the circumstances of the case and the skills which the defendant holds himself out as possessing. Thus a surgeon carrying out an operation is required to demonstrate the skills and knowledge of a reasonably competent surgeon. On the other hand the degree of care expected of a hospital porter is not so exacting. Whilst the standard of care required of a skilled defendant such as a professional person will be high, the reverse cannot be said to be true. An inexperienced or unskilled defendant will not be able to argue that the standard of care which he is required to demonstrate is correspondingly low.

> The principle was applied by the Court of Appeal in *Wilsher v. Essex Area Health Authority* 1986 when it held, by a majority of two judges to one, that inexperience was no defence to an action in negligence against a junior doctor, who would be in breach of his duty of care if he failed to demonstrate the skill of a reasonably competent qualified doctor. On the facts of the case, however, the junior doctor had discharged his duty by asking a more senior colleague to check his work.

In determining whether a duty of care has been broken the court must assess the conduct of the defendant and decide whether he acted reasonably or unreasonably. This assessment allows the judge a large measure of discretion in an individual case, although it could be argued that it also produces some uncertainty in the law. The main factors which the court will take into account in deciding whether there has been a breach of the duty of care are:

- the extent of the risk created by the defendant's conduct − whether the risk was serious or obvious;
- the nature of the harm which is likely to be caused to the plaintiff;
- the practicability and expense of taking steps to minimise the risk;
- the particular circumstances of the case.

A good example of the way in which the courts attempt to balance these factors is provided by the case of *Bolton v. Stone* 1951.

> In *Bolton v. Stone* the plaintiff was standing on the highway outside her home and was struck by a cricket ball hit by a visiting batsman off the pitch of the local cricket club. She sued the members and committee of the cricket club. The ground had been used for cricket since 1864, well before the surrounding houses were built. Balls were rarely hit

out of the ground and onto the highway, perhaps only six times in the previous thirty years, and there was no record of any previous accident. The ball in question had travelled seventy-eight yards before passing over the fence and about twenty-five yards further before hitting the plaintiff. The top of the fence was seven feet about the highway and seventeen feet above the pitch. The House of Lords held that the defendants were not liable because they had taken reasonable care. The chances of such an accident were so slim that the reasonable man would have done no more than the defendants had done to prevent it from happening. In the course of his judgment, Lord Ratcliffe stated:

"A breach of duty has taken place if the defendants are guilty of a failure to take reasonable care to prevent the accident. One may phrase it as 'reasonable care' or 'ordinary care' or 'proper care' – all these phrases are to be found in decisions of authority – but the fact remains that, unless there has been something which a reasonable man would blame as falling beneath the standard of conduct that he would set for himself and require of his neighbour, there has been no breach of legal duty. It seems to me in this case that a reasonable man, taking account of the chances against an accident happening, would not have felt himself called upon either to abandon the use of the ground for cricket or to increase the height of his surrounding fences."

Proof of the defendant's breach of duty

The normal rule in a civil case is that the plaintiff must adduce evidence to prove his case on balance of probabilities. It will therefore be the plaintiff's job, in a negligence case, to show that the defendant did not act in a reasonable way. If he is unable to do this his claim will fail.

In *Wakelin v. London and South Western Railway Co*. 1886 the body of the plaintiff's husband was found near a level crossing on a railway. He had been hit by a train but there was no evidence to suggest what had happened. The accident could have been his own fault or it could have been attributable to the fault of the defendant. As the plaintiff was unable to prove that the defendant acted in an unreasonable manner, her claim failed.

Res ipsa loquitur

In some cases the plaintiff may be relieved of the burden of proving negligence if the court accepts a plea of res ipsa loquitur (the thing speaks for itself). This is a rule of evidence which applies where the plaintiff's injury is one that would not in the ordinary course of events have happened without negligence and there is no satisfactory alternative explanation for the injury other than negligence by the defendant.

The effect of the rule is that the court will infer negligence on the part of the defendant without the need for the plaintiff to pin-point the cause of the injury or explain how the defendant failed to take reasonable care. The defendant will be liable unless he furnishes evidence to show that his negligence did not cause the plaintiff's loss.

The rule will be of great assistance to the plaintiff where it seems to be obvious that the defendant was negligent but the plaintiff is unable to pin-point the exact nature of the defendant's breach of duty.

In *Scott v. London and St. Catherine Docks Co*. 1865 a customs officer was injured when six sacks of sugar fell on him as he was passing the defendant's warehouse. The court held that the res ipsa loquitur rule applied and inferred negligence on the part of the defendant which it was unable to disprove. During the course of his judgment, Erle, CJ stated:

"Where the thing is shown to be under the management of the defendant, or his servants, and the accident is such as, in the ordinary course of things, does not happen if those who have the management use proper care, it affords reasonable evidence, in the absence of explanation by the defendant, that the accident arose from want of care."

In *Ward v. Tesco Stores* 1976 the plaintiff was injured when she slipped on a pool of yoghurt which had previously been spilled onto the floor of the defendant's supermarket and had not been cleaned up. The Court of Appeal applied the res ipsa loquitur rule and the defendant was held liable as it was unable to show that it had taken reasonable care.

Fatal accidents

Where the defendant's breach of duty has resulted in death, legal action may be brought on behalf of the estate of the deceased person under the Law Reform (Miscellaneous Provisions) Acts 1934 and 1970. The dependants of the deceased will have a separate claim under the Fatal Accidents Act 1976 as amended by the Administration of Justice Act 1982.

Resulting Damage

The third essential element of liability in negligence is that the defendant's breach of duty resulted in foreseeable loss or damage to the plaintiff. In reality this involves two separate issues – the issues of causation and remoteness of damage.

Causation of damage

The causation issue is concerned with the question of cause and effect: was the defendant's breach of duty the operative cause of the plaintiff's loss? The plaintiff's claim will fail if he is unable to prove this link. He must show that but for the defendant's negligence his loss would not have occurred.

> In *Barnett v. Chelsea and Kensington Hospital Management Committee* 1969 the plaintiff's husband was a night watchman, who called at the defendant's hospital in the early hours of the morning complaining of vomiting. He was sent home without being examined and was told to contact his own doctor later that day. He was suffering from arsenic poisoning and died a few hours later. The court held that the defendants were in breach of their duty of care, but the claim failed because the negligence of the hospital had not caused the death. The court accepted on the evidence that even if he had been examined immediately, the plaintiff's husband would still have died from arsenic poisoning.

Remoteness of damage

Where the plaintiff proves that his injuries were caused by the defendant's breach of duty, he can recover damages provided that his injuries were not too remote a consequence of the breach. The law does not necessarily impose liability for all of the consequences of a negligent act. Some damage may be too remote. Only damage which was reasonably foreseeable at the time of the negligent act can be recovered by the plaintiff.

In *The Wagon Mound* 1961 a large quantity of fuel oil was carelessly spilled by the defendant's employees while a ship was taking on fuel in Sydney Harbour. Some of the oil spread to the plaintiff's wharf where welding operations were taking place. The plaintiff stopped welding temporarily, but recommenced after receiving expert opinion that fuel oil would not ignite when spread on water. Two days later the oil ignited when a drop of molten metal fell onto a piece of waste floating in the oil, causing extensive damage to the plaintiff's wharf. The court found as a fact that it was not reasonably foreseeable that the oil would ignite in these circumstances. It was held that the damage to the wharf was too remote, and the plaintiff's claim failed.

The plaintiff's damage may be held to be too remote where an unforeseen new independent act, outside the defendant's control, intervenes to break the chain of causation. If the plaintiff's damage is caused by such a *'novus actus interveniens'* the defendant will not be liable for it. For example an employer's liability for injury suffered by an employee at work will not extend to further injuries received in the course of negligent medical treatment in hospital.

In *Cobb v. Great Western Railway* 1894 the defendant allowed a railway carriage to become overcrowded. As a result the plaintiff's pocket was picked and he lost nearly £100. It was held that the act of the thief was a novus actus interveniens and therefore that the plaintiff's loss was too remote.

Defences to a Negligence Action

Contributory negligence

Where the plaintiff has successfully established all of the elements of a negligence action, but has in some way contributed to his injuries by his own negligence, the defendant may raise the defence of contributory negligence.

Section 1(1) of the Law Reform (Contributory Negligence) Act 1945 provides:

> *"Where any person suffers damage as the result partly of his own fault and partly of the fault of any other person or persons, a claim in respect of that damage shall not be defeated by reason of the fault of the person suffering the damage, but the damages recoverable in respect thereof shall be reduced to such extent as the court thinks just and equitable having regard to the claimant's share in the responsibility for the damage."*

The effect of this provision is simply that the plaintiff's damages will be reduced in direct proportion to the extent to which he is to blame for his injuries.

In *Stapley v. Gypsum Mines* 1953 the plaintiffs were miners who, contrary to specific instructions by their employer, worked under a dangerous roof. They were injured when the roof collapsed and fell in on them. Their damages were reduced by 80% for contributory negligence.

In *Froom v. Butcher* 1976 it was held that the failure to wear a seat belt was contributory negligence and that the appropriate reduction in damages was 25% if the seat belt would have prevented the injury altogether, or 15% if it would merely have reduced the extent of the injury.

Voluntary assumption of risk (volenti non fit injuria)

This defence, which is universally referred to by its Latin name *volenti non fit injuria*, is available to the defendant where the plaintiff freely and voluntarily accepts a risk of which he has full knowledge. In modern times the courts have been reluctant to apply the defence, which has the effect of completely defeating the plaintiff's claim, other than in exceptional circumstances. The reason for this is that the type of behaviour which would come within the defence would also usually amount to contributory negligence. The courts probably take the view that a more just outcome can be achieved by applying the rules of contributory negligence.

In *Smith v. Charles Baker & Sons* 1891 the plaintiff was employed in the excavation of a railway cutting. He was injured by a stone which fell from an overhead crane. He had known that there was an element of risk in working beneath the crane but had not objected to his employer. As a defence to his action for compensation, the employer argued that the plaintiff had voluntarily undertaken the risk of injury. The House of Lords held that the employer was liable. The defence failed because mere knowledge of the risk was not the same as consent to the danger. Lord Herschell stated the volenti rule in the following terms:

"One who has invited or assented to an act being done towards him cannot, when he suffers from it, complain of it as a wrong ... if then, the employer thus fails in his duty towards the employed, I do not think that because (the employee) does not straightaway refuse to continue his service, it is true to say that it is willing that his employer should act thus towards him. I believe it would be contrary to the facts to assert that the plaintiff in this case either invited or assented to the employer's negligence."

The defence of *volenti non fit injuria* will not usually be available where the plaintiff has been injured while attempting to rescue someone from a peril created by the defendant's negligence. In these circumstances the rescuer cannot normally be regarded as having freely consented to the risk of injury.

Exclusion of liability for negligence

Under the rules of common law it used to be possible for a defendant to exclude his liability for negligence, either by including an appropriately worded term in a contract, or by displaying a notice to that effect.

In *White v. Blakemore* 1972, for example, the plaintiff's husband, a member of a racing club, stood next to the ropes near a stake watching a race. The wheel of a racing car caught on the rope pulling the stake out of the ground. The stake killed the plaintiff's husband. Notices had been displayed by the defendant in prominent positions excluding all liability for accidents howsoever caused. It was held that the notices were effective to protect the defendant from liability.

Since the introduction of the Unfair Contract Terms Act 1977, however, the scope of the common rules have been considerably cut down. Under s.2 of the 1977 Act liability for death or personal injury caused by negligence cannot be excluded, but that it may be possible to exclude liability for other types of damage or loss. Such an exclusion will only be effective however if the defendant can prove that it is fair and reasonable to allow reliance on it in the circumstances of the case.

Time limits for claims in negligence

The Limitation Act 1980, as amended by the Latent Damage Act 1986, provides that no legal action may be taken in respect of certain types of claim unless proceedings are issued within the limitation period. After this time the claim is said to be statute barred and the court will refuse to entertain it. The limitation period varies according to the legal basis of the claim and the type of injury or damage suffered by the plaintiff.

Business Premises and Liability

Occupiers of business premises whether freeholders or business tenants have duties placed upon them to ensure the safety of all lawful entrants by virtue of the Occupiers Liability Act 1957 and in some cases an obligation to take reasonable care extends to uninvited visitors under the Occupiers Liability Act 1984.

Under the Occupiers Liability Act 1957 an occupier of business premises owes the common duty of care to all his lawful visitors and that is to take such care as in all the circumstances is reasonable to provide for their safety. Notice that the duty is owed by the occupier, the person in control of the premises and he would certainly include the owner in possession or a business tenant or licensee. The business landlord however is regarded as the occupier in relation to parts of the premises which remain under his control, e.g. entrance hall, lifts, forecourt or other common parts. Also if the landlord is under an obligation to repair, he may under s.4 Defective Premises Act 1972 be made liable for injuries that occur as a result of his failure to fulfil a repair obligation. Where the premises are let therefore, both the landlord and the tenant may be regarded as occupier of the premises for different purposes under the Act.

The obligation of the occupier in these circumstances is to take reasonable care in entrusting the work to an independent contractor and to take such steps as he reasonably ought in order to satisfy himself that the contractor was competent and that the work had been done properly. The occupier will have acted reasonably if he selected a reputable organisation to do work on the premises rather than a local handyman.

> In *O'Connor v. Swan & Edgar* 1963 the plaintiff was injured by a fall of plaster when she worked as a demonstrator on the first defendant's premises. The fall of plaster was due to the faulty workmanship of the second defendants who had been engaged as contractors to work on the premises. The court held that as the first defendants had acted reasonably in entrusting the work to a reputable contractor then as an occupier he had satisfied the duty of care which was owed. The second defendants however were held liable in the tort of negligence for faulty workmanship.

Following the Unfair Contract Terms Act 1977 it is no longer possible for an occupier of business premises to exclude the common duty of care in relation to his visitors. To fulfil the duty owed it is necessary to ensure that premises are indeed reasonably safe or alternatively ensure that visitors are safe by giving adequate warning of any dangers. The 1957 Act mentions two categories of visitor in particular, children and independent contractors. It says that in relation to child visitors an occupier must be prepared for them to be less careful than adults. This suggests that for instance that an occupier of retail premises to which the public have access will owe a higher standard of care towards children than adults. The requirement of parental control however is a significant factor in establishing liability for injury caused to child visitors.

> In *Simkiss v. Rhondda B.C.* 1983 a seven year old suffered injury when she fell 30 or 40 feet after sliding on a blanket down a steep slope owned by the council. The High Court found the council liable for breach of the common duty of care in failing to either ensure that the mountainside was safe for children to play on or alternatively fencing it off. The Court of Appeal took a different view of the matter however and pointing out

that adults would have realised that the mountainside must have been an obvious danger, the council was entitled to assume that parents would have warned their children of the danger. In reversing the decision of the High Court, the Court of Appeal stressed that the council's duty of care was not broken by failing to fence the mountain. To require a local authority to fence every natural hazard under its control would impose too onerous a burden.

Not only children but independent contractors are also singled out for mention in the Act. Such persons engaged to carry out specialist work should be aware of the risks inherent in their own trades.

This is reflected in *Roles v. Nathan* 1963 where, despite being warned of the danger, two chimney sweeps carried on working on a boiler and were killed by carbon monoxide poisoning entering from the ventilation system. The employer/occupier was held in the circumstances not to be liable. Ld. Denning MR stated that *"when a householder calls in a specialist to deal with a defective installation on his premises he can reasonably expect the specialist to appreciate and guard against the dangers arising from the defect"*.

In *Rae (Geoffrey) v. Mars (UK)* 1990 an experienced surveyor was instructed to survey business premises and given the assistance of a graduate trainee by the defendant to show him round. The surveyor fell and suffered severe injuries when entering a printing ink store, the floor of which was three feet below the level of the door. No warning of the danger had been given by the trainee. In an action for damages under the Occupiers Liability Act 1957 the court held that notwithstanding his specialist expertise the surveyor, like all visitors should have been given a warning of the exceptional nature of the hazard and the occupiers were accordingly in breach of their duty. By failing to switch on his torch however, while entering the store room, the surveyor was also at fault and the damages awarded were reduced by one third to reflect his contributory negligence.

In relation to uninvited visitors it was not until 1972 that the courts finally recognised that in some circumstances an occupier of business premises could be found liable in damages for injuries caused to a child trespasser.

In *British Railways Board v. Herrington* 1972 British Rail had negligently failed to maintain fencing which ran between their railway track and a park frequently used by children. A six-year old climbed through the fence, wandered onto the track, and suffered severe injury on the electrified rail. The House of Lords held the Board liable in negligence to the child trespasser. The Court stated that, *"... if the presence of the trespasser is known or ought reasonably to be anticipated by the occupier then the occupier has a duty to treat the trespasser with ordinary humanity."*

It should be noted that the duty owed to a trespasser is a restricted duty and much less than the standard of care owed to a lawful visitor. In addition, the court pointed to the economic resources of the occupier as a factor to determine whether he had acted reasonably. The rule in *British Railways Board v. Herrington* had been applied in later cases.

In *Pannett v. McGuinness Ltd.* 1972 a demolition contractor was made liable for injuries caused to a five-year old trespasser by an unguarded fire. This was despite the fact that the contractor, aware of the danger, had posted workmen to guard the fire. The fact that the workmen were absent when the injury occurred meant, as far as the injured child was concerned, nothing was done to safeguard him.

In an attempt to clarify the rules relating to the liability of an occupier towards trespassers, the Occupiers Liability Act 1984 was passed. The Act replaces the common law, which includes the rules laid down by the House of Lords in Herrington's case, 1972.

Under the 1984 Act the occupier will owe a duty to trespassers if:

(a)   he is aware or ought to be of danger; and

(b)   knows or has reasonable grounds to believe that the trespasser is or may be in the vicinity of danger; and

(c)   may reasonably be expected in all the circumstances to offer some protection to the trespasser against the danger.

Having established the existence of a duty the Act goes on to provide that the duty extends to taking such care as in all the circumstances is reasonable to see that the trespasser does not suffer injury by reason of the danger concerned. It is also provided that the duty may in an appropriate case be discharged by warning.

The existence of a duty of care still demands a consideration of *"all the circumstances"* to determine whether the trespasser deserves protection. This may well involve a consideration of the circumstances identified in Herrington's case such as the resources of the occupier, the extent of likely harm, the frequency of trespass etc. In addition the 1984 Act has confined itself to personal injury and so the common law is still relevant if the claim involves damage to the property of the trespasser.

Other examples of tortious liability

The freedom to use premises for business purposes is subject to constraints imposed by both the criminal and civil law. An occupier of land may be restrained by injunction from using his property in such a way as to cause a nuisance to his neighbours, adjoining occupiers or to the public as a whole.

> In *Halsey v. Esso Petroleum* 1961 the plaintiff was the owner of a house on a residential estate and the defendant owned and occupied an oil storage depot on the river bank nearby. On various occasions noxious acid smuts were emitted from metal chimney stacks at the depot which caused damage to the plaintiff's washing, and the paint work of his car. There was also a particularly pungent oily smell from the depot of a nauseating character but which was not a health risk. Further cause for complaint was the noise emitted from the boilers during nightshift which varied in intensity but at its peak reached 63 decibels causing the plaintiff's windows and doors to vibrate. The noise was exacerbated by the arrival of heavy tankers at the depot, sometimes in convoy and as many as fifteen in one night. It was on the basis of these complaints that the plaintiff brought an action alleging nuisance and claiming damages and injunctions to restrain the activity. The Court held that:
>
> 1.   The acid smuts emitted from the chimneys constituted the crime of public nuisance and as the plaintiff had suffered special damage in relation to his motor car he could recover damages for the tort of private nuisance.
>
> 2.   Acid smuts which arise from a non natural use of land and then escape to adjoining land and cause damage will also give rise to strict liability in tort based on the principles laid down in the case of *Rylands v. Fletcher* 1868

3. Injury to health is not a necessary ingredient in the cause of action and since the particularly pungent smell from time to time emitted from the depot went far beyond a triviality, and was more than would effect a sensitive person, it was an actionable nuisance.

4. The noise from the boilers at night disturbed the resident's ordinary comfort and use of their property as did the noise from the vehicles and both would constitute a private nuisance.

5. Injunctions and damages were awarded to restrain the unlawful activities to the extent that they constituted an actionable nuisance.

Certain activities on land have also been made unlawful by statute and may constitute a *statutory nuisance*. From the 1st January 1991 a range of provisions formerly contained in the Public Health Act 1936 and the Public Health (Recurring Nuisances) Act 1969 cease to have effect and are replaced and extended by the Environmental Health Act 1990. Under s.79(1) a list of circumstances may amount to a statutory nuisance including emissions of smoke, gas, fumes, dust, steam, smells or other effluvia and noise from premises which are prejudicial to health or a nuisance. Detection and enforcement of the law is in the hands of local authorities, in particular environmental health officers. They are charged with the duty of inspecting their areas and also investigating complaints with the aim of preventing and eliminating statutory nuisances. Their powers extend to serving abatement notices on individuals or organisations requiring the abatement, prohibition or restriction of the nuisance and the execution of works or the taking of other necessary steps. Contravention of a notice or failure to comply with its terms is also a criminal offence and could lead to a prosecution in the Magistrates Court and a fine of up to £2000 for each offence.

Vicarious Liability

There are some situations where the law is prepared to impose vicarious (substituted) liability on an individual who is not at fault for the commission of the wrongful (tortious) act of another. The best known example of this situation is the common law rule which imposes vicarious liability on employers in respect of torts committed by their employees during the course of their employment. Accordingly, if one employee (Jones) by his negligent act causes harm to a fellow employee Smith then in addition to the possibility of (Smith) pursuing a legal action against Jones he may have the further option of suing his employer who will have become vicariously liable if the negligent act occurred during the course of Jones's employment. The same principle applies equally where the injuries are caused by an employee to some third party. However, while employers have a choice as to whether they insure against the risk of injury to third parties, under the Employer's Liability (Compulsory Insurance) Act 1969, an employer is required to insure himself in respect of injuries caused by his employees to their colleagues.

The imposition of vicarious liability does not require proof of any fault on the employer's part, or any express or implied authorisation to commit the wrongful act. All that must be proved for the purpose of vicarious liability is:

1. an actionable wrong committed by the worker;

2. that the worker is an employee;

3. that the wrongful act occurred during the course of his employment.

What then is the theoretical basis for imposing liability in these circumstances? A number of reasons have emerged, such as he who creates and benefits from a situation should assume the risk of liability arising from it. There is also the idea that if an organisation embarks on an enterprise and as a result harm is caused by one member of the organisation, it should be the responsibility of the organisation to compensate for the harm.

It is after all the employer who selects and controls the employees who work for him. The employer has the responsibility of training staff and can of course dismiss those whose work is performed incompetently. The practical reason for vicarious liability is of course that if the employee were solely liable he would have to insure himself, and the cost of this would be indirectly borne by the employer in the form of higher wages. Under the present system insurance costs are borne directly by the employer who, as a principle of sound business practice, will normally carry adequate insurance.

To determine an employer's liability it is first necessary to establish the employment status of the worker who is alleged to have committed the wrongful act. This is because the legal position differs dramatically depending on whether the worker is employed as an employee under a contract of service rather than as a self employed contractor under a contract for services. Usually this issue may be settled without argument but in the small proportion of cases where there is doubt the courts are left with the task of identifying the true contractual status of the worker. Obviously the express terms of the contract will be a strong indicator of the parties status but in some cases it is only by examining the substance of the relationship that the true position can be determined.

As a general principle an employer is vicariously liable for the tortious acts of his employees committed during the course of their employment. The phrase 'course of employment' has produced numerous interpretations in the courts, but essentially it concerns the question of whether the employee was doing his job at the time of the tortious act. It should be emphasised that an employee will have both express and implied authority to perform work for his employer and while he will normally have no authority to commit torts, he may nevertheless be guilty of a tortious act in the performance of his authorised duties.

> In *Century Insurance Ltd. v. Northern Ireland Road Transport Board* 1942 a tanker driver while delivering petrol at a garage, lit a cigarette and carelessly threw away the lighted match which caused an explosion and considerable damage. His employer was held to be vicariously liable for his negligence as the employee had acted within the course of his employment. By supervising the unloading, the employee was doing his job, but by smoking he was doing it in a grossly negligent manner.

Even if an employee is carrying out an act outside the basic obligation of his contract of employment, his employer may nevertheless be made vicariously liable if the act is carried out for the benefit of the employer.

> In *Kay v. ITW* 1968 the employee injured a colleague when he negligently drove a five ton diesel lorry which was blocking his way. Despite the fact that he was contractually authorised to drive only small vans and trucks, his employer was held to be vicariously liable for his action.

If an employee is doing something of purely personal benefit at the time of the negligent act then he may be regarded, to quote from the colourful language of the Victorian era as "off on a frolic of his own", and his employer will not be responsible.

> In *Hilton v. Thomas Burton (Rhodes) Ltd.* 1961 the plaintiff's husband was a demolition worker who was killed through the negligent driving of one of his colleagues. The defendant employer denied vicarious liability as, at the time of the accident, the van was being driven from a cafe on an unauthorised break. The court held that although the van had been driven with the permission of the employer, at the time of the incident the driver was not doing that which he was employed to do. Accordingly the employer was not liable for the negligent driving.

The extent to which an express prohibition by the employer will prevent vicarious liability will depend upon the nature of the prohibition. If it merely attempts to instruct the employee how he is to do his job, the employee may still be within the course of his employment for the purposes of vicarious liability.

> In *Rose v. Plenty* 1976 a milkman, contrary to an express prohibition, engaged a thirteen year old boy to help him deliver the milk. The boy was subsequently injured by the milkman's negligent driving and sued both the milkman and his employer. The Court of Appeal held that despite the prohibition of the employer, he remained vicariously liable as the milkman had acted within the course of his employment. Scarman L J having considered the prohibition stated that *"There was nothing in the prohibition which defined or limited the sphere of his employment, the sphere of his employment remained precisely the same as before the prohibition was brought to his notice. The sphere was as a roundsman to go the rounds delivering milk, collecting empties and obtaining payment. Contrary to instructions the roundsman chose to do what he was employed to do in an improper way. But the sphere of his employment was in no way affected by his express instructions"*.

It seems therefore that only an express prohibition which effectively cuts down the 'sphere of employment' will prevent the establishment of vicarious liability. The fact that contemporary courts seem to favour the idea of a very wide sphere of employment in individual cases, severely limits the opportunity of employers to restrict liability by express instruction. It is only by deciding the authorised parameters of an individual's job, and deciding that the act complained of fell outside these parameters that vicarious liability can be successfully denied.

If the act is done on the employer's premises with the employer's interest in mind, the employer may be made liable provided the act has a close connection with the employee's job.

> In *Compton v. McClure* 1975 the employer was held to be vicariously liable for the negligence of an employee who, when late for work, caused an accident when driving negligently on the factory road.

While it may be reasonable for an employee to use a degree of force in protection of his employer's property, or to keep order, an employee who commits an assault which has no connection with his work will be solely liable for his conduct.

> So in *Warren v. Henleys Ltd.* 1948 the employer was held not to be vicariously liable for a physical attack by a petrol pump attendant on one of his customers. The claim that the attendant was acting within the scope of his employment was rejected, for while the attack developed out of an argument over payment for petrol, it was in reality motivated by an act of private vengeance.

An employer can be vicariously liable for acts of sex or race discrimination committed by employees during the course of employment unless he can show that he took such steps as were reasonably practicable to prevent the employee from committing the act of discrimination.

> In *Bracebridge Engineering v. Dorby* 1990 the complainant was the victim of serious sexual harassment by her supervisor which constituted unlawful discrimination. The employer was vicariously liable for the misconduct as at the time the act of sexual harassment took place the perpetrators were supposedly engaged in exercising their disciplinary and supervisory functions and were in the course of their employment.

Certainly to impose liability on an employer for the tortious or criminal acts of an employee under his control, there must be a connection between the act complained of and the circumstances of employment. The fact that employment gives the employee an opportunity to commit the wrongful act is insufficient to impose vicarious liability on the employer.

> In *Heasmans v. Clarity Cleaning Company* 1987 the Court of Appeal found it possible to absolve the defendant cleaning company from liability for the acts of one of their cleaners who, while employed on the plaintiff's premises, used the plaintiff's telephone to make international telephone calls to the value of £1,411. The mere fact that the cleaner's employment provided the opportunity to fraudulently use the plaintiff's telephone was not itself sufficient to impose liability on the defendant.

> In *Irving & Irving v. Post Office* 1987 the complaint of race discrimination was based on the conduct of an employee of the post office who when sorting the mail had written a racially insulting comment on a letter addressed to his neighbours who were of Jamaican origin. The issue before the Court of Appeal was whether the employee was acting in the course of his employment so that the Post Office could be made vicariously liable for the discriminatory act. The employee's act of writing on the mail was clearly unauthorised so the question was whether the act was an unauthorised mode of doing an authorised act. Here the misconduct formed no part of the postman's duties and could not be regarded as an unauthorised way of performing his work. *"An employer is not to be held liable merely because the opportunity to commit the wrongful act had been created by the employee's employment, or because the act in question had been committed during the period of that particular employment".*

The increasing practice of employees contracting out areas of work to contractors and sub contractors has important implications when determining liability for injuries caused due to negligence at the workplace.

> In *Sime v. Sutcliffe Catering Scotland Ltd*. 1990 an employee brought a claim alleging negligence by the above catering company when, carrying out her work as a canteen assistant she slipped on some food dropped by a fellow worker and suffered injury. The case was complicated by the fact that the employee was not directly employed by the catering company but by a paper manufacturer, Tullis Russell and Company. Previously the paper manufacturer had contracted out the management of the canteen to the above company, but following pressure from the trade union, had agreed to retain existing canteen staff, including the employee. It was never established whether the worker who had dropped the food was an employee of the catering company or not. The issue therefore was whether the catering company could be held liable vicariously to a worker for the possible negligent act of a worker who they did not employ. The Scottish Court of Session held that responsibility should be with the employer in control. Although not directly employed by the catering company, whether the employer relationship is *"such as to render the company liable for the negligence depends upon whether the substitute employer has sufficient power of control and supervision purely to be regarded as the effective employer at the critical time"*. As the *"whole day to day management of the catering operation and staff was undertaken by the catering company and the canteen manager had complete control over the way in which all the canteen workers did their job"*...and *"since one of the employed persons caused the accident by being negligent in dropping food stuff onto the floor and failing to clean it up the company had to accept responsibility for that negligence"*. The fault of the injured employee was also recognised

and damages were reduced by twenty five percent to reflect her contributory negligence. *"Where a person is working in or near a kitchen where a number of people are working with food or dirty dishes and where it is quite predictable that food might be spilt it is reasonably necessary that a look out be kept for any wet or slippery patches on the floor."*

Generally vicarious liability has been confined to the employer/employee relationship and where contractors are employed, responsibility for their wrongful acts is solely their own. The justification for not extending vicarious liability to employers of contractors, other than in exceptional cases, stems from the fact that the contractor is not subjected to his employer's control in the same way as an employee.

There are then certain legal duties that cannot be delegated, and if the wrongful act of a contractor constitutes a breach of such a duty, owed by an employer to a third party, then the contractor's employer may be made vicariously liable for the default.

> In *Rogers v. Nightriders* 1983 a mini cab firm undertook to provide a hire car to the plaintiff for a journey and did so by engaging a contractor driver. The plaintiff was injured in an accident caused by the negligent maintenance of the mini cab by the contractor. In an action against the mini cab firm the court held that they were not liable as an employer could not be made vicariously liable for their contractor's default. On appeal however, it was held that as the employer had undertaken to provide a vehicle to carry the plaintiff, and since they ought to have foreseen harm to the plaintiff if the vehicle was defective, they owed a duty of care to the plaintiff to ensure that the vehicle was reasonably fit. Such a duty could not be delegated to a contractor and accordingly the employers were liable for breach of the primary duty that they owed to her.

This case is a further example of the distinction that must be drawn between vicarious and direct or primary liability previously considered. By providing a negligent contractor, the employer in *Rogers v. Nightriders* had failed to fulfil a direct duty of care he owed to those he could reasonably foresee being affected.

Criminal Liability in Business

In addition to the potential civil liabilities faced by a business in conducting its affairs, it may also be subject to criminal liability as well. We shall now examine some of the circumstances in which such liability can arise.

Consumer protection

Most, but not all, of the criminal offences designed to protect the consumer apply only to persons supplying goods or services in the course of a trade or business. Enforcement of the criminal law in this area is, as we have seen, primarily the function of trading standards departments. Traders who are charged with criminal offences will be prosecuted in the Magistrates or the Crown Court. If convicted, they will be liable to a fine or, in some cases, imprisonment. Following a conviction the criminal courts also have power to make a *compensation order* to the victim of the crime. In this context the victim will be the consumer who has suffered loss as a result of the offence.

The power to make a compensation order is contained in s.35 of the Powers of Criminal Courts Act 1973. This provides that any court convicting a person of an offence may, in addition to its sentencing power, make an order requiring the offender to pay compensation for any personal injury, loss or damage resulting from the offence or any other offence taken into consideration.

In deciding whether to make an order the court must take account of the ability of the defendant to pay. There is a limit of £1,000 compensation for each offence of which the accused is convicted. Under s.67 of the

Criminal Justice Act 1982 the power to make compensation orders was extended. They may now be made "instead of or in addition to" a fine.

The power to make compensation orders is particularly useful from the point of view of the consumer. It saves him the trouble and expense of bringing proceedings in the civil courts. It will be used only in relatively straightforward cases, however. It is not designed to deal for example with complicated claims involving issues of causation or remoteness of damage.

Two important pieces of legislation that create criminal offences in relation to consumer protection are the Food Safety Act 1990 and the Trade Descriptions Act 1968.

The Food Safety Act 1990

The Food Safety Act 1990 is designed to strengthen consumer protection in relation to food safety, an area of increasing concern in recent years. The Act consolidates existing provision in this areas, adds a number of new regulatory powers and substantially increases the penalties for offences relating to the quality and safety of foods.

It is an offence to process or treat food intended for sale for human consumption in any way which makes it injurious to health. Food is injurious to health if it causes any permanent or temporary impairment of health. The offence can be committed by any business involved in food production or supply, such as food manufacturers, food handlers, retailers or restaurants. The offence may be committed, for example, by adding a harmful ingredient, or subjecting food to harmful treatment such as storing it at an incorrect temperature or storing cooked meat alongside uncooked meat.

Under the Act, food intended for human consumption must satisfy the *food safety requirement*. It is an offence to sell, offer or have in one's possession for sale, prepare or deposit with another for sale any food which fails to meet this requirement. Food which is injurious to health, unfit for human consumption, or so contaminated that it is not reasonable to expect it to be eaten, will fail to satisfy the food safety requirement.

> In *David Greig Ltd. v. Goldfinch* 1961 a trader was convicted of selling food which was unfit for human consumption (under an equivalent provision in the Food and Drugs Act 1955). He sold a pork pie which had small patches of mould under the crust. The fact that the mould was of a type which was not harmful to human beings was held to be no defence to the charge.

It is a further offence, of the Act, for a supplier to sell, to the prejudice of the consumer, any food which is not of the nature, substance or quality demanded. The gist of the offence is the supply of something which is different from that which the consumer has requested. An offence may be committed where no illness or injury results, although often it may.

> In *Meah v. Roberts* 1978 an employee of a brewery cleaned the beer pumps and taps in a restaurant with caustic soda. He placed the remaining fluid in an empty lemonade bottle labelled 'cleaner' which he left for use by the restaurant. The caustic soda was mistakenly served to a customer who order lemonade. The customer became seriously ill as a result. It was held that the restaurant proprietor was guilty of the offence because the food was not of the nature demanded.

Liability for this offence is strict and the trader may be guilty even though he has taken reasonable care.

> In *Smedleys Ltd. v. Breed* 1974 a customer was supplied with a tin of peas which contained a small green caterpillar. The caterpillar had been sterilised in the defendants'

processes and did not constitute a danger to health. The defendants had an extremely efficient system for eliminating foreign bodies from their products. They were found to have taken all reasonable care to avoid the presence of the caterpillar in the tin. Nevertheless, their conviction for supplying food which was not of the substance demanded was upheld by the House of Lords.

The Act creates a number of offences relating to the false description of food; including the publication of misleading advertisements, selling food which is falsely described, presenting food in a misleading way or selling food with a label which is likely to mislead the consumer as to its nature, substance or quality.

In *Van den Berghs and Jurgens v. Burleigh* 1987 the issue was whether a blend of buttermilk, vegetable oil and butter marketed under the name "Emlee" with the words "single or whipping" on the packaging, which also suggested the countryside, misled the public that the product was cream. Despite a statement that the product was a "real alternative to cream" the Crown Court on appeal held that the facts disclosed a breach of both the Food Safety Act and the Trade Descriptions Act in that the label applied a false description and was calculated to mislead as to nature, substance or quality. The general appearance of the packaging was such that it associated in the mind of average customers with cream.

As with many other statutes creating criminal offences of strict liability, a number of defences are available, for example it is a defence to a show that the commission of the offence was due to the act or default of another or that it was committed as a result of reliance on information supplied by another. Similarly, if the defendant can show that he exercised all due diligence and all reasonable precautions to avoid the commission of the offence, he will escape liability.

The Trade Descriptions Act 1968

Earlier in the chapter we examined the circumstances in which a person would be regarded as transacting in the course of a trade or business. An important application of this question arises in relation to criminal liability under the Trade Descriptions Act 1968 for false statements made in business transactions. There can be no liability under the 1968 Act unless the person applying the false description does so within the course of a trade or business rather than a private sale. This is one reason why the Business Advertisements (Disclosure) Order 1977 requires a trader to identify himself as such when he advertises in the classified advertisements in newspapers. The fact that a business organisation is the vendor or purchaser does not automatically mean that a sale is in the course of a trade. The transaction must be of a type that is a regular occurrence in that particular business, so that a sale of business assets would not normally qualify as a sale in the course of a trade or business.

The two principal offences under the Trade Descriptions Act 1968 relate to false description of goods, and making misleading statements about services. A number of defences are also provided for. A further offence of giving misleading price indications is contained in the Consumer Protection Act 1987.

Under the Trade Descriptions Act 1968 it is an offence of strict liability to falsely describe goods or supply goods to which a false trade description has been applied in the course of business.

Goods were falsely described in *Roberston v. Dicicco* 1972 where a second-hand motor vehicle was advertised for sale by a dealer and described as "a beautiful car". The car, although having a visually pleasing exterior was unroadworthy and not fit for use. The defendant was charged with an offence. He argued that his statement was true as he had intended it to refer only to the visual appearance of the vehicle. It was held that he was guilty because the description was false to a material degree. A reasonable person would have taken the statement to refer to the mechanics of the car as well as its external appearance.

A person may be guilty of an offence even though he does not know the description is false, provided he knows that the description has been applied to the goods by another person. This situation may arise for example where a car dealer sells a car which records an incorrectly low mileage on its mileometer. If a dealer is uncertain as to the accuracy of the recorded mileage, he may try to ensure that a false trade description is not applied by displaying a notice disclaiming the accuracy of the mileage reading.

In *Norman v. Bennett* 1974 a customer bought a second-hand car with a recorded mileage of 23,000 miles. In fact the true mileage was about 68,000 miles. He signed an agreement containing a clause which said that the reading was not guaranteed. It was held that this was not an effective disclaimer. Lord Widgery, the Lord Chief Justice, stated that, in order to be effective, a disclaimer:

"must be as bold, precise and compelling as the trade description itself and must be effectively brought to the notice of any person to whom the goods may be supplied. In other words, the disclaimer must equal the trade description in the extent to which it is likely to get home to anyone interested in receiving the goods".

A false trade description may be applied verbally or in writing, for example in a label on goods or in an advertisement, communicated by pictorial representation or even by conduct.

In *Yugotours Ltd. v. Wadsley* 1988 a photograph of a three-masted schooner and the words "the excitement of being under full sail on board this majestic schooner" in a tour operator's brochure was held to constitute a statement for the purpose of the Act. By providing customers who had booked a holiday relying on the brochure with only a two masted schooner without sails the tour operator was guilty of recklessly making a false statement contrary to the Trade Descriptions Act.

The above case is an example of a prosecution being brought for the offence of applying a false trade description in relation to the supply of services rather than goods. The main difference between the offences is that for services the prosecution must establish that the statement was made knowingly or recklessly to secure a conviction.

A statement is made recklessly if it is made regardless of whether it is true or false. It need not necessarily be dishonest. The knowledge or recklessness must be present at the time the statement is made.

In *Sunair Holidays Ltd. v. Dodd* 1970 the defendant's travel brochure described a package holiday in a hotel with "all twin bedded rooms with bath, shower and terrace". The defendant had a contract with the hotel owners under which they were obliged to provide accommodation of that description. A customer who booked the package was given a room without a terrace. The defendant had not checked with the hotel to make sure that its customers were given the correct accommodation of that description. It was held that the statement was not false when it was made, and therefore the defendant was not guilty of an offence.

It must be shown that the trader, at the time the statement is made, either knows that it is false or is reckless as to its truth or falsity; and that the statement actually *is* false. Subsequent developments are irrelevant if these elements are present at the time the statement is made.

In *Cowburn v. Focus Television Rentals Ltd.* 1983 the defendant's advertisement stated: "Hire 20 feature films absolutely free when you rent a video recorder". In response to the advertisement a customer rented a video recorder. The documentation supplied with it indicated that he was entitled only to 6 films, and that they were not absolutely free because he had to pay postage and packing. When he complained, the defendant refunded his postage and packing and supplied 20 free films to him. It was held that the defendant was guilty of an offence because the statement in his advertisement was false and recklessly made. The fact that he subsequently honoured the advertisement provided no defence, as this was done after the offence had been committed.

Conduct of the defendant subsequent to the false statement is relevant however to determine whether an inference of recklessness can be maintained.

In *Yugotours Ltd. v. Wadsley* 1988 (mentioned previously) the fact that statements in a holiday brochure and accompanying letter were clearly false and known to be so by the company meant that when the company failed to correct the statement it was guilty of an offence. The court stated that there was sufficient material before the court to infer recklessness on the part of the maker of the statement. *"If a statement is false and known to be false, and nothing whatever is done to correct it, then the company making the statement can properly be found guilty of recklessness notwithstanding the absence of specific evidence of recklessness".*

In *Wings Ltd. v. Ellis* 1984 the false nature of a statement in their travel brochure was not known by a tour operator when its brochure was published. Some 250,000 copies of the brochure contained an inaccurate statement that rooms in a hotel in Sri Lanka were air conditioned. The brochure also contained a photograph purporting to be a room in the same hotel which was of a room in a different hotel. When the mistake was discovered, reasonable steps were taken to remedy it by informing agents and customers who had already booked by letter. Despite this, a holiday was booked by a customer on the basis of the false information. It was held by the House of Lords that the tour operator was guilty of an offence because the statement was made when the brochure was read by the customer, and at the time the defendant knew that it was false. The fact that the tour operator was unaware that the uncorrected statement was being made to the customer did not prevent the offence being committed.

For corporate liability the prosecution must establish that a high ranking official of the company had the necessary mens rea. The Chairman of a company would certainly suffice but not the "Contracts Manager" in *Wings Ltd. v. Ellis* who had approved the photograph of the hotel which gave a wrong impression.

Where an offence of strict liability is created a number of defences are normally available. Under the Trade Descriptions Act 1968 s.24 there is a defence if the defendant can prove:

"(a) That the commission of the offence was due to a mistake or to reliance on information supplied to him or to the act or default of another person, an accident, or some other cause beyond his control; and

(b) that he took all reasonable precautions and exercised all due diligence to avoid the commission of such an offence by himself or any person under his control".

In order to have an effective defence under s.24, the onus is on the defendant to prove any one of the reasons listed in paragraph (a) above and all of the elements in (b). He must also supply to the prosecution, at least 7 days before the hearing, a written notice giving such information as he has to enable the other person to be identified.

> In *Baxters (Butchers) v. Manley* 1985 the defendant was accused of offences under the 1968 Act in relation to the pricing and weight of meat exposed for sale in his butcher's shop. He claimed that the offences were due to the act or default of the shop manager. This claim was accepted by the court, but the defence under s.24 failed because he was unable to prove that he had taken reasonable precautions to avoid the commission of the offence by his manager. In particular he had failed to give the manager any detailed instructions or guidelines on the requirements of the Act; there was no staff training; and the standard of supervision by a district manager was inadequate.

> In *Lewin v. Rothersthorpe Road Garage* 1984 the s.24 defence was raised in response to a prosecution for selling a motor car to which a false trade description had been applied. The defendant was a member of the Motor Agents Association, and had adopted the code of practice drawn up by the Association in consultation with the Office of Fair Trading. Staff had been instructed in the contents of the code of practice. The court held that he had taken reasonable precautions to avoid the commission of an offence by his employee.

To establish that he took all reasonable precautions and exercised all due diligence the defendant needs to show that he has an effective system of operation. A court should also bear in mind the size and resources of the organisation in determining the steps you would expect a reasonable business to take.

In relation to enforcement of the 1968 Act, wide investigatory powers are conferred on local authority trading standards officers. Before a prosecution is brought, however, the local authority is required to inform the Department of Trade. This is to prevent numerous unnecessary prosecutions for the same false trade description.

> The legality of bringing a second prosecution where there are a number of complaints in relation to the same false statement was at issue in *R. v. Thomson Holidays Limited* 1973. In this case a misleading statement in a travel brochure constituted an offence. The Court of Appeal held that a separate offence was committed every time someone read the brochure, and that it was not necessarily improper to bring more than one prosecution in these circumstances.

Misleading price indications

The offence of giving a misleading price indication is contained in s.20 of the Consumer Protection Act 1987, which provides:

> *"A person shall be guilty of an offence if, in the course of any business of his, he gives (by any means whatever) to any consumers an indication which is misleading as to the price at which any goods, services, accommodation or facilities are available".*

The types of statements which would be caught by s.20 include:

(a)   false comparisons with recommended prices, for example a false claim that goods are £20 less than the recommended price; or

(b)   indications that the price is less than the real price, for example where hidden extras are added to an advertised price; or

(c) false comparisons with a previous price, for example a false statement that goods were £50 and are now £30; or

(d) where the stated method of determining the price is different to the method actually used.

Recently in *R v. Warwickshire CC ex parte Johnson* 1993 the House of Lords confirmed that the liability to honour a price offer under the term of s.20 of the 1987 Act falls on the owners and controllers of business and not on their employees. Here a store manager had refused to sell a television under the terms of a national price reduction offer. He was subsequently charged and convicted of an offence under s.20. On appeal the House of Lords held that employees were exempt from liability for price offers made by their employers. To enable the court to reach this conclusion the 1987 Act was interpreted by reference to a statement made by Ministers during the bills passage through parliament applying the decision in *Pepper v. Hart* 1992.

The Secretary of State, after consulting the Director General of Fair Trading, has issued a code of practice designed to give practical guidance on the requirements of s.20. It aims to promote good practice in relation to giving price indications. Breach of the code will not, of itself, give rise to criminal or civil liability, but may be used as evidence to establish either that an offence had been committed under s.20, or that a trader has a defence to such a charge.

The following cases, decided under previous legislation, illustrate the type of behaviour which will be contrary to s.20.

In *Richards v. Westminster Motors Ltd.* 1975 the defendant advertised a commercial vehicle for sale at a price of £1,350. When the buyer purchased the vehicle he was required to pay the asking price plus VAT, which made a total price of £1,534. It was held that the defendant was guilty of giving a misleading indication as to the price at which he was prepared to sell goods.

In *Read Bros. Cycles (Leyton) v. Waltham Forest London Borough* 1978 the defendant advertised a motor cycle for sale at a reduced price of £540, £40 below the list price. A customer agreed to purchase the motor cycle and negotiated a £90 part exchange allowance on his old vehicle. The defendant charged him the full list price for the new cycle, and stated that the reduced price did not apply where goods were given in part exchange. It was held that the defendant was guilty of giving a misleading price indication.

In one significant respect the offence under s.20 is narrower than the offences which it replaced. This is that s.20 only applies to consumer transactions. For the purpose of s.20, the expression 'consumer' means:

(a) in relation to any goods, any person who might wish to be supplied with the goods for his own private use or consumption;

(b) in relation to any services or facilities, any person who might wish to be provided with the services or facilities otherwise than for the purposes of any business of his; and

(c) in relation to any accommodation, any person who might wish to occupy the accommodation otherwise than for the purposes of any business of his.

A consequence of the narrowing down of the offence is that misleading price indications to business customers will not be caught by it. On the facts of *Richards v. Westminster Motors*, for example, the defendant would not now be guilty of an offence under s.20 because the customer was not a consumer.

Unit Test Questions

1. Give three examples of legal relationships that exist in a business organisation.
2. How are company directors appointed and how may they be removed?
3. What is meant by the expression 'apparent authority'?
4. State the basic principles laid down in *Royal British Bank v. Turquand.*
5. When would a director be in breach of his duty to act in good faith for the benefit of the company?
6. What offence is created by the Financial Services Act 1986?
7. What is the standard of care that must be exercised by a company director?
8. On what grounds could a person have a disqualification order made against them?
9. What is the role of company auditors?
10. What are the main rights of a company shareholder?
11. What is the significance of a share certificate?
12. Explain the meaning of the statutory contract.
13. State the form of company resolution to sanction an alteration of the articles of association.
14. How can company members exercise control over the directors?
15. What general principle was laid down in *Foss v. Harbottle*?
16. What can the court do if it finds that the company affairs have been conducted in a prejudicial manner in relation to minority shareholders?
17. Explain what is meant by a contract which is uberrimae fidei?
18. What is the difference between the actual and apparent authority of an agent?
19. Who is responsible for the debts of a partnership firm?
20. How can a retiring partner discharge himself from possible liability for the firm's debts?
21. Why is it important to distinguish between a business purchaser and a consumer purchaser?
22. State four common law duties of an employee and four common law duties of an employer?
23. Name and define three different torts.
24. How can a business minimise the potential liabilities to which it may be exposed?
25. Name five types of insurance cover relevant to a business.
26. What must be proved to succeed in a claim in negligence?
27. What factors will the court take account of in deciding whether a duty of care has been broken?
28. In your own words explain the defence of contributory negligence.
29. What is the purpose of the Occupiers Liability Act 1957?
30. Explain what is meant by vicarious liability.
31. Name two statutes that impose criminal liability in relation to consumer protection.

Assignment   *Trouble at Mills*

In 1985 Mark Mills, together with his cousin Bryan and a business associate of Bryan's, an accountant called Peter Marshall, decided to form a company to deal in personal insurance services. The company received its certificate of incorporation at the end of 1985. It was called Mills & Co. (Insurance Services) Ltd. and its premises were in Leeds. Mark and Bryan took up 35% of the shares each, Peter took the remainder. The company objects stated that it could carry on the business of providing "personal insurance of any kind".

In 1988 Peter was anxious that his wife should join the company, and each of the existing shareholders agreed to transfer some of their shares to her. As a result she obtained a 25% stake, Mark, Bryan and Peter's shareholding being reduced to 25% each.

Mark was happy with the company structure, since Peter's wife brought to the business considerable commercial expertise, and he received a large sum for the shares he transferred to her. Within a year however, the relationship between the shareholders had deteriorated. In particular Mark felt increasingly isolated. He was anxious that the company expand its insurance business to provide insurance facilities for commercial as well as personal customers. The other shareholders however were of the view that the company, which was suffering a reduced level of profit, should diversify, and move into the lucrative field of marketing, the area in which Peter's wife had previously worked.

By 1993 Mark had decided to form a separate business to offer a complete range of insurance facilities. He formed a partnership with James Blake-Smith, an old schoolfriend, to carry on the additional business. He did not reveal the existence of this business to his fellow shareholders in Mills & Co. Ltd., assuming that since it was based in Barnsley, a town twenty miles away from the company's place of business in Leeds, it had nothing to do with them. No partnership articles were drawn up.

The other members of Mills & Co. Ltd. recently discovered the existence of Mark's new firm. They responded by calling a company meeting, at which, during very stormy business they resolved to alter the company articles to enable it to pursue marketing work, to sell off the company's present business undertaking at a figure well below what Mark believes to be its true value, and to remove him as a director. In addition they are threatening to take away his voting rights. Marks problems have been compounded by problems in the partnership. He has discovered that James Blake-Smith has been in financial difficulties, and that bankruptcy proceedings have been commenced against him this week. He has also purchased, in the firm's name, an expensive computer system, despite a recent partnership meeting at which it was agreed to defer the expenditure until the next financial year.

In an effort to clarify the legal position in relation to these business difficulties Mark has sought your help, as someone with a business of your own and a knowledge of the legal principles applicable to business organisations. Prior to meeting Mark in a couple of days time, you have decided to analyse the legal position he has found himself in, in order to fully advise him as to the extent of his rights and liabilities.

Task

Draft an outline report which you can give to Mark at your meeting with him, that expresses your considered legal opinion on his present business problems.

Assignment *The Wandering Child*

Fiona Berry and John Cheng are business partners who run a number of travel agency related outlets in Lancashire. One such agency Fiesta Travel is situated in premises in Bolton held on a 21 year lease from North Western Properties Ltd. The lease has now run for six years and despite repeated requests by Fiona, the landlords seem reluctant to fulfil their clear repairing obligation in relation to the plaster work on the ceiling of the main office which is in a dangerous state of disrepair. A further cause for anxiety is the condition of the electrical wiring in the building, which again falls within the landlords responsibility.

Concerned at the time it takes for the landlord to respond to requests to repair, Fiona decided to hire Gerry, a local odd job man, to carry out wiring work in the premises. In addition, North Western Properties finally responded to the request for repairs to the ceiling by hiring Joplings, a well known building contractor to carry out the work. Because of pressure of work, Joplings decide to sub contract the work to Tom and Jim, a couple of lads who are "quick and cheap and can manage small jobs".

The events of the last two weeks have driven Fiona to despair! The first replastering work while completed in good time has not been a success. Firstly Sheila, a prospective customer suffered head injury caused by a fall of plaster when she was glancing at travel brochures in the premises. Furthermore Jim in carrying out the replastering work sustained a violent electric shock when he touched exposed electric cables to a light fitting which Gerry had not properly insulated. The icing on the cake was an incident yesterday. Wayne, a six year old on the premises with his parents there to book a holiday, wandered through a door marked 'private' apparently in search of toilets. He fell down the steps inside the door leading to the cellar and suffered a broken arm. The stairs were not lit.

Fiona and John feel that they may face potential legal claims for these incidents and fix an appointment with Masters & Milburn a local firm of solicitors to seek legal advice. Despite their problems they don't wish to leave the Bolton Premises.

Task

You are working for Masters and Milburn as part of a work experience programme and have been asked to interview Fiona and John and to follow up the interview with a written report to one of the senior partners Janet Stephenson. You need to include in the report your assessment of the legal position in relation to liability. Your task is to produce the report for Ms Stephenson. The report should clearly state the legal arguments both for and against the likelihood of Fiona and John incurring liability for the injuries to Sheila and Wayne.

Development Task

Look at the kinds of warning notices displayed in commercial premises and places such as building sites. Using your knowledge of the law concerning occupiers liability and exclusion clauses consider how far the notices you have looked at are lawful.

Element 9.3

Investigate contractual agreements made in business

Performance Criteria

1. The nature and scope of contractual agreements are described
2. The legal requirements of a valid contract are identified
3. The effects and implications of defects in contractual agreements are explained

Range

Nature:

Oral/written; express/implied; standard form/negotiated

Scope:

Goods; services; employment; credit

Legal Requirements:

Form; legality; essentials; restrictions on use and scope of terms and conditions; certainty

Defects:

Non compliance with formalities; absence of essentials; uncertainty; vitiating factors; non-compliance with legal requirements concerning scope of terms and conditions

Evidence Indicators

An analysis of one example of a standard from contract and one negotiated agreement used in business. The examples will have been chosen by the student and used to demonstrate their ability to identify and illustrate the legal requirements of a valid contract

Chapter 4

Contractual Agreements in Business

The Nature and Scope of Contractual Agreements

Economic activity, which we may regard as the acquisition, use and disposal of resources, is one of the most fundamental characteristics of human patterns of behaviour. Organisations and individuals all participate to a greater or lesser extent in this activity, and a nation's material well-being is usually judged in terms of its economic fitness, in other words how economically active it is. There are many factors contributing towards a fit and flourishing economy. They include the presence of natural physical resources, the skills and mobility of the labour force, and the devices used by government to manage the economy. These factors are examined in the Mandatory Units of the GNVQ. What we are concerned with here is a less obvious but nonetheless indispensable component of the economic process, namely the rules and principles which govern the conduct of the participants engaged in negotiating and carrying out the millions of business transactions by which economic objectives are achieved. This body of rules and principles is referred to collectively as the law of contract.

Without an effective legal framework to regulate the enormous number of transactions which an industrialised economy demands each day to function effectively, economic activity would go into decline. The reason for this is that most industrial and commercial organisations would be unwilling to take the financial risks inherent in trading, if it were not for the existence of well established, formalised rules of trading, supported by legal sanctions if they are broken. Although it is not possible to prevent a fellow trader from breaking promises, if those promises are included in a contract, then at least one has the reassurance of knowing that since a legal obligation has been broken, court action can if necessary be taken to obtain redress. The remedy which is sought in such cases is usually that of damages, the legal expression used to describe any form of monetary compensation. Thus if a bank is to grant a mortgage, a civil engineering company to construct a motorway, a landowner to grant a lease of land or an employer to take on staff, there needs to be a measure of confidence underlying such agreements so that if they are not carried out a legal remedy is available to the injured party. Without the security of a binding contract there would be little confidence in forming trading bonds. In the absence of any legal sanction the only security likely to exist would depend upon whether the other party either;

- felt a moral obligation to meet the promises given, or
- believed it could be damaging to its business reputation and standing if it became known that it did not honour its agreements.

It is not only in the economic sphere that contractual ground rules are important. There also are social implications associated with contractual activities. Some examples may help to illustrate this point. If a manufacturer of children's toys produces items which are dangerous to their users, or an employer dismisses an employee out of spite, or a tour operator sells holidays which it knows do not meet the claims made in the brochure, most people will view this as socially unacceptable conduct in terms of the consequences likely to result from it. As a society it concerns us if children are hurt when playing with dangerous toys whose design faults could not have been discovered at the time their parents purchased them. We would conclude, no doubt, that whatever the manufacturer's legal responsibilities may be, he has been grossly socially irresponsible. Similarly it concerns us that the employee has lost his job without good cause, and the family on holiday with young children find the beach is not 100 metres away from the hotel as they were promised, but 2 kilometres away. In each case there is a social cost, not merely a financial one. The redundant employee cannot find alternative employment nearby, and has to move with the family to another part of the country, disturbing the children's education, incurring debts and creating conditions of stress, whilst the family on holiday suffer considerable disappointment and inconvenience.

Sometimes particular forms of contractual activity may be both economically and socially undesirable. Suppose for example that a major UK employer were to insist on all employees signing an undertaking not to seek further employment with any rival organisation anywhere in the UK, for a period of ten years after leaving the present employer. The effect is likely to be:

(i)   to create an unfair trading advantage to the present employer, gained by excluding similar employers who may operate their business more efficiently drawing from the full pool of skilled labour potentially available;

(ii)   to prevent employees from exercising the freedom of opportunity to obtain the best salaries that their skills can command; and

(iii)   in general economic terms to distort the mobility of labour.

Arguably in circumstances of this kind the desirability of giving the employer the freedom to set employment terms which grant him business protection is offset by the undesirability of allowing him to interfere in the free operation of this particular market.

The need to regulate agreements

It is clear then that rules are necessary to regulate the agreements used in transacting. These rules are needed in order to:

* provide a legal framework that offers security and enables commercial activity to expand and prosper;

* restrict activities which are economically harmful;

* pursue the aims of social justice where appropriate, and

* identify the technical means by which parties who wish to do so can make agreements which the law will enforce. An agreement which is legally enforceable is known as a contract.

Before examining the concept of the contract in more depth it is helpful to say a little about the thinking which has guided the lawmakers in creating and developing the principles and rules which make up this vital body of law. As we shall see the law of contract is founded upon common law principles, having been developed by the courts rather than by Parliament.

The Concept of Freedom of Contract

Contracting parties have never enjoyed unlimited freedom to make whatever bargain they choose. Throughout the long development of the English law of contract, which has taken place over many centuries, certain restrictions have always existed. No court, for example has ever been prepared to enforce a contract whose purpose is unlawful, such as an agreement to commit a criminal offence. However the extent of contractual regulation has varied over time, reflecting the thinking current during different periods.

Under the capitalist philosophy of the nineteenth century a laissez-faire approach to the development of the economy was advocated. This involved leaving the markets for goods and services, as far as reasonably practicable, to regulate themselves. The idea of a free market, which should be left to control itself unhindered by the interventions of the courts or Parliament, helped to reinforce the view that had been influential since the eighteenth century of *freedom of contract*. The advocates of freedom of contract considered that as few restrictions as possible should be placed upon the liberty of individuals to make agreements. The Master of the Rolls, Sir George Jessel, expressed it in the following way in 1875: *"If there is one thing which more than any other public policy requires it is that men of full age and understanding shall have the utmost liberty of contracting and their contracts when entered into freely and voluntarily shall be held sacred and shall be enforced by the courts of justice."*

There appear to be some compelling reasons for supporting this view. Firstly the law of contract is a part of private law, which means that the creation and performance of contracts is the responsibility of parties themselves. As we shall see later, contractual rights and obligations only attach to the actual parties entering the contract, although this principle is subject to certain exceptions. Consequently contractual rights and obligations are purely personal. If a contract is broken the only person with the right to a remedy is the injured party. No one else can sue the contract breaker. Secondly it is the parties themselves who are best able to judge their own contractual needs. If their negotiations are not concluded to their mutual satisfaction then they will not go ahead and complete the contract. If on the other hand they are both in agreement they will be happy to bind themselves formally, and incur contractual obligations. They should be left alone to make the contract that suits them, free from external interference.

The objectives of freedom of contract

The underlying reasons for allowing a wide measure of contractual freedom include:

- *market needs:*
  in the interests of healthy markets the participants in market activity should be allowed to trade unhindered. The able will survive and the weak will flounder. External intervention in this process will tend to weaken rather than strengthen economic performance by the artificial distortion of the bargaining process ;

- *personal liberty:*
  interference in contract making is an infringement of individual liberty. In the same way that a person chooses when to marry, or for whom to vote, they should be allowed the freedom to make the contracts of their choosing. If subsequently the choice turns out to be a bad one it is of concern to nobody but the contract maker. The contract is a private, not a public event;

- *knowledge:*
  contracting parties can be assumed to know what they are doing. They act in a rational manner and will therefore ensure that the contract they make is the contract they want.

Nobody else is better placed to identify contractual wants and needs than the parties who are making the contract.

On closer analysis however, it is possible to identify major weaknesses which are inherent in the factors referred to above. In simple terms the underlying flaw in all of them is that they do not reflect the reality of modern contract making. It is important to an understanding of the law of contract to appreciate why the ideas upon which the notion of freedom of contract are based, are in reality largely myths.

The role of consent

In one sense there is complete contractual freedom. Individuals and organisations alike are free to choose whether to enter into a contractual relationship. It cannot be forced on them for consent is a precondition of the relationship. But what precisely does consent mean? To answer this question we need to examine how the courts discriminate between situations where there is a genuine consent, and those in which the consent is in reality artificial. Where the consent is unreal there is no *consensus ad idem*, or meeting of the minds of the parties, even though on a mechanical level they have gone through the motions of reaching an agreement. Circumstances in which the courts will be prepared to consider a claim that the consent is unreal are in cases of misrepresentation, mistake, fraud, duress or undue influence. They are referred to technically as vitiating (invalidating) elements. Once established they have the effect of either invalidating the contract in its entirety in which case the contract is said to be *void*, or of entitling the injured party to escape from the contract if he or she wishes to do so. In such circumstances the contract is said to be *voidable* in their favour. To vitiate literally means to make invalid or ineffectual.

Vitiating elements are dealt later, but we may note here that by granting relief where consent is a sham because a person has been misled, tricked, coerced or mistaken, the courts are demonstrating that they will look at what the parties believed they were agreeing to when the contract was made. Equally of course, the notion of freedom carries with it responsibility, and it is certainly not the role of the courts to repair bad bargains made through lack of prudence. The balance between intervening in an attempt to right legitimate wrongs, and leaving the parties to learn from their trading mistakes is not easily achieved. The point is that the courts are prepared in the right circumstances to untie the bond that has been made, thereby protecting parties in a limited way from the consequences that complete freedom of contract would otherwise produce.

Bargaining inequality

A further important element in examining the concept of freedom of contract is the matter of bargaining power. True consensus is only possible where the parties meet as bargaining equals, but it is commonplace to find that there is an inequality of bargaining power so that one party is able to dominate the other. The result is that far from arriving at agreement through a process of negotiation, the contract is a one sided arrangement in which the dominant party presents terms to the weaker party on a take-it-or-leave it basis. Commonly the dominant party will only be prepared to do business on the basis of standard terms designed to provide it with a high level of commercial protection. If the dominant party is a monopoly supplier, like British Gas or British Rail, the consumer is unable to shop around for a better deal. Even in a reasonably competitive market situation, however, it is often the case that suppliers of goods or services trade on the same or very similar terms, for instance by using a contract designed by the trade association of which they are a member. Contracts arising in this way are sometimes referred to as contracts of *adhesion*, for the weaker party is required to adhere all the terms imposed by the stronger party. When employers recruit staff they are usually employed on contractual terms which are prescribed by the employer and subject to limited negotiation. This becomes more obvious where the supply of labour far exceeds the demand from employers.

To help redress such imbalance Parliament has used legislation to bolster the rights of consumers, whether they be businesses or individuals. This legislation is considered in Chapter 5, but the most notable examples are the Consumer Credit Act 1974, the Unfair Contract Terms Act 1977, and Sale of Goods Act 1979, the Supply of Goods and Services Act 1982 and the Consumer Protection Act 1987.

Even the courts have been prepared to intervene in circumstances of exceptional exploitation. To do so they have applied an equitable principle known as *undue influence*.

> A good illustration is provided by the decision of the Court of Appeal in *Lloyds Bank Ltd. v. Bundy* 1975. Here an elderly farmer, who was ill and had little business knowledge, agreed with the bank to guarantee the account of his son's company. The company was in difficulties, and over a period of time the father increased the size of the guarantee, which was secured by a mortgage on his house, so that eventually the mortgage on the property was for more than the property was worth. This arrangement had been made by the father in consultation with the bank manager, upon whom he implicitly relied. The company's debts remained outstanding, and the bank sought to sell the father's house in order to realise the guarantee. The Court of Appeal unanimously set aside the agreement between the father and the bank. In the course of his judgment Lord Denning MR made the following important observations: *"no bargain will be upset which is the result of the ordinary interplay of forces. There are many hard cases which are caught by this rule . . . yet there are exceptions to this general rule . . . in which the courts will set aside a contract, or a transfer of property, when the parties have not met on equal terms, when the one is so strong in bargaining power and the other so weak that, as a matter of common fairness, it is not right that the strong should be allowed to push the weak to the wall . . . . English law gives relief to one who, without independent advice, enters into a contract on terms which are very unfair or transfers property for a consideration which is grossly inadequate . . . "*

The Legal Requirements of a Valid Contract

Classifying contracts

It is a commonly held view that a contract is not valid unless it is written. This is simply not the case, as can be illustrated by the number of times we make purchases of goods or pay for services without even contemplating the need for a written contract. Indeed contracts are invariably carried out by parties who are not even aware that they have been involved in a legal relationship at all. If written contracts were necessary to effect all transactions, a moment's reflection will demonstrate how time consuming, wasteful of paper and largely irrelevant to our needs such a requirement would be. There are, however, some sound reasons in support of the view that a written contract may nevertheless be worthwhile;

(a)   because the writing would stand as evidence of the transaction should anyone challenge its existence, and

(b)   because the task of reducing an agreement into writing would presumably prompt the parties into expressing themselves clearly, and thinking about the nature of the transaction they are involved in. It would indicate the rights and obligations of the people making it.

But what exactly is a contract? A contract may be simply defined as a legally enforceable agreement. We need therefore to ascertain what it is that makes certain agreements legally enforceable, and since most of these agreements come into being as simple contracts, the logical starting point is to examine the nature of the simple contract.

Activity

> Referring back over the last seven days try to establish how many contracts you have made during that time. See if you can identify what the obligation of the other party were towards you, and what your obligations were towards them. Obligations are simply the promises or undertakings which were exchanged between you. Have all the contracts you have been able to identify been fully completed, or is there anything left to be carried out under them?

Simple Contracts

At common law, parties are free to express a contract in any way, hence the term *'simple'* meaning non-technical. These contracts may be oral, written, or even be inferred from the conduct of the parties. Most simple contracts are oral agreements; buying food, petrol, a record or tape, clothes and so on. Those that are commonly expressed in writing include taking a package holiday, arranging for credit facilities, having building work carried out, joining a bookclub, employing staff, and opening a bank account. There are of course many more. Sometimes the contract may be part written and part oral. Two companies may for instance enter into an agreement where some of the terms such as price are in writing, but others such as delivery arrangements are left to be orally negotiated. Even contracts arising out of conduct are not uncommon. An example will help to illustrate how such a situation can occur. Let us suppose a fuel supplier provides a customer with a fixed quantity of oil each month, under an agreement to run for a year. In the event that the supplier delivers the same quantity of oil in the first month of the following year, and the oil is used by the customer, a new contract would be inferred from the conduct of the parties, even though they have not met face to face. The terms of the new contract will be those of the original.

Whilst the law adopts a flexible attitude towards the means by which a contract can be formed, it is most particular about the components which must be present if the transaction is to be legally enforceable. At common law a simple contract must include:

- an agreement between the contracting parties;
- the provision of consideration to support the contract;
- an intention to become legally bound; and
- legal capacity held by the parties.

These four components are essential. The absence of any one of them will prevent the creation of a contract.

A simple contract which meets these requirements may however still fail for some other reason. Whatever the reason for the failure, it is of the greatest importance to be certain of the effect it has on the contract. The specific nature of the failure determines whether, and if so how, the contract survives, and this in turn tells us about the liabilities of the parties. For the moment, though, we need to concentrate on the classifications applied to contracts generally, and then go on to examine how a contract is formed.

Speciality contracts, or deeds

Speciality contracts, which are commonly referred to as deeds, are formal contracts. Up until 1989 a deed had to meet the requirements of being in writing, and signed, sealed and delivered by the person or persons making it. The Law of Property (Miscellaneous Provisions) Act 1989 has abolished the need for a seal when an individual executes a deed, and also the need for a deed to be written on parchment or paper. The only formalities which now must be met are that the signature of the person making the deed be witnessed and attested. The deed must of course be in writing however this writing may be expressed in any form provided it is clear on the face of the document that it is intended to be a deed.

There are relatively few circumstances in which the law demands the use of a deed to give the effect to a contract. A deed is required under the Law of Property Act 1925 to transfer legal ownership in freehold land, and to create a lease of more than three years duration. Although most deeds will arise out of agreements between parties who have exchanged promises of value, a deed is valid without the need for consideration to support it. Validity is achieved by the technical form of the document. Although it was originally necessary for corporate bodies to contract using the corporate seal, the Corporate Bodies Contracts Act 1960 specifies that a corporation can make contracts as though it were an individual, thus there are no longer any special formal requirements attached to corporations and their contract making. It is not uncommon however to find that under their internal rules corporations are obliged to use the corporate seal for contracts above a certain financial amount, for security reasons.

Void, voidable and unenforceable contracts

Sometimes a contract will fail in such a fundamental way as to render it *void*. A void contract carries no contractual rights or obligations, so if goods have been transferred under such a contract, ownership in them will not pass and they can be recovered from the person in possession of them. Where services are rendered under a void contract, a reasonable sum is recoverable for the work done.

> This occurred in *Craven-Ellis v. Canons Ltd.* 1936 where it was found that the plaintiff, who had worked for some time as the managing director of the defendant company, had in fact been employed under a deed which was void because he had failed to take up shares in the company as required by the company's articles. Nevertheless, he was entitled to remuneration for the work he had done.

The term 'void contract' is really a contradiction in terms, since if the contract is void there is no legally enforceable agreement amounting to a contract. An example of a void contract is one whose purpose is illegal, such as an agreement to commit a criminal act, or trade with an enemy alien during time of war. Sometimes the contract will not be void but merely *voidable*. Where this is so, one of the parties has the option of avoiding the contract, but until this is done the contract still stands. An example is provided in the case of contracts induced by fraud, where the deceived party can avoid the contract.

Finally, a contract may be *unenforceable*. Where this is so the court is unable to enforce it, if called upon to do so by one of the parties. In other respects however it may possess some effect. For instance if a collateral contract such as a guarantee is built upon it the unenforceability will not invalidate the collateral contract. Unenforceability can occur because of a failure to satisfy some technical requirement, such as the need for written evidence to support certain types of contract.

There is a significant difference between merely requiring written evidence of an agreement, and requiring the entire contract to be in writing. In particular the burden of satisfying the former requirement is less onerous than it is to satisfy the latter.

Contracts where writing is necessary

Statute requires that certain contracts be made in writing. The reason for demanding this is, in some cases, to provide the consumer with a measure of protection, but more usually it is required in an effort to oblige parties involved in technical transactions to record their respective obligations. Examples include:

- Hire purchase and conditional sale agreements. Under s.65(1) of the Consumer Credit Act 1974 such an agreement cannot be enforced unless it is properly executed. It is properly executed when a legible document containing all the express terms of the agreement and in the prescribed form is signed by the parties.

- The transfer of shares in a registered company. This is required under s.183 Companies Act 1985, which states that a *"proper instrument of transfer"* must be delivered to the company. The company cannot register the transfer until this is done.

- An acknowledgement of a debt which has become statute-barred, under the Limitation Act 1980.

- An assignment of copyright, under s.90 Copyright Designs and Patents Act 1988.

- Cheques, bills of exchange and promissory notes, under the Bills of Exchange Act 1882.

- Contracts for the sale or other disposition of land under the Law of Property (Miscellaneous Provisions) Act 1989. The writing required under the Act must incorporate all the terms expressly agreed by the parties and appear in a single document, or where contracts are exchanged, in both.

Failure to comply with these statutory requirements renders the contract invalid.

There remains one type of contract which still only requires written evidence of its existence, rather than a written contract containing it, the contract of guarantee. Such contracts are covered by the Statute of Frauds 1677 (as amended). A contract of guarantee is a *"promise to answer for the debt, default or miscarriage of another person"* and the guarantor's liability arises only upon the failure of the debtor to pay.

Contrary to popular belief, apart from merchant seaman and apprentices, there is no legal requirement that a contract of employment be in writing. While there are problems associated with identifying the terms of an oral agreement, nevertheless, given the fluid nature of a contract of employment there is no guarantee that a requirement to reduce the original contract to writing would solve all the problems of interpreting its content.

Under the Employment Protection (Consolidation) Act 1978, there is a statutory requirement on employers to provide their employees within thirteen weeks of the commencement of employment with a written statement of the main terms of employment. Certain classes of employees are excluded including registered dock workers, Crown employees, employees who work wholly or mainly outside Great Britain and part time workers. The objective is to ensure that employees have written confirmation and a source to scrutinise at least the main terms of their employment contracts. Particulars which must be included in the statutory statement include:

- reference to the parties and the dates on which the period of continuous employment began (stating whether a previous period of employment is included as part of continuous employment);

- the scale of remuneration and the method of calculation;

- the intervals at which remuneration is paid (whether weekly or monthly or some other period);

- the terms and conditions relating to hours of work;

- the terms and conditions relating to holidays and holiday pay (sufficient to enable the employee's entitlement to accrued holiday pay on the termination of employment to be precisely calculated);

- the terms and conditions relating to sickness or injury and sickness pay;

- the terms and conditions relating to pension and pension scheme;

- the length of notice which the employee is obliged to give and entitled to receive;

- the title of the job which the employee is employed to do;

- a note containing a specification of any disciplinary rules or reference to an accessible document containing such rules;

- the name of the person to whom the employee can apply if she/he is dissatisfied with any disciplinary decision relating to him/her;

- the name of the person to whom the employer can apply to seek the redress of any grievance;

- whether a contracting out certificate under the provisions of the Social Security Act 1975 is in force in relation to the employment.

Under the Employment Act 1989 an employer is exempt from the requirement to include a note on disciplinary proceedings in the written statement where that employer (together with any associated employer) has less than twenty employees on the date when the employee's employment began.

You often hear people talk about "terms and conditions" of employment and yet there has been no attempt in statute or common law to satisfactorily distinguish between these expressions. The prevalent view seems to be that *terms* are those parts of the contract that are mutually agreed, expressly or by implication and are found in the contract, in collective agreements and occasionally in statutory provisions. *Conditions* on the other hand have a lower status and are unilateral instructions from the employer specifying how and when employment duties are to be fulfilled. Conditions are usually found in work rules, disciplinary and grievance procedures and job descriptions.

To satisfy the requirements of the Act it is not sufficient simply to be told or shown the above particulars of employment. The employer must present the employee with a document containing the information or at least make such a document available for *inspection* (e.g. a collective agreement and a rule book). It should be stressed that a statutory statement is not the contract of employment but rather strong prima facie evidence of its terms. Certainly the mere acknowledgement of its receipt does not turn the statement into a contract.

Contractual terms we shall discover, are often the subject of change, in which case an employer is obliged to notify the employee of changes in the statement within one month of the change. An employer who fails to comply with obligations in relation to the statutory statement could be the subject of a complaint to the Industrial Tribunal. The Tribunal has power to determine what particulars ought to have been included, in a case where no statement has been supplied, or where the statement supplied is incomplete or inaccurate. With no effective sanction available for employers who fail to comply, complaints to Tribunals are rare, and usually only arise in connection with other complaints, for instance in relation to unfair dismissal. Finally it should be mentioned that those employers who provide their employees with a written contract of employment which covers all the matters which must be referred to in the statutory statement, do not have to supply their employees with a separate statutory statement.

Formation of Contracts

Agreement

A contract cannot be created without the parties reaching an agreement. The idea of agreement is therefore central to an understanding of the law of contract. In the business context there are two basic legal questions which arise in respect of all transactions. These are firstly whether a legally enforceable agreement has been made, and secondly what are the terms upon which it is based.

The answer to the second question will reveal the specific obligations each party has towards the other, a matter of considerable importance to them both. It is only by identifying the content and extent of their mutual undertakings that the parties are able to know when they have discharged their responsibilities under the contract, and freed themselves from their legal bond. The two questions are, of course, very closely connected, because it is through the process of reaching their agreement that the parties will expressly fix the terms that are to regulate their contract. In other words, agreements are arrangements to do, or sometimes refrain from doing, specific things, and these specific things are the terms of the contract.

It may be that most people can instinctively tell whether they have an agreement or not, however for legal purposes it is not sufficient to rely upon subjective judgments to decide such significant events. If a disputed agreement comes before a court, obviously the court cannot get inside the minds of the parties to discover their actual intentions. At best all that can be achieved is to look at the way they have conducted themselves, examining what they have said and done, in order to decide the issue on the basis of what a reasonable person would assume.

What the courts do is objectively to assess the evidence and to apply established criteria to help resolve contractual disputes. These criteria take the form of fixed and certain rules, which over a long period have been developed and refined by the judiciary and which are used by all courts to determine what constitutes an enforceable agreement. It follows that a person may find himself legally bound by an agreement, which, in his own mind, he does not consider he has made. How important then, for organisations and individuals alike, to know and understand these rules. Certainly no business can effectively conduct its affairs without the application of such knowledge.

For the sake of convenience agreements can be divided into two separate components:

    (i)   an offer, made by one party to the other; and

    (ii)   an acceptance by the other of the terms contained in the offer.

If a court cannot identify the presence of these two components in a transaction, a simple contract will not have materialised, although as we have seen a person can become bound contractually by expressing a promise in the form of a deed. This is not a common practice, and all we need to note here is that the validity of a deed lies in the specialised form in which the promise is made, rather than in the need for agreement.

The process of negotiation

The person making an offer is referred to as the *offeror*, and the person to whom it is addressed is the *offeree*. In business it is usual to find the parties reaching agreement following a period of negotiation. Such negotiations will be concerned with the details of the proposed transaction, and are likely to include matters such as price, specifications regarding the subject matter of the agreement, and the time and place for performing it. Often during these negotiations offers will be made by one party to the other which are rejected, or met by a fresh offer. Thus either of the parties to the transaction is able to make an offer, not just the one who wishes to sell the goods or services in question or who is the owner or supplier of them.

Examining the negotiating process is important for four reasons:

(i)   because it enables us to identify which party made the final offer;

(ii)   because it enables us to identify the time at which the contract is made;

(iii)   because having established who made the offer we can identify the terms upon which the offer was based, and hence on which the contract is founded; and

(iv)   because during negotiations false statements are sometimes made by one of the parties which induce the other to enter into the contract. These are referred to as misrepresentations.

Characteristics of a Valid Offer

To be legally effective an offer must satisfy the following requirements:

(a)   the offer must be firmly made;

(b)   the offer must be communicated;

(c)   the terms of the offer must be certain; and

(d)   the offer must not have terminated.

Firm offer or invitation to treat

The offeror must intend his offer to be unequivocal, so that when acceptance occurs he will be bound. The difficulty that can arise here lies in distinguishing firm offers from statements which do not carry the full legal status of offers. Sometimes what appears to be a firm offer is merely an incentive or encouragement designed by the person making it to stimulate the making of offers to him and is certainly not intended to be legally binding. A statement of this kind is known as an invitation to treat. It is an indication that the person is willing to do business with anyone who is interested.

> In *Pharmaceutical Society of Great Britain v. Boots Cash Chemists (Southern) Ltd.* 1953 one of the shops in the company's chain had been converted into a self-service supermarket. Some of the shelves carried poisons which by statute were required to be sold in the presence of a qualified chemist. The chemist was in attendance at the checkout. The Pharmaceutical Society which had a duty to enforce the statutory provisions claimed that the company was in breach of them. The Society argued that the contract was made at the shelves where there was no pharmacist in attendance. The court however held that the goods displayed on the shelves were merely invitations to treat. The contract was made at the checkout. The customers made the offer when presenting the goods for payment and the offer was accepted by the cashier.

> Clearly there can be no real distinction between goods displayed on shelves inside a shop and goods displayed in the window. Thus in *Fisher v. Bell* 1961 a shop keeper who was prosecuted for displaying a flick-knife inside his shop window with a price ticket attached, was found by the court not to have committed the offence of offering for sale an offensive weapon contrary to the Restriction of Offensive Weapons Act 1959. The display was simply an invitation to treat.

Advertisements are also generally regarded as constituting invitations to treat. In *Partridge v. Crittenden* 1968 the Divisional Court of the Queen's Bench Division was asked to determine whether an advertisement in a magazine which read, *"Bramblefinch cocks, bramblefinch hens 25/- each"*, constituted the offence of offering to sell wild birds contrary to the Protection of Birds Act 1954. The court quashed the conviction against the defendant which had been issued in the Magistrates Court. The advertisement was simply an encouragement to stimulate the market into making offers. Members of the public responding to the advert made the offers, but of course they could not commit an offence since they were offering to buy, not to sell. The defendant should have been charged with the separate offence contained in the Act of selling wild birds.

The legal inference that advertisements will not normally amount to firm offers to sell is of some value to businesses that trade on a mail-order basis. For instance a company that takes out advertising in a newspaper or colour supplement cannot be sure of the demand for its goods that will result. If the advertisement were to constitute an offer, then the response of a member of the public in sending a cheque or postal order to buy the advertised goods would amount to an acceptance. The company could find itself overwhelmed by the demand, and under a legal obligation to supply goods it simply does not have if its stocks are exhausted.

Perhaps the clearest example of an invitation to treat can be seen in an auction sale. This occurs when the auctioneer presents items in the auction, and asks for bids from those who are present, using expressions such as *"how much am I bid for . . .?"* and *"do I see £20?"* The auctioneer is testing demand, and having assessed it will try to increase it and push the price up. The auctioneer is certainly not offering to sell. The bids themselves constitute offers which the auctioneer is able to accept or reject.

Further examples of the invitation to treat are advertisements inviting suppliers of goods and services to submit tenders, and prospectuses issued by limited companies inviting members of the public to subscribe for shares.

Tenders

The use of tenders is a common commercial practice. Indeed local authorities are required by the Local Government Act 1972 to contract in this way. Under s.135 a contract made by an authority must comply with its standing orders and these standing orders must include provisions for securing competition and for regulating the manner in which tenders are invited in the case of contracts for the supply of goods or materials or for the execution of works. This is usually satisfied by inviting tenders from contractors on an approved list maintained by the authority. The Local Government Act 1988 imposes particular restrictions on local authorities by requiring that certain activities cannot be carried out by the council's own workforce without first going to competitive tender, which will involve the authority itself in making a written bid for the work. The activities covered by the Act include contracts for the collection of refuse, school and other catering arrangements, ground maintenance and the repair and maintenance of motor vehicles. Under the tendering process a tender is an offer and an invitation to tender is an invitation to treat. It is merely an invitation by an individual or organisation wishing to purchase goods or services to request suppliers to submit a contractual offer in the form of a tender.

In appropriate circumstances however it is possible to treat an invitation to tender as giving rise to a binding contractual obligation. If there is clear evidence from what the parties have said and done that a contractual obligation to consider a particular tender in conjunction with all other tenders meeting the tendering requirements was intended, then the Court will enforce it.

In *Blackpool and Fylde Aero Club v. Blackpool Borough Council* 1990 the local authority owned and managed an airport. The plaintiff flying club had for some years operated pleasure flights from the airport. When the grant of the club's concession came up for renewal the council prepared invitations to tender. These were then sent to the club and six other parties. The forms sent out stated that the council did not bind itself, *"to accept all or any part of any tender"*. The form added, *"No tender which is received after the last date and time specified shall be admitted for consideration."*

The plaintiffs delivered their tender to the council offices before the deadline. However because council staff failed to empty the council letter box when they should have done, the council received the tender too late to be considered, and accepted a tender from another tenderer lower in value than the plaintiff's tender. The club sued for damages alleging breach of contract and negligence. The Court held that although contracts in such circumstances should not be freely implied, the evidence here was of a clear intention that the council was contractually obliged to consider the plaintiff's tender with the other tenders, or at least that it would be considered if all the others were. The claim for breach of contract was successful. The question of whether the council would have owed the plaintiffs a duty to take reasonable care to consider a tender submitted within the stated time limit, in the absence of an implied contractual obligation to do so, was not decided.

If the invitation to tender stipulates expressly or impliedly that the goods or services will be required, then an acceptance of the tender will create a binding contract. Alternatively, the invitation may stipulate that the goods or services *may* be required, in which case an acceptance of the tender results in a standing offer to supply as and when required. A failure to order by the buyer in such circumstances will not result in a breach of contract.

It should be noted however that the invitation to treat is not devoid of legal effect. It can give rise to legal liability in the following ways:

(a)   As a statement it can amount to an actionable misrepresentation (see later).

(b)   It may also give rise to criminal liability under the Trade Descriptions Act 1968, if it constitutes a false trade description, or under the Consumer Protection Act 1987 if it gives a false or misleading indication as to the price of goods or services (see Chapter 3).

(c)   Under specific legislation it may give rise to legal liability. For instance in the case of a company prospectus, s.166 Companies Act 1985 provides that the person responsible for a prospectus is liable to compensate anyone acquiring shares to which the prospectus relates, if they suffer loss as a result of an untrue or misleading statement in it.

An offer must be communicated

The party to whom an offer is directed must be aware of it. An offer will normally be made to a single individual or organisation, however there is nothing to prevent an offer being directed to a specific group of individuals, any one or more of whom may choose to accept it. For instance a private limited company that is going public may offer some of its shares at favourable rates to the members of its workforce.

It is possible to make an offer to the public generally, where the offeror is not able at the time the offer is made to identify who the possible recipients are. This principle has been in existence for a long time, and seems to be derived from the willingness of the courts to recognise a contractual obligation on the part of someone offering to pay any member of the public a reward, for example in return for information or the return of property. It is not uncommon to find banks offering financial rewards for information leading to the conviction of bank robbers by displaying notices inside the banks. In such circumstances anyone who satisfies the terms of the offer will be entitled to the reward, as long as they were aware of the offer beforehand. One of the most celebrated instances of an offer made to the public at large, occurred in *Carlill v. Carbolic Smokeball Co.* 1893 which is considered later.

What constitutes communication is a question of fact for the court.

The terms of an offer must be certain

In the event of a dispute between the parties as to the meaning of a term it will ultimately fall to the court to decide the question. The courts will always endeavour to find certainty so that the contract is able to survive wherever possible but if a term is obscure or meaningless then it will fail. This may not prove fatal to the contract if the term constitutes only a minor part of the overall obligations, but where the term is central to the functioning of the contract, uncertainty as to its meaning will defeat the contract as a whole. The following case illustrates the position.

> In *Scammel v. Ouston* 1941 an agreement for the sale of a van where the balance of the price was to be met *"on hire purchase terms over a period of two years"* also failed. Since there was no previous course of dealing between the parties to enable the court to identify what these "hire purchase" terms might be, the only alternative would have been to treat the terms as standard hire purchase terms. Unfortunately, as the court observed, hire purchase terms are not standardised and identical, but vary from agreement to agreement so that for example rates of interest will vary from company to company.

A meaningless term can however often be ignored.

> In *Nicolene Ltd. v. Simmonds* 1953 a contract was made for the sale of 3000 tons of steel bars. The seller then broke the contract, and when the buyer sued for damages the seller argued there was no contract between them, relying on a statement in one of the contractual documents that, *"we are in agreement that the usual conditions of acceptance apply"*. The court, whilst recognising that there were no "usual conditions of acceptance" between the parties, found that the contract was in every other respect clear as to the obligations of the parties. The meaningless term could be cut out from the rest of the contract. In the course of his judgment Lord Denning MR commented that, *"A clause which is meaningless can often be ignored . . . ; whereas a clause which has yet to be agreed may mean there is no contract at all."*

A common example of a clause or term which the parties have yet to agree is price, and price is obviously a vital term in any contract. In the unlikely event that the parties have reached agreement whilst overlooking the question of price altogether how will this affect their agreement? In such circumstances it may still be possible to enforce the agreement. In the case of sales of goods, the Sale of Goods Act 1979 provides under s.8 that if the parties have not agreed price, or arranged a method for fixing price, or previously dealt with each other so that there is a price level in existence, then the buyer is bound to pay a reasonable price. This will usually be the market price. A similar rule applies in relation to those contracts which are covered by the Supply of Goods and Services Act 1982. The most difficult situation to overcome is one in which an agreement has been made to settle price at a later date.

> In *May and Butcher v. R.* 1929 Lord Buckmaster said of this situation, *"It has long been a well-recognised principle of contract law that an agreement between two parties to*

enter into an agreement in which some critical part of the contract is left undetermined is no contract at all."

It is an entirely different matter however, if machinery has been agreed which can be used to fix the price, or indeed resolve any other aspect of uncertainty.

In *Sykes (F & G) Wessex v. Fine Fare* 1967 a supplier of chickens undertook to supply a supermarket chain with between 30,000 and 80,000 birds each week over a period of one year. The agreement also provided that for a further four years the supplier would provide chickens in quantities *"as might be agreed"*. The court held that since the contract provided for arbitration to settle disagreements, the contract was not void on the basis of the uncertainty of the term as to quantity.

Since the introduction of the Law of Property (Miscellaneous Provisions) Act 1989 a contract for the sale of land must be made in writing, signed by the parties and contain all of the express terms in order to be valid.

Recently in *Pitt v. PHH Asset Management* 1993 the Court of Appeal considered the validity of a "lock out agreement" entered into by a vendor and a prospective purchaser of property under which the vendor agreed that he would not deal with any other potential purchaser for a stipulated period. The vendor had accepted the appellant's offer for a property subject to contract, but in a separate agreement promised not to consider further offers if contracts were exchanged within two weeks of draft contracts being drawn up. When the vendor broke that agreement and sold to another purchaser the appellant sued for breach of contract. The Court of Appeal held that the lock out agreement was not a contract for the sale of land and so did not have to comply with the requirements of s.2 of the Law of Property (Miscellaneous Provisions) Act 1989. Furthermore the agreement had all the characteristics of a binding contract and thus the appellant was entitled to damages when it was broken.

The offer must not have terminated

If the offer has come to an end in some way before the offeree accepts it, the acceptance is of no legal effect for there is no longer an offer to accept. However we need to look closely at how offers once made can legally be regarded as at an end. This can occur in the following ways: where the offeror has revoked the offer; or where the offer has lapsed; or where the offer has been accepted or met with a counter offer.

Where the offeror has revoked the offer

Revocation is permissible at any time before the offeree has accepted it, and the revocation can be effective even if it is not communicated directly by the offeror, provided it is communicated through some reliable channel. However, like an offer, a revocation will only be effective when it is actually communicated by being brought to the attention of the offeree. The following cases illustrate these points.

In *Dickinson v. Dodds* 1876 an offer to sell some houses was expressed to remain open until 9 a.m. on Friday. The offeree however learnt from a reliable third party on Thursday that the offeror had negotiated a sale to another purchaser. This was held to be sufficient to amount to a revocation .

In *Byrne & Co. v. Leon Van Tienhoven & Co.* 1880 an offer to sell tin plate was received by the offeree on 11 October, and immediately accepted by telegram. The offeror however had posted a revocation which the offeree received on 20 October. It was held the revocation was only effective when actually received, and was therefore too late.

Does actual receipt mean physical delivery to the business premises of the offeree or must it in addition be opened and read? The House of Lords has suggested that it will be effective even if it has not been opened, provided that it would have been opened, *"if the ordinary course of business was followed"*. This comment, which was made in *Eagleshill Ltd. v. J Needham (Builders) Ltd.* 1972 makes clear that a business which for whatever reason fails to promptly deal with its mail may nonetheless find itself bound by the contents of any letters of revocation it has received. The *Blackpool and Fylde Aero Club* case referred to previously, provides a further illustration of the possible consequences of failing to deal with mail promptly.

If the offeror seeks to revoke an offer made to the world at large, although there is no decided case on the point, it is likely that the revocation can be effected by using the same publicity as that afforded to the original offer. For instance if a new supermarket which is to open next week advertised in the local paper that the first twenty customers taking goods to the checkout on opening day would receive a free bottle of champagne, then a further advertisement in the same paper informing the public that no champagne will be available should be a sufficient act of revocation. It may however do little for business goodwill.

Sometimes an offeror may seek to revoke the offer after the offeree has started to perform the act required by the offeror, but has not yet completed it. Suppose for example that in an attempt to increase the sales, a national newspaper offers £100,000 to the first person to produce a pollution free petrol engine by a certain date. Before this date the newspaper, which is in financial difficulties announces that it is withdrawing its offer. In the meantime an engineer has made considerable progress on a pollution free engine design. It seems that the revocation will not be effective as regards the engineer, on the grounds that the offer carried with it an implied undertaking that it would remain open until the specified date, and that in any event once the engineer starts to carry out the work he has accepted the offer which cannot thereafter be revoked.

Where the offer has lapsed

An offer will lapse automatically in the following circumstances:

- after a stated time limit for which it was to be held open has passed;
- if there is no such time limit, after a reasonable time;
- if the situation on which it was based has fundamentally changed, as for example where the property which has been offered for sale has been destroyed by fire, or has been stolen before acceptance occurs;
- where the offeror has died, if this is known to the offeree before acceptance. If the offeree is unaware of the offeror's death the latter's estate will be bound by the contract.

There is no legal obligation on an offeror to keep the offer open for any particular length of time, unless some separate contract has been entered into between the offeror and the offeree to this effect.

Characteristics of a Valid Acceptance

Acceptance is defined as the unconditional assent to all the terms of the offer. As we have already seen a conditional acceptance will occur when a potential purchaser of land agrees to buy it subject to contract. This is acceptance subject to happening of a future event which may or may not occur, and is not therefore binding.

The following points provide an indication of how to determine whether an acceptance is valid.

It must be unconditional

It is surprisingly common to find people believing that they have accepted the offer, when in fact they have made a fresh offer themselves by accepting on conditions. The general position regarding the need for unconditional assent is as follows:

- a conditional acceptance will constitute a counter offer. Thus a conditional acceptance does not complete the transaction but rather continues the negotiations;

- a counter offer both rejects and extinguishes an original offer.

In *Hyde v. Wrench* 1840 the defendant offered his farm to the plaintiff for £1,000. The plaintiff replied offering £950. The defendant subsequently rejected this, so the plaintiff purported to accept the original £1,000 offer. It was held that there was no contract since the original offer had been extinguished by the counter offer. Although expressed as an acceptance, it was in fact a fresh offer;

- any alteration to the terms of the offer will render the acceptance invalid.

For instance in *Northland Airlines Ltd. v. Dennis Ferranti Meters Ltd.* 1970 which involved negotiations for the purchase of an aircraft by Northland from Ferranti, a telegram from Ferranti stated, *"confirming sale to you - aircraft - £27,000. Winnipeg. Please remit £5,000 for account of . . . "* to which Northland replied by telegram, *"This is to confirm your cable and my purchase - aircraft on terms set out in your cable. Price £27,000 delivered Winnipeg. £5,000 forwarded to your bank in trust for your account pending delivery. Balance payable on delivery. Please confirm delivery to be made 30 days within this date. "* This was held by the Court of Appeal to be a counter offer, for it contained new terms provisions regarding delivery, and payment of the deposit in trust rather than outright, so that it did not transfer to the seller until physical delivery had occurred;

- in commercial dealings between parties each trading on their standard terms, the terms which apply to the contract will often be those belonging to the party who fired the last shot. This situation has become known as the 'battle of the forms'.

In *Butler Machine Tool Co. v. Ex-Cell-O Corporation (England) Ltd.* 1979 the plaintiffs offered to sell a machine tool to the defendants in a quotation. This contained a price variation clause, which by means of a specific formula enabled the plaintiffs to raise the quoted price between contract and delivery if their own costs rose. The defendants ordered the goods but on their own standard terms which did not include a price variation clause. The plaintiffs, on receipt of the order form, signed and returned an acknowledgement slip which it contained. The plaintiff's costs rose considerably between contract and delivery. The Court of Appeal regarded the defendant's order as a counter offer, and the return of the acknowledgement slip as the plaintiff's acceptance. The contract between them did not therefore contain a price variation clause.

The acceptance must be communicated

It is open to the offeror to stipulate the method by which acceptance may be made. If no stipulation is made, anything that achieves communication will suffice; words, writing or conduct. If it is clear that the offeror demands a particular method of acceptance only, then no other method will be effective. In most cases however, the offeror is likely to do little more than to give a general indication of the form of acceptance to be used. Where this occurs but the offeree adopts a different method of acceptance which is as quick or quicker than the specified method, the acceptance will be effective, since no disadvantage will have been caused to the offeror.

> Consequently the Court of Appeal in *Yates Building Co. v. R J Pulleyn & Son (York)* 1976 held that an acceptance by means of ordinary post was effective, despite the offeror directing that registered post or recorded delivery should be used.

Given the need for positive action in communicating, it follows that silence can never amount to an effective acceptance of the offer. This holds true even if the parties have, in advance, agreed upon such procedure. For instance, if following an interview, an employer says to the interviewee that the job is his or hers if they hear nothing from the employer in the next five days, the interviewee agrees this arrangement, and the five days elapse without word from the employer, a binding contract will not have come into existence. What the law requires is some positive act.

> In *Felthouse v. Bindley* 1862 an uncle wrote to his nephew offering to buy the nephew's horse for £30.15s. and stating *"If I hear no more about him I shall consider the horse mine at that price"*. The nephew gave instructions to the defendant, an auctioneer, not to sell the horse as he intended it for his uncle. The defendant inadvertently sold the horse, and the uncle sued him in the tort of conversion. The court held that action must fail. The horse had not become the uncle's for there was not a contract.

The existence of this common law principle did not in the past act as a disincentive to curb the practice of inertia selling, and it was not until the passing of the Unsolicited Goods and Services Act 1971 (as amended) that the practice was effectively controlled. Inertia selling involves sending goods by post to recipients who have not requested them. Usually an accompanying letter will indicate that if the goods are not wanted they should be returned, but that if the recipient retains possession of them beyond a stated period (usually between seven and twenty one days) this will be treated as acceptance, and payment should then be made. Prior to 1971 this type of 'hard sell' was widespread: it is an example of the way in which the less scrupulous try to take advantage of the public's absence of legal knowledge and awareness. The 1971 Act provides that the recipient of unsolicited goods can treat them as an unconditional gift after six months have elapsed. The period is reduced to thirty days if the recipient serves notice on the sender asking that that goods be collected and the sender fails to do this .

There are two circumstances in which acceptance can operate without communication occurring at the same time, firstly in cases where the post is used to create the contract and secondly where the nature of the offer makes formal notification of acceptance unrealistic.

Transactions using the post

Transactions effected by means of correspondence in the form of letters, fax's, invoices, quotations and share applications are obviously very common in commercial life. From a practical standpoint a business organisation will wish to keep records of its business activities, and the use of written correspondence is an effective way of achieving this.

Where the post is used there will always be a period during which the letter is in transit when the person to whom it is addressed is unaware of its contents. In the case of an offer or revocation of an offer made by post the communication is effective only when it is received by the party to whom it is sent. However, in the case of an acceptance by post the courts have laid down a rule that the letter is effective at the time and place of posting, provided it was correctly addressed and pre-paid. This rule applies even if the letter of acceptance is lost or destroyed in the post.

> The case of *Henthorn v. Fraser* 1882 illustrates the practical application of the post rules. Fraser offered to sell some houses to Henthorn and gave him fourteen days to consider. The following day Fraser decided the price he had quoted was too low and wrote to Henthorn revoking the offer. After the letter of revocation had been posted but before he had received it, Henthorn decided to buy the houses, and posted his letter of acceptance at 3.50 p.m. It was held that a binding contract had come into existence at 3.50 p.m. The letter of revocation was ineffective, for it had arrived too late.
>
> This position was confirmed in the case of *Brinkibon Ltd. v. Stahag Stahl und Stahlwarenghandel* 1983. The parties had contracted using telex facilities. The plaintiffs were in London and the defendants in Vienna. The acceptance was telexed from London to Vienna. The defendants were alleged by the plaintiffs to be in breach of contract and the plaintiffs sought leave to serve a writ on the defendants. Since the defendants were outside the jurisdiction of the English Courts, having their business in Austria, the only way the writ could be served under the rules of the Supreme Court was if the contract had been made in England. The House of Lords held that the contract had been made in Vienna.

It is, of course, open to the parties to vary these rules if they wish to do so, and it may be prudent for an offeror to stipulate that an acceptance in writing which is posted to him shall not be effective until it is actually received. It is common to find terms in standard form business contracts to this effect, and the courts seem willing to infer a variation of the post rules whenever possible.

> In *Holwell Securities Ltd. v. Hughes* 1974 an option (offer) provided that it should be exercisable *"by notice in writing"*. The court held that this requirement effectively excluded the postal rule and that actual receipt of the letter of acceptance was necessary to conclude a contract.

Sometimes the circumstances of the offer are such that the courts will regard conduct which occurs without the knowledge of the offeror as a sufficient method of acceptance. Although in a sense this is not the same as silence, from the offeror's point of view it amounts to the same thing, since if the offeree does not have to make contact with the offeror, the offeror remains in the dark. Where an offer has been made to the public at large the courts may take the view that the offeror could not possibly have expected to receive an acceptance from every person who has decided to take up the offer. This would be a commercial nonsense.

> In *Carlill v. Carbolic Smokeball Co.* 1893 the defendant company advertised a medical preparation which they manufactured, and claimed in the advertisement that they would pay £100 reward to anybody who contracted *"the increasing epidemic of influenza"* after purchasing and using the product as directed. The advertisement added that £1000 was deposited with the Alliance Bank *"showing our sincerity in the matter"* The plaintiff purchased a smokeball, used it as directed, then caught influenza. She sued for her £100 reward. The court held that the advertisement constituted a firm offer intended to be legally binding, since the bank deposit indicated an intention to meet claims, the offer could be made to the public at large, and acceptance of the offer in such circumstances could be implied by the conduct of those like the plaintiff, who performed the stated conditions. In consequence the company was held liable.

Consideration

Under English law the simple contract has always been seen in terms of a bargain struck between the parties. The bargain is arrived at by negotiations and concluded when a definite and certain offer has been made which has been met with an unequivocal acceptance. Millions of transactions of this kind are made each day.

Making an agreement, as we have already seen, involves giving undertakings or promises. The offeror makes his promise, and indicates what the offeree must do in return. For instance the seller of goods undertakes to transfer ownership in the goods, and specifies the price to be paid by the buyers for acquiring ownership. The employer indicates the type of work the employee will be required to perform, and promises a certain wage rate or salary for doing it. The idea of a contract as an exchange of promises is fundamental to an understanding of the simple contract. We have already encountered a basic definition of a contract as being a legally enforceable agreement. There are others however. A definition provided by Sir Frederick Pollock, a leading legal writer, described the contract as *"a promise or a set of promises which the law will enforce"*. Pollock was seeing the 'agreement' of our first definition as something always made up of promises.

Bilateral and unilateral contracts

If promises are exchanged the contract is said to be *bilateral*. This is the most common type of arrangement. For instance, if a partnership offers a person a place in the business if they are prepared to contribute £5,000 to the capital of the business, and the prospective partner undertakes to do so the contract is a bilateral one. If however the offeror, rather than requiring a promise in return requires of the offeree some other act, then the contract is said to be *unilateral*. An example of a unilateral contract occurs where a company promises to make payment or provide goods to any of its customers who collect a certain number of tokens from buying the company's products. Petrol companies frequently use this type of device to compete with their rivals, so that by the time a customer has purchased a specific quantity of petrol they become entitled to items such as glasses or cutlery. The customer has made no promise to the garage, but is certainly entitled to the advertised items if he satisfies the requirements stipulated by the petrol company to qualify for the 'gifts'.

Executory and executed consideration

Consideration, and hence the contract itself, is said to be *executory* where the promises that have been made are to be performed in the future. An example is an agreement whereby the seller promises to deliver goods next week, and the buyer agrees to pay for them on delivery. Consideration is said to be *executed* where in return for a promise the offeree provides the required consideration which also acts as acceptance of the offer. This would occur, for instance, in the case of a member of the public who provides the Post Office with information that leads to the conviction of those responsible for an armed robbery at a sub-post office, where the Post Office has offered a reward for such information.

An agreement in which the consideration exchanged is entirely executory is fully enforceable, although legal action for breach of contract can only be commenced after the date for performance has passed, or if before this time one of the parties has made clear that they will not perform their obligations when they fall due.

There are a number of important principles which apply to consideration and we now need to examine them in more detail.

Consideration is needed to support all simple contracts

In the absence of valid consideration passing between the parties the general rule is the agreement they have made will be of no legal effect. If however their agreement is expressed in the form of a deed, the absence of a valuable promise made by the promisee to the promisor does not invalidate the contract. If a person executes a deed under which he promises to make a payment or transfer property to someone else a future date, the promise will bind him, and be enforceable by the promisee, despite the absence of any consideration provided by that person.

Consideration need not be adequate but must have some value

The word *adequate* in this context means equal to the promise given. The principle of adequacy of consideration has developed to cope with contractual disputes in which one of the parties is arguing that the contract is bad because the value of the consideration provided by the other party is not the economic equivalent of the value of the promise given in return.

The courts are not prepared to defeat an agreement merely on the grounds that one of the parties has, in effect, made a bad bargain. Bad bargains are a fact of commercial life. A deal that is struck where one of the parties has entered it in haste, or without proper enquiry, or has been swayed by convincing salesmanship, may be bitterly regretted subsequently, but it is certainly not possible in such circumstances to escape liability on the grounds that "I gave more than I got". Consequently there is no relief for the business or the individual who is at the receiving end of a hard bargain. For instance, suppose a company is in need of a specific item of machinery without which the manufacturing process cannot function. It eventually locates suitable machinery owned by the seller, with whom the company negotiates to make a purchase. The seller is aware of the company's pressing need, and responds by raising the price to a figure well beyond the usual selling price. The company agrees to buy at this price, but before receiving delivery discovers another machine of the same type which is available from an alternative supplier at the usual selling price. Can the company escape from its original contract on the grounds that the cost of the machinery was well in excess of the usual market price, and therefore that the consideration it will receive (the machinery) is not adequate to sustain the promise of payment it has made? The answer is clearly no. The parties fixed their price by agreement. The company received what it wanted, and the price level merely reflected the sellers bargaining strength and the buyers urgent need.

> The case of *Haigh v. Brooks* 1839 provides a useful illustration of the idea of the bargain taken to its most extreme position. The plaintiffs were owed large sums of money by a third party, and the defendant agreed to guarantee these debts. He later asked the plaintiffs if they would cancel the guarantee. This they agreed to, provided that in return the defendant would pay off certain debts they owed. He agreed, and the guarantee was returned to him. On examination the defendant discovered that because the written guarantee failed to meet certain statutory requirements it was unenforceable, and indeed always had been. He refused to pay the debts on the grounds that all he had received in return was a worthless piece of paper. The court held that the agreement was binding. Even though the guarantee was legally invalid the defendant had received what the bargained for - his release from the supposed liability. Lord Chief Justice Denman remarked, *"The plaintiffs were induced by the defendant's promise to part with something they might have kept, and the defendant obtained what he desired by means of that promise"*.

However apparently insignificant the consideration may be, as long as it has some discernible value it will be valid.

> In *Chappell and Co. Ltd. v. Nestlé Co. Ltd.* 1960 the defendants, as part of a sales promotion, offered a record at a reduced price if their chocolate bar wrappers accom-

panied the payment. The plaintiffs held the copyright in the record, and argued that the royalties they were entitled to should be assessed on the price of the record plus the value of the wrappers, which the defendants in fact simply threw away when they had been received. The House of Lords agreed with the plaintiffs, seeing the subsequent disposal of the wrappers as irrelevant, since each wrapper in reality represented the profit on the sale of a bar of chocolate, and was therefore part of the consideration.

Adequacy is not determined solely by economic criteria. It is enough, for instance, that the promise is a promise to refrain from doing something which the promisor is legally entitled to do. It may be a promise not to take legal proceedings, or not to exercise a legal right such as a right of way. Previously we considered the case of *Pitt v. PHH Asset Management Ltd.* 1993 where the Court of Appeal held that a lock out agreement negotiated by a vendor and a prospective purchaser of property constituted a binding contract. The court found that the contract was supported by valuable considertation namely the removal of the purchaser's threat to seek an injuction to prevent a sale to another buyer and the purchaser's further pressure to exchange contracts on the purchase of the property within a two week period. Even where the promise is related to a positive act the act may have little to do with anything capable of economic valuation, yet still be good consideration in the eyes of the law. A parent may undertake to pay a sum of money to a son or daughter in the event of them marrying, or graduating, and the marriage or graduation will be valid consideration in these circumstances.

Moreover it is not necessary that the promisor should obtain direct personal benefit from the consideration provided by the promisee. Thus a parent's promise to a son or daughter to pay them £10,000 to help them set up in business is enforceable if the business is established, whether or not the parent has a financial stake in it.

The question of whether a forbearance will operate as adequate consideration may in particular cases be of some concern to those engaged in business and commercial activity. Suppose for example that the owner of the only retail travel agency in a small town is approached by a larger company, with a number of agencies in the area. The owner is told that in consideration of the payment of £30,000 by him to the company, it will not set up a competing business in the town. Would this be a valid agreement? In *Thorne v. Motor Trade Association* 1937 Lord Atkin, commented, *"it appears to me that if a man may lawfully, in the furtherance of business interests, do acts which will seriously injure another in his business he may also lawfully, if he is still acting in the furtherance of his business interests, invite that other to pay him a sum of money as an alternative to doing the injurious acts".*

Consideration must be sufficient

Consideration is treated as insufficient, and therefore incapable of supporting a contract, when it involves the promisor undertaking to do something he is already obliged to do legally. The rationale here is that since the promisor is bound to carry out the promise anyway, there can be no true bargain in using performance of this promise to support another contract. Consideration is insufficient where the promisor has an existing contractual or public obligation to carry out the promise offered as consideration.

> In *Stilk v. Myrick* 1809 a promise by a ships captain to pay sailors an additional sum for working the ship on the return voyage was unenforceable, even though they had to work harder due to the desertion of two crew members. The court found that their existing contracts bound them to work the ship home in such circumstances, thus they had provided no new consideration to support the promise of extra wages.

In dramatically changed circumstances it may be possible to show that a fresh contract has been negotiated.

In *Williams v. Roffey Bros. & Nicholls (Contractors) Ltd.* 1990 the defendants had a contract with a housing association for the refurbishment of a number of flats. They subcontracted the joinery work to the plaintiff. After performing most of his obligations under the contract the plaintiff found himself in financial difficulties, for the agreed price of £20,000 was too low. The defendants were anxious for their contract with the housing association to be completed by the agreed date, since under a penalty clause they would suffer financially for late completion. The defendants met the plaintiff and agreed to pay him an additional £10,300 for completion of the joinery work. He then carried out most of the remaining work, but refused to complete it when the defendants indicated that they would not pay him the additional agreed sum. They argued that he was under a contractual obligation to carry out the work arising from the original contract. He had given no new consideration for the promise of extra payment.

The Court of Appeal held that the new agreement was binding on the defendants. By promising the extra money they had received a benefit, namely the avoidance of a penalty payment, or alternatively the need to employ another sub-contractor. This benefit was consideration to support the new agreement even though the plaintiff was not required to any more work than he had originally undertaken. The court approved the decision in *Stilk v. Myrick*, however on its facts the Williams case seems to suggest that the courts are now prepared to take a more liberal approach in their willingness to recognise a fresh contract and what can be properly regarded as good consideration.

Of further relevance to the question of how to assess sufficiency is the old common law principle that payment of a lesser amount to a creditor than the full debt cannot discharge the debtor from liability for the full amount even though the creditor agrees it, and accepts the lesser amount. This is known as the rule in *Pinnel's Case* 1602. It is based upon the view that there can be no real bargain in a person agreeing to accept a lesser sum than they are legally entitled to. But if the varied agreement contains an additional element, such a promise to pay the reduced sum earlier than the date on which the full debt is due, then provided the creditor agrees it, this will be binding. It may be of considerable commercial advantage to receive a smaller amount immediately than have to wait for the full sum, where, for example, the creditor is experiencing cash flow problems.

In addition to early payment of a reduced amount if agreed by the creditor, there are certain other exceptions to the rule in Pinnel's case. They include:

- Substituted performance. This arises where the creditor accepts some other form of consideration instead of money, such as the delivery of goods. Alternatively payment of a lesser sum together with an additional element, such as a promise to repair the creditor's car, would suffice.

- Payment of a lesser sum by a third party. Such an arrangement operates to discharge the full debt.

- A creditor's composition. This occurs where two or more creditors whose full debts cannot be met by the debtor agree between themselves to accept a reduced payment, and the debtor pays this to each of them. Such an arrangement is an alternative to bankruptcy proceedings, or a winding up, and usually it will involve the debtor paying off the debts according to a fixed percentage, for instance, 50p in the £. Where a composition is made, creditors are precluded from subsequently pursuing the debtor for the outstanding amount.

- Payment of a lesser sum where the debtor is disputing the value of the work that has been performed, and the creditor accepts the reduced amount. The reason why the creditor is bound by such an arrangement is that if the dispute were to be resolved by court action, the court might determine the value of the work performed as worth even less than the debtor has offered to pay, hence accepting the reduced sum may be seen as a new bargain.

Performance of a public duty as a means of furnishing consideration is insufficient to support the contract.

> This is demonstrated in the case of *Collins v. Godefroy* 1831. The plaintiff had received a *subpoena* (a court order) to give evidence in court. He then agreed with the defendant to give the evidence in return for his expenses. The court held that there was no contract for the payment of expenses, as the promise of payment was not supported by sufficient consideration. The plaintiff was under an existing duty to give evidence.

However if the promisor performs some act beyond the public duty, this will operate as valid consideration.

> In *Harris v. Sheffield United F C* 1987 the football club challenged its contractual liability to pay for the policing of its football ground during home matches. It was held that the contract between itself and the police authority was valid. The number of officers provided was in excess of those who would have been provided had the police simply been fulfilling their public obligation to keep the peace and prevent disorder.

Consideration must be legal

If it is illegal the whole contract will be invalidated.

There are two classes of illegal contract, those existing under the common law and those made illegal by Parliament. Illegality at common law arises in cases where the contract is regarded as being contrary to public policy, for example contracts involving sexual immorality, contracts involving the commission of crime and contracts associated with corruption in public life. In these cases it is the moral wrongdoing associated with them that has lead the judiciary to regard the nature of the promises being exchanged between the parties as unlawful and thus unenforceable. Amongst those contracts rendered illegal by parliament are agreements made between the suppliers of goods to refuse to sell to retailers who are not prepared to comply with minimum resale price arrangements under the Resale Prices Act 1976 such arrangements, by means of which retailers are effectively blacklisted, are regarded by Parliament as morally reprehensible, and thus illegal. It is however the case that both Parliament and the judiciary also recognise further classes of contracts which whilst not unlawful, are nonetheless void and unenforceable because their effects are regarded as undesirable for social or economic reasons. Contracts falling within this category are not therefore tainted by being regarded as morally reprehensible. They include contracts in restraint of trade. The question of illegality and public policy is considered later in the chapter. It should be noted that attempting to enter into an illegal contract may itself give rise to criminal liability.

Consideration must not be past

A party to contract cannot use a past act as a basis for consideration. Therefore, if one party performs an act for another, and only receives a promise of reward after the act is complete, the past act would be past consideration. What is required is that the promise of one of the parties to the alleged contract is given in response to the promise of the other. If an act is carried out with no promise of reward having been made, it will be treated as purely gratuitous.

In *Roscorla v. Thomas* 1842 the seller of a horse, after the buyer had purchased it, promised the buyer that it was sound and free from vice. It was not, and the buyer sued the seller on the promise. The action failed. The promise was supported by no new consideration.

The principle of past consideration has relevance in business dealings for it is common to find statements that amount to promises being given after the contract is concluded, for instance car salesmen giving undertakings after the customer has bought the vehicle and builders making claims about their properties to purchasers moving into the new house.

There are exceptions to the rule:

- where the work has been performed in circumstances which carry an implication of a promise to pay.

In *Re Casey's Patents, Stewart v. Casey* 1892 the joint owners of a patent agreed with Casey that he should manage and publicise their invention. Two years later they promised him a third share in the patent, *"consideration of your services as manager"*. The court rejected the view that this promise was supported by past consideration from Casey. The request to him to render his services carried an implied promise to pay for them. The promise of a third share was simply the fixing of the price.

By way of contrast in *Re Magrath* 1934 Durham County Council agreed with its treasurer in 1931 to pay him an additional £700, representing extra work he had carried out between 1920 and 1925, but which had not been recognised in his salary. The payment was successfully challenged as being unlawful, for it was not supported by consideration, thus making the payment a gratuity to the treasurer. The payment of gratuities to council officers is illegal. Council members who had voted for the payment were surcharged. Lord Maugham stated: *"It is, I think, clear that the local authority cannot out of public moneys give gratuities to their officers and servants over and above their fixed salaries and wages... Different considerations might well apply to a case where the officer or servant was asked to perform extra services in respect of a specified job or undertaking, on the understanding that as soon as the work was complete the authority would determine the amount of his special remuneration"*.

- where a debt, which has become unrecoverable by operation of the limitation period (i.e. statute barred) is revived by a subsequent acknowledgement of it by the debtor, which is made in writing. In such circumstances the Limitation Act 1980 states that no consideration of any kind need be sought to enforce the debt;

Only the parties to the agreement who have provided each other with consideration can sue on the contract. A person who has provided no consideration does not have the right to sue on the contract, for that person is not a party to it. This principle is known as privity of contract.

Intention to Create Legal Relations

Having established the existence of a valid agreement supported by consideration, a contract may still fail unless it is able to satisfy a further legal test. The additional requirement is that the parties intended their agreement to have legal consequences. Many agreements are made in which it is abundantly obvious from the context of the event that it was never in the contemplation of the parties to bind themselves legally. How then can a court discriminate between those arrangements when the parties did intend their agreement to be legally enforceable, and those where this was not the intention? To answer this question the court will look at all the available evidence, and in particular whether the parties have expressly indicated their intention. For instance committing an agreement into written form may suggest a more formal type of relationship.

Common law presumptions regarding intention

At common law certain presumptions regarding intention are applied by the courts. If the subject matter of the agreement is of a social or domestic kind, where the context of the agreement or the relationship between the parties is such as to suggest an absence of full legal commitment, then the courts will presume there was no intention to create a contract. This does not mean, for example, that it is impossible for members of the same family to contract each with the other, and certainly many families are participants in joint business ventures such as partnerships which are founded on a contractual relationship. Rather it is simply a requirement of the common law that there is clear evidence of such an intention. This must be sufficient to rebut the presumption that the parties did not intend to contract.

> Thus in *Snelling v. John G. Snelling Ltd.* 1972 the court had to identify the nature of an agreement between the plaintiff and his two brothers, who together were all directors of the defendant company. Each of them had provided loans to the company, and when they took a further loan from a finance company the brothers agreed not to reduce their own loan until the amount borrowed from the finance company had been repaid. By a separate agreement made between the three of them they undertook that if any of them resigned voluntarily as a director before repayment to the finance company had been made, repayment of the loan to the defendant company would be forfeited. The plaintiff voluntarily resigned and sued the company for the return of his money. The court held that the agreement between the brothers was intended to create legal rights, not least because it had emerged out of strong disagreements between the brothers.

Commercial transactions

In relation to commercial contracts the courts will presume an intention that they are intended to be legally binding. So whenever there is a business dimension to the agreement the only way in which it is possible to prevent the judicial presumption from operating is to indicate clearly that the agreement is not intended to be a contract. The inclusion of the phrase *"binding in honour"* on a football coupon was held by the court in *Jones v. Vernons Pools Ltd.* 1938 to amount to clear evidence that there was no intention to create a contract.

> In *Rose and Frank Co. v. Crompton Bros* 1923 a written agreement entered into by two commercial organisations included the following clause *"This arrangement is not entered into, nor is this memorandum written , as a formal or legal agreement... but... is only a definite expression and record of the purpose and intention of the ... parties concerned, to which they each honourably pledge themselves"*. This clause, the court held, was sufficient evidence to overturn the presumption that the commercial agreement was intended to be legally binding.

Since 'honour clauses' have the effect of making an otherwise legally enforceable agreement unenforceable by means of court action, they need to be treated with some care. There may appear to be sound reasons for their use in the right circumstances, but the inability to bring a claim for breach of the terms of the agreement before the courts does have the effect of leaving the parties commercially vulnerable. Suppose such a term is included in an agreement between the sole supplier of a particular type of goods and a customer who makes his profits form reselling these goods. The customer has no legal protection against the supplier unilaterally determining the agreement, leaving the customer with orders that cannot be met and the task of finding a new type of business. Of course the supplier may be left with a large quantity of goods he will have to find new outlets for. This may be difficult or even impossible at short notice, however he will be unable to recover his losses by legal action.

Clauses ousting the courts jurisdiction and arbitration clauses

It is important to bear in mind that a term which attempts entirely to exclude the court's jurisdiction will be void on the grounds that its effect would be to prevent a court from even determining the preliminary issue of the nature of the agreement itself. It is quite legitimate however to insert an arbitration clause into the contract. Arbitration clauses are a common feature of business agreements, for they provide a dispute solving mechanism which is generally cheaper, quicker and more private than court proceedings. The rights of consumers as regards agreements they have entered into which contain arbitration clauses are now protected under the Consumer Arbitration Agreements Act 1988. The Act provides that where a consumer has entered into a contract which provides for future differences between the parties to be referred to arbitration, the arbitration arrangements cannot be enforced against him unless, under s.1:

(a) he has consented in writing after the difference has occurred to the use of the arbitration; or

(b) he has submitted to the arbitration; or

(c) the court has made an order under s.4. This enables the court to determine that the consumer will not suffer a detriment to his interests by having the difference determined by the arbitration arrangements rather than by court proceedings.

The court must consider all relevant matters, including the availability of legal aid (i.e. financial support provided by the State for meeting the costs of court proceedings).

A consumer is someone who enters into the contract without making the contract in the course of a business or holding himself out as doing so, the other party does make the contract in the course of a business, and if the contract is a sale of goods transaction the goods are of a type ordinarily supplied for private use or consumption.

The Act is designed to deal with contracts where an arbitration clause is being used by a business as a mechanism for preventing a dispute from being heard before the courts, so that the consumer is bound to follow arbitration arrangements which may well be weighted against him.

Collective agreements

Contractual intention is also of significance in relation to collective agreements, A *collective agreement* is one between trade unions and employers' organisations by which an agreement or arrangement is made about matters such as terms and conditions of employment. It is estimated that as many as 14 million employees within the United Kingdom are employed under contracts which are regulated in part by collective agreements. The Trade Union and Labour Relations (Consolidation) Act 1992 provides that a collective agreement is presumed not to have been intended by the parties to be a legally enforceable contract unless the agreement is in writing and contains a statement that the parties intend it to be legally enforceable. Often the statutory statement of the particulars of the employment which the employer is legally obliged to give the employee will make express reference to a collective agreement in operation within the particular employment sector involved, and this will have the effect of incorporating it into the individual contract of employment. Once this has occurred changes in the contract of employment created by re-negotiation of the collective agreement will automatically vary the individual employee's contractual relationship with the employer.

Capacity to Contract

Capacity is an expression that describes a person's ability to do something. In legal terms this covers the ability to make contracts, commit torts and commit crimes.

The general rule under English law is that anyone can bind himself by a contract, as long as it is not illegal, or void for public policy. There are however exceptions to the rule, of which the most significant are contracts made by corporations and contracts made by minors.

Corporations

The nature of corporate bodies was dealt with in Chapter 2, and it will be recalled that they are regarded as legal persons in their own right, thus enabling them to make contracts, commit torts (and some crimes), and hold land. Since they enjoy legal rights and are subject to legal obligations they can sue, and be sued, in respect of these rights and obligations.

Whilst corporations are created in different ways, for example by registration in the case of limited companies and by specific statute in the case of state corporations, they share certain common characteristics, and as far as their capacity is concerned they are all subject to the principle of ultra vires, although in the case of registered companies the Companies Act 1989 has severely limited its scope.

The Doctrine of ultra vires

A corporation must be formed with stated objectives. These are located in the documents which create the organisation: its charter, the statute which establishes it or its memorandum and articles of association. If the corporation acts outside these objectives it is said to be acting ultra vires - beyond its powers - and at common law it cannot be bound. It lacks the capacity to do anything that its stated objectives do not authorise. Equally all activities falling within these objectives can be validly achieved, for they are intra vires - within the powers. Other than in the case of a registered company, no action can be brought to enforce a contract which is ultra vires a corporation: if there is any liability it will rest with those who have authorised or carried out the ultra vires activity. The issue of ultra vires will emerge either where a corporation is using it as a defence in circumstances where it is refusing to perform its contractual obligations, or where a challenge is being brought against the corporation by someone with a legal interest in doing so, in an attempt at preventing the corporation from carrying out an alleged ultra vires act.

> In *Attorney General v. Fulham Corporation* 1921 the corporation had power by statute to operate wash-houses where its inhabitants could wash their own clothes. The corporation established a municipal laundry, acting under these statutory powers, where the washing work could be carried out by employed staff. A ratepayer challenged the legality of this action, and through the Attorney General proceedings were brought against the corporation. The court held that the statutory powers did not extend to the running of a laundry, and therefore the activity was ultra vires. An injunction was granted restraining the corporation from running it.

A further possibility is the use of ultra vires as a defence raised not by the corporation itself but by the other party.

> In *Bell Houses Ltd. v. City Wall Properties Ltd.* 1966 the objects clause in the memorandum of association of Bell Houses stated the principal object to be the developing of housing estates, but in addition it could *"carry on any other business*

whatsoever which can, in the opinion of the board of directors, be advantageously carried out by the company in connection with or as ancillary to the general business of the company ". The company entered into a transaction with City Wall Properties to introduce it to a financier who would be able to provide financial help for property development. City Wall Properties refused to pay an agreed commission of £20,000 for the work done by the company on the grounds that the transaction was ultra vires the company. Bell Houses sued. The Court of Appeal held that the company was entitled to its fee, on the grounds that the agreement was within the company's powers provided the directors honestly believed it to be advantageous to the company, in relation to its principal business objects.

Minors

The law has always sought to protect minors from the consequences of entering into transactions which are detrimental to them. The aim has been to provide minors with some protection from their lack of commercial experience, whilst at the same time recognising circumstances where it is appropriate that they should be fully accountable for the agreements they make. The result is a mixture of common law and statutory rules which seek to achieve a balance between these conflicting objectives. The expression *minor* refers to anyone under the age of eighteen, this being the age of majority under the Family Law Reform Act 1969. There are three categories of contracts which may be entered into by a minor. They are:

(a) Valid contracts, which include beneficial contracts of employment, and contracts for necessaries. A beneficial contract of employment is one which is substantially for the minor's benefit. Benefit is invariably taken to mean that the contract must include some element of training or education,although this will probably be easily established. The court will set aside a contract of employment which viewed overall is not beneficial.

In *De Francesco v. Barnum* 1890 a minor's contract of apprenticeship provided that she was to be totally at the disposal of her principal, who had no obligation to pay her. The court held the contract to be invalid, since its terms were harsh and onerous.

In *Roberts v. Gray* 1913 the defendant, a minor, with a view to becoming a professional billiards player, had entered an agreement with the plaintiff, himself a leading professional, to accompany the plaintiff on a world tour. The plaintiff spent time and money organising the tour, but following a dispute the defendant refused to go. The plaintiff sought damages of £6000 for breach of contract. The Court of Appeal held that the contract was for the defendant's benefit, being in the nature of a course of instruction in the game of billiards. The plaintiff was awarded £1500 damages.

Necessaries are defined in s.3 Sale of Goods Act 1979 as *"goods suitable to the condition in life of the minor ... and to his actual requirements at the time of sale and delivery."* This is a subjective test of the minors needs, found by reference to his economic and social status.

(b) Voidable contracts, which bind the minor until he repudiates them. This may be done before reaching majority or within a reasonable time thereafter. If a repudiation has not taken place after this time the contract becomes valid. Contracts falling within this category are those of a long term nature, such as non-beneficial contracts of employment, contracts for a lease, contracts to take shares in a company, and partnership agreements.

(c)   Contracts of what have been described as a *negatively voidable* kind, that is contracts which the minor can enforce to a certain extent, but which cannot be enforced against him. As a general principle contracts that do not come within the previous two categories fall within this one. In particular it includes contracts for non-necessary goods, and contracts in which the minor has set up in business as a trader. Originally the common law regulated the position regarding these contracts. Then the Infants Relief Act 1874 altered the common law position by providing that contracts for the repayment of money lent or to be lent, contracts for non-necessary goods, and accounts stated were, in the words of the Act *"absolutely void"*. If such a contract was ratified by the minor on reaching the age of majority a new contract was required, involving fresh consideration.

Following recommendations made by the Law Commission in 1984 concerning reform of the law in this area, the Minor's Contracts Act 1987 was enacted. The effects of the Minor's Contracts Act can be summarised as follows:

(i)   the provisions of the Infants Relief Act 1874 no longer apply (except in Northern Ireland), thus restoring the original common law position. This means that in the case of those contracts coming under the old 1874 Act, the 'absolutely void' category mentioned above, if a minor makes such a contract it (a) is binding on the other party, (b) is not binding on the minor unless ratified on reaching the age of majority, in which case it becomes binding without the need for a fresh contract. Ratification may be express or implied;

(ii)   a guarantee entered into by an adult to support a loan to a minor is enforceable against the adult guarantor. It is common to find contractual documents which require a parent or guardian to sign them if the other party to the agreement is a minor, the adult being obliged either to act as the other party in place of the minor, or act in the capacity of guarantor;

(iii) if the minor performs the contract, that is carries it out, then he is in exactly the same position as an adult would be, so the only circumstances in which he can recover money or property he has transferred is when there has been a total failure of consideration;

(iv)   property acquired by the minor under a contract which does not bind him and in which he defaults may be recovered by the other party if the court considers this to be *"just and equitable"*. Alternatively if the original property has been exchanged for other property by the minor, or he has obtained cash by selling it and the cash can be identified, the exchanged goods or cash can be recovered. This is provided for by s.3 of the 1987 Act, which allows an adult to recover money or property acquired as a result of fraud under the equitable doctrine of restitution.

Consequently the circumstances in which a claim against the minor will clearly not succeed are those in which the court would not regard it as just and equitable to exercise the powers under s.3, or where the minor has consumed the goods or otherwise dealt with them so that recovery has been frustrated. For instance, a minor who buys on credit bottles of vintage wine which are drunk at a party he holds for his friends will not be liable to compensate the unpaid seller.

The lowering of the age of majority in 1969, together with the reluctance of many organisations such as mail order companies to deal with minors has meant that the law as it affects negatively voidable contracts is no longer probably of great significance.

Defects in Contractual Agreements

So far we have considered the fundamental issues of how and when a contract is made. It would be encouraging to discover that no further contractual issues are ever likely to arise. The parties to the agreement, having met the basic legal requirements and formed their contract will simply carry out their respective responsibilities to their mutual satisfaction and performance will have been completed. This is indeed what usually happens. The contract is made and performed. Each side is satisfied. The transaction is completed.

But contracts do not always run so smoothly. They can go wrong, sometimes for technical reasons and sometimes for practical reasons. Among the more common claims that arise are the following:

- that the contract is not binding because there was not true consent given to it. Such a possibility was mentioned in the discussion of freedom of contract. It may be alleged that the contract was induced by the making of false statements, or that one or even both parties were mistaken in reaching their agreement. A further possibility is an allegation that one side exerted unfair influence over the other, or perhaps even made threats against the other;

- that the contract is invalid because its purpose is something contrary to the public interest, for instance because it imposes an unreasonable restraint upon trading freedom;

- that the obligations arising under the contract have not been performed either partially or in total, so that there has been a breach of contract;

- that some event has occurred which has brought the contract to an end, without performance having been completed.

Of these various possibilities the most frequent are claims of breach of contract. Whatever the nature of the claim may be, however, it will always involve the innocent party seeking some remedy; perhaps financial compensation, or a court order enforcing the performance of the contract, or placing the parties in the position they would have been in had the contract been carried out.

Sometimes what appears superficially to be a properly constituted contract, proves on closer examination to contain some defect which was present when the agreement was made. Certain defects of this kind the law recognises as sufficiently serious to either partially or wholly invalidate the contract. Such defects are referred to as *vitiating* (invalidating) factors, and they occur in circumstances of misrepresentation, mistake, duress and undue influence.

Misrepresentation

Before arriving at a contractual agreement the parties will often be involved in a process of negotiation. Negotiations can range over any issues which the parties think are relevant to the protection of their interests, but they are certainly likely to cover questions of payment, when and how the contract is to be performed, and what terms will be attached to it. The aim of negotiating is both to obtain information and to drive a good bargain, and negotiating skill is a valuable commodity in most areas of commercial and industrial life. Not all contracts are preceded by negotiations however, and as a general rule the more marked the imbalance in trading strength is between the parties the less likely serious negotiation of terms and conditions will be. Thus transactions between large organisations on one side, and small organisations or private consumers on the other tend to be characterised by the dominant party presenting the weaker party with a set of terms which are not open to discussion but have to be accepted in their entirety if a contract is to be made.

The nature of representations

Statements made during the bargaining process may become a part of the contract itself, that is, they may become terms of the contract and rise to an action for breach of contract if they prove untrue. But in many cases there will be no intention by the maker of the statement that the statement should be absorbed into the contract at all. It will be made merely to induce the other party to make the contract. Statements of this sort are known as *representations*. If a representation is untrue for any reason it is referred to as a *misrepresentation*, and it will be actionable. The injured party (the misrepresentee) will base a claim not on breach of contract, but on the law applicable to misrepresentation. The reason is that the misrepresentation, whilst influential in the creation of the contract, has not been incorporated as a part of it. The contract itself has not been broken, but rather an assertion that was made in advance of it. It may however be possible to satisfy the court that in the particular circumstances a representation has become a contractual term, and in that event the action brought will be a contractual one. The important distinction between representations and terms is considered in more detail later.

A representation is a statement or assertion of fact made by one party to the other before or at a time of the contract, which induces the other to enter into a contract. The statement can be in any form. Thus it can be in writing, such as a company prospectus containing details of the company's trading activities, or it can be spoken, or be implied from conduct. The definition enables us to distinguish a number of statements whose form or content excludes them from being treated as representations.

Statements of opinion

It frequently occurs that during the negotiation process statements are given which are based upon the opinion of the maker. Since the representation must be one of fact, a statement expressed as an opinion cannot become a representation. It can be a difficult task to clearly discriminate between what is, or can be fairly regarded as an issue of fact rather than opinion.

> In *Esso Petroleum Co. Ltd. v. Mardon.* 1976 Mardon took a tenancy of a filling station owned by Esso, having been given a forecast by an experienced Esso sales representative of the quantity of petrol the station could be expected to sell annually. This quantity was never reached during the four years Mardon remained as tenant, and the business ran at a loss. The Court of Appeal decided that the company had made a misrepresentation, since the sales representative's knowledge of such matters made the forecast a statement of fact rather than opinion, and the sales representative was acting in the capacity of an agent of the company. Mardon's claim for damages was successful. The misrepresentation was regarded as a negligent one, and the court also took the view that the representation amounted to a contractual warranty, that is a contractual promise. In his leading judgment Lord Denning MR commented: *"it was a forecast made by a party, Esso who had special knowledge and skill. It was the yardstick by which they measured the worth of a filling station. They knew the facts. They knew the traffic in the town. They knew the throughput of a comparable station. They had much experience and expertise at their disposal. They were in a much better position than Mr. Mardon to make a forecast. It seems to me that if such a person makes a forecast - intending that the other should act on it and he does act on it - it can well be interpreted as a warranty that the forecast is sound and reliable in this sense that they made it with reasonable care and skill. That warranty was broken. Most negligently Esso made a 'fatal error' in the forecast*

they stated to Mr. Mardon, and on which he took the tenancy. For this they are made liable in damages".

Clearly it is not possible to avoid liability for a statement which is expressed as, or is subsequently claimed to be an opinion, when the knowledge and experience of the representor in the matter is far greater than that of the representee.

Advertising and sales boasts

Although there is no rule of law which prevents such statements from amounting to representations they will be seen as no more than sales boasts, provided they are not capable of substantial verification. They do not attract any legal consequences. They are regarded simply as the over inflated belief the seller has in the product in his efforts at sales promotion. Examples include the estate agents, *'most desirable residence'*, and the carpet company's *"We cannot be equalled for price and quality"*. However to advertise that "'interest free credit is available on all items bought this month"', or that a motor vehicle has returned "31 mpg at a constant 75 mph" are clearly statements of fact. If untrue they give rise to a criminal offence under the Trade Descriptions Act 1968 as well as amounting to misrepresentations.

A false statement of law cannot constitute a misrepresentation. This is based upon the general legal proposition that ignorance of the law does not excuse an otherwise unlawful act. The assumption is that the representee knows the law, and cannot therefore rely upon a plea that he relied upon inaccurate statements of law. Of course it would be quite different if these statements were being made by his legal adviser, upon whom he is placing reliance.

A statement of future intention is not a statement of fact and is therefore not actionable. This is not so however where the statement of future intention conceals the present state of mind of the misrepresentor, which may constitute a fact.

> In *Edgington v. Fitzmaurice* 1885 the directors of a company invited a loan from the public to finance expansion. However their real intention was to use the money raised to pay off debts. This statement of intention was held to be a statement of fact which was false and actionable. Bowen LJ in the course of his judgment, remarked *"The state of a man's mind is as much a state of fact as the state of his digestion. It is true that it is difficult to prove what the state of man's mind at a particular time is, but if it can be ascertained it is as much a fact as anything else. A misrepresentation as to the state of a man's mind is, therefore, a misstatement of fact".*

It might be thought that a representation could not arise in a situation where no statements of fact are made. However, although generally a non-disclosure cannot amount to a representation, there are some important exceptions to this rule. In contracts *uberrimae fidei* (of the utmost good faith) duties of full disclosure are imposed.

The obligation of disclosure under such contracts is based on the nature of this particular class of agreement. They are in general contracts where one party alone has full knowledge of all material facts. Insurance contracts and contracts for the sale of shares through the issue of a prospectus are examples of contracts uberrimae fidei. If full disclosure is not made in such cases the injured party can rescind the contract. Thus before entering into an insurance agreement the party seeking cover must disclose all facts which are material to the nature of the risk which is to be insured. In the case of a company issuing a prospectus, the Financial Services Act 1986 s.162 requires that the document must contain information prescribed under rules made by the Secretary for Trade and Industry (for instance the financial record of the company and details of contracts it has entered into.) A general duty of disclosure is laid down in s.163 which covers any information potential investors, or their professional advisers, would reasonably require in order to make an informed assessment of (a) the company's financial position and (b) the rights attaching to the shares to be issued. In determining what information comes within the general duty to disclose, the following matters are required by statute to be considered:

(i)   the nature of the shares and who issued them;

(ii)   the nature of those who are likely to acquire them;

(iii) the fact that certain matters (i.e. of an investment nature) may reasonably be expected to be known by the professional advisers likely to be consulted by the acquirers of shares; and

(iv)   information available to investors or their professional advisers under statute.

In contracts for the sale of land the vendor is under an obligation to disclose any defects in his title, that is in his ownership of the property, although the obligation does not apply to defects in the property itself, for instance dry rot or damp.

In relation to a contract of employment there is no duty on a job application to volunteer information which is not requested during the recruitment process which includes the completion of an application form.

> In *Walton v. TAC Construction Materials Ltd.* 1981 the complainant was dismissed after working for thirteen and a half months when the employer discovered that he was a heroin addict. During a medical inspection prior to employment the employee had answered "none" when asked to give details of serious illnesses and failed to reveal that he was injecting himself with heroin. While the tribunal decided that it was fair to dismiss him because of the deception *"it could not be said that there is any duty on the employee in the ordinary case, though there may be exeptions, to volunteer information about himself otherwise than in response to a direct question"*.

If a statement is true when made but becomes untrue before the contract is concluded, the representor will be under a duty to disclose this alteration to the other party.

> In *With v. O'Flanagan* 1936 the purchaser of a doctor's practice was able to rescind the contract because, despite being told accurately during negotiations that the annual income of the practice was £2,000, he was not informed prior to the sale, which took place some months later, that the income of the practice had fallen sharply because of an illness which prevented the doctor from working.

The Financial Services Act 1986, also deals with this possibility in relation to the issue of a prospectus. It requires the issue of a supplementary prospectus if a *"significant change"* occurs or a *"significant new matter"* arises after the issue of the original prospectus, whilst the offer for shares is still open.

Inducement

The representation must induce the person to enter into the contract. There can be no inducement in cases where the other party is unaware of the representation or does not believe the statement, or has relied on his own skill and judgment. In such cases no action will lie in misrepresentation.

> In *Attwood v. Small* 1838 during the course of negotiations for the sale of a mine, the vendor made exaggerated statements of its capacity. The buyers subsequently appointed their own experts to investigate the mine, and the agents reported back to the buyers that the vendor's statements were true. As a result the buyers purchased the mine, only to

discover that the statements were inaccurate. It was held that the buyers had no remedy in misrepresentation. They placed reliance upon their own independent investigation.

The representation need not be the sole or major inducement. It will be enough that it had a material affect upon the person's mind, in their decision to reach an agreement.

Types of misrepresentation

Actions for breach of contract and misrepresentation differ in an important respect. If a term of a contract is broken it is irrelevant to consider the state of mind of the contract breaker in establishing the existence and extent of liability. If however a mere representation has proved to be untrue and has become a misrepresentation, the effect this has on the liability of the misrepresentor depends on the state of mind accompanying it.

A misrepresentation may be made innocently, negligently or fraudulently.

A misrepresentation is innocent if the person making it had reasonable grounds for believing it to be true, and negligent where there was a lack of reasonable care taken to determine the accuracy of the statement. In contrast, a fraudulent misrepresentation is a representation which a person makes knowing it to be untrue, or believing it to be false, or which is made recklessly where the person making it does not care whether it is true or false. Thus it is a representation which is not honestly believed by the person making it, or where there has been complete disregard for the truth.

> Fraudulent misrepresentation was considered in the leading case of *Derry v. Peek* 1889. Under a private Act of Parliament a company was granted power to operate horse-drawn trams, and could run steam powered trams with the Board of Trade's consent. This the directors applied for, and in the belief that the consent would be granted, they went ahead and offered shares to the public through a prospectus that stated the company had power to run trams by steam. Shares were taken up. The consent was not given, and in consequence the company was wound up, many investors losing their money. Action was brought against the directors in the tort of deceit. The House of Lords defined a fraudulent misrepresentation as stated above, and having found that the directors believed the consent was simply a formality, held that the tort had not been committed. The directors were inaccurate but not dishonest, and inaccuracy without more is not fraud. They were not liable to pay damages.

At common law it has been possible since 1964 to claim damages in the tort of negligence for a negligent misrepresentation under the principle laid down in *Hedley Byrne v. Heller* 1964. This case provides that where there is a *special relationship* between the persons making a statement and the recipient of it, a duty of reasonable care is owed in making it. If a duty is broken damages will be available, representing the loss suffered. The 'special relationship' concept is central to the decision. The quality of this relationship was referred to by Lord Morris when he stated:

> *"Where in a sphere in which a person is so placed that others could reasonably rely on his judgment or his skill or on his ability to make careful inquiry, a person takes it on himself to give information or advice to, or allows his information or advice to be passed on to another, who, as he knows or should know, will place reliance on it then a duty of care will arise".*

The reliance placed on the statement by the recipient of it must be reasonable. In Hedley Byrne itself, a disclaimer of liability was enough to prevent reliance on a financial reference that had been given by a bank to a third party being reasonable. Following the decision in *Esso Petroleum v. Mardon* 1976 the Hedley Byrne principle has been extended to apply to a pre-contractual relationship, in addition to a non contractual relationship of the kind that appeared in Hedley Byrne.

Remedies available for misrepresentation

A variety of remedies are available to the misrepresentee. They include common law and equitable remedies, and the remedies available under the Misrepresentation Act 1967. At common law, as we have seen, damages are available in the tort of deceit for fraudulent misrepresentation, and in the tort of negligence for negligent misrepresentation. In equity *rescission* is available in any case of misrepresentation. This is a remedy which seeks to put the parties back to their pre-contractual position. If this cannot be achieved, for instance where the subject matter of the contract has been altered, lost or sold to a third party, rescission is not available. Nor can it be claimed if it would be inequitable to grant it. Thus if a person in full knowledge of the misrepresentation affirms the contract, i.e. expressly or by implication indicates that he intends to continue, the right to rescind will be lost. Affirmation can occur through delay in bringing an action.

> In *Leaf v. International Galleries* 1959 the plaintiff bought from the defendants a picture described as a Constable, and was held unable to rescind the contract some five years later when he discovered on trying to re-sell it that it was not a Constable after all. The plaintiff also argued, unsuccessfully, that the contract was affected by mistake (see later). It can be of advantage to a plaintiff to plead alternative legal arguments in this way, for if one proposition fails the other might succeed, and clearly a plaintiff would not choose to bring two separate actions, or even more, if the matter can be dealt with in one trial.

Unlike the common law remedy of damages, which are available as of right once liability has been established, rescission, being an equitable remedy, is discretionary. The court exercises this discretion in accordance with certain principles, referred to as *equitable maxims*. Essentially these principles are concerned with ensuring that in awarding equitable relief the court should be satisfied not only that the plaintiff has acted fairly, but also that the defendant will not be unfairly treated if the remedy sought by the plaintiff is granted. This is the justification for the restrictions on the granting of rescission, which have previously been referred to.

Under statute, damages are available under the Misrepresentation Act 1967 in respect of negligent and innocent misrepresentation. Under s.2(1) damages are available for negligent misrepresentation. It is a defence for the maker of the statement to show that up to the time of the contract he believed that the statement was true and that there was reasonable cause to believe this. Obviously such a belief will depend upon the steps taken by representor to verify the statement. There is an important difference between a claim brought for negligent misrepresentation under s.2(1) and a claim founded in the tort of negligence, which is that the burden of proof lies with the misrepresentor under s.2(1), but with the misrepresentee in negligence.

Under s.2(2), where a misrepresentation is a purely innocent one, damages may be awarded; however, the section requires that the party seeking relief must ask the court to rescind the contract. If the court is satisfied that grounds for rescission exist it may award damages instead, if it is of the opinion that it would be equitable to do so. The aim of this provision is apparently to cover cases where the misrepresentation is of a minor nature and give the court the discretion to award damages, whilst leaving the contract intact.

Mistake

Traditionally the courts have shown reticence in treating mistake as a ground for the avoidance of contractual liabilities. We have already seen that a contract will remain valid despite its proving to be economically disadvantageous to one of the parties because of what is, in effect, a mistake as to the value or quality of the subject matter. It is not the responsibility of the courts to interfere with such agreements where the parties openly and voluntarily make their bargain. Where goods are the subject matter of the contract the common law rule was expressed as *caveat emptor* (let the buyer beware) and despite considerable erosion of this rule, principally through the passing of legislation such as the Sale of Goods Act 1979, certain aspects of it still remain. The purchaser of an item he believes is a valuable antique has no remedy when the mistake is discovered, finding he has paid far more than the item is worth. It may of course be different if the seller made false representation before the sale. The converse is also true where an item such as a painting, which is sold by its owner for next to nothing, subsequently realises many thousands of pounds at auction for its new owner. The original owner can only lament the error of judgment made in selling it in the first place. The caveat emptor rule remains of considerable importance in private sales. It is of less significance where the seller is a business, for Parliament has sought to provide protection for consumers who buy from businesses, and will not generally permit business sellers to hide behind the caveat emptor rule.

The following types of mistake will not effect the validity of a contract:

(a)   A mistake of law.

(b)   An error of judgment about the value of the subject matter of the contract, unless a misrepresentation was made.

(c)   A mistake about the meaning of a trade term. In *Harrison & Jones Ltd. v. Bunten & Lancaster Ltd.* 1953 a buyer purchased 100 bales of 'Sree brand' kapok from the seller. Both parties believed that this type of kapok was pure, but when the buyer discovered that Sree brand was a mixture of different types of kapok he claimed that the contract was void for mistake. The court, however, held that the contract was valid, being unaffected by the mistake.

(d)   A mistake about ability to perform the contract within a certain time, e.g. in a building contract.

Despite this wide range of mistake situations which are ignored in law, there are nevertheless circumstances where the mistake is regarded as of so fundamental a nature that the courts will treat it as affecting the contract. Such mistakes are known as *operative* mistakes, and they render the contract void. The following is an outline of the types of operative mistakes which are recognised.

Mistake about the nature of a signed document

We are brought up on words of warning about care in signing documents, for good reason, since it will be no defence for the signatory to say he failed to read, or did not understand, the document. A defence known as *non est factum* (not my deed) is available, however, if the following conditions are satisfied:

(i)   that the document signed is fundamentally or radically different from the one the signatory believed it to be; and

(ii)   that the signatory exercised reasonable care in signing the document; and

(iii) that fraud was used to induce the signature.

In *Saunders v. Anglia Building Society* 1974 the House of Lords indicated the narrow limits of the defence of non est factum. The facts were that a 78 year old widow signed a document which a Mr. Lee had told her was a deed of gift of her house to her nephew. She did not read the document since, *"at the time of signing her glasses were broken."* The document in fact transferred her property to Lee, who subsequently mortgaged the property to a building society. The widow now sought to recover the deeds, pleading non est factum. The action failed. The document had been signed with carelessness, and furthermore it was not substantially different from the one she believed she was signing: they were both assignments of property.

There will sometimes be grounds other than mistake on which a person who has signed a contractual document can rely to avoid the contract. For example, in the case of consumer credit agreements such as hire-purchase agreements, the Consumer Credit Act 1974 grants a five-day period after the agreement is made within which the debtor can cancel the agreement, provided it was signed somewhere other than on the creditor's premises. Putting a signature to a contract which is void at law, such as an illegal contract, will incur no contractual liability.

Mistake as to the identity of the other party

Mistake of this kind is usually unilateral, where only one of the parties is mistaken about the identity of the other party to the contract. When this occurs the contract will be void if the mistaken party can show that the question of identity was material to the making of the contract, and that the other part knew or ought to have known of the mistake. The majority of cases in which this type of mistake has occurred involve fraud, so the requirement of knowledge of the mistake will have been satisfied, and the mistaken party will be left with the difficult task of trying to show that he would not have made the contract if the true identity of the other party had been known.

> In *Cundy v. Lindsay & Co.* 1878 the respondents, a firm of linen manufacturers in Belfast, received an order for 250 dozen handkerchiefs from a rogue called Blenkarn whose address was 38 Wood Street, Cheapside. He signed the order to make it appear that it had come from a firm called Blenkiron and Company who traded at 123 Wood Street, Cheapside. The respondents knew Blenkiron and Company to be a reputable firm, and therefore sent the goods, together with an invoice headed Blenkiron and Company, to 37 Wood Street. Blenkarn then sold the goods to the appellant, who was unaware of the fraud. Lindsay & Company were held to be entitled to the goods since their contract with Blenkarn was void. His existence was entirely unknown to them; they intended to deal only with Blenkiron and Company.

If the parties deal face to face, mistake about identity will be far more difficult to establish. In a shop, for instance, the shopkeeper presumably intends a contract with the person on the other side of the counter, irrespective of what the person calls himself.

> In *Phillips v. Brooks* 1919 a rogue called North entered a jeweller's shop where he represented himself to be a gentleman called Sir George Bullough. He purchased a ring for £450, for which he gave the jeweller a worthless cheque. The following day North sold the ring to a firm of pawn brokers. On discovering his loss later, the jeweller traced the ring to the pawnbrokers and sought to recover it from them, alleging that his original contract with North was void for mistake. The court disagreed, since the parties had dealt face to face. The contract was, however, voidable on the grounds of fraud. Unfortunately, this did not help the jeweller, as he had not taken steps to avoid the contract until after the ring had been purchased by the pawnbroker, who now has a good title (i.e. legal ownership) to it.

The expression voidable contract was considered earlier. A voidable contract, such as one induced by fraud, gives the fraudulent party ownership of the goods until the innocent party takes action to avoid the contract, for example by informing the police of the loss. If before the contract has been avoided the rogue has sold the goods to a third party who buys in good faith and is unaware of the fraud, that third party becomes the owner of the goods, and the original owner cannot reclaim them. This was the position that Phillips the jeweller found himself in.

Bilateral mistakes

The instances of mistake considered so far concern mistakes made by just one of the parties. These are consequently known as unilateral mistakes. In cases of bilateral mistakes both the parties are mistaken, either about the same thing, *common* mistake, or about something different, *mutual* mistake.

Mutual mistake

Where a mutual mistake occurs the parties are at cross purposes, and in cases of fundamental error arguably there can be no contract in existence anyway, on grounds of the uncertainty of their agreement. For example if one company agrees to sell a machine to another, and the description of it is so vague that the seller believes he is selling an entirely different machine to the one the buyer believes he is buying, there is no effective agreement within the process of offer and acceptance. The approach applied by the courts in these circumstances is an objective one.

> In *Raffles v. Wichelhaus* 1864 the buyer purchased a cargo of cotton from the seller, to arrive *"ex Peerless from Bombay"*. Remarkably there were two ships named Peerless sailing from Bombay, one in October which the buyer had in mind and one in December which the seller had in mind. The court held that no contract had been entered into. Viewed objectively the facts denied the existence of an offer and an acceptance for there was no consensus ad idem.

Common mistake

> An example of a common mistake occurred in *Couturier v. Hastie* 1856. A contract was made for the sale of some wheat which at the time was being carried on board a ship. Unknown to both parties, when they made the agreement the wheat had already been sold by the ship's captain because during the voyage it had started to overheat. The court held the contract to be void, since it was a contract of impossibility.

There are some significant exceptions to this type of claim. At common law relief from a contract affected by a common mistake will not be available where the mistake:

- *Occurs after the contract is made*. In *Amalgamated Investment & Property Co. Ltd. v. John Walker & Sons Ltd.* 1976 the defendants sold the plaintiffs a warehouse for £1.7m. The defendants knew the plaintiffs intended to redevelop the site, and both knew planning permission would be necessary. Contracts were exchanged on 25 September. On 26 September the defendants were informed by the Department of the Environment that the building had become 'listed'. This made development consent most unlikely, and without it the property was worth £200,000. The plaintiffs sought to rescind the contract. The Court of Appeal rejected the claim. There was no mistake in the minds of the parties when the contracts were exchanged sufficient to set the contracts aside;

- *Relates to quality*. An example of a mistake about quality is seen in *Leaf v. International Galleries* 1950 where the purchaser believed he was buying a Constable painting only to discover later that Constable was not the artist. The mistake was not operative, since the purchaser had received under the contract what he had bargained for, namely the painting.

A further illustration occurred in *Bell v. Lever Bros. Ltd.* 1932. Bell, who was the managing director of a company controlled by Lever Bros. Ltd., became redundant as a result of company amalgamations, and Lever Bros. Ltd. paid him, £30,000 as compensation for his loss of office. It was subsequently discovered that as managing director he had committed serious breaches of duty by secret trading and could have been summarily dismissed without compensation. Although Bell had not revealed his misconduct to the company before he received the compensation, he was not acting fraudulently because he was unaware that what he had done rendered him liable to dismissal without compensation. The company sought to recover the compensation it had paid to Bell on the grounds of mistake. The House of Lords decided that it could not do so, since the company had paid the compensation in the belief that Bell was an employee who had carried out his duties in a proper way. They were therefore mistaken about the quality of their employee, which was insufficient to give rise to an operative mistake.

Remedies

At common law

The effect of an operative mistake at common law is to render the contract void *ab initio* – from the outset. The true owner is thus entitled to the return of goods, or damages from whoever is in wrongful possession.

In equity

The position in equity is different however, for equity recognises certain types of operative mistake, which the common law does not grant relief for, in particular in cases involving mistake as to quality. The following cases illustrate the position.

In *Solle v. Butcher* 1950 the parties entered into a lease in the mistaken belief that, due to substantial improvements carried out to it, the flat being let was not subject to rent control legislation. The tenant had been paying rent at the agreed rate of £250 p.a. when it was discovered that the flat was subject to rent control. The maximum rent recoverable was £140 p.a., although if the landlord had served a statutory notice on the tenant before the lease had been executed, he would have been entitled legitimately to charge £250 p.a., the extra amount representing the value to the tenant of the improvements. The tenant claimed to the overpayment of rent. The landlord counterclaimed for possession. The Court of Appeal found itself unable to grant relief at common law for the mistake was one of quality. However exercising its equitable jurisdiction the court allowed the lease to be rescinded on condition that a new lease on the same terms at the higher rent be offered to the tenant, the new lease enabling the landlord to serve the relevant notice on the tenant.

In *Magee v. Pennine Insurance Co. Ltd.* 1969 a proposal for insurance for a motor car had been incorrectly completed without the insured's knowledge. Following a crash, a claim was made and the insurance company agreed to pay £385 which the insured was willing to accept. On discovery of the material inaccuracy in the policy however, the company withdrew their offer of payment for which they were then sued. The Court of

Appeal held that under the common law the common mistaken belief that the policy was valid was inoperative and the contract of the insurance was valid. In equity however the agreement to pay £385 would be set aside as there had been a fundamental misapprehension, and the party seeking to rescind was not at fault.

Rectification

In the context of considering equitable relief where parties to a contract have been in error, the equitable remedy of rectification is worth noting. Where it applies the court will rectify a written document so that it accords with the true agreement of the parties. For rectification to operate there must be:

(i) agreement on the particular aspect in question,

(ii) which is certain and unchanged at the time of writing, and

(iii) the writing must fail to express the agreement.

> In *Craddock Bros. v. Hunt* 1923 an oral agreement for the sale of a house expressly excluded an adjoining yard and yet the later written agreement and conveyance included the yard. The court ordered a rectification of the documents in order to express the parties' true original intention.

The equitable remedy of rectification will not be available however simply because one party has made a miscalculation and the agreement entered into does not express his intention.

> In *Riverplate Properties v. Paul* 1975 the plaintiff granted a long lease of a maisonette to the defendant and had intended that the lessee should pay half the cost of exterior and structural repairs that were required. The lease however put the entire burden on the plaintiff. The defendant believed that she was not responsible for those repairs and the plaintiff claimed for rectification or rescission of the lease. The court held that a unilateral mistake of this kind could have no impact on the terms of the lease agreed by the parties. There was no justification for equity to disrupt the transaction actually entered into and the mistake was inoperative. The error in failing to include a suitable term in the lease was the plaintiffs.

Duress and Undue Influence

The term duress at common law involves coercion of a person into making a contract by means of actual or threatened violence to them. The threat must be illegal. The plea of duress is an extremely unusual one, although it was raised in a case that was heard by the Privy Council in 1976.

> *Barton v. Armstong* 1976 involved death threats made by Armstrong against Barton, designed to force Barton to purchase Armstrong's shares in a company of which they were both major shareholders. There was evidence that Barton regarded the acquisition as a satisfactory business arrangement in any event. He subsequently sought to have the deed by which he purchased Armstrong's share declared void. By a majority the court held the agreement to be void, although the minority view was that the claim should fail. This was because it seemed that although Barton took the threats seriously, the real reason for making the purchase was commercial.

A more subtle form of improper pressure is undue influence, which equity recognises as giving the innocent party the right to rescind the contract. In some relationships a presumption of undue influence arises. This is the case where there is a fiduciary relationship, or where one person is in a position of dominance over the other e.g. parent and child, solicitor and client, doctor and patient, trustee and beneficiary. The dominant party who attempts to uphold a transaction entered into in such a relationship must rebut the presumption of undue influence by showing that he has not abused his position in any way. Evidence that the innocent party has taken independent advice will go a long way to rebutting the presumption and saving the contract.

> In *Lancashire Loans v. Black* 1934 the Court of Appeal recognised that the presumption of undue influence between a parent and a child can transcend the child marrying and leaving home. Here a married daughter, without independent advice, had contracted to pay off part of her mother's debts. The court held that the transaction could be set aside as the daughter had not exercised her free will but acted under the influence of her mother.

The courts are still prepared to recognise new relationships where the doctrine applies, for example an influential secretary companion and his elderly employee in *Re Craig* 1971, and a banker who sought to obtain a benefit from his customer in *Lloyds Bank v. Bundy* 1975.

> In *National Westminster Bank plc v. Morgan* 1985 a wife, as joint owner of the matrimonial home, had been advised to execute a second mortgage to refinance the old mortgage of the property. The advice had been given by the manager of the bank mortgagee who had assured the wife that the mortgage did not cover business debts. Although made in good faith this statement was untrue and the wife subsequently applied to have the mortgage set aside when the husband died, on the grounds of undue influence. The court held that the relationship had raised the presumption of undue influence as the manager's advice was relied on and the bank mortgagee had gained an advantage. Also the failure to suggest independent advice on these facts meant that the mortgage could be set aside on the ground of undue influence.

In modern times the courts have demonstrated an increased willingness to see the principles underlying duress and undue influence as elements in a broader principle of law which Lord Denning referred to in *Lloyds Bank v. Bundy* 1975 as *"inequality of bargaining power."* It may be useful to refer to his judgment, which is contained earlier in this chapter.

The idea of economic duress falls under this broad terminology. The following cases provide a clear illustration of situations in which the courts have been prepared to recognise economic duress.

> In *Clifford Davies Management Ltd. v. WEA Records Ltd.* two composer members of a pop group entered into an agreement with their manager to assign the copyright in all their work to him for a period of ten years, for a very small financial consideration and his promise to use his best endeavours to publish the work they composed. The Court of Appeal found that on the basis of bargaining inequality the contract could be set aside at the option of the composers. The factors cited by the court that pointed to the inequality were:
>
> • the overall unfairness of a ten year tie, supported by vague consideration offered in return by the manager;
>
> • the conflict of interest arising from the manager acting as the business adviser to the composers, whilst at the same time representing his own company's interests in negotiating with them; and

- the absence of any independent advice available to the composers, and their reliance upon the manager who exerted undue influence over them.

In *Atlas Express v. Kafco (Importers and Distributors)* 1989 the defendants were a small company involved in the import and distribution of basketware. They sold a quantity of their goods to Woolworths, and agreed with the plaintiffs, a national road carrier, for deliveries to be made by them. The plaintiffs depot manager quoted a price for deliveries based upon his guess as to how many cartons of goods would be carried on each load. In the event he overestimated how many cartons would be required to be carried on each load, and now refused to proceed with the contract unless the defendants agreed to a minimum payment for each load of £440, in substitution for the original arrangement of £1.10 per carton. Anxious to ensure the goods were delivered on time, and unable in the circumstances to find an alternative carrier, the defendants agreed to the new arrangement, but later refused to pay. The plaintiff's claim for breach of contract failed. The court took the view that the plaintiff's threat to break the contract together with their knowledge of the defendants dependency on them represented a clear example of economic duress.

The Effect of Public Policy on Contracts

We have already seen that while contracts are part of the private law, this does not mean contract making is the exclusive domain of the parties themselves, allowing them complete freedom to make whatever type of contract they choose. At common law certain types of contract are regarded as illegal on the basis that they are contrary to public policy. The list of illegal contracts has been added to by statute.

Public policy is a vague term which has never been clearly defined. The legal writer Pollock saw it as *"a principle of judicial legislation or interpretation founded on the current needs of the community."* This appears to mean that it is concerned with the public good, rather than with what is politically appropriate; and in practice public policy involves the court in applying economic, moral and other criteria to the contract in question to decide whether it is desirable in the general public interest. By these means the courts have held many types of contract to be illegal including contracts to commit criminal and tortious acts, contracts for trading with the enemy in times of war, and contracts which oust the jurisdiction of the courts.

The effects of declaring a contract illegal will vary. Sometimes a party who is unaware of the illegality will be allowed to sue on the contract, but where the parties are fully aware of the illegal nature of the transaction the court will deny them any remedy.

In *Foster v. Driscoll* 1927 a group of people entered into a partnership agreement in England, the object of which was to smuggle a ship-load of whisky into the USA. This was a violation of the prohibition laws then in force in the USA, so the partnership was illegal on the grounds of public policy, and it was held that no action could be brought in respect of any matter arising out of the agreement.

Contracts in Restraint of Trade

One aspect of common law illegality which is of particular application within the sphere of business and commerce involves contracts that are regarded as being in restraint of trade. This area of law is of sufficient importance that some types of restraints contained in a contract are regulated by statute. The essence of such a contract is that it contains an agreement by one of the parties to it to restrict that party's freedom of trade with others outside the contract in the future. What constitutes such a contract can be discovered only by applying the principles set out by the courts, and in more recent times by Parliament. These are considered below. It should be borne in mind that because the doctrine of restraint of trade is guided by considerations of public policy, the categories of contract to which it applies alter as economic and social conditions change. Examination of the law regarding restraints tends to show that what the courts and Parliament are largely seeking to prevent are practices which restrict competition to the detriment of the public.

For convenience restraints are considered below under two headings:

(a)   restraints controlled at common law; and

(b)   restraints controlled by statute.

Restraints at common law

The leading authority here is the decision of the House of Lords in the Nordenfelt case.

> In *Nordenfelt v. Maxim Nordenfelt Guns and Ammunition Co. Ltd.* 1894 the seller of a gun and ammunition manufacturing business agreed with the buyer not to manufacture guns or ammunition anywhere in the world, or compete in any way, for a period of twenty five years. Although the undertaking not to compete in any way was considered unreasonable by the court as being too wide, it was severed from the rest of the restraint, which was considered to be a reasonable protection for the buyer. The seller, who was an inventor, had a worldwide reputation in the field of munitions, and this helped to explain the length and geographical location of the restraint clause. In the course of his judgment Lord MacNaghten laid down the following principle:

> *"The public have an interest in every person's carrying out his trade freely; so has the individual. All interference with individual liberty of action in trading, and all restraints of trade themselves, if there is nothing more, are contrary to public policy, and therefore void".*

> This is a *prima facie* presumption i.e. one made on first sight. It can be rebutted where the restraint can be shown to be reasonable.

Restraints take many forms, but among the more important are the following:

- Restraints on employment. These are imposed by employers as a device to prevent employees from setting up in competition when they leave the employment.

- Restraints on the sale of a business. It is usual practice to impose a restraint on the vendor of a business to protect the goodwill that the purchaser has acquired.

- Agreements between suppliers and retailers under which the retailer agrees to sell only the supplier's goods. Most cases have involved *solus* agreements under which petrol stations have agreed to sell only the petrol and other products of a particular petrol company.

- Price fixing agreements and agreements which seek to regulate or limit supplies of goods. Such agreements are governed by statute and should be considered in the mandatory unit Business in the Economy.

As noted above, whilst there is an assumption that a contract in restraint of trade is void, if the restraint can be shown to be reasonable both in the interests of the parties to it and in the interests of the public generally, then it will be treated as valid and will survive.

Restraint on employment

An express term found in many contracts of employment is a clause which purports to restrict the freedom of the employees, on the termination of employment, from engaging in a competing business or working for a competitor for a specified period. Provided such a clause is inserted to protect a genuine proprietary interest of the employer and is reasonable in extent, the express restraint will be valid and enforceable. A restraint clause which purports to restrict the free choice of an ex-employee as to the employment options open is prima facie void as a contract in restraint of trade. Such a contract is nevertheless valid and enforceable if reasonable in the circumstances because:

(a)   the employer has a genuine proprietary interest worthy of protection such as clientele, confidential information, or trade connection; and

(b)   the restraint clause is drafted in such a way that it is no wider than is reasonably necessary to achieve the desired objective.

If the court is satisfied that the purpose of the restraint clause is no more than to prevent healthy competition then it will be declared void and of no legal effect.

> In *Strange v. Mann* 1965 the manager of a bookmakers agreed not to engage in a similar business to that of his employer within a twelve mile radius on the termination of his employment. In an action to enforce the clause, the court held that, as the bookmaker had little or no influence over the firm's clientele and in fact communicated with them mainly by telephone, the employer had no valid interest to protect. As the primary aim of the clause was simply to prevent competition it was declared void.

A distinction must be drawn between an attempt by an employer to prevent his ex-employee revealing trade secrets or lists of clients to competitors and simply preventing an ex-employee putting into practice the knowledge, skills and abilities that he acquired during his period of employment.

> In *Herbert Morris Ltd. v. Saxelby* 1916 a seven year restraint on the employee was held to be void as simply an attempt to prevent the employee making use of the technical skill and knowledge which he acquired with his employer if he took up employment with a rival firm.

> In *Forster and Sons v. Suggett* 1918, on the other hand, a covenant which was aimed at preventing the defendant divulging a secret glass making process to any rival organisation in the United Kingdom, was held to be valid and enforceable.

Having identified a proprietary interest worthy of protection, the next step is to analyse the restraint clause to discover whether it is reasonable in the circumstances. A number of factors are deserving of attention to assist in the analysis, such as the area of the restraint, the length of time it is to run and the nature of the work which the employer is attempting to restrain. The wording of the restraint clause is therefore crucial, for if it is too extensive in the geographical area of protection, or too long in time, it will be unenforceable. Each case turns on its own facts and all the circumstances are considered.

> In *Fitch v. Dewes* 1921 a lifetime restraint on a solicitor's clerk from working for another solicitor within a radius of seven miles of Tamworth Town Hall was nevertheless held to be valid. The House of Lords felt that the modest area of the restraint which the employer relied on for his clientele justified even a lifetime restraint.

In *Fellows & Sons v. Fisher* 1976 a conveyancing clerk employed by a firm in Walthamstow agreed that for five years after the termination of employment he would not be employed or concerned in the legal profession anywhere within the postal district of Walthamstow and Chingford or solicit any person who had been a client of the firm when he had worked there. Not only was the five year restraint thought to be too long, bearing in mind the large population in the areas identified, but the attempt to exclude any work in the legal profession, which would include legal work in local government and the administration of justice, was also thought to be unreasonable and the restraint was declared void.

It is crucial to the validity of a restraint clause that the employer limits its extent to protect the clientele and business locations which apply to the employee's term of employment. It would be unreasonable for an employer to attempt to prevent competition in geographical locations into which it has not yet operated.

In *Greer v. Sketchley Ltd.* 1979 the restraint clause purported to prevent the employer competing nationwide when in fact the employer's business was limited to the Midlands and London. The argument that an employer is entitled to seek protection in geographical areas in which he intends to expand, was rejected.

In *WAC Ltd. v. Whillock* 1990 the Scottish Court of Session emphasised that restrictive covenants must be construed fairly and it is *"the duty of the Court to give effect to them as they are expressed and not to correct their errors or to supply their omissions"*. Here the clause in question specifically prevented any ex-company-shareholders for two years carrying on business in competition with the company. The clause did not impose any restriction on the right of an employee to be a director or employee of another company which carried on business in competition and so could not prevent the employee/shareholder from becoming a director of a competing company.

If a restraint clause is drafted in such a way that it is reasonable in extent, then provided it does not offend the public interest it will be binding and can be enforced by means of an injunction. In practice such injunctions are rarely granted for the very presence of the clause acts as a sufficient deterrent.

In *Lawrence David Ltd. v. Ashton* 1989 the Court of Appeal emphasised that the decision whether or not to grant an interlocutory (temporary) injunction to enforce a restraint of trade clause should be taken in accordance with the principles laid down in *American Cyanamid Company. v. Ethicon Ltd.* 1975 (see later). In restraint of trade cases, the most relevant criterion is whether or not an employer would have any real prospect of succeeding in a claim for a permanent injunction at the trial.

There have also been a few exceptional cases where the courts have determined that part of a restraint clause is unreasonable but other separate parts of the clause are reasonable and would be valid and enforceable. In such circumstances, rather than declare the whole clause to be void and unenforceable, the courts have severed the unreasonable part of the contract and, provided that what remains can stand alone, declared it to be valid and enforceable.

In *Lucas T & Company v. Mitchell* 1974 the defendant salesman contracted that he should not for one year after the determination of his employment:

- solicit orders within his trading area from present customers and those whom his employer supplied during the previous twelve months; and

- deal in the same or similar goods to those that he sold.

In an action for breach of contract, the court found that two obligations were severable so that the second clause against dealing was unreasonable and void but the first clause not to solicit orders was valid and enforceable.

Restraints on the sale of a business

Where a person sells a business the buyer will usually seek some form of protection to prevent the seller setting up in competition. Restraints that are imposed in such cases are more likely to survive than those imposed on employees, since the buyer and the seller will be negotiating on an equal footing. Nevertheless if the clause is too wide it will fail.

> In *British Reinforced Concrete Engineering Co. Ltd. v. Schelff* 1921 the defendant who operated a business selling road reinforcements in the UK, sold his business to the plaintiff. In the contract of sale the seller agreed not to compete for a specified period in the *"sale or manufacture of road reinforcements"* in the UK. The defendant took employment in the same type of business working for a competitor, and the plaintiff sued to enforce the restraint clause. The court held that had the clause been confined to 'sales' it would have been valid, but to include 'the manufacture of reinforcements' made the restraint wider than was necessary, and therefore void.

Solus agreements

In the case of solus and similar agreements there is no rule of law which prevents a supplier and a dealer from entering into an agreement under which the supplier is to be the retailer's sole supplier, but the duration of such an agreement must not be for an unreasonable length of time, or the restraint will be void as being against the public interest.

> In *Esso Petroleum Co. Ltd. v. Harpers Garage (Stourport) Ltd.* 1968 Harpers Garage entered into a solus agreement with Esso for the supply of Esso petroleum to two garages owned by Harpers. They received a discount from Esso for agreeing for take only Esso petroleum and for undertaking to keep the two garages open at all reasonable hours. The House of Lords held that the restraint which tied one garage to the agreement for four years and five months was valid, but the restraint which tied the other garage to take only Esso petroleum for twenty one years, in return for a £7000 loan to assist in the purchase and improvement of the garage, was too long and therefore invalid.

Contract Terms

The terms of a contract are the obligations owed by the parties to each other under it. All contracts contain terms. In transactions involving large sums of money, or where the agreement is of a complex or technical nature, the terms are likely to be numerous and detailed. By inserting terms into the contract the parties will be trying to clarify their mutual obligations. They will be attempting to define the nature and scope of the contract, and will try to anticipate eventualities which may possibly emerge after the contract as been made but before it has been carried out. Thus they may make provision for such contingencies as shortages of labour or materials. Different types of contract obviously reflect different sets of terms appropriate to the nature and purpose of the agreement. For example if the contract involves the construction of a building or a ship its terms will seek to clearly identify the specifications involved. On the other hand the granting of a lease or tenancy will concentrate on matters such as who has responsibility for carrying out repairs, and how the property should be used. It is not only large organisations which are involved in detailed and technical contracts;

even small organisations will encounter documents such as leases when they set up in a business and seek accommodation. Clearly not all contracts contain detailed terms. In the simplest contracts terms will be single promises made by each party to the other. In more complete agreements the contract may run into many pages. A set of contract terms is given below.

Standard form contracts

Clearly it makes commercial sense to set out precisely and exhaustively the terms which are to apply to the contract, and the means used by the majority of organisations to achieve this in the standard form contract. A standard form contract is a printed document consisting of a uniform set of terms for use by an organisation as the basis upon which it trades. A standard form agreement is of advantage in business in two ways:

- it helps to save time by removing the need for the regular negotiations of terms; and

- it will seek to provide the organisation with the maximum amount of commercial protection possible, by relying on terms which are favourable to it, for instance, by enabling it to cancel the agreement in specified circumstances, raise its price in line with increases in manufacturing costs, and so on.

We have already referred to the imbalance in trading strength that frequently occurs in contract making with the dominant party dictating terms to the weaker party. We have seen that contracts, usually of a standard form kind, in which this dominance is asserted are often referred to as contracts of adhesion, for the weaker party is unable to negotiate but must simply adhere to the stronger party's terms. The danger of this type of economic oppression was pointed out by Lord Diplock in *Schroeder Music Publishing Co. Ltd. v. Macauley* 1974 when he stated:

> *"The terms of this kind of standard form of contract have not been the subject of negotiation between the parties to it, or approved by any organisation representing the interests of the weaker party. They have been dictated by that party whose bargaining power, either exercised alone, or in conjunction with others providing similar goods or services, enables him to say: "If you want these goods or services at all, these are the only terms on which they are available. Take it or leave it"."*

As we shall see, some of the more obvious abuses which were present at one time in this type of contract are now controlled by legislation; for example extortionate credit bargains by the Consumer Credit Act 1974, and exclusion or limitation of liability by the Unfair Contract Terms Act 1977.

The use of standard form agreements does not always indicate a situation of dominance by one party over the other. The standard agreement may be the basis upon which negotiations are conducted, or it may be that both sides have equal bargaining strength and both will try to insist on the use of their own form of agreement. In some areas of commercial and industrial activity standard terms are devised by organisations to represent the interests of the sector generally. For example local authorities may together produce sets of terms which they can all use in their dealings with suppliers of goods or services. In the building industry there are such arrangements. The present standard contract in use is called the Joint Contracts Tribunal (JCT) form. Where parties of relatively equal bargaining strength deal with each other over a long period of time, standard form agreements may evolve by negotiation. Far from being oppressive, this type of standard form contract provides a framework of certainty for business transactions and an appropriate division of rights and responsibilities between the parties. It may take into account possible occurrences and contingencies. The apportionment of risks under it can be linked with the insurance arrangements of the parties. Such an agreement will be designed to avoid the risk of litigation between the parties, for example by use of arbitration and liquidated damages clauses.

A standard form contract for the sale of goods is set out below.

1. (a) THIS AGREEMENT is made the   day of   19
BETWEEN   of
(referred to in this agreement as ''the seller'') and
of
(referred to in this agreement as ''the buyer'')

WHEREBY IT IS AGREED that the seller shall sell and the buyer shall purchase the goods described in condition 2 in accordance with the terms of this contract.

(b) No amendments or modifications to these conditions and, in particular, no terms or conditions of purchase of the buyer shall form part of the contract or be binding upon the seller unless expressly agreed to in writing and signed by the seller.

2. (a) Description of goods:

 (b) The description of the goods in condition 2(a) above is believed to be correct as to weights, dimensions, capacity, composition, performance and otherwise. Any error, omission or mis-statement therein (whether or not it materially affects the description of the goods) shall not annul the sale nor entitle the buyer to be discharged from the contract or to claim any compensation in consequence thereof. Provided that nothing in this condition shall oblige the buyer to accept any goods which differ substantially in any of the above-mentioned respects from the goods agreed to be sold if the buyer would be prejudiced by reason of such difference. In that event the buyer shall be entitled to rescind the contract and to claim repayment of the price, but the seller shall incur no further liability in respect thereof.

3. (a) In addition to the price of the goods, the buyer shall pay

(i) Vat or other taxes payable in respect of the goods;

(ii) the cost of insurance under condition 8; and

(iii) the cost of delivery under condition 4.

(b) The price of the goods is :
     add V.A.T :
     insurance :
      delivery :
   total amount due :

(c) Where the date of delivery specified in condition 4 is more than six months from the date of this agreement, the seller reserves the right to increase the price of the goods in proportion to any increase in costs to the seller of materials labour and other inputs between the date of this contract and the date of delivery.

(d) The buyer will pay the price of the goods and any other sums due to the seller under this contract within 30 days of the date of delivery. In the event of a failure to make payment by the due date interest at the rate of 10% per annum shall be payable on any sums outstanding.

4. (a) The delivery date is   . This date is given as way of an estimate only and the seller shall not be liable for failure to deliver on time.

    (b) Unless the seller is notified otherwise in writing at least seven days before the delivery date, the seller shall deliver the goods to the buyer's place of business. The cost of transportation and insurance up to the time of actual delivery will be paid by the buyer in accordance with condition 3.

    (c) The seller shall be entitled at its sole discretion to make partial deliveries or deliveries by instalments.

    (d) Deviations in quantity of the goods delivered (representing no more then 10% by value) from that stated in condition 2 shall not give the buyer any right to reject the goods or to claim damages. The buyer shall be obliged to accept and pay at the contract rate for the quantity of goods delivered.

5. (a) The seller reserves the right to modify the specification or design of the goods in whole or in part without prior notification to the buyer. The buyer shall accept such modified goods in performance of the contract.

    (b) The buyer shall be deemed to have accepted the goods unless within 14 days of delivery written notice is received by the seller to the contrary.

6. (a) The property in the goods shall remain with the seller until the seller has received payment in full for the goods and all other sums owing to the seller on whatever grounds.

    (b) If the buyer sells the goods prior to making payment in full for them, the rights of the seller under this condition shall attach to the proceeds of sale or to the claim for such proceeds. The buyer shall, if required to do so by the seller, formally assign any such rights.

    (c) For so long as the property in goods remains with the seller, the buyer shall store the goods separately so that they may readily be identified as the property of the seller. The seller shall during this time have the right to retake possession of the goods. For this purpose the buyer hereby irrevocably authorises the seller or his agents to enter upon any premises occupied by the buyer.

    (d) The seller may maintain an action for the price notwithstanding that property in the goods may not have passed to the buyer.

7. The goods shall be at risk of the buyer in all respects from the date of this contract or, if later, the date of manufacture by the seller.

8. Unless the buyer notifies the seller in writing to the contrary, the seller shall at the expense of the buyer insure the goods to the full replacement value thereof until the time of delivery.

9. (a) In the event that the goods supplied to the buyer fail to comply with the terms of this contract, or prove to be defective, the liability of the seller is limited to the replacement of the goods or, at the seller's option, the refund of all payments made by the buyer in respect of the goods.

    (b) Except as otherwise provided in condition 9(a), the seller shall be under no liability of whatsoever kind whether or not due to the negligence or wilful default of the seller or its servants or agents arising out of or in connection with any breach of the seller's obligations under this contract. All conditions, warranties or other terms, express or implied, statutory or otherwise, are hereby expressly excluded.

    (c) Nothing in this condition shall exclude or restrict any liability of the seller for death or personal injury resulting from the negligence of the seller or its servants or agents.

    (d) If it should be held in relation to any claim that the preceding provisions of this paragraph are ineffective, the buyer shall not be entitled to reject the goods and any damages recovered by the buyer shall be limited to the reasonable cost of remedying the breach of contract provided that the seller shall first be afforded the opportunity of itself carrying out such remedial work.

(e) Nothing in this condition or in conditions 2(b) or 4(d) shall exclude or restrict any liability of the seller for breach of its implied undertakings as to title; and, where the buyer deals as a consumer, any liability of the seller for breach of its implied undertakings as to description, quality, fitness for purpose, or correspondence with sample.

(f) In the case of transactions covered by paragraphs (4) and (5) of the Consumer Transactions (Restrictions on Statements) Order 1976 the provisions of this contract shall not affect the statutory rights of the consumer.

10. The seller shall not be liable for non-performance in whole or in part of its obligations under this contract due to causes beyond the control either of the seller or of the seller's suppliers including any Act of God, fire, flood, tempest, act of state, war, civil commotion, embargo, accident, plant breakdown, hindrance in or prevention from obtaining any raw materials or other supplies, interference by labour disputes, inability to obtain adequate labour, manufacturing facilities or energy, or any other like cause. If any such event continues for a period of more than 6 weeks, the seller may cancel this contract or vary condition 4(a) hereof by notice in writing to the buyer without liability on the part of the seller.

11. (a) The seller shall have the right to terminate this contract by notice in writing in the event of the buyer's insolvency and the buyer shall indemnify the seller against all losses and damage suffered by reason of such termination.

(b) Termination of the contract under this condition shall not affect the accrued rights of the parties arising in any way out of the contract as at the date of termination.

(c) In the event of termination under this condition the seller shall have the right to enter any business premises occupied by the buyer and recover any goods which are the seller's property.

12. In the event of cancellation of this contract by the buyer for whatever reason, the buyer agrees to pay 20% of the purchase price to the seller by way of liquidated damages.

13. The benefit of this contract shall not be assigned or transferred by the buyer without the prior written consent of the seller. The seller shall have the right to assign to any of its associated companies all of the rights, powers, duties and obligations under this contract without the consent of the buyer. In the event of any such assignment by the seller references in this contract to the seller shall be deemed to be references to any company taking under the assignment.

14. If any difference shall arise between the seller and the buyer upon the meaning of any part of this contract or the rights and liabilities of the parties hereto, the same shall be referred the arbitration of two persons (one named by each party) or their umpire in accordance with the provisions of the Arbitration Act 1950 or any amending or substituted legislation for the time being in force.

SIGNED for and on behalf   )

of the SELLER:)

SIGNED for and on behalf   )

of the BUYER:)

Commentary and analysis on the standard form contract

The terms of this standard form contract were drawn up by the seller, and it is clear that most of its contents are weighted in his favour. We shall now examine selected clauses of the agreement in order to see what they are attempting to achieve, and comment on any legal rules which may affect their validity. You may find it helpful to refer to Chapter 5, which contains a fuller account of the provisions of the Sale of Goods Act 1979 to which many references are made in this commentary.

Clause 1(b) attempts to exclude any conflicting terms of business on which the buyer usually trades, or any other variation of the terms set out in the seller's standard form. As we saw earlier in the chapter, where there is a battle of forms like the one which occurred in *Butler Machine Tool Co. Ltd. v. Ex-Cell-O Corporation Ltd.* 1979, the rules of offer and acceptance will determine whether clause 1(b) is actually effective.

Clause 2(b) is an attempt to deal with the problem posed by s.13 of the Sale of Goods Act 1979, which provides that compliance with description is a condition of the contract. Under s.13 anything less than strict compliance with the contract description gives the buyer the right to reject the goods and rescind the contract, even if he suffers no loss as a result. This happened for example, in *Re Moore & Landauer* 1921 and *Arcos v. Ronnaasen* 1933. Clause 2(b) is a limitation of liability and will be subject to the controls in s.6 of the Unfair Contract Terms Act 1977.

Clause 3(c) is a price variation clause. This type of clause is particularly significant when the rate of inflation is high. It allows the seller to pass onto the buyer any increase in costs between the date of the contract and the date of delivery. Increases cannot be passed on under clause 3(c) if delivery takes place within six months of the making of the contract. Obviously the longer the period of time between contract and delivery, the more the price will increase. A buyer faced with this type of term will usually try to negotiate an upper limit on any price increase if he cannot persuade the seller to withdraw it altogether.

Clause 3(d) provides for the payment of interest in the event of late payment of sums due to the seller from the buyer. This is an attempt by the seller to ensure a steady cash flow in his business. In the absence of a contractual right to interest:

(i)   no interest will be payable by the buyer in respect of late payments, unless the seller actually issues legal proceedings against him to recover the debt; and

(ii) the buyer can avoid having to pay interest by paying the money at any time before legal proceedings are issued.

Clause 4(a) makes provision for the date of delivery. Under a commercial contract, the agreed delivery date is usually a condition rather than a warranty, unless the parties agree otherwise. This was established in the case *Hartley v. Hymans* 1920. Under clause 4 (a) the delivery date in any contract made by reference to these standard terms is a warranty only. The clause goes even further, however, and excludes the liability of the seller for failure to deliver on time. This exclusion of liability will be covered by s.3 of the Unfair Contract Terms Act 1977.

Clause 4(b) fixes the place of delivery. Where no provision is made for this in a contract, s.29 of the Sale of Goods Act 1979 provides that the place of delivery is the seller's place of business if he has one, and if not, his residence; except that, if the contract is for the sale of specific goods, which to the knowledge of the parties when the contract is made are in some other place, then that place is the place of delivery.

Clause 4(d) excludes the seller's liability for delivery of the wrong quantity if the amount delivered is within 10% of the amount ordered, and obliges the buyer to take and pay for the quantity actually delivered. Without this clause, and clause 2(b) with which it overlaps, the buyer would be entitled, under s.30 of the Sale of Goods Act 1979, to choose, in the event of delivery of the wrong quantity, between:

(i) rejecting all of the goods delivered; or

(ii) rejecting any excess over the contractual quantity; or

(iii) accepting all of the goods delivered and paying for them at the contract rate in the event of short delivery.

Clause 5(b) limits the time during which the buyer can repudiate the contract by rejecting the goods for breach of condition. Once a buyer has accepted goods, he is entitled to sue for damages only in the event of a breach of condition by the seller. Acceptance denies him the right of repudiation.

Clause 6 is a retention of title clause, under which the seller retains ownership of the goods until they have been paid for.

Clause 7 transfers risk to the buyer on the making of the contract. The transfer of risk, at this stage we need only comment that the buyer should insure the goods once risk is transferred to him: a matter which is provided for in clause 8.

Clause 9 is an elaborate limitation of liability clause designed to minimise the seller's liability for breach of contract. As such it is covered by s.3 and s.6 of the Unfair Contract Terms Act 1977. The purpose of each subclause should become clear when you have studied the text on exclusion clauses and the Unfair Contract Terms Act 1977 later in this chapter.

Clause 10 is a force majeure clause which aims to make provision for events which otherwise could frustrate the contract.

Clause 12 is a liquidated damages clause. This type of clause aims to quantify the amount recoverable by one of the contracting parties where the other is in breach of contract. At common law a liquidated damages clause is valid if it represents a genuine pre-estimate of the amount of money which would be lost in the event of a breach of contract. If, however, it provides for a payment which is out of proportion to the actual losses which are likely, the clause will be void as a penalty. In *Dunlop Pneumatic Tyre Co. v. New Garage Motor Co.* 1915, Lord Dunedin stated that a liquidated damages clause:

> *"will be held to be a penalty if the sum stipulated for is extravagant and unconscionable in amount in comparison with the greatest loss that could conceivably be proved to have followed from the breach."*

Where the clause is held to be a penalty it is void and the innocent party can sue only for the loss actually sustained. On the other hand if the clause is valid and not a penalty, he can sue for the stipulated sum only, whether his actual loss is greater or smaller.

Clause 13 restricts the rights of the buyer to transfer the benefit of the contract. The buyer's rights under a contract are a form of intangible business property (a chose in action) which can be sold or transferred to another person.

Clause 14 is an arbitration clause. It enables either party to refer any dispute arising from the contract to arbitration. The process of arbitration is examined in Chapter 5 , which also gives an assessment of the advantages and disadvantages of arbitration as compared to legal action in the courts. It will be recalled that under the Consumer Arbitration Agreements Act 1988, this type of clause can only be enforced as against a consumer in limited circumstances.

Where an agreement is made by reference to a standard form contract the express terms set out in the document will determine the rights and obligations of the parties, and will be referred to in the event of a dispute. It may still be possible however to challenge the contract. On the facts of a case it may be possible to show that the entire document failed to be incorporated into the agreement made by the parties. This happened in *Thornton v. Shoe Lane Parking* (discussed later). Alternatively there may be grounds for challenging a particular term, for instance because it is not appropriately worded.

Activity

Try to obtain your own copies of different types of standard form agreements. You may find that you already have some at home, for instance if members of the family have obtained goods on credit, or taken out insurance policies. Examine the agreements you have found and try to analyse them, to discover what they are actually saying.

The classification of terms

The terms of a contract vary in importance. Sometimes the contract itself will say how much importance is attached to a certain term, while in other cases it may be left to the court to decide the question because the parties to the contract have not made it clear. The value that is attached to each term is of great significance because it determines what the consequences will be if the particular term is broken.

Major terms are called *conditions*. A condition is a term which is said to go to the root of the contract, and where performance is essential to the contract. If it is broken the innocent party has the right to treat the contract as repudiated and to refuse to perform his or her obligations under it. In addition the injured party may sue for damages.

Minor terms are called *warranties*. They are terms which are said to be collateral to the main purpose of the contract. In consequence, if a warranty is broken the contract still stands, and the innocent party does not have the right to treat the contract as being at an end, merely the right to damages.

Where breach of a condition occurs the injured party is not bound to repudiate the contract. As an alternative the injured party can elect to treat the contract as subsisting, treating the breach of condition as if it were a warranty. The obligation that had been broken is then referred to as an *ex post facto* warranty, and only damages will be available. There may be sound commercial reasons for treating a breach of condition as one of warranty, and letting the contract stand. The innocent party may realise that if the contract is repudiated it will be difficult to obtain an alternative supplier of the goods and services in question, or undue delay and inconvenience will be caused if the goods have to be disassembled, removed from the premises and returned to the supplier.

Two similar cases illustrate the distinction between conditions and warranties. In *Bettini v. Gye* 1876 the plaintiff, an opera singer agreed in writing to sing in various concerts and operas over a period of three and a half months, and to be present at rehearsals for at least six days before the engagements were due to begin. Due to illness he arrived with only two days of rehearsals left, and as a result the defendant terminated the agreement. Looking at the contract as a whole, the court decided that the rehearsal clause was not a condition, but merely a warranty, for which damages alone was the remedy.

The contract had been wrongfully terminated and the plaintiff could counter-claim for damages.

In *Poussard v. Spiers and Pond* 1876 an opera singer was unable to take part in the first week of performances due to illness. In the meantime the management had engaged a substitute and refused the original singer the part when she arrived. They were held to be entitled to do so, for her non-attendance at the performances was a breach of a vital term of the contract.

Sometimes it is impossible to say whether a term is a condition or a warranty when it is first created because it will be so broadly framed that it could be broken in a major respect or a minor respect, and therefore it is only possible to say after the event what effect the particular breach should have on the contract. Such terms are referred to as *innominate*, meaning intermediate terms.

The position is illustrated in *Hong Kong Fir Shipping Co. Ltd. v. Kawasaki Kaisen Kaisha Ltd.* 1962. Here a ship was chartered on terms that stated what it would be *"in every way fitted for ordinary cargo service"*. Inefficient engine-room staff and old engines contributed to a number of breakdowns so that during the first seven months of the charter the ship was only able to be at sea for eight and a half weeks. The charterers repudiated the contract. The Court of Appeal decided that this particular breach did not entitle the charterers to repudiate. Diplock J stated that the terms in the contract were not really either a condition or a warranty but rather *"an undertaking, one breach of which may give rise to an event which relieves the charterer of further performance … if he so elects and another breach of which may not give rise to such an event but entitle him only … to damages."*

Terms and Conditions of Employment

While terms of employment contain the mutual rights and obligations of the parties conditions of employment refer to matters over which the employer alone has control and are subject to unilateral change. A contractual term could include a condition of employment which would entitle an employer to require the employee's compliance.

> In *White v. Reflecting Road Studs Ltd.* 1991 a term in the employee's contract provided that *"the company reserves the right when determined by requirements of operational efficiency to transfer employees to alternative work and it is a condition of employment that they are willing to do so when requested"*. This means that the employee could be lawfully transfered from one department to another without his consent.

It is common practice in many spheres of employment for the employer to issue work rules by printing notices or handing out rule books. Such rule books often contain instructions as to time-keeping, meal breaks, disciplinary offences and grievance procedure, sickness and pension rights, job descriptions, and the employer's safety policy. Although there is still some doubt as to the legal status of work rules, the present view is that such documents are unlikely to contain contractual terms. One school of thought is that work rules should be regarded as 'conditions' rather than 'terms' of employment, and as such they should be subject to unilateral change by the employer. For example, while the number of hours worked would normally be the subject of express agreement and constitute a contractual 'term', instructions as to when these hours should be worked will normally be contained in a rule book and as a 'condition' be liable to unilateral change.

> In *Cadoux v. Central Regional Council* 1986 the employee's contract of employment was to be subject to the Conditions of Service laid down by the National Joint Council for Local Authorities' Administrative, Technical and Clerical Services, as supplemented

by the Authorities Rules, as amended from time to time. The issue in the case was whether, under the Authorities' rules, the employer was entitled to introduce a non-contributory life assurance scheme for staff and then subsequently unilaterally withdraw it. The Scottish Court of Session held that here the "Authorities' Rules" were clearly incorporated into contracts of employment. They were however, made unilaterally by the employer, and although introduced after consultation, they were the "Authorities' Rules" and not subject to mutual agreement. Consequently there was *"no limitation on the employer's right to vary, alter or cancel any of the provisions of the Rules. The reference to the Authorities Rules, "as amended from time to time", led to the clear inference that the employer could alter their rules at their own hand"*. In the present case therefore the employer was entitled unilaterally to withdraw the provision of the non-contributory life assurance scheme.

In *Secretary of State for Employment v. ASLEF (No 2)* 1972 Lord Denning expressed the view that rule books issued to railwaymen by their employers did not contain contractual terms but rather instructions to an employee as to how he was to do his work.

More recently in *Dryden v. Greater Glasgow Health Board* 1992 the Employment Appeal Tribunal decided that an employer was entitled to introduce a rule imposing a smoking ban at the workplace and the staff had no implied right to smoke. *"An employer is entitled to make rules for the conduct of employees in their place of work within the scope of the contract"*.

Where, however, a rule book is given or referred to by the employer at the time the contract of employment is formed, the fact that the employee has agreed that it is to be part of the contract and acknowledges that fact by his signature would more than likely give the rule book contractual effect. Certainly there is case law authority which suggests that by posting a notice of the fact that the rule book has contractual effect, an employer would ensure that the rules become incorporated into individual contracts of employment.

How terms originate

So far the examples of terms that have been considered are those which have been expressly agreed between the parties. There are however two additional sources of contract terms, the courts and Parliament. Both these law making institutions are responsible for inserting terms into contracts, independent of the wishes of the parties involved, and the broad justification for doing so appears to be desire to enable the contract to 'work' and to achieve a level of protection for the consumer of goods and services. How contractual terms arise, is considered below.

Express terms

These are the terms which have been specifically detailed and agreed upon by the parties. The parties are free to classify them in advance as being conditions or warranties if they so wish. If they fail to do so it will be left to the court to decide how significant a particular breach is by looking at the term in relation to the contract as a whole. Even where the contract does classify a term or terms, the court still reserves the right to construe the meaning of the term looking at the contract as a whole.

In *L Schuler AG v. Wickham Machine Tool Sales* 1973 the appellant company, a German organisation, by an agreement, granted sole selling rights over their panel presses in England, to the respondents Wickham. The agreement provided that Wickham's representatives should visit six named firms every week for the purpose of seeking orders.

Clause 7(6) indicated the status of this particular obligation stating that *"it shall be a condition of this agreement"*. On certain occasions Wickham's employees failed to satisfy the requirement, and Schulers responded to this by claiming that they could repudiate, arguing that a single failure would be sufficient to constitute a breach. The House of Lords rejected this argument. Such a construction was so unreasonable that the parties could not have intended it.

As we have seen some statements made prior to contract will constitute representations. Sometimes a representation will actually become a term of the contract. This being so, if the term is broken the innocent party will be able to bring an action for breach of contract, rather than for misrepresentation. It is often difficult to determine whether a representation has in fact become a term where there has been no express incorporation of it, and the courts will take into consideration a number of factors. For instance, a representation will be presumed not to have become a term if a formal written contract is executed after the representation and does not contain it. There is, however, one main test to be applied: whether the person making the statement was promising its accuracy. If so, the statement will become a contractual term.

> How difficult it can be to draw a distinction between representations and terms is illustrated by *Oscar Chess Ltd. v. Williams* 1975. The defendant wished to take a new car on hire-purchase terms from the from the plaintiffs, who were car dealers. In part exchange he offered them his own car, which was described in the log book as a 1948 Morris. He confirmed the vehicle to be a 1948 model, honestly believing this to be so, and received £290 part-exchange allowance. Eight months later the plaintiffs discovered that the car was a 1939 model, for which only £175 should have been allowed. They sued the defendant for the difference, i.e. £115. The Court of Appeal decided by a majority that the defendant's statement about the age of the car was not a term of the contract. Lord Denning made the point that, *"as motor dealers, the plaintiffs could without difficulty have checked the true age of the car with the manufacturers by giving them the engine chassis numbers."*

If the parties to a contract of employment have included their respective rights and obligations under it in a signed document called the contract of employment, then this document will contain the express terms of the agreement. In many cases however the express term of a contract of employment can only be determined by establishing the content and status of the various documents transferred during the recruitment process and what the parties orally agreed at the inteview. Express terms will be found in the statutory statement of the main term and conditions of employment, a job application form and in rare cases even a job advertisement.

> In *Holliday Concrete v. Wood* 1979 a job advertisement indicated that a fifteen month contract was available and this was held to be the period of employment.

> In *Joseph Steinfeld v. Reypert* 1979 the fact that a post was advertised as "sales manager" indicated the contractual status of the successful applicant.

In the event of conflict between the writing and what was orally agreed the written statements will normally have priority. However the express terms are decided by discovering the intention of the parties to the contract and it could be the case that an oral promise has more significance because of the importance attached to it.

> In *Hawker Siddely Power Engineering Ltd. v. Rump* 1979 the complainant was employed as a heavy goods vehicle driver in 1973 and signed a contract of employment which stated that he would be liable to travel all over the country. The obligation was confirmed in a later statement of terms and conditions of employment issued in 1976 and signed

by the complainant. In fact the complainant had made it clear when he took the job that because of his wife's illness he would not travel beyond the south of England and that had been orally agreed by the manager when he signed the contract. When finally in 1978 the complainant refused to obey an instruction to travel to Scotland and this led to his dismissal. One issue before the Tribunal was whether he was contractually obliged to do so. The Tribunal thought not deciding that the promise to work only in the south was an oral contractual term. Here *"there was a direct promise by the employers which must have become part of the contract of employment because it was following upon the promise that the employee signed the contract"*. Even the subsequent written statement which included a mobility clause signed by the employer was insufficient to exclude the oral term previously agreed, for the employee *"had no notice that the oral term that he had secured was going to form no part of his new contract. The mere putting in front of him a document and invitation for him to sign it could not be held to be a variation by agreement so as to exclude the important oral term which he had previously secured"*.

Terms implied by the courts

It is not the task of the courts to insert new terms into contracts, but rather to interpret those that already exist. But they will sometimes imply a term to give a contract 'business efficacy'. The rationale underlying such an approach is that since the parties clearly intended to create a binding agreement, they must have intended to include terms to make the contract 'work'.

> Thus in *The Moorcock* 1889 a term was implied by the court in a contract between a ship owner and a firm of wharfingers. The contract was to use their wharf on the Thames for the discharging and loading of his vessel, the Moorcock. He was going to pay a charge for the use of the cranes alongside the wharf. While the vessel was moored there she was damaged when the tide ebbed and she came to rest on a ridge of hard ground. The Court of Appeal held that the wharfingers were liable for breach of an implied term that the mooring was safe for the vessel. *"In business transactions such as this,"* said Bowen LJ, *"what the law desires to effect by implication is to give such business efficacy to the transaction as must have been intended at all events by both parties who are businessmen."*

> In *Irwin v. Liverpool City Council* 1977 the defendant council let a flat in an upper floor of a block of flats to the plaintiff tenant. A term was implied by the Court into a tenancy agreement between the plaintiff and the defendant Council to the effect that the defendants had an obligation to keep in repair the stairs and the lift in the block of flats which they owned, thus ensuring that the plaintiff could gain access to his property.

> In *Baylis v. Barnett* 1988 the plaintiff lent the defendant a sum of money. The defendant knew this involved the plaintiff in borrowing the money from a bank. Although the parties did not discuss the question of interest the Court held there was an implied term that the defendant would indemnify the plaintiff for any interest he owed to the bank.

Two fields in which the courts have been active in implying terms are in the employment relationship, and in the landlord and tenant relationship. Thus at common law there are certain fundamental obligations owed by the employer to the employee and vice versa, which are implied by the courts. For instance the employee owes a duty of good faith to the employer at common law, whilst the employer has an obligation to provide for the employee's safety.

In *Creswell v. Board of Inland Revenue* 1984 the court held that in every contract of employment there is an implied term that employees are required to be flexible and adapt to new methods and techniques introduced in the course of employment.

In *Woods v. W H Car Services Ltd.* 1982 it was recognised that in every employment contract there is an implied term of great importance, that of trust and confidence between the parties. Such a term requires that employers *"will not without reasonable and proper cause, conduct themselves in a manner calculated or likely to destroy the relationship of trust and confidence between employer and employee"*.

In the landlord and tenant relationship the common law imposes an obligation upon the tenant not to commit waste, (physical harm), to the premises being occupied, and upon the landlord to provide the tenant with quiet enjoyment, i.e. not to interfere with the tenant's occupation of the premises. Parliament has also legislated to insert terms into certain categories of contract, primarily with the view to protecting the weaker party from exploitation by the stronger.

Statutory implied terms

Parliament has been particularly active during the post-war period in its use of legislation to introduce specific terms into particular types of contractual agreement. As a result statutory implied terms are now many and varied and, because they are statutory, the obligations they impose tend to be detailed. In many cases statutory terms are implied as a legislative attempt to counter-balance the inequalities that exist in a particular bargaining situation, for example by restricting the ability of organisations which trade on the basis of their own standard form contracts to exclude liability for breaches of contract which they have caused. In other cases statutory terms can be seen as a vehicle for effecting profound social and economic change, such as the insertion of the equality clause in contracts of employment. Yet again, there are those statutory terms which simply represent a codification of judicially recognised mercantile custom, for example under the Sale of Goods Act 1979.

Statutory terms implied under the 1979 Act are considered in Chapter 5, in conjunction with an examination of other implied statutory terms which grant rights to consumers.

The exclusion and restriction of liability

We have seen how a contract creates obligations which the parties making it are obliged to meet, and that failure to do so constitutes a breach of contract which can possibly lead to a claim for damages. It follows that a prudent person, recognising the potential liabilities involved in entering into a contract, will try to reduce or perhaps entirely remove any such risk. How far this is possible depends upon whether the clause in the contract excluding or restricting liability is successfully incorporated into the contract, and if it has been whether it satisfies certain tests of validity laid down by both Parliament and the courts. The account below provides a summary of its main features. The diagram on the next page (Figure 4.1) indicates the questions which have to be answered in order to determine whether a clause excluding or restricting liability will work.

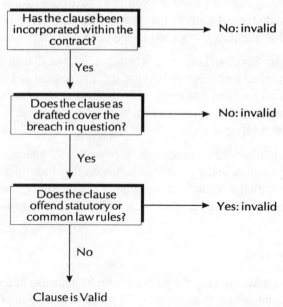

Figure 4.1 *The Exclusion of Contractual Liabilities*

Activity

Clauses excluding and restricting liability are very common. You can find them contained in contractual documents and on public notices. See how many of them you can discover. A common location of exclusion notices is at the entrance to car parks, inside sports and leisure centres, and on documents such as tickets. Consider what the clauses you have discovered are actually trying to achieve, and whether , as drafted, they are lawful.

Incorporation and drafting of the terms

To become a part of a contract a term must be included in the contractual offer. We saw in Chapter 5 that a term is only valid if it is certain. In other words it must have a clear meaning which a court can, if needs be, specifically identify. So if a term does not form a part of the contractual offer, or is in some way unclear, it will be ineffective.

A good example of terms failing to become part of the contract occurs where the terms in question are introduced after the contract has been made.

> This happened in *Thornton v. Shoe Lane Parking* 1971 where the terms of the contract were contained on the back of a parking ticket. They could only be read therefore after the customer had inserted the money into the machine, and thus subsequent to the making of the contract.

Where the term is contained in an unsigned document, or on a notice, it will be effective only if the person relying on it took reasonable steps to bring it to the attention of the other party, and where the document or notice containing it might reasonably be regarded as contractual and likely to contain contractual terms. If a document containing contractual terms has been signed then in general the signatory will be bound by its terms whether or not they have been read.

The need to express contractual terms clearly is very important. This is especially so when the term is an attempt by one of the parties to exclude liability. As Scrutton LJ pointed out in *Alison (J Gordon) Ltd. v. Wallsend Shipway and Engineering Co. Ltd.* 1927 *"if a person is under a legal liability and wishes to get rid of it, he can only do so by using clear words."*

The courts use the following tests for determining whether the exclusion clause is valid:

a)   does it clearly and unequivocally cover the breach of contract in question. This is a rule of strict interpretation;

(b)   is it ambiguous or doubtful?

Statutory control of exclusion clauses

One of the features of exclusion clauses is that they are a standard component in contracts of adhesion, the 'take it or leave it' contracts mentioned earlier in the chapter. A person who is in a weak bargaining position may have no effective control over the power of the stronger party to insert such exclusion clauses.

Under the Unfair Contract Terms Act 1977, Parliament has come to the aid of the weaker party. The Act applies not only to contractual exclusions but also tortious ones, for example a notice at the entrance of a public park that attempts to exonerate the council from liability for any harm suffered to the members of the public whilst in the park. The main provisions of the Act are set out below.

Under s.2 a person cannot either by a contractual term or by notice, exclude or restrict his of her liability in contract or tort for death or personal injury arising from negligence. Liability for other loss or damage arising from negligence can still be excluded, provided the exclusion can be shown to be reasonable.

The kind of term that will be caught under the first limb of the section would be one which attempted a blanket exclusion such as *"any liability in respect of any personal injury howsoever arising is hereby excluded".*

An example of the second limb of the section being applied by the court is found in *Philips Products v. Hamstead Plant Hire* 1983. The hire company hired out a JCB to the plaintiffs under a standard term agreement. A driver was included, but the company excluded any liability in negligence for the driver's acts. In the event whilst he was working under the plaintiff's directions the driver damaged their factory through his own negligence. The court held the exclusion clause to be unreasonable and therefore invalid. It was unreasonable because the hire was for a short period giving the plaintiffs little opportunity to insure. They did not select, nor effectively control the driver, and moreover their experience of such hiring arrangements was very limited.

Under s.3 , where a person inserts in their own written standard terms of business any term purporting to exclude or restrict liability for breach of contract, the term must satisfy the test of reasonableness. If the other contractual party is a consumer the rule applies, even if the contract is not based upon the other's written terms. An example of the application of this section would be where a time limit is placed upon the period for making claims.

Section 5 of the Act deals with guarantees. It provides that where goods are of a type ordinarily supplied for private use or consumption, a term contained in a guarantee of the goods cannot exclude or restrict liability for loss or damage caused by the negligent manufacture or distribution of the goods, where the defect occurs when the goods are in consumer use.

Finally section 6 deals with exclusions of the implied conditions of the Sale of Goods Act 1979 (see Chapter 5). Originally it was quite permissible for a seller to exclude the statutory implied conditions from a contract of sale, but under the 1977 Act the position is very different. Section 6 provides that if there is a sale to a consumer any clause excluding the terms implied by sections 12 to 15 of the Sale of Goods Act is ineffective. A person buys as a consumer if the goods are of a type ordinarily sold for private use or consumption by a seller in the course of business to a person who does not buy them in the course of business. In a non-consumer sale, for instance between two businesses, any attempt to exclude s.12 of the Sale of Goods Act is absolutely void, although sections 13, 14 and 15 can be excluded if the seller can show that this is reasonable. Whether it is reasonable to do so is determined by a number of guidelines laid down by the Act. These are:

- The respective bargaining strengths of the parties relative to each other. This involves considering possible alternative sources of supply. For instance a monopolist seller may have difficulty in establishing the reasonableness of a widely drafted exclusion clause.

- Whether the customer received an inducement to agree the term, or in accepting it had the opportunity of entering into a similar contract with other persons but without having to accept a similar term. The reference to other persons involves account being taken of the suppliers within the market and their terms of trading. Sometimes suppliers combine to produce standardised terms of trading, giving buyers no opportunity of finding improved terms. An example of an inducement would be a reduction in price.

- Whether the customer knew or ought reasonably to have known of the existence of the term. This involves the customer's knowledge of the trade in general, its terms and customs, and knowledge of the seller, with whom the customer may have previously traded on the same terms.

- Where the term excludes or restricts any relevant liability if some condition is not complied with, where it is reasonable at the time of the contract to expect that it would be practicable to comply with the condition. It might not be practicable, for example, to require the buyer to notify the seller of defects occurring in a large consignment of goods within a limited time period with a proviso that failure to notify in time will relieve the seller of any liability.

Discharge of Contract

Since a contract gives rise to legally enforceable obligations, contracting parties need to know how and when these obligations have been discharged and cease to be binding on them. Only then have their duties been discharged. Discharge may occur in any of the following ways:

(a) Discharge by performance

The general rule is that complete performance, complying precisely to the contractual terms, is necessary to discharge the contract.

An illustration of this common law rule in the case of *Sumpter v. Hedges* 1898. Here the plaintiff builder agreed to erect some houses for a lump sum of £565. Having carried out half the work to the value of £333 the builder was unable to complete the work because of financial difficulties. In an action by the builder to recover compensation for the value of the work done, the Court of Appeal confirmed that he was not entitled to payment. The legal position was expressed by Smith, LJ who stated *"The law is that*

> *where there is a contract to do work for a lump sum, until the work is completed, the price of it cannot be recovered".*

On the face of it this decision appears harsh in its effect upon the builder. In fact the difficulty for the court is that a single sum has been arranged in consideration for the completion of specified works. If these works are not completed in their entirety the court would be varying the clearly expressed intentions of the parties if it was to award the builder payment of a proportionate part of the lump sum. In other words, by agreeing a lump sum the parties have impliedly excluded that possibility of part payment for partially fulfilled building work. Such a contract is said to be an *entire* contract.

The obligation on a contracting party to provide precise, complete performance of the contract before the contractual obligations can be treated as discharged can obviously produce injustice.

There are however two exceptions that grant limited relief to the party obliged to perform, where the contract is divisible, and where there has been substantial performance.

(i) A divisible contract. In some circumstances the courts are prepared to accept that a contract is a divisible one where part of the performance of the contract can be set off against part of the consideration to be given in return. Had the parties in *Sumpter v. Hedges* agreed a specified sum to be paid on completion of certain stages of the house building, then the builder could have recovered compensation for part of the work done. In practice it is usual in a building contract to provide for payment of parts of the total cost at various stages of completion.

It is not necessary for the parties to formally specify that the contract is a divisible one, although in contracts involving substantial work, such as civil engineering operations, or shipbuilding, it would be most unusual not to find that the contract has been split into stages, with payment due on completion of each stage. The courts seem willing to recognise a divisible contract wherever possible, and will, for example, regard a contract based upon an estimate or quotation given in advance, which itemises the work to be performed and with a breakdown of the costs as a divisible contract.

(ii) Substantial performance. If a party to a contract has substantially performed his contractual obligations subject only to minor defects, the courts have recognised that it would be unjust to prevent him recovering any of the contractual price. Therefore under this exception the contractual price would be recoverable, less of course a sum representing the value of the defects. It must be stressed that the exception will only operate where the defects are of a trifling nature. This question is determined by considering not only the nature of the defects but also the cost of rectifying them in relation to the total contract price.

> A claim of substantial performance of the contract was made in *Bolton v. Mahadeva* 1972. Here the plaintiff, a heating contractor, had agreed to install a central heating system in the defendant's house for £560. On completion of the work the system proved to be so defective that it would cost £174 to repair. The defendant refused to pay the plaintiff any of the cost of the work and the plaintiff sued. The County Court accepted the plaintiff's claim of substantial performance and awarded him the cost of the work less the cost of the repair. On appeal however, the Court of Appeal held that in the circumstances the plaintiff had not substantially performed the contract and he was not therefore entitled to recover any of the cost of the work. The exception would not operate where there were numerous defects requiring a relatively high cost of repair.

From the consumer's point of view it can be difficult to ascertain whether incomplete performance of the contract is nevertheless sufficient on the facts to amount to substantial performance. A refusal of payment may well be met with a legal action by the contractor to recover the debt owed. Further complications may be caused where the contractor offered to remedy the customer's complaint free of charge and the customer has refused to accept the offer. As we saw earlier in the event of a dispute concerning the value of work performed, an offer of reduced payment by the debtor to the creditor will be binding on the creditor, an example of one of the exemptions to Pinnel's case.

> In *Lawson v. Supasink Ltd.* 1982 the plaintiff's employed the defendants to design, supply and install a fitted kitchen. The total cost was £1,200, and the plaintiffs had to pay a deposit. After the kitchen units had been fitted, but before work on the kitchen was completed, the plaintiffs informed the defendants of their dissatisfaction with the standard of workmanship. In response the defendants undertook to remedy the faults free of charge, but the plaintiffs later rejected this, asked for the units to be removed and for the return of their deposit. The defendants refused. The Court of Appeal, having accepted that the shoddy work did not amount to substantial performance, then considered the offer to remedy made by the defendants. The question was whether they had failed to mitigate their loss, that is minimise the damage they had suffered. In *Fayzu Ltd. v. Saunders* 1919 Scrutton LJ commented, *"... in commercial contracts it is generally reasonable to accept an offer from the party in default."* In *Lawson* the Court held that the plaintiffs had not acted unreasonably for, in the words of Shaw LJ *" I do not see how the plaintiffs could be required ... to afford the defendants a second opportunity of doing properly what they singularly failed to do adequately in the first instance."*

The acceptance of partial performance

If a party to a contract partially performs his obligations and the other party accepts the benefit, then he is obliged to pay a reasonable price for it. In such circumstances the courts would allow an action on a quantum meruit basis (as much as he deserves). This exception however will only operate where the party receiving the benefit has the option of whether or not to accept or reject it. In *Sumpter v. Hedges* the owner had no choice but to accept the work done on the half completed houses and was therefore not obliged to pay for it. In a situation like that in *Lawson v. Supasink* the units were capable of being removed and returned.

A contract of employment is often described as a wage/work bargain. The employee is entitled to be paid the agreed wage if he satisfactorily performs the work required under the contract. If an employee fails to fully perform his contractual obligations, for instance during a period of industrial action an employer has the option of accepting the past performance, but withholding wages to reflect the work not performed.

> This was the case in *Miles v. Wakefield Metropolitan District Council* 1987 where the plaintiff, a superintendent registrar acting in accordance with NALGO instructions, refused to perform marriages on a Saturday morning although he was willing to perform other duties. The Council made it clear that if he was not willing to perform the full range of his duties on a Saturday morning his wages would be reduced. Subsequently the employer withheld 3/37ths of his pay and so withheld the total wage for Saturday morning work. The plaintiff's claim to recover the wages withheld was eventually dismissed by the House of Lords. Their Lordships stressed the point that in a contract of employment *"wages and work go together and if the work declines the employer need not pay"*. Here the employer had made it clear that he was not willing to accept the plaintiff's partial performance so that his position was on Saturday mornings as if he was refusing to work at all. The employer was entitled to withhold the whole of remuneration due for the periods the employee had made it clear that he was not ready and willing to perform the full range of work he could properly be required to do. *"Since*

the plaintiff could not successfully claim that he was at the material time ready and willing
to perform the work which he was properly required to do on Saturdays his action for
the remuneration attributable to that work must fail."

Certainly for an employer to be lawfully justified in making a deduction from the wages of an employee pursuing limited industrial action it is necessary to show that the work not performed falls squarely within an employee's contractual obligation.

Where performance is prevented

Obviously if a party to a contract is prevented from fulfilling his contractual obligations by the other party then he will not be in default. If in a building contract the owner prevents the builder from completing, in these circumstances the builder can recover a reasonable price for the work done on a quantum meruit.

As well as the above exceptions to the general rule that the performance of contractual obligations must be precise, it is important to note that if a party to a contract makes a valid tender (offer) of performance this may be regarded as equivalent to performance. The refusal of the other party to allow performance to take place will discharge any further obligations on the part of the tenderer. Thus if a seller of goods attempts to deliver them at the agreed time and place and the goods meet contract description, the refusal of the buyer to accept them will,

(i)   amount to a valid tender of performance;
      and

(ii) entitle the seller to sue the buyer under s.50 Sale of Goods Act 1979 for damages for non-
      acceptance of the goods.

Despite the problems that can occur in performance, most contracts are satisfactorily discharged in this way.

(b) Discharge by agreement

This method of discharge occurs where the parties to a contract agree to waive their rights and obligations under it. It is called bilateral discharge. To be an effective *waiver* the second agreement must be a contract, the consideration for which is the exchange of promises not to enforce the original contract. The situation however is more complex where one party to a contract has already executed or partly executed his consideration under it. Here for a waiver to be effective it must be embodied within a speciality contract or be supported by fresh consideration. This is called unilateral discharge and can only be achieved by *accord* and *satisfaction*. The accord is simply the agreement to discharge and the satisfaction is the consideration required to support it, e.g. X contracts to sell goods to Y for £50. X delivers the goods to Y and then hearing of Y's financial difficulties agrees to waive payment. Here the agreement of X to waive payment (the accord) is not enforceable unless supported by fresh consideration furnished by Y (the satisfaction). The fresh consideration of course must be of value but need not be adequate. As we saw in our examination of the principles of consideration, at common law the rule in *Pinnel's case* provides that there is no value in a creditor taking as satisfaction payment of a lesser sum than he was due under the original agreement.

A creditor's promise to accept a reduced amount may however be binding on him, through the operation of the equitable doctrine of *promissory estoppel*, established in *Hughes v. Metropolitan Railway Co.* 1877 by the House of Lords, and by Denning J as he then was in *Central London Property Trust Ltd. v. High Trees House Ltd.* 1947. Here the defendant company took a 99-year lease on a block of flats from the plaintiff company at an annual rent of £2,500. The lease was granted in 1937. By 1940 the evacuation of large numbers of people out of London because of war meant that the defendant company was unable to let all the flats and could not meet the annual rent out of the profits it was making. As a result, the plaintiff company agreed to accept a reduced annual rent of £1,250. By the beginning of 1945 the flats were fully let again. An action was brought by the plaintiff company to recover the difference between the reduced rent and the full rent for the last two quarters of 1945. The action succeeded, for the court considered that the agreement of 1940 would continue only as long as wartime conditions prevailed. The Court also considered whether the plaintiffs could recover the remaining arrears from the defendants, relying on *Pinnel's case*. It took the view that such action would be inequitable, even though permissible at common law. In equity the creditor would be estopped, or denied the right of disowning his promise to accept the reduced amount, where the debtor had to the creditor's knowledge relied on the promise, and acted on it to his detriment. This rule is consequently referred to as promissory estoppel. It was said in the later case of *Combe v. Combe* 1951 that the doctrine is a shield rather than a sword, meaning that the person receiving the promise cannot sue on it, the 'sword', but can raise it as defence, 'the shield', if action is brought to recover the outstanding payment. The doctrine only arises within the context of a pre-existing contractual relationship, and does not remove consideration as a requirement of the simple contract.

It is worth pointing out that the High Trees decision is an authority which also supports the view that a deed can be varied by a simple contract. Prior to 1947 it has always been considered that because a simple contract is inferior to the more formal deed, that only a deed could vary a deed.

Being a form of equitable relief, it is only possible for a person to raise promissory estoppel as defence if he has acted in an equitable manner himself.

In *D & C Builders v. Rees* 1965 Mr. & Mrs Rees exacted a promise from D & C Builders to accept a reduced amount than that originally agreed, for building work carried out to the Rees's home. They claimed the building work was substandard, but in fact they were simply attempting to escape the full payment due, using their knowledge that the builders were in financial difficulties and desperate for cash. Sometime after the reduced payment had been made the company sued for the outstanding balance, and the defendants pleaded promissory estoppel. The Court refused to allow Mr. & Mrs Rees the equitable defence, on the grounds of their own lack of equity.

If the parties to a contract of employment, without duress and after taking proper advice, enter into a separate contract, supported by good consideration, with the objective of terminating the employment relationship by mutual consent, the contract will be valid and enforceable.

(c) Discharge by breach

If a party to a contract fails to perform his obligations under it or performs his obligations in a defective manner then he may be regarded as being in breach of contract. Generally, the remedy of an innocent party to a contract who has suffered as a result of a breach is to sue for damages. For some breaches of contract however, the innocent party is given the additional remedy of treating the contract as repudiated, in other words terminated, and thus discharging himself from the obligations under it. As previously mentioned terms in a contract are classified into different categories and it is only when a condition has been broken that repudiatory breach has occurred. If a breach of contract occurs before the time set for performance of the contract it is called an *anticipatory breach*. This will occur where a party to a contract expressly declares that he will not perform his part of the bargain. Once an anticipatory breach has occurred the innocent party does not have to wait for the date set for performance but has the option of immediately suing for breach of contract.

> In *Hochester v. De La Tour* 1853 the defendant agreed in April to engage the plaintiff for work to commence in June. The defendant told the plaintiff in May that he would not require his services. The court held that a cause of action for breach of contract arose on the anticipatory breach in May.

Thus in such circumstances the injured party can commence legal action at the time of the anticipatory breach. Alternatively he can wait until performance is due to see if it is in fact carried out, and if it is not, commence action thereafter.

(d) Discharge by frustration or subsequent impossibility

A contract may be discharged by frustration where as a result of an event subsequent to making the contract, performance of the contract can no longer be carried out. The event must be subsequent to the contract for if the contract is impossible to perform at the time it is made there is no contract. Originally the common law did not take such a lenient view of changes in circumstances and required that the parties to a contract should provide for all eventualities. If because of a subsequent event performance of an obligation became impossible, the party required to perform the impossible obligation would be liable to pay damages for non performance.

> In *Paradine v. Jane* 1647 the King's Bench Court held a tenant liable to pay three years' arrears of rent to a landlord despite the fact that the tenant had been dispossessed of his house by soldiers during the Civil War.

Today however the courts recognise that certain supervening events may frustrate a contract and thus release the parties from their obligation under it. Were the facts of *Paradine v. Jane* to come before a modern court, the outcome would probably be quite different.

> In *National Carriers Ltd. v. Panalpina (Northern) Ltd.* 1981 the plaintiffs leased a warehouse in Hull to the defendants. The lease was for ten years, however for a period of twenty months the only access road to the premises was closed by the local authority due to the poor state of a listed building nearby. The defendants refused to pay any further rent to the plaintiffs. The House of Lords accepted the defendant's argument that a lease could, in law, become frustrated, but felt that twenty months out of a ten year period, was not sufficiently substantial to frustrate the contract.

There are a number of grounds upon which a contract may become frustrated. They include:

(i) Changes in the law. If because of new legislation performance of the contract would become illegal this would be a supervening event to frustrate the contract.

> In *Denny, Mott and Dickson Ltd. v. James B. Fraser Ltd.* 1944 the House of Lords held that a contract for the sale of timber was frustrated because of the subsequent passage of various Control of Timber Orders rendering performance of the contract illegal.

(ii) Destruction of subject matter. If the subject matter or means of performance of the contract is destroyed this is an event which frustrates a contract.

> In *Taylor v. Caldwell* 1863 the plaintiff agreed to hire the defendant's music hall to give some concerts. Prior to performance the hall was destroyed by fire and this event, the court held, released the parties from their obligations under the contract.

(iii) Inability to achieve main object. If as a result of change in circumstances performance of the contract would be radically different from the performance envisaged by the parties then the contract is frustrated. It must be shown that the parties are no longer able to achieve their main object under the contract.

In *Krell v. Henry* 1903 the defendant hired a flat for two days to enable him to watch Edward VII's Coronation procession. Due to the King's illness the Coronation was cancelled and the defendant naturally refused to pay. The Court of Appeal held that as the main object of the contract was to view the procession, and this could no longer be achieved, the foundation of the contract had collapsed. The contract was thus frustrated and the parties released from their obligations under it.

A further claim of frustration as a consequence of the cancellation of the Coronation was brought in *Herne Bay Steamboat Co. v. Hutton* 1903. Here a steamboat had been chartered to watch the naval review as part of the Coronation celebrations and also for a day's cruise round the fleet. The Court of Appeal had to determine whether the cancellation of the naval review released the defendant from his obligation to pay the hire charge. The Court held that there has not been a sufficient change in circumstances to constitute a frustration of the contract. Here the defendant could have derived some benefit from the contract and was therefore liable to pay the hire charges. A further distinction between *Henry* and *Hutton* is that in *Henry* the claim was brought by a private individual whereas in *Hutton* the hirer was engaged in a commercial enterprise, using the hired boat to take trips of sightseers to Spithead. Frustration is not available in a commercial transaction merely because the contract turns out to be less profitable than one of the parties expected.

(iv) Death or illness. In a contract for personal services the death or illness of the person required to perform will frustrate the contract. Temporary illness or incapacity will generally not release a party from his obligations. The illness must be such that it goes to the root of the contract.

It is difficult in any given case to say whether the circumstances of an illness are such that it is no longer practical to regard the contract of employment as surviving. Obviously the seriousness and length of the illness are crucial factors but generally all the circumstances are relevant, including the nature of the job, the length of employment, the needs of the employer and obligations in relation to replacement, and the conduct of the employer.

In *Notcutt v. Universal Equipment Company* 1986 the Court of Appeal considered the position of a worker who, two years from retirement and with 27 years' service, suffered an incapacitating heart attack with a medical prognosis that he would never work again. A finding that the contract was terminated by frustration meant that the employee was not entitled to sick pay during his statutory period of notice. The court held that *"there is no reason in principle why a periodic contract of employment determinable by short or relatively short notice should not in appropriate circumstances be held to have been terminated without notice by frustration, according to the accepted and long established doctrine of frustration in the law of contract. The coronary which left the complainant unable to work again was an unexpected occurrence which made his performance of his contractual obligation to work impossible and brought about such a change in the significance of the mutual obligations that the contract if performed would be a different thing from that contracted for."*

Non frustrating events

The common law doctrine of frustration will not apply in the following circumstances:

(a) If performance of the contract has become more onerous on one party or financially less rewarding.

   In *Davis Contractors Ltd. v. Fareham UDC* 1956 the plaintiff building company claimed that a building contract should be regarded as discharged by frustration due to the shortage of available labour and resultant increased costs. The House of Lords rejected the arguments that frustration had discharged the contract. Performance of the contract had simply been made more onerous than originally envisaged by the plaintiffs.

(b) If the parties to a contract have made express provision for the event which has occurred then the common law doctrine of frustration is inapplicable. The courts will simply give effect to the intention of the parties expressed in the contract.

(c) A distinction must be drawn between a frustrating event over which the parties have no control and a *self-induced* frustration. If it can be shown that a party to the contract caused the supposed frustrating event by his own conduct then there will be no frustration but there may be a contractual breach.

   In *Maritime National Fish Ltd. v. Ocean Trawlers Ltd.* 1935 the appellants had chartered a trawler from the respondents. The vessel was fitted with an otter trawl, which it was unlawful to use without a government licence from the Minister. The appellants used five vessels for fishing and applied for five licences, but were granted three and were allowed to nominate which vessel the licence would cover. They did not nominate the vessel chartered from the respondents, and refused to pay the charter fee. The Court held that they were liable to pay it. They could not claim frustration since it was a self-induced situation which prevented them from using the vessel.

Consequences of frustration of contract

To determine the rights and duties of the parties following frustration it is necessary to consider the position at common law and under statute. Frustration of course will terminate a contract. However under common law it does not discharge the contract *ab initio* (from the outset) but only from the time of the frustrating event. Therefore, if before that date work had been done or money transferred, the common law rule is simply that losses lie where they fall. It is thus not possible to recover money due or paid prior to frustrating events, except if there is a total failure or consideration, for example if there has been performance of consideration by one party and non performance of consideration by the other.

The common law position has been altered to some extent by the Law Reform (Frustrated Contracts) Act 1943. The Act however does not apply to certain contracts such as insurance, charter-parties (shipping contracts) and contracts for the sale of specific goods, so the common law position is still relevant. Under the Act the following conditions apply:

- Money transferred prior to the frustrating event may be recovered.

- Money due prior to the frustrating event is no longer due.

- Expenses incurred prior to the frustrating event may be deducted from money to be returned.

- Compensation may be recovered on a quantum meruit basis where one of the parties has carried out an act of part performance prior to the frustrating event and thus conferred a benefit on the other party.

Remedies for Breach of Contract

No account of the principles of the contract is complete without some mention of the various remedies available to an innocent party in the event of a breach. The options available are to claim damages and/or treat the contract as discharged under the common law, or pursue an equitable discretionary remedy.

Damages

The usual remedy is to sue for *unliquidated* damages under the common law. Unliquidated damages are damages whose level is determined by the court, exercising its own discretion. It is sometimes possible for a plaintiff to quantify the measure of damages being sought concisely, in which event the plaintiff will claim a *liquidated* amount e.g.: three weeks loss of salary where the salary is of a fixed amount.

The aim of awarding damages

Damages awarded under an unliquidated claim, should amount to a sum of money which will put the innocent party in the position he would have been in had the contract been performed properly, that is the loss resulting from the breach directly and naturally. Consequently a plaintiff should not be awarded damages when the result would be to put him in a better position financially than would have been the case if the contract had not been broken.

> In *C & B Haulage v. Middleton* 1983 the Court of Appeal refused to grant damages to an engineer, who was evicted from the business premises he occupied before the contractual licence he held had expired. The reason for the refusal was that he was working from home, and thus relieved from paying any further charges under the licence. Damages would make him better off.

> In *Paula Lee Ltd. v. Robert Zehil & Co. Ltd.* 1983, under an agreement made between the parties the defendants had undertaken to take 16,000 dresses from the plaintiff manufacturers each season, which they would sell in the Middle East. The dresses in question covered a range of prices. The defendants terminated the agreement with two seasons left, and were only willing to pay compensation representing loss of profit to the plaintiffs on the sale of 32,000 of their cheapest dresses. The Court took the view that for the purposes of determining the measure of damages a term could be implied into the original agreement that the 32,000 garments involved would have been selected in a reasonable manner from the various price ranges involved, thus increasing the damages beyond the minimum level suggested by the defendants.

Damages may be refused where the court is of the view that they are too speculative.

> On this basis the court awarded only nominal damages to the plaintiffs in *Entertainments Ltd. v. Great Yarmouth Borough Council* 1983. The council had repudiated an agreement under which the plaintiffs were to put on summer shows in the town. The judge, Cantley J took the view that as it had not been established as probable that the shows would have made the plaintiffs a profit, to award anything other than nominal damages would be speculative.

Remoteness of damage

The consequences of a contractual breach can often extend well beyond the immediate, obvious losses. A failure to deliver goods may for example result in the buyer being unable to complete the work on a particular job, which will in turn put him in breach with the party who had contracted him to carry out the job. That party may in turn suffer further consequences, thus the original breach leads to a chain of events which become increasingly remote from it. Damages will only be awarded for losses which are proximate. The courts take the view that it is unfair to make a contract-breaker responsible for damage caused as a result of circumstances of which he was unaware.

> In *Hadley v. Baxendale* 1854 the plaintiff mill owner contracted with a defendant carrier who agreed to take a broken millshaft to a repairer and then return it. The carrier delayed in delivery of the shaft and as a result the plaintiff sought to recover the loss of profit he would have made during the period of delay. The court held that this loss was not recoverable as it was too remote. The possible loss of profit was a circumstance of which the carrier was unaware at the time of the contract. The result would have been different however had the plaintiff expressly made the defendant aware that this loss of profit was the probable result of a breach of contract.

The decision in *Hadley v. Baxendale* has been approved by the House of Lords on many occasions and knowledge of the circumstances which could produce the damage it still a crucial factor in determining the extent of the liability for the breach.

> In *Czarnikow v. Koufos (The Heron II)* 1969 a shipowner delayed in delivering a cargo of sugar to Basrah. The sugar was to be sold by the cargo owners at Basrah, where there was an established sugar market. During the nine days the ship was delayed the market price fell. The cargo owners successfully sued for their loss. The House of Lords considered that the loss ought to have been within the reasonable contemplation of the shipowners as a consequence of the delay. It was felt that the shipowners should have appreciated that a market for goods is something which by its nature fluctuates over time.

Other principles applicable to a claim for damages

Where a breach has occurred the innocent party, if he accepts that the breach discharges the contract, must take all reasonable steps to mitigate the loss resulting from the breach. There is no requirement for the injured party to act immediately to take on a risky venture but rather act reasonably in order to minimise the loss rather than 'sitting on the breach'. For instance an hotel would be expected to try and relet a room that a customer, in breach of contract, had failed to use.

> In *Moore v. DER Ltd.* 1971 the plaintiff, a dentist, ordered a new Rover 2000 as a replacement for the one he had which was a total loss following an accident. He could have purchased a second-hand car. The Court of Appeal took the view that he had acted reasonably, for his practice was a busy one and he needed a car that was completely reliable. Nor did this arrangement prevent him from recovering the costs of hiring another vehicle during the period he was waiting for the new car, even though he could have bought a second-hand car much sooner.

By way of contrast in *Luker v. Chapman* 1970 the plaintiff lost his right leg below the knee following a motor accident partly caused by the negligence of the defendant. This injury prevented him from continuing his work as a telephone engineer, but he was offered clerical work as an alternative. He refused it, choosing instead to go into teacher training. It was held that he could not recover as damages the loss of income suffered whilst he underwent the teacher training.

Damages are not limited to the pure economic cost of the loss of the bargain but may also be recovered for inconvenience, discomfort, distress or anxiety caused by the breach.

> In *Jarvis v. Swans Tours Ltd.* 1973 the Court of Appeal held that the plaintiff was entitled to damages for mental distress and disappointment due to loss of enjoyment caused by breach of a holiday contract.

> In *Perry v. Sidney Phillips & Son* 1982 a surveyor negligently failed to notify his client of defects in a house which the client subsequently bought. The defects included problems with a septic tank which caused offensive smells and violated health legislation. Damages for the client's distress and upset were granted.

In substantial contracts involving large sums, such as building contracts, it is usual to attempt to liquidate damages payable in the event of a breach. This is achieved by the parties expressly inserting a clause into the contract providing for a sum of compensation to be payable on a breach. Generally, provided such clauses represent a genuine pre-estimate of the future possible loss rather than amounting to a penalty to ensure performance of contract, they are enforceable by the courts.

A term will generally be regarded as a penalty clause if

(i)   the amount involved is regarded as extravagant. In *Dunlop Pneumatic Tyre Co. Ltd. v. New Garage & Motor Co. Ltd.* 1915 the appellants supplied tyres to the respondents at a trade discount on terms that if the respondents sold the tyres below list price they would pay the appellants £5 per tyre. The House of Lords treated this as a genuine estimate of the harm which Dunlop would suffer by undercutting, and thus enforceable. However in *Ford Motor Co. v. Armstrong* 1915 Armstrong, a motor retailer, agreed to pay £250 to Fords for every car he sold below their list price. The Court of Appeal regarded this as an extravagant sum which was thus void as a penalty.

(ii)   A fixed sum is payable on the occurrence of any one of several events, some of which may be minor breaches and some of which may be more serious.

(iii)   The amount payable is greater than the maximum amount of loss that is likely to be sustained.

Once the court decides however that the sum stipulated represents a liquidated damages clause, rather than a penalty, it will be enforced, even though the actual loss sustained may be larger, or smaller, than damages specified.

> Thus in *Cellulose Acetate Silk Co. Ltd. v. Widnes Foundry Ltd.* 1933 the foundry had agreed to pay £20 for every week of delay in completing the construction of premises for Cellulose Acetate. Delays amounted in total to 30 weeks, and Cellulose Acetate sought £6,000 compensation for the actual losses they had suffered. The Court held that Widnes Foundry were only liable for damages of £600 (£20 x 30 weeks) as agreed.

Liquidated damage clauses are a common commercial device. If you have ever looked at a holiday booking form you will have seen the graduated cancellation charges inserted by the holiday company, which increase in amount the closer to the holiday the cancellation occurs. This reflects the anticipated difficulty the operator is likely to experience in reselling the holiday at short notice.

The right to treat a contract as discharged will depend upon the nature of the breach. For breaches of condition the innocent party may sue for damages and/or treat the contract as repudiated, whereas for less important terms the innocent party is limited to an action for damages.

Quantification of damages in relation to goods or land is essentially a question of assessing the market price and then determining the actual loss. The Sale of Goods Act 1979 provides for a number of remedies, including damages, available to an injured party to a sale of goods transaction.

Discretionary remedies

These remedies are available because of the intervention of the Court of Chancery. They include the injunction, specific performance and the remedy of quantum meruit.

Injunctions

An injunction is an order of the court which directs a person not to break his contract, and is an appropriate remedy where the contract contains a negative stipulation.

> This can be seen in *Warner Bros. Pictures v. Nelson* 1937. The defendant, the actress Bette Davis, had agreed to work for the plaintiff company for twelve months, and not to act or sing for anyone else or be otherwise employed for a period of two years, without the plaintiff's written consent. It was held that she could be restrained by injunction from breaking the negative aspects of her undertaking, thus preventing her from working under a new acting contract in England where she was earning more money. The injunction was however confined to her work as an actress, for it was recognised that if the negative terms in her contract were fully enforced it would have the effect of either forcing her to work for Warner Bros. or starve, and this would mean the injunction acting as a device for specific performance of the contract. Equity will not order specific performance of contracts of a personal kind which would involve constant supervision, and which, by their nature, depend upon the good faith of the parties. Similarly in *Page One Records Ltd. v. Britton* 1968 an injunction was applied for to prevent the Troggs pop group from engaging anyone as their manager other than the plaintiff. An injunction on these terms was refused, for to grant it would indirectly compel the pop group to continue to employ the plaintiff.

Types of injunction

There are three types of injunction which may be applied for:

(a) **an interlocutory injunction**. This is designed to regulate the position of the parties pending trial, the plaintiff undertaking to be responsible for any damage caused to the defendant through the use of the injunction if in the subsequent action the plaintiff is unsuccessful. In *American Cyanamid v. Ethicon* 1975 the House of Lords said that an interlocutory injunction should only be granted where the plaintiff can show that the matter to be tried is a serious one and that the balance of convenience is in his favour. One rarely used option for an employee who feels that his employer is unreasonably requiring him to do work which is not part of his contactual obligations is to seek an injunction to maintain the status quo at work.

In *Hughs v. London Borough of Southwark* 1988 a number of social workers applied to the High Court for an injunction to stop their employers requiring them to staff community areas on a temporary basis and so terminate their normal hospital work. The High Court held that the employer's instruction was in breach of contract and the plaintiff social workers were entitled to an injunction to restrain the breach. The Court of Appeal in *Powell v. The London Borough of Brent* 1987 had previously held that the court has power to grant an injunction to restrain the breach of a contract of service provided that there was mutual confidence between the employer and employee. Here, despite the dispute, the employers retained confidence in the social workers. In this case the employers had *"failed to consult with the hospital or have sufficient steps in investigation properly to inform themselves as to the balance of work priorities.*

In certain circumstances a specialised kind of interlocutory injunction, known as a *Mareva injunction*, may be sought. The Mareva injunction takes its name from the case in which it was first successfully applied for, *Mareva Compania Naviera v. International Bulk Carriers* 1980, and it is used when the subject matter of a contract is in danger of being removed from the area of the courts jurisdiction. If the action which is to be heard involves a claim for damages and the sale of the subject matter is likely to be used to pay them, a Mareva injunction can be used to restrict the removal of these assets from the courts' jurisdiction. This is a valuable protection in cases where the defendant is a foreign organisation. s.37 Supreme Court Act 1981 grants the High Court the power to issue such injunctions.

(b)   **a prohibitory injunction**. This orders a defendant not to do a particular thing. The injunction sought in the *Nelson* case (above) was of this kind. Much of the case law concerning prohibitory injunctions is concerned with employment contracts, and as we have seen such an injunction can only be used to enforce a negative stipulation. In addition the remedy of a prohibitory injunction will not be given where a court is of the opinion that damages would be an adequate remedy, although in the words of Sachs LJ in *Evans Marshall v. Bertola SA* 1973 *"The standard question in relation to the grant of an injunction, are damages an adequate remedy? might perhaps, in the light of the authorities of recent years, be rewritten: is it just, in all the circumstances, that a plaintiff should be confined to his remedy in damages."*

A prohibitory injunction was used in *Decro-Wall International v. Practitioners in Marketing* 1971 where a manufacturer was restrained from breaking a sole distributorship agreement by an order preventing him from disposing of the goods to which the agreement related in any other way. The Court was not however prepared to order him to fulfil the positive part of the agreement which was to maintain supplies of the goods to the distributor, for this would have amounted to specific performance of the contract (see below).

In cases involving land an injunction may be used where for example, the purchaser has undertaken contractually with the vendor not to build on the land, but after the contract has been made seeks to break the promise.

(c)   **a mandatory injunction**. This is used to order that a positive act be done, for example that a fence blocking a right of way be taken down.

In *Sky Petroleum Ltd. v. VIP Petroleum Ltd.* 1974 the parties entered into a ten year agreement in 1970 under which VIP undertook to supply all Sky's petrol requirements. Following a dispute in 1973 VIP refused to continue its supplies to Sky, and because of an oil crisis at the time Sky found itself unable to secure any other source of supply. The Court granted a temporary injunction against VIP restraining it from withholding a reasonable level of supplies.

Specific performance

The decree of specific performance is an order of the court requiring a party who is in breach of contract to carry out his promises. Failure to comply amounts to a contempt of court. As an equitable remedy it will only be granted if certain conditions apply. These are:

- Where damages would not provide an adequate remedy. Usually in commercial transactions damages will be adequate, and will enable the injured party to purchase the property or obtain the services from some alternative source. However where the subject matter of the contract is unique, for example a painting, specific performance will lie. The item must however be unique, and in *Cohen v. Roche* 1927 specific performance was not ordered of a contract to sell some rare Hepplewhite chairs since it was difficult, but not impossible, to buy similar chairs on the open market.

Land is always regarded as unique, and it is in the enforcement of contracts for the sale of land that specific performance is most commonly used.

A contract for the purchase of shares or debentures can also be specifically enforced.

- Where the court can properly supervise the performance.

In *Ryan v. Mutual Tontine Association* 1893 the Court of Appeal held that despite the fact that a lessor of a service flat was in clear breach of his obligation to provide a porter who was to be *"constantly in attendance"*, an application for specific performance of the lease was refused. This was on the ground that to ensure compliance constant supervision by the Court would be required. Damages only therefore should be awarded.

- Where it is not just and equitable.

In *Malins v. Freeman* 1837 the Court refused the remedy where a bidder at an auction erroneously and carelessly bought property believing he had put in a bid for an entirely different lot. Damages was felt to be an adequate remedy against the bidder, who refused to complete the contract.

Further the plaintiff must satisfy the various equitable maxims which demand high standards of behaviour if relief is to be granted. Thus for example it is said that *"he who comes to equity must come with clean hands"*, meaning that the plaintiff's behaviour must be beyond reproach.

Quantum meruit

- A quantum meruit claim (i.e. for as much as is deserved) is available where:
- damages is not an appropriate remedy. This could occur where performance of a contract has begun, but the plaintiff is unable to complete the contract because the defendant has repudiated it, thus preventing the plaintiff from obtaining payment.
- where work has been carried out under a void contract.

In *British Steel Corporation v. Cleveland Bridge and Engineering Co. Ltd.* 1984 steel had been supplied to the defendants by the plaintiffs whilst the parties were still negotiating terms. The negotiations subsequently failed, and no contract was concluded between them. The court held that the plaintiffs were entitled to claim on a quantum meruit for the price of the steel supplied to the defendants and used by them.

Conclusion

The contract law we have explored in this chapter represents the culmination of centuries of legal development. Its breadth and depth reflects the significance of contract making to a country whose wealth was founded upon trade. The law of contract continues to evolve. You will have noticed that many of the cases we have used, have been decided within the last few years. One of the fields in which this evolution can be most clearly seen is that of consumer protection. The next chapter is devoted to exploring aspects of modern consumer protection law.

Unit Test Questions

1. Why is written contract useful?

2. Identify the four essential components which a simple contract must include.

3. How does a simple contract differ from a deed?

4. Distinguish between void, voidable and unenforceable contracts.

5. Give three examples of contracts which the law requires to be in writing.

6. What characteristics make up a valid offer?

7. What is the difference between an invitation to treat and a tender? Is it true that an invitation to treat carries no legal consequences?

8. Does a meaningless term in a contract invalidate the contract?

9. When an offer is made how long does it remain valid?

10. Is it true to say that silence can never amount to acceptance?

11. What are the effects of the post rules in contract making?

12. Explain the meaning and effect of the expression "the battle of forms".

13. What does the expression "consideration" mean in contract making?

14. Give an example of consideration which is regarded by the courts as not sufficient.

15. State the principle contained in Pinnels Case.

16. When is consideration regarded as past?

17. Which categories of contract are binding on minors?

18. How is misrepresentation defined?

19. Give two examples of statements which do not constitute a representation.

20. Distinguish between innocent, negligent and fraudulent misrepresentation.

21. What must be proved to escape from liability under a signed document.

22. How do you establish an operative mistake as to identify ?

23. How does mutual mistake differ from common mistake?

24. What is undue influence and how does it affect a contract?

25. Give two examples of a contract in restraint of trade.

26. What is the commercial value of a standard form contract?

27. Define the expression condition and identify how conditions are distinguished from warranties.

28. In what circumstances will a court be prepared to imply a term into a contract?

29. Identify the four ways in which a contract can be discharged and state what thee expresion "discharged" means.

30. When is the concept of substantial performance applied to a contract?

31. What is accord and satisfaction?

32. On what grounds can a contract be said to be frustrated?

33. State the principles which a court will follow when it is asked to award unliquidated damages.

34. Describe two types of injunction which may be granted as a contractual remedy.

35. What does quantum meruit mean and when can it be claimed?

Assignment *Are We Agreed?*

You work as a legal assistant in the legal department of Anglo-Amalgamated Metal Industries plc. On returning from your summer holiday you find two files in your in-tray. They are accompanied by a memorandum from your superior, one of the company's lawyers, which states, "Please respond to the letters contained in the attached files. See me if you have any difficulties."

The first file contains the following letter from a solicitor:

I represent Miss Sally Goldwell. I understand from my client that she was interviewed for a clerical post with your company. Following the interview she was asked if she would be willing to accept the post, and she indicated that she would. Two days later, on 10th September 199X, she received a formal offer of the post from your company's Personnel Officer. She was asked to reply in writing within five days. She was ill at the time and arranged for a friend to notify you of her acceptance by phone. Her friend telephoned sometime after 7 pm on 13th September 199X. This was a Friday, and her friend had to leave a message on the Personnel Department's answerphone. I gather that the Personnel Department closes from 4.30pm on Friday, until 8.30 the following Monday, and that the message only reached the Personnel Officer at Midday on Monday 16th September. He had that morning telephoned another interviewee to offer her the job, which she accepted. My client subsequently heard from you that the post was no longer available for her.

I am of the opinion that a contract exists between my client and yourselves, in respect of which you are in breach. I look forward to your prompt response.

Yours faithfully,

Roger Major

The second file contained the following letter from one of the company's suppliers, Humberside Steels Ltd.:

We refer to our offer to supply you with 40 tonnes reinforced steel bars, to which you responded with an order (68747/5/NX) for the goods to be delivered to you on 1st May. We replied immediately informing you that due to circumstances beyond our control delivery would be on the 24th May. We heard nothing from you, and delivered the goods on 24th May, only to find that you rejected them on the basis that they had not been ordered. We are at a loss to understand your action, particularly as we have often varied the delivery date with you in this way in the past, without complaint by you.

We should be grateful therefore to receive your remittance in due course.

Yours faithfully

James Leach pp
Humberside Steels Ltd.

Tasks

1. Draft replies to each of these letters, in which you state the legal basis upon which the company challenges the contractual claims they make.

2. In the form of a memorandum to your superior, Jane West, state the action you have taken, and indicate any weakness you feel may exist in the company's legal position in respect of the two claims.

Development Task

The local citizens advice bureau has approached you to give a short talk to its voluntary workers concerning the way in which contractual agreements are made. Produce a short information sheet outlining the nature of a contract which you can give to the workers at the end of a meeting.

Assignment　*An Arabian Tale*

Thompsons Importers was owned and managed by Michael Thompson. Michael had decided to sell the business, having reached an age at which he felt he ought to be taking life more easily. The major activity carried on by Thompsons was the import into the United Kingdom of luxury goods from the Middle East and India.

The business was put on the market, and one of Michael's trading competitors, Arabian Exportex Ltd. expressed an interest in acquiring it. The managing director of the company, Alan Naseem, indicated to Michael that the company would require a report on the condition and future prospects of the business and Michael agreed to this.

The report was prepared by Rupert Gray, an accountant with Frayne and Company a reputable firm of accountants in Birmingham. Alan Naseem happened to know Rupert Gray, and encouraged him to make the report, "as pessimistic in assessing the future prospects of Thompsons as you feel truth will permit."

Rupert Gray's report contained a number of reasons for doubting the future viability of Thompsons. In particular it contained statements that: "the business is unlikely to withstand competition from foreign competitors whose profit margins and overheads are lower, and who are attracting an increasing share of the market"; and "import duties on luxury goods from outside the EEC are to be increased from next year."

Rupert Gray actually had no knowledge or information about foreign competition either for the present of the future, but had relied on observations made by Alan Naseem during a conversation with him. He had however read an article in Accountancy World in which it was stated that "import duties on some luxury items brought into the United Kingdom from outside the EEC are to be revised." Arabia Exportex Ltd. sent a copy of the report to Michael Thompson, who in consequence dropped his price by £100,000. Arabia Exportex Ltd. purchased at the lower price.

Two years after selling out to Arabia Exportex Ltd., Michael happened to meet a former business colleague who knows the import business well. Michael discovered that no changes had been made to import duties since he sold the business, and the foreign competition referred to in the report had not materialised. Following an angry phone call to Alan Naseem, Mr. Naseem has revealed the instruction he gave to Rupert Gray regarding the report, and says his company cannot be held responsible for a report produced by an independent professional.

Task

You are employed by a large firm of accountants who for many years have handled Michael Thompson's affairs. You are called upon to provide legal advice from time to time, and the senior partner has passed on to you the situations described above, as told to him by Michael Thompson. The senior partner suggests that probably a solicitor needs to be involved, but has asked you to arrange to meet Mr. Thompson to discuss the matter when he calls in to the office next week, or alternatively to write advising him.

Prepare notes on the issues involved as a preliminary to meeting and discussing the matter with Mr. Thompson.

Assignment   *A Bad Week at Britech*

The Managing Director of Britech Systems Ltd., an electronics company based in West London and for which you work, has asked you to look into two problems facing the company which have blown up over the last week and are causing him considerable anxiety. One of these problems concerns a major contract negotiated between the company and an international telecommunications organisation ITTB. The contract involves the construction, installation and maintenance by Britech of a highly sophisticated computer monitoring system to control signals beamed to and from the United Kingdom and North America using ITTB's own satellite. The system was due to be installed and be fully operational by the beginning of December, eight months away, but work has been halted due to the commercial collapse of Modem plc, which is only UK supplier of certain vital microelectronic components used by Britech in the construction of the monitoring system. Modem went into liquidation two weeks ago, and it is unclear whether there is any chance of receiving the components ordered by Britech from Modem. ITTB, aware of the problem, is arguing that its contract with Britech has been frustrated, and has indicated that it is seeking another company to supply the system as a matter of urgency.

Additionally one of Britech's senior employees, who left the company six months ago, has just set up his own business as a microelectronics consultant. In common with other senior staff the employee, Gerry McBain, had agreed to a clause in his contract of employment which stipulated, "The employee agrees and undertakes that in the event of the termination of his/her employment with the company, he/she will not compete in any way with the business of the company or so act as to cause damage to the interests of the company, for a period of five years, to run from the date of termination, such undertaking to extend to the whole of England and Wales."

The managing director of Britech has arranged to meet you tomorrow to discuss the legal position in relation both to ITTB and to Mr McBain.

Tasks

Analyse the two situations described, and produce notes on them in which you seek to clarify the company's position, in order to advise the managing director (a) whether the company has a contractual claim against ITTB, and if it has what the measure of damages is likely to be, and (b) what the likelihood is of the company being able to successfully obtain an injunction to prevent the business activities of Mr. McBain.

Element

9.4 Investigate the rights of business customers and consumers

Performance Criteria

1. The nature and scope of consumer protection is investigated
2. Key rights of consumers are identified
3. Procedures for dispute settlement between customers and business are described

Range

Nature and scope:

Statutory framework i.e. Sale of Goods Act 1979, Supply of Goods and Services Act 1982, Consumer Credit Act 1974, Consumer Protection Act 1987, Data Protection Act 1984, European Community regulations related to consumer protection

Key rights:

In relation to sale of goods; consumer credit transactions; supply of goods and services; product liability, use of data

Procedures:

Arbitration, small claims, civil courts

Evidence Indicators

A case study containing consumer problems which the student will identify, suggest solutions to and explain the procedure to be followed to attain a successful outcome

Chapter 5

Rights of Business Customers and Consumers

Consumer Protection

The primary objective of business activity is the provision of goods and services for consumers. Consumption of goods and services meets the private needs of individuals. All of us act as private consumers in this way. We make regular purchases of goods and services to satisfy our demand for a wide range of necessaries and luxuries, from food and clothing to motor cars, video recorders and holidays. Goods and services are also demanded by business organisations, who acquire them to meet their own internal requirements, as well as for the purpose of resale to other businesses in the chain of production or to consumers. The legal rules relating to inter-business contracting are, in many cases, identical to those which apply where a business deals with a private consumer. However the law has increasingly sought to compensate for the relative economic weakness of individual consumers, by developing a framework of consumer protection.

The protection of the consumer has been sought by a combination of legal devices. These include:

(i) conferring remedies which are available by legal action in the civil courts, for example under the Sale of Goods Act 1979;

(ii) regulating certain types of trading activities, for instance through the licensing requirements under the Consumer Credit Act 1974 or registration under the Data Protection Act 1984; and

(iii) imposing criminal liability in respect of certain types of unacceptable trading practices, for example under the Trade Descriptions Act 1968.

A number of key consumer protection measures imposing criminal liability on the trader are examined in Chapter 3. In this chapter it is proposed to deal principally with the civil law rights and remedies of the consumer and to examine the nature and scope of consumer rights arising from the implementation of EC directives on product liability and package travel.

Figure 5.1 on the next page is designed to provide an overview of the major features of consumer protection under the civil and criminal law.

	Civil Law	Criminal Law
Enforcement	Recission of contract Sue for damages (or defence to an action for damages) in the County Court or High Court Arbitration	Local Authority: Trading Standards Department Prosecution in the Magistrates and Crown Courts Compensation orders under the Powers of Criminal Courts Act 1973 Director General of Fair Trading Data Protection Registrar
Defective Products	Sale of Goods Act 1979 Supply of Goods and Services Act 1982 Tort of Negligence Consumer Protection Act 1987 Codes of Practice	Consumer Protection Act 1987 Food Safety Act 1990 Road Traffic Act 1988 and other specific legislation Health and Safety at Work Act 1974
Defective Services	Supply of Goods and Services Act 1982 Professional Negligence Regulation by trade or professional associations Codes of Practice Package Travel Regulations 1992	Trade Descriptions Act 1968 Consumer Credit Act 1974 Health and Safety at Work Act 1974 Package Travel Regulations 1992
False Statements	Misrepresentation Breach of Contract Negligent mis-statement Tort of Deceit Data Protection Act 1984	Trade Descriptions Act 1968 Consumer Protection Act 1987 Weights and Measures Act 1985 Fair Trading Act 1973 Data Protection Act 1984
Exclusion of Liability	Common Law rules of incorporation and interpretation Unfair Contract Terms Act 1977	Consumer Transactions (Restrictions on Statements) Order 1976 and (Amendment) Order 1978

Figure 5.1 *Consumer Protection under the Civil Law and the Criminal Law*

Consumer protection by means of statutory implied terms

Key consumer rights, for example in relation to faulty or shoddy goods or those which have been wrongly described or labelled, derive from the statutory implied terms contained in sections 12 to 15 of the Sale of Goods Act 1979 and equivalent provisions in other Acts.

In the last chapter we saw that obligations may arise under a contract in two different ways. First because the law imposes them, for example by Act of Parliament, and second because the parties expressly agree to them.

In a contract for the sale or supply of goods the law imposes obligations on the supplier by the legal mechanism of implied terms in the contract of supply. These statutory implied terms operate as if the seller had said to the buyer "I promise you that…". Most of these terms are conditions, which, if broken, will give rise to the right to repudiate the contract, reject the goods and sue for damages. There are a small number of implied warranties also. The buyer's remedy in the event of a breach of warranty is damages. In the case of a breach of condition, as we shall see later in the text, the buyer may lose the right to reject the goods in certain circumstances.

The implied terms contained in Sections 12 to 15 of the Sale of Goods Act 1979 automatically become part of any contract for the sale of goods. Equivalent terms have been introduced into most other types of contract involving the supply of goods. The Supply of Goods (Implied Terms) Act 1973 and the Supply of Goods and Services Act 1982 have followed the model originally laid down in the Sale of Goods Act with the result that the full range of contracts under which goods are supplied are now covered by the same terms. For convenience we shall refer to the 1979 Act for the purpose of examining the detailed content of the implied terms below.

Consumer protection where the seller of goods has no right to sell

Under s.12 of the 1979 Act there is an implied condition that the seller has the right to sell the goods. If this is broken, for example because the goods belong to someone else, the buyer will be able to repudiate the contract and recover in full the price he paid.

> In *Rowland v. Divall* 1923 three months after buying a motor car the purchaser discovered that it had been stolen before it came into the seller's possession. The seller therefore had no right to sell it. The purchaser returned the car to its original owner and sued the seller under s.12. It was held that he was entitled to the return of the price because he had suffered a 'total failure of consideration'. The fact that the buyer had used the car for over three months did not affect his right to recover the full purchase price.

Where the seller is the true owner of the goods he may nevertheless have no right to sell them if for example they infringe intellectual property rights held by another person.

> In *Niblett v. Confectioners Materials Co.* 1921 the purchaser of a quantity of tins of preserved milk could not resell them without infringing the Nestle Company Trade Mark. This infringement arose because the labels placed on tins by the manufacturer bore the name 'Nissly Brand'. The seller was held to be in breach of s.12.

Under s.12 there is also an implied warranty that the goods are free from any potential claims by any third parties which had not been disclosed to the buyer. There is also an implied warranty that the buyer will enjoy quiet possession of the goods.

> In *Microbeads v. Vinhurst Road Markings* 1975 the seller sold road marking machines to the buyer. After the sale a third party obtained a patent on the machine. The continued use of the machine by the buyer was then in breach of the third party's patent rights. The buyer sued the seller under s.12 claiming that he was in breach of the implied condition that he had the right to sell, and of the implied warranty that the buyer would enjoy quiet possession. The Court of Appeal held that there was no breach of condition. At the time of the sale there was no infringement of the patent and therefore the seller had the right to sell. However, the seller was liable in damages for breach of the warranty that the buyer would enjoy quiet possession of the goods.

Consumer protection where goods are wrongly described or labelled

Where there is a contract for the sale of goods by description, s.13 of the 1979 Act implies a condition that the goods will correspond with the description. Whenever the buyer has not seen the goods before the contract is made the sale is obviously a sale by description. Also, if goods are packaged, for example food inside a tin or cardboard box, there is a sale by description. The buyer will only be able to see the goods after he has purchased them and opened the package. The vast majority of sales will be made by description. The 1979 Act provides in s.13(3) that a sale of goods is not prevented from being a sale by description by reason only that the goods are selected by the buyer after being exposed for sale, for example in a self-service store. The description can extend to such things as weight, size, quantity, composition and age.

> In *Dick Bentley Productions Ltd. v. Harold Smith Motors Ltd.* 1965 a car dealer sold a second-hand car with a recorded mileage of 30,000. In fact the true mileage was nearer 100,000. The seller was held liable for a breach of s.13.

Similar conduct today could make the seller criminally liable under the Trade Descriptions Act 1968 (considered in Chapter 3). One significant difference between the Sale of Goods Act and the Trade Descriptions Act is that the latter only applies where the sale is made in the course of a trade or business. Section 13 applies both to private and business sales.

> In *Beale v. Taylor* 1967 the buyer purchased a car advertised as a 1961 Herald Convertible having had a trial run in it as a passenger. The buyer soon found the car to be unsatisfactory. On an examination by a garage it was discovered that the car had been made up of halves of two different cars. The rear portion was part of a 1961 Triumph Herald 1200 model while the front was part of a earlier 948 model. The two portions had been welded together unsatisfactorily into one structure, and the vehicle was unroadworthy and unsafe. The Court of Appeal held that the seller had broken the promise implied into the contract by s.13 and was liable in damages to the buyer.

The seller will be in breach of s.13 if he does not comply strictly with the contract description.

> In *Arcos Ltd. v. E.A. Ronaasen & Son* 1933 the buyer agreed to purchase a quantity of wooden staves, half an inch thick, for making cement barrels. When they were delivered only 5% of them were exactly half an inch and the vast majority were nine sixteenths of an inch in thickness. An arbitrator found that the staves were still reasonably fit for making cement barrels. The House of Lords held that the buyers were entitled to reject the goods because the seller had not strictly complied with the contract description. Lord Atkin observed:
>
> *"a ton does not mean about a ton, or a yard about a yard. Still less when you descend to minute measurements does half an inch mean about half an inch. If the seller wants a margin he must and in my experience does stipulate for it".*

Very small deviations from the contractual specification can however be disregarded for example where a delivery of 250 gallons of oil is 2 pints short.

Where the seller does not comply with the contract description the buyer is entitled to reject the goods even though he suffers no damage.

> In *Re Moore & Co. Ltd. and Landauer & Co.* 1921 the buyer purchased a quantity of canned fruit. The contract stipulated that each case should contain thirty tins but on delivery about half the total quantity of tins were packed into cases of twenty four. The

court held that the buyer was entitled to reject the goods, even though there was no evidence that the buyer would suffer any loss.

Although the vast majority of sales will be made by description, it is possible even where the seller has applied a description to goods in the course of negotiations or in the contract itself, that the court may find that the sale is not made 'by' description. This can occur where the buyer places no reliance on the description and the court imputes no common intention that the description is an essential part of the contract.

> In *Harlingdon & Leinster Enterprises Ltd. v. Christopher Hull Fine Art Ltd.* 1990 the plaintiffs were art dealers at a London gallery specialising in the German expressionist school. The defendants, who were dealers specialising in contemporary British artists, were asked to sell an oil painting described in an earlier auction catalogue as the work of Gabriele Munter, an artist of the German expressionist school. During the course of negotiations for the sale of the painting, it was made clear to the plaintiffs that the defendants did not know much about the painting and had no expertise in relation to it. It was described during negotiations and on the sales invoice as a Munter. Subsequent to the sale it was discovered to be a forgery and the plaintiffs sued to recover the purchase price under s.13. The Court of Appeal held that the plaintiffs' claim failed because the sale was not made 'by' description. The plaintiffs had not relied on the description but had bought the painting purely on their own assessment of it.

Consumer protection and faulty goods

Merchantable quality

Section 14(2) of the 1979 Act provides:

> *"Where the seller sells goods in the course of a business there is an implied condition that the goods supplied under the contract are of merchantable quality, except that there is no such condition:*
>
> *(a)   as regards defects specifically drawn to the buyer's attention before the contract is made; or*
>
> *(b)   if the buyer examines the goods before the contract is made, as regards defects which that examination ought to reveal".*

There are a number of important features of s.14(2) which should be noted:

(a)   the seller must be a business seller. The implied condition does not apply to private sales;

(b)   the seller may be anyone in the chain of distribution, such as a manufacturer, wholesaler or retailer;

(c)   the condition does not apply where a defect has been drawn to the buyer's attention prior to the sale, or where the buyer has examined the goods before buying them and ought to have discovered the defect: (see *R & B Customs Brokers v. United Dominions Trust* 1988 and *Crow v. Barford and Holttum* 1963 discussed later in the text);

(d)   in order to comply with this section, some system of quality control will need to be introduced. This is particularly so where the seller is also the manufacturer;

(e)   liability under the section is strict:

In *Frost v. Aylesbury Dairies Ltd.* 1905 the dairy supplied milk contaminated with typhoid germs and was held liable despite establishing that it had used all reasonable care to prevent such contamination.

The expression merchantable quality is defined in s.14(6) which provides:

"Goods of any kind are of merchantable quality if they are as fit for the purpose or purposes for which goods of that kind are commonly bought as it is reasonable to expect having regard to any description applied to them, the price (if relevant) and all other relevant circumstances".

Under this definition the standard of quality will vary according to the circumstances of the case. Goods must be reasonably fit for their ordinary uses, although account may be taken of any description applied to them and, where relevant, the price. Clearly if goods are described as 'seconds' or 'manufacturer's rejects' they will not be expected to be of perfect quality. Similarly, the standard of quality and durability expected of shoes priced at £18 will be lower than that expected of those priced £58. However if the £58 shoes had been reduced in a sale to a price of £18, the sale price would probably not be relevant in determining the standard of quality expected.

In *Bartlett v. Sydney Marcus Ltd.* 1965 the seller, who was a car dealer, warned the buyer that a second-hand car had a defective clutch. The buyer was given a choice of purchasing it for £550 as it was, or £575 after the seller had repaired it. The buyer opted to take the car as it was. The repairs cost more than the buyer expected. He sued the seller alleging that, for this reason, the car was not of merchantable quality. The Court of Appeal held that the seller was not liable as there was no breach of the implied term.

In *Crowther v. Shannon Motor Company* 1975 it was held that a second-hand car which needed a replacement engine after three weeks was not of merchantable quality. The car had been described as being in excellent condition.

The requirement of merchantable quality extends not only to the goods themselves but also to their packaging and any instructions supplied with them.

In *Wormell v. RHM Agriculture (East) Ltd.* 1987 the plaintiff was a farmer who purchased a chemical spray from the defendant in order to kill wild oats. The instructions provided with the spray indicated that its use outside a certain period carried the risk of injury to the crop. The plaintiff was aware of the warning and decided to take that risk. In fact, because of the late application, the spray was totally ineffective. The plaintiff claimed damages for the costs of the spray and the wasted labour in applying it. The Court of Appeal accepted that, as a matter of principle, any instructions supplied with goods would be treated as part of the goods themselves in assessing merchantability or fitness for purpose. On the facts, however, it was held that the seller was not liable as the instructions had clearly stated that spraying after a certain period of growth was not recommended. The seller was not bound to give full and exhaustive reasons for the instructions given.

The wording of s.14(2) makes it clear that the obligation applies to all goods which are supplied under the contract.

In *Geddling v. Marsh* 1920 mineral water was sold in bottles which were to remain the property of the manufacturer. The buyer was injured when a defective bottle burst. It was held that he was entitled to damages under s.14 even though the bottles were loaned rather than sold to him under the terms of the contract.

This rule applies even if the item which causes the harm was mistakenly supplied with the contract goods:

> In *Wilson v. Rickett, Cockerell and Co. Ltd.* 1954 a delivery of 'Coalite' included a detonator from the mine, which exploded when it was put onto a household fire. The Court of Appeal held that the sellers were liable for a breach of s.14(2).

Goods may be unmerchantable even if they can easily be put right.

> In *Grant v. Australian Knitting Mills Ltd.* 1936 the buyer purchased underpants which contained a chemical. This caused dermatitis, a skin disease, when the buyer wore them. The chemical would have been removed if the buyer had washed them before he wore them. It was held that the goods were not of merchantable quality, and the seller was liable.

The seller will not be liable, however, if the defect in the goods is caused by the way in which the buyer treats them.

> In *Heil v. Hedges* 1951 the buyer was infected with tapeworms after eating a pork chop which had been undercooked. It was held that the seller was not liable because the meat would have been quite safe if it had been properly cooked.

It appears that a seller will not be liable under this section solely because there are no spare parts available to service the goods which he has supplied.

> In *L. Gent v. Eastman Machine Co. Ltd.* 1985 the plaintiff purchased a knitting machine from the defendant. Not long afterwards spare parts were required and it took four months for the spares to be supplied. It was held that the knitting machine was not rendered unmerchantable by the seller's failure to be able to supply spare parts within a reasonable time.

In 1983 the Law Commission published a working paper, no. 85, entitled The Sale and Supply of Goods, followed by a report (Cm 137) in 1987. This recommended a clarification of the seller's obligations in relation to the quality of goods supplied. The phrase merchantable quality should be replaced with *'acceptable quality'*. Goods would be of acceptable quality if they were of a standard that a reasonable person would regard as acceptable, taking account of any description applied to them, the price, and all other relevant circumstances. Relevant circumstances would extend beyond the question of fitness of the goods for their common purposes, and include matters such as the appearance of the goods, their finish, suitability for immediate use, freedom from minor defects, safety, and durability. It is likely that legislation will incorporate the recommendations of the Law Commission eventually but, in the meantime, the Court of Appeal appears to have taken a lead in the same direction.

> In *Rogers v. Parish (Scarborough) Ltd.* 1987 the plaintiff bought a new Range Rover from the defendant's garage. Although it was driveable and roadworthy the car had a number of defects in its engine, gearbox, oil seals and bodywork. The defendant argued that the car was of merchantable quality within the definition in s.14(6) as it could be driven in safety on a road and therefore was "fit for the purpose for which goods of that kind are commonly bought". The Court of Appeal rejected the defendant's argument on the grounds that it was based upon too narrow an interpretation of s.14(6). Mustill LJ, declared that:
>
> *"the purpose for which goods of that kind are commonly bought would include not merely the purpose of driving the vehicle from one place to another but of doing so with the*

appropriate degree of comfort, ease of handling, reliability and pride in the vehicle's outward and interior appearance".

In two further cases, the Court of Appeal has made it clear that the principles laid down in *Rogers v. Parish* are equally applicable to sales of second hand cars.

In *Business Applications Specialists v. Nationwide Credit Corporation Ltd.* 1988 the plaintiff purchased a second-hand Mercedes motor car for £14,850. It was two years old and had a recorded mileage of 37,000. The plaintiff drove the car for 800 miles when it broke down due to burnt out valves and worn valve guides and guide seals. The cost of repairs was £635. The County Court judge dismissed the action on the grounds that the car was roadworthy despite the defects. The plaintiffs appeal was dismissed by the Court of Appeal which held that although judge had applied the wrong test he had reached the correct conclusion. He ought to have applied the test laid down in *Rogers v. Parish*.

In *Shine v. General Guarantee Corporation Ltd.* 1988 a second-hand Bertoni-bodied Fiat X19 had been advertised as 'superb' and described verbally as 'nice car, good runner, no problems'. In fact the car had been written off after having been submerged in water for 24 hours. The Court of Appeal held that, comparing the purchaser's reasonable expectations at the time of sale with the actual condition of the car, it was not of merchantable quality. In the words of Bush J:

"He was buying potentially a 'rogue car' and irrespective of its condition it was in fact one which no member of the public, knowing the facts, would touch with a barge pole unless they could get it at a substantially reduced price to reflect the risk they were taking.... A car is not just a means of transport, it is a form also of investment (though a deteriorating one) and every purchaser of a car must have in mind the eventual saleability of the car as well as, in this particular case, his pride in it as a specialist car for the enthusiast".

Fitness for notified purpose

Where the buyer requires the goods for a special or unusual purpose, the seller may be liable for a breach of s.14(3) if the goods are not fit for that purpose. Under s.14(3):

"Where the seller sells goods in the course of a business and the buyer, expressly or by implication, makes known ... to the seller ... any particular purpose for which the goods are being bought, there is an implied condition that the goods supplied under the contract are reasonably for that purpose, whether or not that is a purpose for which such goods are commonly supplied, except where the circumstances show that the buyer does not rely, or that it is unreasonable for him to rely, on the skill or judgment of the seller".

Consumers sometimes place reliance on the expertise of the seller, for example when a customer goes into a shop and asks whether the shop has something that will perform a particular task, say fixing a broken ornament or removing stains from a carpet. A business may describe its accounting procedures to a supplier of office equipment, relying on the supplier to provide a suitable system to cope with these procedures. In these cases the seller will be liable under s.14(3) if the goods, even though of merchantable quality, do not fulfil the purpose for which the buyer requires them.

In *Cammell Laird & Co. Ltd. v. Manganese Bronze & Brass Co. Ltd.* 1934 the buyers supplied the sellers with a specification for ships' propellers which they were to manufacture for the buyers. Reliance was placed upon the sellers regarding matters outside the specification, including the thickness of metal to be used. The propellers were found on delivery to be too thin. The buyer's action was successful on the ground that the unfitness concerned a matter on which the buyers had relied upon the seller's skill.

There will be no liability under s.14(3) where the circumstances show that the buyer does not rely on the skill or judgment of the seller.

> In *Teheran-Europe Co. Ltd. v. ST Belton Tractors Ltd.* 1968 industrial equipment was sold to the plaintiff buyer for the purpose of exporting and resale in Persia. The seller knew this but was not familiar with the Persian market, unlike the buyer who carried on a business there. The equipment infringed Persian regulations and the plaintiff sued the seller for breach of s.14(3). The Court of Appeal held that the seller was not liable as the buyer had relied on his own skill and judgment as to whether the equipment was suitable for resale in Persia. There was no reliance on the skill or judgment of the seller.

When the product only has one purpose the buyer will be held to have impliedly made known to the seller the purpose for which he wants the goods.

> In *Priest v. Last* 1903 the buyer was held to have made known impliedly to the seller the purpose for which he required a hot water bottle. The seller was liable under s.14(3) when the bottle burst after a few days injuring the buyer.

The seller will not be liable however, where the buyer does not tell him of any particular requirements.

> In *Griffiths v. Peter Conway Ltd.* 1939 the buyer, who had particularly sensitive skin, developed dermatitis as a result of wearing a coat which she bought from the defendant. The coat would not have had this effect on a normal person and the buyer had not told the seller about her sensitivity. It was held that the seller was not liable under s.14(3).

Consumer protection where goods are sold by sample

This is a form of protection which will apply mainly to the business customer, for example where raw materials or large quantities of goods are purchased after a sample has been examined and perhaps tested for its suitability for the customers purpose. It can also apply to consumer situations, for example, where a new carpet or a made to measure suit is purchased by an individual. The sample acts as a sort of three dimensional description of the final product which can be touched or tasted or in some other way give the potential buyer a fuller appreciation of the nature of the product on offer.

Under s.15 of the 1979 Act, where goods are sold according to a sample, there are implied conditions that:

(a)   the bulk of the consignment will correspond with the sample in terms of quality;

(b)   the buyer shall have a reasonable opportunity of comparing the bulk with the sample; and

(c)   the goods shall be free from any defect rendering them unmerchantable which would not be apparent on a reasonable examination of the sample.

The function of a sample was described by Lord MacNaghten in *Drummond v. Van Ingen* 1887 when he stated:

> *"The office of a sample is to present to the eye the real meaning and intention of the parties with regard to the subject matter of the contract which, owing to the imperfections*

of language, it may be difficult or impossible to express in words. The sample speaks for itself".

Claims based on more than one ground

Where a person is injured by defective goods there may be a number of alternative grounds upon which he could sue. There is a considerable degree of overlap between s.14(2) and s.14(3), so that, for example the sellers in *Frost v. Aylesbury Dairies* 1905 and *Priest v. Last* 1903 were in breach of both implied conditions. The seller in *Beale v. Taylor* 1967 was found to be in breach of s.13, and would probably have been in breach of s.14 if he had sold the car in the course of a business. There is also a considerable overlap between the law of contract and the tort of negligence in this area. In *Grant v. Australian Knitting Mills* 1935 the retailer was liable because the goods were not of merchantable quality, and the manufacturer was liable in negligence.

Later in this chapter a number of cases are examined in the field of product liability, for example *Lambert v. Lewis* 1981, in which the injured party's claim is based both in negligence and in contract. Part 1 of the Consumer Protection Act 1987 gives additional remedies for injury by defective products. It is quite conceivable that an injured party would have a claim in contract, in negligence and under the 1987 Act. Figure 5.3 (later) provides a comparison between these three alternatives. Of course the injured party can only recover damages once, but he may bring his claim under all of these headings by 'pleading in the alternative'. If he fails in one aspect of his claim, he can still recover damages if another succeeds.

The rule of privity of contract means that only the buyer can claim for breach of the implied terms. If this claim against the seller succeeds then liability can be passed down the line through the chain of distribution. The seller can sue his supplier for an indemnity based upon the supplier's breach of contract. He is in effect trying to drop out of the picture by saying "if I am liable then as my supplier you are liable on the same basis". This process, known as third party proceedings, continues until the manufacturer is sued. Only an effective exclusion of liability clause can break the chain of indemnity.

> In *Godley v. Perry (Burton & Sons Ltd., Third Party; Graham, Fourth Party)* 1960 a boy of six lost the sight of one eye when firing a catapult which he had bought for 6d from the defendant's shop. The catapult fractured below the point where the handle joined the fork. The evidence showed that is was made of cheap brittle polystyrene, indifferently moulded and containing internal voids. The retailer had purchased the catapult from a wholesaler who had purchased it from an importer. The importer had bought the goods from a manufacturer in Hong Kong. The plaintiff sued the defendant shopkeeper who issued third party proceedings against the wholesaler. The wholesaler in turn claimed against the importer. The court decided that the catapult was not of merchantable quality, and that the retailer was liable to the purchaser. Liability passed up the line so at the end of the day the importer (or his insurers) were left either to bear the loss or pursue the manufacturer in the Hong Kong courts.

Exclusion of liability for breach of statutory implied terms in contracts for the supply of goods: Sections 6 & 7 Unfair Terms Act 1977

Section 6 of the 1977 Act applies to contracts for the sale of goods and hire purchase agreements, while s.7 applies to all other contracts under which the possession or ownership of goods passes to the customer. The rules contained in each section are very similar, although there are some minor differences between them.

The extent of the protection given to a customer under these rules depends on whether or not he deals as a consumer.

Exclusion where buyer is a consumer

Where the customer deals as a consumer, there can be no exclusion of the terms implied under Sections 12 to 15 of the Sale of Goods Act 1979 and the equivalent provisions in the Supply of Goods (Implied Terms) Act 1973 and the Supply of Goods and Services Act 1982. As a result a purchaser who deals as a consumer obtains a high level of protection. The circumstances in which a purchaser will be dealing as a consumer are set out in s.12 of the 1977 Act which states:

"*a party to a contract deals as a consumer in relation to another party if:*

(a) *he neither makes the contract in the course of a business nor holds himself out as doing so; and*

(b) *the other party does make the contract in the course of a business; and*

(c) *where the contract involves the supply of goods, the goods are of a type ordinarily supplied for private use or consumption*".

Three aspects of the transaction must be examined in order to see whether the buyer deals as a consumer: the buyer, the seller and the goods themselves. If the buyer buys for his business or from a private seller or if the goods are of a type which would not usually be purchased for private use then the buyer cannot deal as a consumer. The courts have been prepared to give a fairly wide interpretation of s.12:

In *Peter Symmonds & Co. v. Cook* 1981 the plaintiffs were partners in a firm of surveyors and they bought a second-hand Rolls Royce in the partnership name with partnership money. The car was intended for use by one of the partners only. The High Court held that the plaintiffs were dealing as consumers in the purchase of the car even though it was to be used partly for business purposes.

In *R & B Customs Brokers Co. Ltd. v. United Dominions Trust Ltd.* 1988 the plaintiff company bought a second hand Colt Shogun car for the use of one of its directors, and signed a conditional sale agreement which excluded liability in relation to quality and fitness unless the buyer was dealing as a consumer. The director discovered that the roof of the car leaked before the defendant finance company signed its part of the agreement thereby concluding the contract. The plaintiff rejected the car for breach of the implied terms relating to merchantable quality and fitness for purpose. At first instance the judge held that the plaintiff could not rely on the implied condition as to merchantable quality as he had notice of the defect before the contract was made, but that the defendant was in breach of the implied condition as to fitness for purpose. The judge took the view that the plaintiff had been dealing as a consumer and accordingly that the exclusion of liability was invalid under s.6 of the 1977 Act. On appeal, the decision of the judge was upheld. The principal issue was whether the company was dealing a consumer. Neil LJ stated:

"*In the present case the director gave evidence on behalf of the company that the car was only the second or third vehicle acquired on credit terms. It follows, therefore, that no pattern of regular purchases had been established for this business, nor can it be suggested that this transaction was an adventure in the nature of trade. I am therefore satisfied that in relation to the purchase of this car the company was dealing as consumer within the meaning of s.12 of the 1977 Act.*"

Where the contract is made at auction or by competitive tender, the customer can never be regarded as dealing as a consumer under the Act.

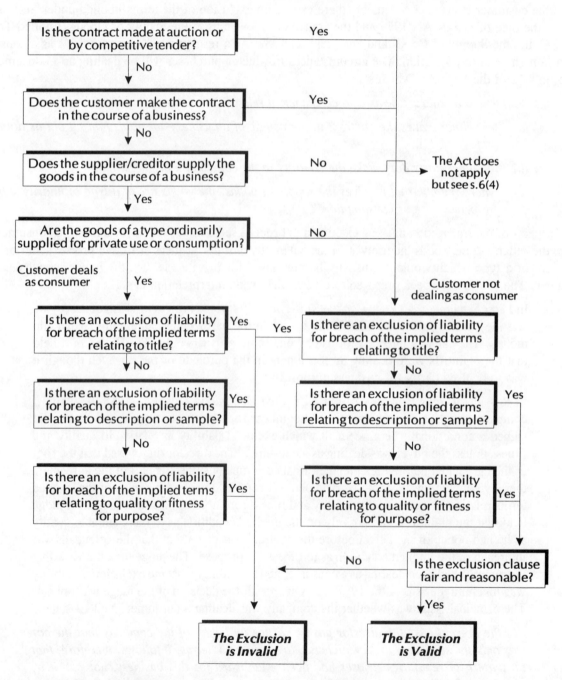

Figure 5.2 *Exclusion of Liability for Breach of Statutory Implied Terms in Contracts for the Sale and Supply of Goods: Section 6 and Section 7 Unfair Contract Terms Act 1977*

Exclusion where buyer is not a consumer

Where the customer deals otherwise than as a consumer, for example because the supplier is not in business or because the goods are of a type which are not normally bought for private use, there can be no exclusion of liability for breach of the implied terms relating to title. The other implied terms can however be excluded as against such a customer, but only if the clause satisfies the test of reasonableness.

In the case of a contract of hire, where there is an exclusion of the implied terms relating to the supplier's right to transfer possession of the goods, this exclusion will be subject to the test of reasonableness and will not automatically be rendered void under s.7(4). This applies whether or not the hirer is dealing as a consumer. Figure 5.2 summarises the application of s.6 and s.7, except as regards the exclusion of the implied terms relating to the transfer of possession in hire contracts.

For the purpose of s.6 and s.7, the Act lays down guidelines which the court may take into account in determining whether an exclusion clause is reasonable. Strictly speaking, the Act does not apply these guidelines to determine reasonableness in relation to the other sections which apply the reasonableness test, but in practice the courts take them into account in those cases also. The factors to be taken into account under the guidelines are:

(a)   the relative bargaining strength of the parties;

(b)   whether there was an opportunity to purchase the product elsewhere without submitting to the clause;

(c)   whether any inducement was given to the buyer in return for accepting the clause;

(d)   whether the goods were made to the buyer's design or specification;

(e)   whether the customer knew or ought reasonably to have known of the existence of the clause;

(f)   the extent to which it was open for the parties to cover themselves by insurance; and

(g)   the particular circumstances of the case.

In *George Mitchell Ltd. v. Finney Lock Seeds Ltd.* 1983 the plaintiff was a farmer who purchased cabbage seed from the defendant. The seeds were described as those of a solid heading late winter cabbage. In fact they were of a different type, of inferior quality and unfit for human consumption. The plaintiff planted 63 acres of these cabbages. They proved to be of no value and had to be ploughed in. The seed had cost £192 but the plaintiff's loss was in excess of £61,000. The plaintiff was not insured for this loss and sued the seller for breach of the term implied by s.13 of the Sale of Goods Act 1979 that the goods would correspond with their description. The defence put forward by the sellers was an exclusion clause limiting liability to either the cost of the seed or its replacement value. The clause read:

"in the event of any seeds or plants sold or agreed to be sold by us not complying with the express terms of the contract of sale or with a representation made by us or by any duly authorised agent or representative on our behalf prior to, at the time of, or in any such contract, or any seeds or plants proving defective in varietal purity we will, at our option, replace the defective seeds or plants, free of charge to the buyer or will refund all payments made to us by the buyer in respect of the defective seeds or plants and this shall be the limit of our obligation. We hereby exclude all liability for any loss or damage

arising from the use of any seeds or plants supplied by us and for any consequential loss or damage arising out of such use or any failure in the performance of or any defect in any seeds or plants supplied by us or for any other loss or damage whatsoever save for, at our option, liability for any such replacement or refund as aforesaid".

The House of Lords affirmed the decision of the Court of Appeal that the clause was ineffective. Lord Denning, in his last judgment before retiring, considered a number of questions relevant to the validity of the clause. The first was whether the clause was part of the agreement. He found that it was since such conditions were usual in the trade, and therefore well known, and in any event the clause was included on the back of the invoice. The second was the wording of the clause, and whether as drafted it covered and effectively limited the supplier's liability. He found that the clause clearly did so. Finally the question arose as to whether the clause was a reasonable one. It had been imposed by the defendant without negotiation. The seedsmen could insure against the risk of crop failure without materially affecting the price of the seeds. The defendants could have tested the seeds but the plaintiffs had no opportunity of discovering the defectiveness of the seed until it was too late. In addition there was evidence that the defendants would usually negotiate a realistic settlement where a claim was justified in similar circumstances. Taking these factors into account the clause was held to be unreasonable and invalid.

In *R. W. Green Ltd. v. Cade Brothers Farms* 1978 the plaintiffs purchased a quantity of seed potatoes from the defendants under the terms of a written standard form contract which included a clause limiting liability of the defendants to a refund of the price. The potatoes were infected with a virus which could only be detected at harvest time. The crop failed and the plaintiffs sued the defendants for breach of the terms implied into the contract by s.14 of the Sale of Goods Act. It was held that the defendants were in breach of the implied terms, but were not liable because the exclusion clause was reasonable in the circumstances of the case. The seed had been sold cheaply because it was uncertified and the plaintiffs could have paid more and bought certified seed potato. The terms of the contract had not been imposed by the seller, rather they were the product of many years negotiation by trade associations and unions representing both sides of the industry.

Criminal liability for the use of invalid exclusion clauses

The Unfair Contract Terms Act 1977 invalidates many exclusion clauses so that they cannot be relied upon as a defence to an action for damages. The Act does not, however, prevent the trader from using invalid clauses. The clause may have no legal validity, but the consumer may be misled because of his lack of legal knowledge. The Consumer Transactions (Restrictions on Statements) Order 1976 (as amended in 1978) was made under the Fair Trading Act 1973 to prevent this unfair trading practice in a limited range of situations. The order applies to any clause in a consumer transaction which purports to exclude liability for breach of Sections 13, 14 or 15 of the Sale of Goods Act 1979. Under the order it is a criminal offence for a person, in the course of a business, to do any of the following:

(a)   display a notice of such a clause at a place where consumer deals are likely to be made,

(b)   publish any advertisement to supply goods which includes such a clause,

(c)   provide the consumer with a written contract or other document containing such a clause, or

(d)   supply goods bearing any statement about the seller's liability in relation to description quality or fitness for purpose, unless the statement makes it clear that it does not affect the statutory rights of the consumer.

Activity

In relation to any products which you use personally or which have been purchased recently for use in your home, examine the packaging or information supplied with the product. Try to find at least two things with printed information which contains statements that the statutory rights of the consumer are not affected.

Write a brief explanation of why you think it has been necessary for this statement to appear as part of the information on those products.

Consumer's right to reject goods

It was noted earlier that the remedy available to a buyer in the event of a breach of any term of a contract by the seller depends upon whether the term is classified as a condition or a warranty. Most of the implied terms by statute into contracts for the supply of goods are conditions, and the buyer's remedy for breach, in addition to damages, will be to reject the goods and recover the price. It is of course open to the buyer to choose to affirm the contract, thereby waiving his right to reject but retaining the right to sue for damages.

The right to reject may also be lost, in the case of a sale of goods contract, where there has been an acceptance of the goods by the buyer. This is provided for in s.11(4) of the Sale of Goods Act 1979, which states:

> *"Where a contract of sale is not severable, and the buyer has accepted the goods, or part of them, the breach of a condition to be fulfilled by the seller can only be treated as a breach of warranty, and not as a ground for rejecting the goods and treating the contract as repudiated, unless there is an express or implied term of the contract to that effect".*

Where the buyer has accepted the goods, then, he loses the right of rejection but still has a claim for damages, which is the normal remedy for breach of warranty. The situations in which the buyer will be deemed to have accepted the goods are set out in s.34 and s.35. Section 34 deals with the buyer's right to examine the goods, and provides:

> *"(1) where the goods are delivered to the buyer, and he has not previously examined them, he is not deemed to have accepted them until he has had a reasonable opportunity of examining them for the purpose of ascertaining whether they are in conformity with the contract.*
>
> *(2) Unless otherwise agreed, when the seller tenders delivery of the goods to the buyer, he is bound, on request, to afford the buyer a reasonable opportunity of examining the goods for the purpose of ascertaining whether they are in conformity with the contract".*

Section 35(1) states:

> *"The buyer is deemed to have accepted the goods when he intimates to the seller that he has accepted them, or (except where s.34 otherwise provides) when the goods have been*

> *delivered to him, and he does any act in relation to them which is inconsistent with the*
> *ownership of the seller, or when after the lapse of a reasonable time, he retains the goods*
> *without intimating to the seller that he has rejected them".*

Clearly a purchaser who retains goods for longer than a reasonable time without giving notice of rejection will be deemed to have accepted them under s.35(1):

> In *Lee v. York Coach and Marine* 1977 a buyer purchased a second hand car which had defective brakes. The seller was therefore in breach of the implied condition that the car would be of merchantable quality. The buyer purported to reject the car some five months after taking delivery. It was held that she had accepted the car by retaining it beyond a reasonable time. Her only remedy was damages as she had lost the right of rejection.

Whilst it would be difficult to argue with the conclusion in the *Lee* case that retention of goods for five months was beyond a reasonable time, the decision in a more recent case that a period of three weeks is to be regarded in the same way is perhaps more surprising.

> In *Bernstein v. Pamson Motors (Golders Green) Ltd.* 1987 the plaintiff purchased a new Nissan car from the defendant for £8,000. The plaintiff was ill at the time of the purchase and consequently did not use the car a great deal. Three weeks after delivery, when the car had done only 140 miles, the engine seized up. The plaintiff rejected the car on the grounds that it was not of merchantable quality, and demanded the return of the purchase price. The defendant repaired the car so that it was as good as new, but the plaintiff refused to take it back. Rougier J., in the High Court, held that the car was not of merchantable quality and that the plaintiff was entitled to damages, assessed at £250. He was not, however, entitled to reject the car because, by driving it for 140 miles, and retaining it for three weeks, he had accepted the car within the meaning of s.35(1).

Product Liability in Negligence

It was seen above that the right to make a product liability claim in contract is confined to an injured person who actually buys the goods himself. The contract claim can be brought against the supplier of the goods only. The supplier is strictly liable, even if he is not at fault. In negligence anyone injured by the product can sue anyone who has failed to take reasonable care in relation to it thereby causing the injury.

We shall now examine those elements of negligence liability which are particularly significant in defective product claims:

The duty of care

In relation to liability for manufactured products we have seen that it was not until as late as 1932 that it was recognised that a general duty of care was owed by manufacturers to consumers. This was established by the decision of the House of Lords in the case of *Donoghue v. Stevenson* the facts of which were described in Chapter 3. The importance of the decision in the field of product liability lies in the fact that, in his judgment, Lord Atkin described the duty of a manufacturer in the following terms:

> *"... a manufacturer of products, which he sells in such a form as to show that he intends*
> *them to reach the ultimate consumer in the form in which they left him with no reasonable*
> *possibility of intermediate examination, and with the knowledge that the absence of*
> *reasonable care in the preparation or putting up of the products will result in an injury*

to the consumer's life or property, owes a duty to the consumer to take that reasonable care."

Although this statement has been developed by subsequent interpretation it can still be regarded as the framework within which a court will decide whether a duty of care exists. Four elements within the framework require closer examination:

(a) Who can be sued

Lord Atkin's reference to *a manufacturer of products* embraces everyone involved in the manufacturing enterprise from design to distribution. It also extends to others who have worked on the goods at any time.

> In *Stennet v. Hancock* 1939, for example, the plaintiff was a pedestrian who was injured when part of the wheel of a lorry broke away whilst the lorry was being driven. The defect in the wheel was the result of a repair which had not been carried out properly. The court held that the repairers were liable under Lord Atkin's manufacturing principle.

(b) What type of defects will give rise to liability

Lord Atkin referred to products which the manufacturer sells *in such a form as to show that he intends them to reach the ultimate consumer in the form in which they left him with no reasonable possibility of intermediate examination.* This has been interpreted as limiting the application of the duty to products with latent defects. Latent defects are faults which are not apparent on an examination of the goods. Lord Wright in *Grant v. Australian Knitting Mills Ltd.* 1936 stated that:

> *"The principle of Donoghue's case can only be applied where the defect is hidden and unknown to the consumer ... the man who consumes or uses a thing which he knows to be noxious cannot complain in respect of whatever mischief follows, because it follows from his own conscious volition in choosing to incur the risk or certainty of mischance."*

> This interpretation of Lord Atkin's principle was followed in the case of *Crow v. Barford (Agricultural) Ltd.* and *H.B. Holttum & Co. Ltd.* 1963. The plaintiff bought a rotary lawn mower known as a Barford Rotomo from Holttum after it was demonstrated to him at home. The machine was designed in such a way that the guard for the blades had an opening to allow the grass to be expelled as it was being cut. To start the lawn mower the user's foot had to be placed on the casing containing the blade. While starting the Rotomo the plaintiff's foot slipped into the opening and two of his toes were cut off.

> The claim against the manufacturer was made on the basis of the principle in *Donoghue v. Stevenson* but the Court of Appeal decided that this did not apply because the danger was "perfectly obvious" and not hidden or unknown to the plaintiff. The claim in contract against the retailer was also unsuccessful because the plaintiff had inspected the lawn mower during the demonstration before he purchased it. This brought the case within the exception contained in s.14(2) of the Sale of Goods Act that the seller does not promise that the goods are of merchantable quality in relation to defects which ought to have been revealed by the buyer's prior examination of the goods.

(c) To whom is the duty owed

Lord Atkin tells us that the duty of care is owed to the *ultimate consumer* of the product. This expression has been interpreted widely so as to include the purchaser, any person injured while using or consuming the product and any other person, such as the plaintiff in *Stennet v. Hancock*, who is injured by the product in circumstances where injury to him ought reasonably to have been foreseen.

> For example, in *Lambert v. Lewis (Lexmead Ltd., third party; Dixon Bate Ltd., fourth party)* 1982 the driver of a car and his son were killed and the plaintiffs, his wife and daughter, were injured when their car was hit by a trailer which had become detached from a farmer's Land Rover and careered across the road into the path of their car. The accident was caused by a design defect in the towing hitch, which was unable to cope with the stresses to which it was subjected in normal use. The evidence showed that part of the towing hitch had been missing for a number of months before the accident and that the farmer should have realised this.
>
> The trial judge decided that the manufacturer was 75% to blame for the accident and that the farmer was 25% to blame and apportioned liability accordingly. The farmer issued third party proceedings against the retailer from whom he had purchased the towing hitch. He was seeking indemnity for the damages for which he was liable and basing his claim in contract on the retailer's breach of the implied terms in s.14 Sale of Goods Act. The retailer in turn issued fourth party proceedings against the manufacturer in contract and in negligence. On appeal the House of Lords decided that the retailer was not liable to the farmer because the farmer's own negligence, rather than the retailer's breach of contract, was the operative cause of his loss. The fourth party proceedings were consequently dismissed because the retailer had no liability to pass on to the manufacturer.

(d) What type of damage is recoverable

In his statement of the duty of care owed by a manufacturer, Lord Atkin confines the scope of the duty to *injury to the consumer's life or property*. Within this damages are recoverable for death, personal injury or damage to property, excluding damage to the product itself.

One category of loss which cannot always be sued for in negligence is pure financial loss. A 1985 case provides a good illustration of this rule in the context of product liability.

> In *Muirhead v. Industrial Tank Specialities (ITT Marlow, third party; Leroy Somer Electric Motors Ltd., fourth party)* 1985, the plaintiff was a wholesale fish merchant who installed in his premises a large seawater tank in which to store lobsters. The seawater had to be filtered, oxygenated and recirculated. This was done by a series of pumps working 24 hours per day. The tank and pumps were installed by I.T.S. Ltd. The pumps were manufactured by Leroy Somer Electric Motors Ltd and supplied to the plaintiff by I.T.S. Ltd. through other suppliers in the chain of distribution. The pumps constantly broke down and on one occasion the recirculation of water was affected so that the plaintiff lost his entire stock of lobsters. The plaintiff successfully sued I.T.S. Ltd. in contract but the company went into liquidation unable to satisfy the judgment against it. The plaintiff then proceeded with action against the manufacturers claiming damages for all of the losses incurred as a result of the defects in the pumps. The vast bulk of the claim was for the loss of profits on intended sales but the Court of Appeal decided that this was pure financial loss and therefore not recoverable in a negligence action. The rest of the plaintiff's claim succeeded.

Breach of duty

Once it has been established that the manufacturer in a given case owes a duty of care to avoid injury to the plaintiff, the second major element of negligence liability which the plaintiff must prove is that the manufacturer was in breach of that duty. A breach of duty is a failure to take reasonable care and involves a finding of fault on the part of the manufacturer. In many cases the task of proving this may be a difficult one for the plaintiff, involving a detailed investigation of the defendant's processes of manufacture design and testing and a comparison with procedures adopted by other producers in the same field. The plaintiff will need to employ expert witnesses who can analyse these processes and procedures and pin-point any lack of care which may have caused the defect in the product and therefore caused the injury. If the plaintiff is unable to prove a breach of duty he may have to bear the loss himself without compensation, unless there is another available legal basis for his claim.

A breach of the duty of care may occur outside the process of development design and manufacture.

> In the case of *Vacwell Engineering v. BDH Chemicals Ltd.* 1971 for example, the manufacturer of a chemical produced for industrial use was held liable in negligence for a failure to give proper and adequate warnings that the chemical would explode when mixed with water. This should have been achieved by clear labelling of the product.

> In *Walton v. British Leyland (UK) Ltd.* 1978 the failure of British Leyland to recall the Austin Allegro car after a large number of 'wheel drift' faults had been reported to the company was held to be a breach of the duty of care. Leyland were held liable to the plaintiffs who were severely injured when the wheel of their Allegro came off as the vehicle was travelling at 60 mph on a motorway. The Judge, Willis J., in the High Court stated:

> *"The duty of care owed by Leyland to the public was to make a clean breast of the problem and recall all cars which they could in order that safety washers could be fitted ... The company seriously considered recall and made an estimate of the cost at a figure (£300,000 in 1974) which seems to me to be in no way out of proportion to the risks involved. It was decided not to follow this course for commercial reasons. I think this involved a failure to observe their duty of care for the safety of the many who were bound to remain at risk ..."*

Res ipsa loquitur

In the context of product liability the principle of res ipsa loquitur is of considerable significance. The tendency in recent times has been for the courts to allow the plaintiff to rely on the rule in many cases involving defective products. Res ipsa loquitur is considered in detail earlier in Chapter 3. Here we may note its application in product liability cases.

> In *Chaproniere v. Mason* 1905 the plaintiff broke a tooth when eating a bread bun which was found to contain a pebble. He pleaded res ipsa loquitur and the defendant baker was held to be liable because he was unable to prove that he had not been negligent.

Where the plaintiff pleads res ipsa loquitur, the manufacturer will need to produce strong evidence if he is to satisfy the court that the injuries were not caused by his negligence. It will not be sufficient for him to show that he has a good system of work and provides adequate supervision during the process of manufacture.

In *Grant v. Australian Knitting Mills* 1936 the plaintiff contracted dermatitis because of the presence in his underwear of excess sulphite after the process of manufacture by the defendant. The defendant's evidence was that he had manufactured over four and a half million pairs of underpants and had received no other complaints. Nevertheless he was held liable because the probability was that someone in his employment for whose acts he was legally responsible had failed to take care.

In *Hill v. James Crowe (Cases) Ltd.* 1978 the plaintiff, a lorry driver, was injured when he fell off a badly nailed wooden packing case on which he was standing in order to load his lorry. The manufacturer of the packing case gave evidence that the standards of workmanship and supervision in his factory were high and argued that he had not failed to fulfil his duty to the plaintiff to take reasonable care in producing the case. The Court held that the defendant was liable for the bad workmanship of one of his employees even though, in general terms, he had a good production system. He had not proved that the plaintiff's injuries were not due to the negligence of one of his employees.

This case provides an example of the manufacturer's liability for a foreseeable misuse of his product.

The extremely high standard of care which the courts are prepared to impose on a manufacturer can be seen in the following case.

In *Winward v. TVR Engineering* 1986 the defendants were in the business of producing specialist sports cars. They were responsible for the design and assembly of the vehicles using components bought in from other sources. The car in question incorporated a Ford engine which was supplied to the defendants fitted with a Weber carburettor. The carburettor had a basic design fault which ultimately caused petrol to leak from it. The plaintiff's wife was injured when leaking petrol came into contact with the hot engine. The defendants argued that it was reasonable for them to rely on the expertise of their supplier, particularly as the design fault had never previously manifested itself. The Court of Appeal held that the defendants were in breach of their duty through their failure to test the component and modify its design.

The Consumer Protection Act 1987 : Strict liability for injury caused by defective products

Part I of the Consumer Protection Act 1987 provides a framework of strict liability for injury and damage caused by defective products. This part of the Act was introduced in order to give effect to the EC Directive on Product Liability (85/374/EEC) and represents a significant extension of consumer protection in this area by providing an additional basis upon which to obtain compensation for injury caused by unsafe or faulty goods.

Liability under s.2(1) of the Act arises *"where any damage is caused wholly or partly by a defect in a product"*. In order to succeed in a claim, the plaintiff must prove two things:

(a)   that the product was defective, and

(b)   that the defect caused the injury or damage.

If the plaintiff can prove these things, the defendant will be liable even though he took all possible care in relation to the product. This is the crucial difference between strict liability under the Act and liability based upon negligence which, as we have seen, depends upon proof of fault by the defendant.

Who is liable?

Liability falls upon all or any of the following persons:

(a) the *producer* – this term is defined in s.1(2) and includes the manufacturer of the product, the producer of any raw materials or the manufacturer of a component part.

(b) the *'own brander'* – any person who, by putting his name on the product or using a trade mark or other distinguishing marks in relation to it, has held himself out to be the producer of the product

(c) the *importer into the EEC* – a person importing the product into the Community from a non Community state for the purpose of supplying it in the course of his business.

(d) any *supplier* who cannot identify the person who produced the product, or supplied it to him. In such circumstances that person will be liable, regardless of whether he was a business supplier, provided he supplied the product to someone else, and the following conditions are met:

   (i) he is requested by a person suffering any damage to identify any producer, own brander or importer into the EEC;

   (ii) the request is made within a reasonable time after the damage occurs;

   (iii) at the time of the request it is not reasonably practicable for the injured party to identify all of the potential defendants; and

   (iv) he fails, within a reasonable time, to comply with the request or to identify the person who supplied the product to him.

Thus it will be imperative, where litigation is threatened, for businesses to be able to identify the supplier of the products or component parts used in any goods sold by the business. It will be particularly important to differentiate, by product coding for example, between the products of two or more suppliers who are supplying identical components for incorporation into the same type of finished product. This will apply to all component parts ranging from electric motors to nuts and bolts.

Where two or more persons are liable for the injury each can be sued for the full amount of the damage. The party who is sued may be entitled to a contribution or indemnity from anyone else who is liable, under the Civil Liability (Contribution) Act 1978. Of course the injured person can only recover compensation once, regardless of the number of possible defendants or the legal basis of his claim. The injured person will usually choose to sue the defendant against whom liability can most easily be established and who is most likely to be able to afford to pay damages or to have insurance cover.

When is a product defective?

In order to succeed in a claim the plaintiff will have to prove that his injury was caused by a defect in the product. Section 3 tells us that a product will be regarded as defective when *"the safety of the product is not such as persons generally are entitled to expect"*. It is clear that the lawnmower in *Crow v. Barford and Holttum* above would be defective under this definition. The question of when a product is defective is likely to be central to much of the litigation under the Act. Section 3(2) gives us some guidance as to the factors which will be relevant in deciding whether a product is defective. It provides:

> *"In determining what persons generally are entitled to expect in relation to a product all the circumstances shall be taken into account, including:*

(a)   *the manner in which, and purposes for which, the product has been marketed, its get-up, the use of any mark in relation to the product and any instructions for, or warnings with respect to, doing or refraining from doing anything with or in relation to the product;*

(b)   *what might reasonably be expected to be done with or in relation to the product; and*

(c)   *the time when the product was supplied by its producer to another person;*

and nothing in this section shall require a defect to be inferred from the fact alone that the safety of a product which is supplied after that time is greater than the safety of the product in question.''

Clearly it is very important for any business to ensure that the packaging of their products is such that it does not suggest or imply that the product can be used in a manner or for a purpose which is unsafe. Appropriate warnings of the dangers associated with the use or foreseeable misuse of the product must be amply displayed on the packaging and, where necessary, on the goods themselves. A further precaution which may be taken by the producer of goods is the date coding of products in order to take advantage of the defence suggested by the final part of s.3(2). Thus if a safer product is subsequently developed and put onto the market, the level of safety provided by the original product cannot be judged solely by reference to improved safety features in the new product.

Defences

A number of specific defences are provided for in s.4 of the Consumer Protection Act. These are in addition to the obvious defences that the product was not defective or that it was not the cause of the plaintiff's loss. Thus it is a defence to show:

(a)   that the defect was attributable to the defendant's compliance with a legal requirement, or

(b)   that the defendant did not supply the goods to anyone.

In this connection it is interesting to notice s.1(3) which says that where a finished product incorporates component products or raw materials, the supplier of the finished product will not be treated as a supplier of the component products or raw materials by reason only of his supply of the finished product. Thus, for example, a builder using high alumina cement could argue that he was not a supplier of that cement for the purposes of the Act. He could invoke this defence if the building subsequently deteriorated due to defects in the cement.

(c)   Section 4 also enables the defendant to escape liability if he can show that he had not supplied the goods in the course of his business and that he had not own branded, imported into the EEC, or produced the goods with a view to profit.

This defence could be invoked, for example, in relation to the sale of home made jam at a coffee morning in aid of charity.

(d)   The nature of the fourth defence under s.4 depends upon whether the defendant is a producer, own brander or importer into the EEC. If he is, he can escape liability by proving that the defect was not present in the product at the time he supplied it. If he is not, he must show that the defect was not present in the product at the time it was last supplied by any person of that description.

(e)   Section 4 provides the *development risks* defence that, given the state of scientific and technical knowledge at the time the product was put into circulation, no producer of a product of that kind could have been expected to have discovered the defect if it had existed in his products while they were under his control.

The development risks defence has provoked much discussion. Its adoption was optional under the terms of the directive. It is argued that the defence reduces the strictness of liability by introducing considerations which are more relevant to negligence. Its main impact will be seen in those areas which are at the forefront of scientific and technical development. The pharmaceutical industry, for example, could benefit from it in relation to the development of new drugs. It may seem ironic that if an event like the Thalidomide tragedy were to re-occur the victims could be prevented from recovering compensation because of the operation of this defence. The tragedy was in fact a major cause of pressure for the introduction of strict product liability laws throughout Europe.

(f)   Where the defendant is a producer of a component product, he will have a defence under s.4 if he can show that the defect in the finished product is wholly attributable to its design or to compliance with instructions given by the producer of the finished product.

Damage

Assuming the plaintiff succeeds in his claim, the question arises as to the types of loss he will be compensated for. Under s.5 damages are recoverable for death or for personal injury. This includes any disease or other impairment of a person's physical or mental condition. The plaintiff will also be able to claim compensation for damage to his property. However, exceptions to this provide significant limitations on liability under the Act. There is no liability for loss of or damage to:

(a)   the product itself,

(b)   any property in respect of which the amount of the claim would be below £275,

(c)   any commercial property – property of a type which is not ordinarily intended for private use, occupation or consumption and which is not actually intended by the plaintiff for his own private use, occupation or consumption.

All of these categories of loss are recoverable in a contract claim, although the first category of loss, or damage to the product itself is not recoverable in negligence.

Contracting out

Section 7 of the Consumer Protection Act provides for an absolute prohibition on the limitation or exclusion of liability arising under the Act.

Time limits for claims

The limitation period provided for in the Act, regardless of the type of damage, is three years from the date on which the right to take action arises, or, if later, three years from the date on which the plaintiff is aware:

(a)   that he has suffered significant damage,

(b)   that the damage is attributable to a defect in the product, and

(c)   of the identity of the defendant.

There is an overall cut off point 10 years after the product is put into circulation. After the 10 year period has elapsed no new claims can be made although any proceedings which have already been started may continue.

	Contract	Negligence	Consumer Protection Act
who is liable	seller; he may claim an indemnity from the previous seller in the chain of distribution	manufacturer; includes designer, repairer, processor and other persons working on goods	producer, own brander, importer into EEC, supplier who refuses to identify previous supplier or producer
who can claim	buyer only	ultimate consumer provided injury to him is foreseeable	any person injured by a defect in the product
basis of liability	strict; if goods not reasonably fit for usual or notified special purposes	fault; failure to take reasonable care in relation to the product	strict; where the product does not provide the safety which persons are entitled to expect
types of loss	personal injury death damage to property financial loss	personal injury death damage to property other than the product financial loss in limited circumstances	personal injury death damage £275+ to consumer property other than product
exclusion of liability	prohibited if buyer dealing as consumer otherwise possible if exclusion is reasonable	prohibited if death or personal injury otherwise possible if exclusion is reasonable	prohibited in all cases
time limit for claims	personal injury; 3 years from the date on which the plaintiff had knowledge of the material facts giving rise to the claim Other claims; 6 years from the date on which cause of action arose; or in negligence cases only, (if later) 3 years from the date of plaintiff's knowledge of the material facts if within 15 years of the negligent act		3 years from the date on which the plaintiff was aware of the damage the defect and the identity of the defendant if no more than 10 years since the product was put into circulation

Figure 5.3 *Comparison of Alternative Forms of Legal Liability: Injuries Caused by Defective Products*

Criminal Liability for Unsafe Goods

Part II of the Consumer Protection Act 1987 replaces earlier legislation on consumer safety including the Consumer Safety Act 1978 and the Consumer Safety (Amendment) Act 1986.

Under s.10 of the 1987 Act it is a criminal offence to supply consumer goods which are not reasonably safe. An offence is also committed by offering or agreeing to supply unsafe goods or exposing or possessing them for supply.

In deciding whether goods are reasonably safe, the court must examine all the circumstances, including:

(a)   the way in which the goods are marketed;

(b)   the use of any mark, for example indicating compliance with safety standards;

(c)   instructions or warnings as to the use of the goods;

(d)   whether the goods comply with relevant published safety standards;

(e)   whether there is a way in which the goods could reasonably have been made safer.

The offence in s.10 can be committed only in relation to consumer goods. Consumer goods are goods which are ordinarily intended for private use or consumption, with the exception of food, water, gas, motor vehicles, medical products and tobacco.

The Secretary of State has power, under s.11, to make regulations for the purpose of ensuring that goods of any particular type are safe. Safety regulations can cover the design, composition or finish of goods; and ensure that appropriate information is given in relation to them. They may also restrict the distribution of particular types of goods or prohibit their supply or exposure for supply.

A considerable number of regulations, made under previous legislation, are still in force. These relate for example to aerosols, babies' dummies, balloons, cosmetics, electrical goods, night-dresses, toys and many other types of product. Breach of safety regulations is an offence under s.12 of the 1987 Act.

Under s.41 of the 1987 Act any person who suffers injury or loss as a result of a breach of safety regulations has the right to sue the trader for damages for breach of statutory duty. This right cannot be restricted or excluded by any term or notice in any contract.

The Secretary of State also has a number of other powers under the 1987 Act. He may, for example, serve a *prohibition notice* on a trader requiring him to stop trading in unsafe goods of a particular description. Alternatively, where a trader has distributed goods which are unsafe, the Secretary of State may serve on him a *notice to warn*. This requires the trader, at his own expense, to publish warnings about the unsafe goods to persons to whom they have been supplied.

Power is also given to local authorities under the Act, to serve a *suspension notice* on any trader. This in effect freezes the goods in the hands of the trader for up to six months. The power to serve a suspension notice arises if the authority has reasonable grounds for suspecting that goods are not reasonably safe under s.10, or are in breach of safety regulations. A trader who fails to comply with a suspension notice is guilty of a criminal offence.

A Magistrates Court has power to order the forfeiture of goods where there has been a contravention of the safety provisions of the 1987 Act. Where goods are forfeit they must, under s.16, either be destroyed, or released for the purposes of being repaired, reconditioned or scrapped.

Consumer Credit

The Consumer Credit Act 1974 was introduced with the aim of ensuring 'truth in lending'. The Act applies to a wide range of types of credit agreement and places strict controls upon persons who provide credit facilities in the course of their business. Overall responsibility for administering the Act lies with the Director General of Fair Trading. The Act creates many criminal offences and enforcement in relation to these is by local authority Trading Standards Officers.

Agreements regulated by the Act fall within two broad categories, consumer hire agreements and consumer credit agreements. Under s.8:

> *"A consumer credit agreement is an agreement between an individual (the debtor) and any other person (the creditor) by which the creditor provides the debtor with credit not exceeding £15,000".*

The agreement must be for the provision of *credit*. This is defined in wide terms by s.9(1) to include *cash loans and any other form of financial accommodation*. Hire purchase, conditional sale and credit sale agreements will all be consumer credit agreements if they satisfy the other elements of the definition. Certain types of credit agreement, particularly those concerned with the purchase and development of land and buildings, are excluded from the operation of the Act and are not consumer credit agreements.

An agreement will not be a consumer credit agreement where:

(a) the debtor is a limited company, and therefore not an individual (a flesh and blood person), or

(b) the amount of credit provided is in excess of £15,000.

In these cases most of the provisions of the Act will not apply and the agreement will be governed by common law principles.

Licensing of creditors

Any person who intends to carry on the business of providing credit cannot do so unless he first obtains a licence from the Director General of Fair Trading. The Director General must grant a licence to any person who makes an application, provided he is satisfied that:

(a) the name under which the business is operating is neither misleading nor undesirable, and

(b) the applicant is a fit person to engage in the activities covered by licence.

A consumer credit agreement made with an unlicensed creditor is not enforceable against the debtor without the consent of the Director General of Fair Trading.

Equal liability of the creditor and the supplier

Earlier in this chapter it was noted that many credit transactions involved three parties: debtor, creditor, and supplier. The policy of the 1974 Act is to make the creditor, in addition to the supplier, answerable to the debtor if anything goes wrong. This applies only where a business connection exists between the creditor and the supplier, for example where the supplier has an arrangement with a particular finance company under which the company provides credit for all suitable customers of the supplier. Because the creditor is responsible for the acts of the supplier, he will be careful to deal only with suppliers who are reputable. The long term aim of this policy is to raise general standards of trading and squeeze cowboy suppliers out of business. The policy is reflected in s.56 and s.75 of the Act.

Where there is a business connection between the supplier and the creditor, the supplier is deemed, by s.56, to be the agent of the creditor when he negotiates with the debtor before a consumer credit agreement is made. If the debtor is induced to enter an agreement by the supplier's misrepresentation, he is entitled under s.56 to exercise a right of rescission against the creditor.

Under s.75 the debtor can claim against the creditor, as well as the supplier, for any breach of contract or misrepresentation by the supplier. Again this applies only where there is a business connection between the creditor and the supplier. At common law the debtor could claim, under the rule in *Andrews v. Hopkinson* 1956, against the supplier only and had no claim against the creditor. The effect of s.75 can be far reaching, for example if goods are purchased with a credit card (such as Access or Barclaycard), the finance company behind the card can be sued for the retailer's breach of contract or misrepresentation.

Where the debtor sues the creditor under s.56 or s.75, the creditor in turn has a right of indemnity from the supplier.

Annual percentage rate (APR)

The Act introduces a uniform system which all lenders must use in quoting the cost of credit. This is the annual percentage rate or APR. It enables the consumer to make a true comparison between interest rates and other costs charged by one lender as against those charged by another.

Prior to the introduction of APR there was no standard method of calculating the percentage rate. At that time loans on identical terms in relation to interest and other costs could be advertised at widely varying rates, depending upon the statistical method used to calculate the rate. Consumers therefore had no reliable yardstick against which the different deals on offer could be measured.

All traders must now calculate the cost of credit using the statistical method laid down by the Act. The APR, arrived at in this way, must be shown on certain types of credit advertisement, for example in newspapers, catalogues or shop windows. In addition, the consumer has the right to ask for a written quotation of credit terms, which must specify the APR, where a trader advertises that credit is available.

Form and content of consumer credit agreements

The Consumer Credit Act lays down strict rules governing the form and content of agreements. The object of the rules is to protect the debtor by giving him the fullest possible information about his rights and obligations.

The agreement must be in a form which complies with regulations made under the Act. It must contain details of such things as:

(a)   the names and addresses of the parties

(b)   the APR

(c)   the cash price

(d)   any deposit

(e)   the amount of credit

(f)   the total amount payable

(g)   the amount of each payment

(h)   repayment dates

(i)   sums payable on default

(j)   certain rights and protections under the Act.

The agreement must be in writing and signed personally by the debtor. If either of these requirements is not met, the creditor will be unable to sue the debtor if he defaults, for example by stopping his payments.

The debtor must receive a copy of the agreement when he signs it, and a further copy as soon as it has been signed by the creditor. If this requirement is not complied with, the creditor cannot sue the debtor, or enforce the agreement in any other way, for example by repossession, unless he previously obtains the permission of the court.

Credit reference agencies

A credit reference agency is an organisation which collects financial information about individuals. This includes a person's record in paying off debts and previous credit agreements, and outstanding judgments recorded against them in the county court. Creditors will usually consult credit reference agencies before entering into agreements with new customers. There are two national credit reference agencies.

These are:

CCM Systems limited,
Talbot House,
Talbot Street,
Nottingham NG1 5HF.

Credit Data Limited,
Regency House,
38 Whitworth Street,
Manchester M60 1QH.

In addition there are a number of local agencies. Where an individual applies for credit he may require the trader to provide him with the name and address of any credit reference agency which has been consulted about him.

An individual has the right, under s.158 of the 1974 Act, to know what information is being held about him by a credit reference agency. He also has the right to correct any false information in the file kept by the agency. To exercise this right he must make a written request, containing sufficient particulars to enable the agency to identify the file, and accompanied by a fee of £1.

The agency must supply the individual with a copy of any file which it keeps relating to him. The copy must be in plain English and accompanied by a notice of the individual's right to correct false information. If the agency does not keep a file relating to the individual, it must write informing him of that fact.

If any of the information in the file is incorrect, the individual can ask the agency to correct it. If the agency refuses to alter the file to the satisfaction of the individual, or if it does not reply within 28 days of a request, the individual can write a note of correction of up to 200 words. The agency must add the note of correction to the file. It also has a duty to send details of the correction to anyone who obtained information from the file within the previous 6 months.

An agency will be guilty of a criminal offence if it fails to comply with a duty imposed on it by the 1974 Act.

Cooling off and cancellation

It is a well established principle of the law of contract that once an agreement has been entered into, cancellation by one of the parties is a breach of contract which entitles the other to sue for damages. The Consumer Credit Act 1974 provides an important exception to this principle.

An agreement will be cancellable under the Act where:

   (a)   statements are made by the trader in the presence of the debtor prior to making the agreement, and

   (b)   the debtor signs the agreement at a place other than the trader's place of business, for example at home.

The right of cancellation typically applies to credit transactions entered into with doorstep salesmen, although the right exists whenever the above conditions are fulfilled. Where an agreement is cancellable, it must contain a notice informing the debtor of his right to cancel. The agreement can be cancelled at any time up to the end of the fifth full day after it has been signed by both parties.

Notice of cancellation must be given in writing. It can be expressed in any manner, so long as it indicates an intention to withdraw from the agreement. Where a debtor exercises the right to cancel, he ceases to be liable under the agreement and is entitled to the return of all sums paid by him.

Default by the debtor

Default notice

Where a debtor is in breach of a consumer credit agreement, the creditor cannot terminate the agreement or demand early payment or recover possession of goods until a default notice has been served on the debtor. The notice must in the form prescribed by the Act. It must specify the nature of the breach, the action required to remedy it, and the date (giving at least 7 days) by which remedial action must be taken.

The creditor cannot take any steps to enforce an agreement until the date specified in the notice has passed. If the debtor complies with a default notice within the required period, the breach of agreement by him is treated as not having occurred.

Protected goods

Where the debtor under a hire purchase or conditional sale agreement has paid at least one third of the total price, the goods are protected goods. If the debtor is in default of the agreement, the creditor at common law has an unrestricted right to repossess the goods because at this stage he still owns them. However, under s.90 of the 1974 Act, the creditor cannot retake possession of protected goods without either a court order or the debtor's permission. If he does so the agreement terminates. The debtor is released from all liability under it. In addition he is entitled to recover from the creditor all sums previously paid by him under the agreement.

> In *Capital Finance v. Bray* 1964 a finance company repossessed a car without a court order. As the debtor had repaid more than one third of the total price, the car was covered by the protected goods rules. The company, realising its mistake, returned the car to the debtor by leaving it outside his house. The debtor used the car for several months but refused to make any further payments. The finance company sued for payment. The debtor counterclaimed for the return of all money paid by him under the agreement. It was held that the finance company had wrongfully repossessed the car and could not

correct the mistake by returning it to the debtor. The debtor was entitled to repayment of all sums which he had paid under the agreement.

Extortionate credit bargains

Under s.137 of the 1974 Act, the courts have power to re-open any credit agreement, whether or not it is a consumer credit agreement, which is part of an extortionate credit bargain, and relieve a debtor from payment of any sum in excess of that which is fair and reasonable. The courts have wide powers under this section and can order a creditor to repay all or part of any sum already paid; or set aside any obligation imposed on the debtor, or alter the agreement in any other way in order to do justice between the parties.

A credit bargain is extortionate under the Act if it requires the debtor to make payments which are *grossly exorbitant* or which otherwise *grossly contravene the ordinary principles of fair dealing*. In order to determine whether a credit bargain is extortionate a number of factors will be taken into account, including:

(a)   interest rates prevailing at the time it was made;

(b)   the age, experience, business capacity and state of health of the debtor;

(c)   the degree and nature of any financial pressure on the debtor when the bargain was made;

(d)   the degree of risk accepted by the creditor and his relationship to the debtor;

(e)   whether or not a cash price was quoted;

(f)   how far any linked transaction was reasonably required for the protection of the creditor, or was in the interest of the debtor.

> In *A. Ketley v. Scott* 1981 the defendant borrowed £20,500 in order to enable him to complete the purchase of a house. The money was released by the plaintiff on the same day that he was approached for the loan. The defendant did not tell him that his bank account was £2,000 overdrawn, the bank had a first mortgage on the house, and he was also liable under a £5,000 guarantee. Nor did he disclose that the house had been valued at £24,000. The loan was for three months at an annual rate of interest of 48%. At the expiry of its term the plaintiff sued for repayment of capital and interest. The defendant counterclaimed for the re-opening of the agreement as an extortionate credit bargain. It was held that the plaintiff was entitled to enforce the agreement. This was not an extortionate credit bargain because the lender had taken a considerable risk; obtained little security; had been deceived by the defendant; had no time to check the defendant's financial position, and advanced the money with extraordinary speed.

Termination by the debtor

A debtor under a hire purchase or conditional sale agreement may terminate the agreement under s.99 at any time before the final payment falls due. He must give notice in writing to the creditor, or to any person authorised to receive payment on the creditor's behalf. The debtor must return the goods to the creditor.

Under s.100 the debtor's liability on termination is limited to:

(a)   any sums already due for payment before the date on which he exercises the right of termination; and

(b) a further sum to bring his total payments up to one half of the total price (or less if the agreement so provides) or any lesser sum which in the opinion of the court represents the creditor's loss on termination; and

(c) if he has broken an obligation to take reasonable care of the goods, compensation for this.

Contracting out

Under s.173 of the 1974 Act it is not possible to insert a term into a consumer credit agreement which takes away any of the protection given to the debtor by the Act. Contracting out is absolutely prohibited.

Consumer Protection in Relation to Services

Consumer protection in relation to services is achieved in a number of ways. One important method is the regulation of those who provide services. This may be done by a statutory system of licensing, for example the licensing of those who sell alcoholic liquor; or the licensing of those who provide credit in the course of a business under the Consumer Credit Act 1974.

Regulation by professional bodies

Many professional service providers such as lawyers, doctors, architects, surveyors and accountants are regulated by professional associations. These associations often have the power to authorise the individual professional to practice his profession, or indeed to withdraw or refuse to give such authorisation. This may be done by the issue of annual practising certificates to those who have demonstrated their fitness to practice and who comply with conditions laid down by the association, for example by providing evidence of adequate professional indemnity insurance cover. Providing professional services without a current practising certificate is usually a criminal offence.

Professional associations are almost invariably authorised, through contractual conditions of membership or by Act of Parliament, to exercise disciplinary powers over members of the profession. These disciplinary powers are usually exercised, in the more serious cases, by a domestic tribunal. The tribunal will act rather like a court and will hear formal complaints against members of the profession. If a complaint is proven, the tribunal will have power to impose punishments ranging from a simple reprimand to the imposition of a fine or the suspension or withdrawal of the right to practise as a member of the profession.

In addition to disciplinary tribunals, many professional bodies sponsor arbitration schemes which provide a means by which compensation claims can be adjudicated without reference to the courts. One example is the Solicitors Arbitration Scheme set up by the Law Society in 1986. The scheme is run by the Chartered Institute of Arbitrators. In order to use the scheme both the solicitor and the claimant must agree. They will be bound by the decision of the arbitrator and neither party can subsequently take the matter to court. The arbitrator will look at written submissions by the parties and other supporting documents. He will decide whether the claim is valid and fix the amount of compensation to be awarded. In exceptional cases, where it appears that a decision cannot be made on the examination of documents alone, there is provision for a verbal hearing with the agreement of both parties. Each party must pay a registration fee in advance but the fee will be refunded to the successful party. The remaining costs of the scheme are paid by the Law Society itself.

Codes of practice under the Fair Trading Act 1973

In those parts of the service sector which fall outside the sphere of the traditional professions, many service providers are members of trade associations. These bodies tend not to have legal powers of the type possessed by professional bodies to regulate the conduct of their members. The Director General of Fair Trading has a duty under the Fair Trading Act 1973 to encourage trade associations and other similar organisations to prepare Codes of Practice and circulate them to their members. The codes should be designed to give guidance to traders relating to the safeguarding and protection of the interests of consumers.

A code of practice is a statement by a trade association which aims to establish and define the standards of trading which it expects from its members. Voluntary codes of this type have been introduced, following consultation with the Office of Fair Trading, to cover many areas of business. Such codes often provide a mechanism for the arbitration of consumer complaints as an alternative to legal proceedings in the courts.

Codes of practice provide a means whereby, in effect, a sector of industry or commerce can regulate itself. There are a number of costs and benefits to this. The main advantages are:

- a code can encourage a positive approach to trading standards and set high standards in excess of the legal minimum;

- a code can be changed fairly quickly in order to meet changing circumstances;

- a code can be expressed in non-technical language and interpreted positively according to its spirit;

- a code normally deals with one type of business or product. It can be drawn up to meet particular problems which are likely to arise in the limited area which it covers. Legislation, on the other hand, usually applies to all sectors of business;

- a code can clarify the rights and obligations of the trader and the customer in simple language;

- a code can often provide procedures and remedies which are appropriate to its subject matter in a more flexible way than legislation.

There are, however, a number of drawbacks associated with self regulation by Codes of Practice. The main disadvantages are:

- limited sanctions are available in the event that a trader does not comply with the provisions of a code. The ultimate penalty is usually expulsion from the trade association. In some sectors at least, this is not a very real punishment;

- the trade association may be in a position of conflict of interests when drawing up a code. Its principal function is the protection of the interests of its members;

- the consumer may not be aware of the existence of a code or the remedies which it offers;

- a code will not apply to a trader who is not a member of the trade association. In some sectors, particularly where the trade association has a high profile, for example ABTA in the travel trade, most traders are members. In other sectors, however, only a minority of traders belong to a trade association.

Contractual liability for defective services

Where services are provided in a manner which is inconsistent with the express terms of the contract, the consumer will be able to sue for damages for breach of contract, and in some cases will be able to withdraw from the contract on the grounds of a breach of condition by the service provider. This will depend upon the exact wording of the express terms of the contract, and the seriousness of the breach. Where the consumer has suffered loss or damage but there has been no breach of an express term, the service provider may still be liable for breach of an implied term in the contract.

The Supply of Goods and Services Act 1982 sets out terms which will be implied both into contracts for the supply of services and into contracts for work done and materials supplied. These terms will apply, for example, to contracts for dry cleaning, entertainment and professional services, home improvements and motor vehicle maintenance. The major areas of concern in relation to this type of contract were identified in a report of the National Consumer Council in 1981 entitled 'Services Please'. These concerns were quality, delay in performance and cost. They are all dealt with by the 1982 Act. The aim of this part of the 1982 Act is simply to codify the common law without changing it. The NCC believed that this was necessary for three reasons: certainty and clarity; ease of reference, and in order to focus attention on the existence of the obligations owed by those who supply services.

Implied duty to use reasonable care and skill

The 1982 Act in s.13 provides:

> *"In a contract for the supply of a service where the supplier is acting in the course of a business, there is an implied term that the supplier will carry out the service with reasonable care and skill".*

The nature of the duty was explained by Lord Denning in *Greaves & Co. (Contractors) Ltd. v. Baynham Meikle and Partners* 1975 in the following terms:

> *"The law does not usually imply a warranty that the professional man will achieve the desired result, but only a term that he will use reasonable care and skill. The surgeon does not warrant that he will cure the patient. Nor does the solicitor warrant that he will win the case .... whether it is a medical man, a lawyer, or an accountant, an architect or an engineer, his duty is to use reasonable care and skill".*

The section has wide ranging application embracing most situations where a client or customer is paying for services. In addition to those professions mentioned by Lord Denning, it applied to builders, hairdressers, dry cleaners, surveyors, auctioneers, tour operators, bankers, car repairers and many others who provide services in the course of their business.

The following cases illustrate the scope of the duty:

> In *Curtis v. Chemical Cleaning and Dyeing Company* 1951 the plaintiff took a wedding dress to the defendant dry cleaners for cleaning. When she came to collect the dress she found that it had been stained. It was held that the company were liable for the damage to the dress which had been caused by their failure to take care of it.

> In *Lawson v. Supasink Ltd.* 1984 the plaintiffs employed the company to design, supply and install a fitted kitchen at a price of £1,200. Plans were drawn up and agreed but the company did not follow them when installing the units. The plaintiffs complained about the standard of work before the installation was complete. After taking independent expert advice the plaintiffs demanded the return of their deposit and asked the defendants to remove the kitchen units. The defendants refused and the plaintiffs sued. The judge found that the kitchen was installed in 'a shocking and shoddy manner' and that the work was 'beyond redemption'. He awarded damages of £500 for inconvenience and loss of the use of the kitchen; damages of the difference between the cost of equivalent units and the contract price; and the return of the deposit. On appeal the defendants argued

that they had substantially performed the contract and were therefore entitled to the contract price less the cost of remedying any defects. This was rejected by the Court of Appeal on the grounds that the standard of workmanship and design was so poor that the doctrine of substantial performance could not be applied, having regard to the large sums which would have to be spent to remedy the defects.

The contract in the *Supasink* case was a contract for work and materials. Section 13 of the 1982 Act applies to the work element in such a contract. In some cases it may be important to know whether the defect complained of is due to fault in the materials themselves or the supplier's failure to take care in doing the work. This is because the nature of the liability for each of the two elements of the contract is different. In relation to the supply of materials, the supplier will be strictly liable, even if he is not at fault (like the defendant in *Frost v. Aylesbury Dairies* 1905 above). If the work is defective the supplier will only be liable if he has failed to take reasonable care. Another reason why the distinction may be important is that different controls on the use of exclusion clauses are applied by the Unfair Contract Terms Act 1977 to each element of contracts of this type.

Where services, or goods and services, are supplied by any person taking on work in connection with the provision of a dwelling house, s.1(1) of the Defective Premises Act 1972 imposes a duty of care on that person. He has a duty to see that the work is done in a workmanlike or professional manner with proper materials so that, in relation to the work he has taken on, the dwelling will be fit for habitation when it is completed.

Exemptions from the operation of s.13 of the 1982 Act have been made for company directors who have a duty to use such care as they would use in relation to their own personal affairs in performance of their duties as directors. A solicitor acting as an advocate before a court is also exempted from the section because of the rule that advocates cannot be made liable for professional negligence.

Implied terms relating to time for performance

Section 14 of the 1982 Act provides:

> *"Where, under a contract for the supply of a service by a supplier acting in the course of a business, the time for the service to be carried out is not fixed by the contract,...there is an implied term that the supplier will carry out the service within a reasonable time. What is a reasonable time is a question of fact".*
>
> In *Charnock v. Liverpool Corporation* 1968 the plaintiff recovered damages for the defendant's unreasonable delay in performing a contract. The defendant took eight weeks to repair the plaintiff's car when a reasonably competent repairer would have completed the repair within five weeks.

If a reasonable time has elapsed within which the contract should have been performed, the customer is entitled unilaterally to serve a notice fixing a time for the performance of the contract.

The new time limit must be reasonable. If the supplier fails to meet it, the Court of Appeal held in *Charles Rickards Ltd. v. Oppenheim* 1950 that the customer is entitled to withdraw from the contract without penalty.

If the time for performance of the contract has been agreed then s.14 does not add an additional requirement that the services should be provided within a reasonable time.

Implied terms relating to the cost of the service

Section 15 of the 1982 Act deals with the cost of services supplied. It provides:

"Where under a contract for the supply of a service, the consideration for the service is not determined by the contract,…there is an implied term that the party contracting with the supplier will pay a reasonable charge. What is a reasonable charge is a question of fact".

Section 15 does not enable a customer to reopen an agreement on the grounds that the charge for the service is unreasonably high, if the customer originally agreed to pay that charge. It applies only where there is no mechanism in the contract for determining the price and limits the amount recoverable to a reasonable sum.

Non-contractual Liability for Defective Services

The vast majority of claims for injury or loss caused by defective services are made by customers of the service provider rather than by third parties who have no contractual relationship with him. Most claims will therefore be based on an allegation of breach of contract, often on a breach of the implied duty to use reasonable skill and care in the performance of the contract. This is usually referred to as *contractual negligence.*

Where the plaintiff has no contractual relationship with the service provider, he will have to establish that the service provider owes him a duty of care under the general principles of the law of negligence examined in Chapter 3. Without a contract he will obviously be unable to rely on s.13 of the 1982 Act. The term *third party negligence* may be used to distinguish this situation from one of contractual negligence. Where the plaintiff suffers personal injury or damage to property, the neighbour principle laid down by Lord Atkin in *Donoghue v. Stevenson* 1932 will be applied by the court to determine whether a duty of care is owed by the service provider in a third party negligence claim. Many claims against members of the medical profession arise as a result of personal injuries suffered by patients in their care. In the case of NHS patients, where there is no contract with the practitioner, third party negligence will be the basis of any such claim. In such cases the existence of a duty of care can readily be shown. Applying the neighbour principle, the practitioner must reasonably foresee that carelessness on his part is likely to injure the patient. The patient is clearly a neighbour as he is closely and directly affected by the practitioner's acts or omissions. In other words there is a very close degree of proximity between them. The injured patient as a plaintiff may however have more difficulty in proving that a breach of duty has occurred.

> In *Bolam v. Friern Hospital Management Committee* 1957 the plaintiff broke his pelvis during electro-convulsive therapy treatment at the defendant's hospital. He claimed that the doctor was negligent principally because he failed to exercise any manual control over the plaintiff during treatment beyond merely arranging for his shoulders to be held, his chin supported, a gag used, and a pillow put under his back. Informed medical opinion consisted of two schools of thought regarding the use of restraint in these circumstances, one view favouring restraint, the other against it. It was held that there had been no breach of duty by the defendants.

McNair J., discussing the standard of care required of a professional man, stated:

> *" where you get a situation which involves the use of some special skill or competence, then the test as to whether there has been negligence or not … is the standard of the ordinary skilled man exercising and professing to have that special skill. A man need not possess the highest expert skill; it is well established law that it is sufficient if he exercises the ordinary skill of an ordinary competent man exercising that particular art …*
>
> *A doctor is not guilty of negligence if he has acted in accordance with a practice accepted as proper by a responsible body of medical men skilled in that particular art. Putting it*

the other way round, a man is not negligent, if he is acting in accordance with such a practice, merely because there is a body of opinion who take a contrary view."

The statements of McNair J., were approved by the House of Lords in *Whitehouse v. Jordan.*

In *Whitehouse v. Jordan* 1981 a senior hospital registrar in charge of a difficult birth used forceps to assist in the birth. The use of forceps was unsuccessful and the baby was eventually delivered by Caesarean section. The baby was born with brain damage. It was alleged that this resulted from the defendant's negligence in pulling too hard and too long with the forceps. The Court of Appeal held that the defendant was not liable in negligence even though he had made an error of judgment. Lord Denning, MR, in a statement which was not accepted as valid by the House of Lords, stated:

"we must say, and say firmly, that, in a professional man an error of judgment is not negligent."

The House of Lords, whilst confirming the decision of the Court of Appeal, disagreed with the statement by Lord Denning. Lord Fraser stated:

" I think that Lord Denning MR must have meant to say that an error of judgment 'is not necessarily negligent' ... Merely to describe something as an error of judgment tells us nothing about whether it is negligent or not. The true position is that an error of judgment may, or may not, be negligent; it depends on the nature of the error. If it is one that would not have been made by a reasonably competent professional man professing to have the standard and type of skill that the defendant held himself out as having, and acting with ordinary care, then it is negligent. If, on the other hand, it is an error that a man, acting with ordinary care, might have made, then it is not negligence."

Where a doctor writes a prescription which is illegible, and as a result a pharmacist dispenses the wrong drugs and the patient is injured, both the doctor and the pharmacist may be liable in negligence.

In *Prendergast v. Sam & Dee Ltd.* 1988 the plaintiff was prescribed a fairly common drug for a chest infection. The doctor's handwriting was not clear, and the pharmacist read it as being a drug for diabetes. It escaped his notice that if it had been the diabetes drug the dosage, the number of tablets and the size of the tablets were wrong. In addition a prescription for diabetes would have been free whereas the plaintiff was asked to pay. As a result of taking the wrong drug the plaintiff suffered brain damage. It was held that the pharmacist fell below the standard of skill of a reasonably competent pharmacist, who would have been alerted by the inconsistencies, and was liable in negligence. The doctor too was negligent, and liability was apportioned 25% to the doctor and 75% to the pharmacist.

Financial loss caused by negligence in providing services

Where the plaintiff is suing for contractual negligence there will be little difficulty in establishing liability for financial loss caused by the defendant's breach of contract, provided that the loss is not too remote. The rules of remoteness of damage in contract were laid down in *Hadley v. Baxendale* 1854 and are examined in Chapter 4.

Where the claim is based upon tortious or third party negligence, the plaintiff may have more difficulty in establishing that the defendant owed a duty of care to avoid causing his financial loss. A claim for financial loss (sometimes referred to as economic loss) usually takes the form of a claim for the loss of profits which the plaintiff would have made but for the defendant's negligence or the loss of money invested as a result of advice or information given by the defendant. As we saw in Chapter 3 a duty of care can readily be established by applying the neighbour principle where the claim relates to personal injury or property damage. Where the plaintiff's loss is financial, however, considerations of public policy may come into play in determining the existence and scope of the duty of care. In this context the courts will distinguish between financial losses caused by negligent statements and those which are caused by negligent acts. The basis and scope of the duty of care will vary according to which of these categories the plaintiff's claim comes within.

Non-contractual liability for financial loss caused by negligent statements

Prior to the decision of the House of Lords in *Hedley Byrne v. Heller* 1964 it was well settled law that there could be no liability in tort for financial loss caused by negligently made statements. In *Candler v. Crane, Christmas & Co.* 1951, for example, the Court of Appeal by a majority held that a false statement, carelessly made, was not actionable in the tort of negligence. Lord Denning dissented and was prepared to recognise the existence of a duty of care where the defendant had some special knowledge or skill upon which the plaintiff relied. He stated:

> *"From early times it has been held that persons who engage in a calling which requires special knowledge and skill owe a duty of care to those who are closely and directly affected by their work, apart altogether from any contract or undertaking in that behalf."*

The judgment of Lord Denning was approved by the house of Lords in *Hedley Byrne v. Heller*, and the decision of the majority in the *Candler* case was overruled.

> In *Hedley Byrne & Co. v. Heller and Partners Ltd.* 1964 the plaintiffs were advertising agents whose clients, Easipower Ltd, were customers of the defendant merchant bank. The plaintiffs had been instructed to buy advertising space for Easipower's products on television and in the newspapers. This involved them in the expenditure of large sums of money. Never having dealt with Easipower before, the plaintiffs sought a reference as to their creditworthiness to the extent of £100,000 from the defendant. The reference was given 'without responsibility on the part of the bank' and stated with reference to Easipower: "Respectably constituted company, considered good for its ordinary business engagements. Your figures are larger than we are accustomed to see". In fact Easipower had an overdraft with the bank, which ought to have known that the company would have difficulty meeting payments to the plaintiff. Within one week of giving the reference the bank was pressing Easipower to reduce its overdraft. Relying on the reference the plaintiffs incurred personal liability by placing advertising contracts. Easipower then went into liquidation due to insolvency and as a result the plaintiffs lost over £17,500. The actual decision in the case was that the defendant was not liable as the disclaimer of responsibility was effective to prevent the bank from assuming a duty of care.

The principal importance of the decision, however, is that the House of Lords recognised the existence, in certain circumstances, of a duty of care in relation to financial loss caused by negligently made statements.

For reasons of public policy, the scope of the duty and the class of persons to whom it is owed was restricted by the House of Lords. The main policy reason for this was a reluctance to create open ended liability by exposing a defendant to claims by numerous plaintiffs for a single instance of negligence.

For this reason the House of Lords held that in order for a duty to arise there must be a *special relationship of reliance* between the parties. This requires a close degree of proximity between the parties and was characterised by Lord Devlin as *'a relationship equivalent to a contract'* albeit lacking the essential ingredient of consideration. A fuller definition of the special relationship of reliance was given by Lord Reid who said that it included:

> *"... all those relationships where it is plain that the party seeking information or advice was trusting the other to exercise such a degree of care as the circumstances required, where it is reasonable for him to do that, and where the other gave the information or advice when he knew or ought to have known that the inquirer was relying on him."*

The test for determining whether a duty of care exists outside a contract in relation to careless statements causing financial loss is whether a special relationship of reliance exists between the parties. This is narrower in its scope than the neighbour principle and under it the duty will be established if the plaintiff can prove:

(i)   that the defendant possessed special skill or knowledge,

(ii)   that the plaintiff relied on the defendant to exercise care,

(iii) that the defendant knew or ought to have know that the plaintiff was relying on him, and

(iv)   that reliance by the plaintiff was reasonable in the circumstances.

> In *Caparo Industries plc v. Dickman* 1990 the plaintiff owned shares in a public company, Fidelity plc, whose accounts for the year ending 31 March 1984 showed profits far short of the predicted figure. This resulted in a substantial drop in the quoted share price. After receiving the accounts for the year, which had been audited by the third defendant, Touche Ross & Co, the plaintiff purchased further shares in Fidelity plc and shortly afterward made a successful takeover bid. The plaintiff sued the auditors in negligence, claiming that the accounts were inaccurate and misleading in that they showed a profit of £1,200,000, when in fact there had been a loss of over £400,000. The plaintiff argued that the auditors owed it a duty of care either as a potential bidder for Fidelity plc because they ought to have foreseen that the 1984 results made Fidelity plc vulnerable to a takeover bid, or as an existing shareholder of Fidelity plc interested in buying more shares. The House of Lords held that a duty of care in making a statement arises only where there is a relationship of proximity between the maker of the statement (in this case the auditors) and the person relying on it (the plaintiff). A relationship of proximity is created where the maker of the statement knows that the statement will be communicated to the person relying on it specifically in connection with a particular transaction and that person would be very likely to rely on it for the purpose of deciding whether to enter into the transaction. Applying this principle to the case, the House of Lords held that no duty of care was owed by the auditors to the plaintiff as there was no relationship of proximity on the facts as the auditors were not aware of the plaintiff or its intentions at the time the statement was made. Although auditors owe a statutory duty to shareholders, this is owed to them as a class rather than as individuals. The nature of this duty was explained by Lord Jauncey who stated:

> *"the purpose of the annual accounts, so far as members are concerned, is to enable them to question the past management of the company, to exercise their voting rights, and to influence future policy and management. Advice to individual shareholders in relation to present or future investment in the company is no part of this purpose."*

Where there is a contract between the service provider and consumer who suffers financial loss as a result of negligent advice or information provided under the contract, there is no need to establish the existence of a special relationship of reliance. The duty of care implied by s.13 Supply of Goods and Services Act 1982 extends to cover financial losses suffered by the consumer or client in this situation.

Non-contractual liability for financial loss caused by negligent acts

It has been a long-standing principle of law of negligence that pure financial (or economic) loss caused by a negligent act rather than a statement is not recoverable where the parties are not in a contractual relationship.

> Thus for example in *Weller Co. v. Foot & Mouth Disease Research Institute* 1965 the defendants carried out research into foot and mouth disease, a highly infectious disease affecting cattle. The virus escaped from their premises and affected cattle in the surrounding area. As a result restrictions on the movement of cattle were introduced and two cattle markets belonging to the plaintiff auctioneers had to be closed. The plaintiffs sued for loss caused to their business. It was held that, because the loss was purely financial and not connected with any physical harm caused to the plaintiffs or their property, no duty of care was owed by the defendants to the plaintiffs, and the claim failed.

The major policy reason for refusing to recognise a duty of care for pure financial loss is that it could lead to open ended liability. In the *Weller* case, for example, the closure of the markets would have affected the businesses of all those who transported cattle to and from the markets; of the shops, cafes and public houses in the vicinity of the markets; of the banks which would have handled the money in the sale and purchase of cattle; and the destruction of cattle caused by the escape of the virus could have adversely affected the economic interests of cattle feed suppliers, agricultural workers and milkmen, with substantial knock-on effects throughout the local economy. If the defendants were not to be liable for all of these consequences, the line of legal liability has to be drawn restrictively. Thus claims can be brought for injury to the person and damage to property, and for financial losses which are closely associated with such injury or damage. However claims for pure financial loss caused by the defendant's negligent act are not allowed. The extent of a plaintiff's financial loss may not readily be foreseen by the defendant before the negligent act occurs and the plaintiff will be in the best position to assess the extent and insure against the risk of financial loss.

Financial loss directly associated with physical injury may be referred to as 'consequential' rather than 'pure' financial loss. Here the defendant may owe a duty to the plaintiff under the neighbour principle. An example of the distinction between these types of financial loss can be seen in *Spartan Steel v. Martin*.

> In *Spartan Steel & Alloys Ltd. v. Martin & Co. (Contractors) Ltd.* 1972 the defendant's employee, while digging up a road with a mechanical excavator, carelessly damaged an electricity supply cable and cut off the power to the plaintiff's factory. In order to prevent damage to a furnace, the molten metal in it had to be poured off before it solidified. The melt was damaged to the value of £368, and the plaintiffs lost the profit of £400 which they would have made had the process been completed. The electricity supply was cut off for 14 hours during which four additional melts could have been processed. The profit on the additional melts would have been £1,767. The Court of Appeal held that the first two items claimed were recoverable – these were damage to property and consequential financial loss. The loss of profits on additional melts, however, was a pure financial loss not sufficiently connected with the physical damage and therefore not recoverable.

Exclusion of liability for negligence in providing services

Section 2 of the Unfair Contract Terms Act 1977 provides

*(1)   "A person cannot by reference to any contract term or to a notice given to persons gener-
ally or to particular persons exclude or restrict his liability for death or personal injury
resulting from negligence.*

*(2)   In the case of other loss or damage, a person cannot so exclude or restrict his liability for
negligence except insofar as the term or notice satisfies the requirement of reasonableness".*

This gives us two important basic rules. First that it is not possible to exclude liability for death or personal
injury resulting from negligence.

The second rule is that liability for loss or damage other than death or personal injury cannot be excluded
unless the exclusion is reasonable. This would apply, for example, to clauses which excluded liability for
damage to property or financial loss caused by negligence. The application of the rule in situations involving
contractual negligence and third party negligence in providing services can be seen in the following cases.

In *Spriggs v. Sotheby Parke Bernet and Co. Ltd.* 1984 the plaintiff, who was a
businessman, deposited a diamond with Sotheby's to be auctioned. He signed a document
which, among other things, excluded Sotheby's liability for negligence. He was given
the opportunity to insure the diamond but did not do so. Whilst the diamond was on view
prior to the auction, it was stolen despite the defendant's fairly comprehensive security
system. The plaintiff sued for negligence and the defendants relied on the exclusion
clause. Under s.2(2) the clause is only valid if the defendant can show that it is reasonable.
The court held that the clause in this case was reasonable and valid. The plaintiff was a
successful and experienced businessman and no doubt was used to contracts containing
exclusion clauses. He could not be regarded as having unequal bargaining power. The
risk was one which could have been covered by insurance but the plaintiff turned down
the opportunity to take this precaution.

In *Smith v. Eric S. Bush (a firm)* 1989 the defendants were engaged by the Abbey National
Building Society to carry out a survey and valuation of a house as required by s.13
Building Societies Act 1986. The plaintiff, who intended to purchase the house, paid for
the inspection. She later purchased without the benefit of any structural survey. Eighteen
months after the purchase, part of the house fell in because the flues in the attic were
left unsupported when the chimney breast in the room below had been taken out, a defect
which the defendants had overlooked when surveying the house.

In *Harris v. Wyre Forest District Council* 1989 the plaintiffs applied to the defendants
for a 90% mortgage to assist in the purchase of their council house. The defendants also
had a statutory duty to obtain a valuation before advancing the money and instructed
their own valuation surveyor to carry it out. After receiving the report they granted the
mortgage to the plaintiffs who assumed therefore that the surveyor had found no serious
defects and purchased the property without their own independent survey. Three years
later they discovered that the house was subject to settlement, was virtually unsaleable
and could only be repaired at a cost greater than the purchase price.

The House of Lords, which considered both cases together, held that a valuer who carried
out a mortgage valuation for a typical house purchase owed a duty of care both to the

lender and to the borrower to carry out his valuation with reasonable skill and care. The valuer would know that the valuation fee had been paid by the borrower and that the valuation would probably be relied upon by him in deciding whether or not to enter into a contract to purchase the house. This knowledge could readily be implied in relation to a borrower within the lower or middle range of the housing market, although the position would be different in the case of very expensive residential property or commercial property. In each case the House of Lords held that the defendants were in breach of their duty to carry out reasonably careful visual inspections of the premises. The scope of the duty was described by Lord Templeman:

"The valuer will value the house after taking into consideration major defects which are, or ought to be, obvious to him in the course of a visual inspection of so much of the exterior and interior of the house as may be accessible to him without undue difficulty."

In the *Bush* and *Harris* cases, the House of Lords had also to deal with disclaimers of liability which were contained in the valuation reports. It was held that such disclaimers were subject to the test of reasonableness under s.2(2) of the Unfair Contract Terms Act 1977. Having regard to the high cost of houses and the high rates of interest charged to borrowers, their Lordships decided that it would not be fair and reasonable for mortgagees and valuers to impose on purchasers the risk of loss arising as a result of incompetence or carelessness on the part of valuers, and that the disclaimers were therefore ineffective.

The reasonableness of a disclaimer of liability in similar circumstances to *Smith v. Bush* was considered in *Stevenson v. Nationwide Building Society* 1984. In this case, however, the purchaser was an estate agent who was well familiar with the difference between a valuation and a structural survey. It was held that the disclaimer was reasonable and effective to protect the defendant, when its staff surveyor failed to notice a substantial structural defect during the course of a visual inspection.

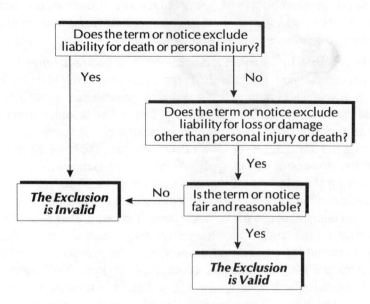

Figure 5.4 *Exclusion of Liability for Negligence: Section 2 Unfair Contract Terms Act 1977*

Consumer Protection in relation to Package Holidays

The Package Travel, Package Holidays and Package Tours Regulations 1992, which we shall call the Package Travel Regulations came into force in December 1992 and are designed to implement the EC directive on Package Travel, Package Holidays and Package Tours (90/314/EEC). The regulations introduce a fairly comprehensive set of rules covering package travel and package holidays which are designed to protect the consumer. A number of the matters covered by the regulations were previously dealt with in the ABTA codes of practice for travel agents and tour operators, although the new regulations go much further in protecting the consumer.

The regulations apply to packages sold or offered for sale in the United Kingdom and, unlike the ABTA codes, apply to domestic packages as well as overseas travel arrangements. The concept of a package is central to the application of the regulations. Only if the travel arrangements fall within the definition of a package will the many elements of consumer protection contained within the regulations apply. A package is defined as:

> *"The pre-arranged combination of at least two of the following components when sold or offered for sale at an inclusive price and when the service covers a period of more than 24 hours or includes overnight accommodation:*
>
> *a. transport*
>
> *b. accommodation*
>
> *c. other tourist services not ancillary to transport or accommodation and accounting for a significant proportion of the package, and*
>
> *i. the submission of separate accounts for different components shall not cause the arrangements to be other than a package,*
>
> *ii. the fact that a combination is arranged at the request of the consumer and in accordance with his specific instructions (whether modified or not) shall not of itself cause it to be treated as other than pre-arranged"*

In order to come within the regulations, the travel arrangements must be *pre-arranged*. This would obviously include the packages which can be bought off-the-shelf, for example a fortnight in Majorca selected from a tour operators brochure. It also includes tailor made travel arrangements put together to meet the needs of a particular client, provided that the arrangements are put together before the conclusion of the contract. The package must be sold at an *inclusive price*. If a customer books travel and accommodation through a travel agent, for example, and pays the travel agent for his air ticket, but pays the hotel direct at the end of his stay, this is not a package and the regulations do not apply. As an anti-avoidance measure, the definition makes clear that the separate invoicing of the individual elements does not of itself prevent the creation of a package. Where transport and accommodation are combined, then provided that the arrangements last for at least 24 hours or include overnight accommodation, a package will come into being. However, if one of these elements is missing, the arrangements must include *other tourist services* which are not ancillary to transport or accommodation and which account for a significant proportion of the package. The other services provided here must be tourist services and not, for example, educational services. If a language summer school is advertised including accommodation and modern language tuition, but excluding transport, this combination is not of itself enough to create a package. The other tourist services must account for a significant proportion of the package. This would not be the case, for example, where a guest could use a swimming pool at a hotel as this is a facility which goes with the use of the hotel and not another tourist service. Neither would it usually be significant.

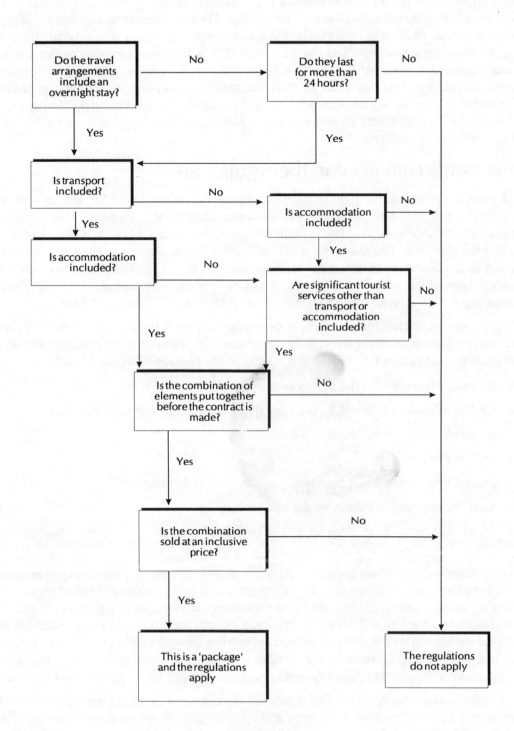

Figure 5.5 *The Package Travel Regulations – when do they apply?*

The person or organisation who puts together the package is known as the *organiser*. This will usually be a tour operator, although the travel agent will come within the definition of organiser where he puts together a package for his customers. This will be so even though the customer may end up with individual direct contracts with the providers of the components that make up the package. The expression *consumer* within the regulations includes the person who takes or agrees to take the package, any person on whose behalf the package is purchased, and any person to whom the package is transferred. This third category of consumer arises because the regulations introduce a new *right to transfer a booking* where the original consumer is *prevented* from proceeding with the package. This may occur for example, due to illness or jury service although the consumer will not be regarded as being prevented from proceeding if he simply changes his mind. The person to whom the package is transferred must satisfy all the conditions applicable to the package, and reasonable notice must be given of the intention to transfer.

Consumer rights contained in the regulations

Regulation 4 gives the consumer the right to sue for compensation where he suffers loss as a result of any misleading description relating to a package or misleading information as to its price. This new right arises in circumstances where an offence would be committed by a trader under s.14 of the Trade Descriptions Act 1968 or s.20 of the Consumer Protection Act 1987, although r.4 is wider in its scope as it applies both to those operating in the course of business and to those who are not. The criminal offences only apply to misleading information which is supplied knowingly or recklessly whereas the regulation applies to information which is misleading even if it is not applied knowingly or recklessly.

Under r.5 it is a criminal offence for an organiser or retailer to make a brochure available to a prospective consumer unless the description of the package in the brochure indicates in an understandable and accurate manner both the price and certain key information relating to the package. This would include:

- the destination and the type of transport used;
- the type of accommodation, its location, degree of comfort and main features;
- the meals which are included;
- the itinerary;
- general information about passports, visas and health formalities;
- when the deposit and balance of the price is due, and
- the arrangements for security for money paid and for repatriation of the consumer in the event of insolvency.

Under r.6 the particulars in a brochure constitute implied warranties for the purposes of any contract to which they relate. Where the brochure states that the information in it may change and the changes are clearly communicated before the contract is made then these will override inconsistent statements in the brochure. Under r.7 a retailer or organiser will be guilty of a criminal offence if they do not provide the intending customer with information in writing or in some other appropriate form about passport and visa requirements, health formalities and the arrangements for the security of money paid over and for the repatriation of the consumer in the event of insolvency. This information must be supplied before the contract is concluded.

It is also a criminal offence, under r.8, to fail to provide the consumer in good time before the start of the journey with written information about the journey and the arrangements for assistance from representatives of the organiser and contact names in the event of difficulties on the tour.

It is an implied condition of the contract that all of its terms should be communicated to the consumer before the contract is made. This does not apply where circumstances make it impracticable, for example in the case of last minute bookings. In any event a written copy of the contract must be supplied to the consumer. The written terms must comply with the regulations and contain certain minimum information. This is similar to, but more detailed than, the information which must be included in a brochure under r.5.

The regulations limit the organiser's ability to increase the price of the package by way of a surcharge. If the contract contains such a clause, it will be void unless the contract allows for the possibility of a price reduction as well as an increase. The contract must state precisely how the revised price is to be calculated. Price changes can only be made to reflect changes in transport or fuel costs, exchange rates, taxes or fees. In any event no price increase may be made in the period of 30 days before departure and the tour operator must always absorb the first 2% of an increase.

If where the organiser, within the terms of the contract, wishes to make a significant alteration to an important term, such as the price, he must notify the consumer as quickly as possible. The consumer will have the option to withdraw from the contract without penalty or to accept the change. If the consumer does withdraw then he is entitled to take an available substitute package of the equivalent quality; a full refund or a lower quality substitute package coupled with a rebate.

Where the organiser is in breach of contract because a significant proportion of the services contracted for are not provided he must make suitable alternative arrangements at no extra cost to the consumer for the continuation of the package. If it is not possible to make such arrangements or if the consumer validly refuses to accept them the organiser must provide the consumer with equivalent transport home or to another destination with the consumers agreement. The organiser may still be liable to compensate the consumer for the difference between the services contracted for and those supplied.

The regulations also make detailed provision for the protection of the consumer in the event of the insolvency of the tour operator or organiser. He is required at all times to be able to provide sufficient evidence of security for the refund of money paid in advance and for the repatriation of the consumer in the event of insolvency. This is important as booking conditions for package holidays will almost invariably require full payment by the consumer eight weeks before departure, and because it provides protection for the holiday maker who would otherwise be stranded abroad if the tour operator becomes insolvent while they are on holiday. This protection is further enhanced by the licensing and bonding requirements in the regulations.

Tour operator's liability

When booking a package holiday, the consumer makes a contract with a tour operator. This contract is usually made through a travel agent, though in the case of direct sell operators the contract may be made without the use of an intermediary. Where a travel agent is involved he will bring together the parties to the contract in return for a commission paid by the tour operator. In accordance with the ordinary principles of the law of agency, the travel agent will not himself be a party to the contract. The tour operator puts together the various elements of the package such as flights, transfers from airport to hotel, hotel accommodation and food; and sells them together as one product. The tour operator will enter into separate contracts with the suppliers of the component parts of the package. In addition to the elements already noted, the package may include other items such as car hire, excursions, tickets for events and holiday insurance, although these may be optional extras.

Where the consumer books a package holiday he is contracting only with the tour operator and has no direct contract with the suppliers of individual components of the holiday. The terms of the contract with the tour operator are set out in the brochure, though not necessarily all on the same page. There will usually be at least one page of general booking conditions, sometimes referred to as a fair trading charter, often towards the back of the brochure. These must be read in conjunction with the information on the booking form itself, and the information in the main body of the brochure about the particular hotel and resort chosen by the consumer which is entered onto the booking form with the holiday dates and the price.

Activity

Obtain a copy of a package holiday brochure from a travel agent. Find the page or pages which contain the booking conditions. Examine the conditions relating to payment and cancellation and any two other printed conditions. Write a brief note on each of the four contract terms explaining what they mean and whether it is the customer or the tour operator which benefits from the particular way in which the conditions are worded.

The tour operator may be liable to pay damages to a dissatisfied consumer if facilities described in the brochure are not available, for example where the consumer books a room in a particular hotel which is specified as having a balcony overlooking the sea and bathroom facilities en suite and this turns out not to be the case. We have already seen that the tour operator may incur criminal liability under s.14 Trade Descriptions Act 1968 in these circumstances. You may refer back to the 1968 Act in Chapter 3 and look at the cases of *Wings v. Ellis, Yugotours v. Wadsley* and *Sunair Holidays v. Dodds*. The tour operator's civil liability for damages will be based upon the breach of an express term of the contract.

In *Jackson v. Horizon Holidays* 1975 the plaintiff had booked a month's holiday in Ceylon staying in an hotel. The defendant's brochure described the hotel facilities. These included a swimming pool, a mini golf course and a hair-dressing salon. The hotel in fact had none of these facilities and the food was poor. The plaintiff's children's room was unusable due to mildew and fungus on the walls, and the sanitary facilities were dirty. The Court of Appeal awarded damages of £1,100 to the plaintiff for breach of contract. This was made up of £600 for the reduction in the value of the holiday and £500 damages for mental distress, vexation and disappointment.

In *Jarvis v. Swans Tours Ltd.* 1973 the plaintiff booked a skiing holiday which was described in the defendent's brochure as a house party in Morlialp. The price included a number of house party arrangements, a welcome party on arrival, afternoon tea and cake, Swiss dinner by candle-light, fondue party, yodel evening, and a farewell party. The brochure also stated that ski packs could be hired in Morlialp, the hotel owner spoke English and the hotel bar would be open several evenings a week. In the first week of the holiday the house party comprised only 13 people, and in the second week the plaintiff was the only guest at the hotel. The hotel owner did not speak English, the bar was only open on one evening, and the plaintiff was unable to hire full length skis except for two days during the second week. The Court of Appeal held that the quality of holiday provided fell far short of that which was promised in the brochure and awarded damages to the plaintiff. This included damages representing the difference between what the plaintiff had paid for the holiday and what he had been supplied with; as well as damages for mental distress, frustration, annoyance and disappointment.

The tour operator may also be liable for breach of an implied term in the contract. As a provider of services in the course of a business, s.13 of the Supply of Goods and Services Act 1982 applies to the tour operator, and implies a term in the contract between him and the consumer that he will use reasonable care and skill in carrying out the contract.

> In *Davey v. Cosmos Air Holidays* 1989 the plaintiff booked a two weeks' package holiday in the Algarve for himself and his family. During the holiday the entire family suffered diarrhoea and the plaintiff's wife and son both contracted dysentery. The evidence showed that the illness was caused by a general lack of hygiene at the resort and the fact that raw sewage was being pumped into the sea just fifty yards from the beach. The defendant tour operators had resident representatives at the resort who knew of the dangers. It was held that the defendants were liable for breach of the implied duty in the contract to take reasonable care to avoid exposing their clients to a significant risk of injury to their health.

The tour operator will not be liable merely because the consumer has suffered injury, provided the tour operator has taken reasonable care. In the Davey case, for example, Cosmos would not have been liable had they warned the plaintiffs of the risks and advised them as to the steps to take to avoid injury.

A tour operator has a duty to exercise reasonable care and skill in selecting the suppliers of components of the package. In order to fulfil this duty he should, for example, undertake thorough inspections of the hotels, not only to verify the availability of facilities for inclusion in the brochure but also to satisfy himself as to the standards of kitchen hygiene, general safety, sanitary conditions and such things as fire escapes.

> In *Wilson v. Best Travel Ltd.* 1993 the plaintiff suffered serious injuries after tripping and falling through glass patio doors at an hotel in Greece. The glass doors were fitted with 4mm glass which complied with Greek safety standards but would not have met equivalent British standards. The plaintiff claimed damages against the defendant tour operators, arguing that the hotel was not reasonably safe for use by the defendants' customers and that they were in breach of their duty of care under s.13 of the Supply and Goods and Services Act 1982. It was held that the tour operators were not liable. They had discharged their contractual duty of care by checking that local safety regulations had been complied with. It was not necessary for them to ensure that the Greek hotel came up to English safety standards provided that the absence of a relevant safety feature was not such that a reasonable holiday maker might decline to take a holiday at the hotel in question. This could be the case, for example, if the hotel had no fire precautions at all even though they were not required under local law.

> In *Wall v. Silver Wing Surface Arrangements Ltd. (trading as Enterprise Holidays)* 1981 the plaintiff holiday maker was injured as a result of the fact that the management at his hotel had locked the fire exit. The evidence showed that the fire escape had not been locked when it was inspected by the defendants. It was locked on the occasion in question for security reasons to prevent unauthorised access into the hotel. It was held that the defendants were not liable as they had exercised reasonable care in selecting a suitable hotel and checking that the safety arrangements were satisfactory. The court rejected the plaintiff's argument that the tour operator had an implied contractual duty to ensure that the plaintiff would be reasonably safe in the hotel. The duty to take reasonable care in selecting the hotel had been fulfilled and the tour operator was not liable.

In circumstances where the tour operator is not shown to have been negligent, the consumer may be left with the difficult task of suing the hotel. As we have seen there is no contract between the consumer and the hotel. The claim could not therefore be based in contract. A major problem for the consumer is that the hotelier's liability will depend on the national law of the country in which the hotel is situated, and whether an equivalent of the English law of third party negligence exists there. There is the additional expense and inconvenience of having to take legal action in a foreign country with an unfamiliar legal system and perhaps in a foreign language.

The consumer's rights in this situation have been greatly improved as a result of the implementation of the Package Travel Directive by the Package Travel Regulations 1992. Under r.15 *the tour operator is legally responsible to the consumer for the proper performance of the obligations arising under the contract*, and it does not matter whether the obligations are to be performed by the tour operator or by other suppliers of services. The tour operator is liable to the consumer for any damage caused by the improper performance of the contract by any of his suppliers. This new right to sue the tour operator where, for example, the consumer is injured by the negligence of the hotelier means that the consumer's position is made much easier as he does not have to face the problems involved in suing abroad. If the consumer is successful in his claim, the tour operator will be able to seek an indemnity from his supplier and unlike the consumer who has no contract with the supplier, the tour operator will be able to base his claim on a breach of contract. Thus in a case such as *Wall v. Silver Wing* the tour operator would be liable to the plaintiff, and in turn would seek an indemnity from the hotel. In *Wilson v. Best,* however, it is probable that the consumer's claim would still fail on the grounds that the supplier had properly performed the contract.

The tour operator will have a defence to a claim by a consumer under r.15 if he can show that the failures in the performance of the contract are attributable to the consumer himself or are unforeseeable or unavoidable and caused by a third party. In such circumstances, except where the problems are entirely due to the consumer, the tour operator still has a duty to render prompt assistance to the consumer.

The tour operator is permitted to limit his liability in line with the levels of compensation provided for in international conventions such as the Warsaw Convention in respect of international flights.

He is also permitted to limit his contractual liability to the consumer for damage other than personal injury, provided that the limitation is not unreasonable. This is in line with the provisions of s.2 Unfair Contract Terms Act 1977, except that the regulations only permit a limitation and not a total exclusion of this liability.

Where the consumer experiences problems when he is actually on the package holiday or tour, he has a duty under r.15 to communicate his complaint to the organiser where he considers that it arises from defective performance of the contract by a component supplier, for example where the hotel room which has been allocated to him is unsatisfactory or is significantly inferior to that which was described in the brochure. The organiser, or his local representative, must then make prompt efforts to resolve the problems in an appropriate way.

Data Protection Act 1984

The widespread use of computers in modern society has meant than an increasing amount of information, much of it about individuals, is collected and stored in computer files by business, the public sector and other organisations. This has given rise to concern about issues such as individual privacy, the possible damage that can arise if errors are made and incorrect information is held about someone, and the use to which information may be put.

The Data Protection Act 1984 provides a legal framework governing the collection, storage and distribution of *personal data*, information relating to identifiable living individuals where this is done using computers. The Act does not, however, apply to records or information held in paper files; or to information about a company or any other body which is not an individual.

The Act provides for the registration and supervision by the Data Protection Registrar of *data users*, that is people and organisations who hold and use personal data; and of *computer bureaux*, people or organisations who process personal data for others or who allow others to use their equipment for this purpose. Certain categories of information, however, are exempt from the workings of the Act, for example, data held by a club about its members in certain circumstances. Other categories of information are subject to a partial exemption, for example, information which is held by the police in relation to crime detection. These are examined below. The Act gives a number of important rights to *data subjects*, the individuals about whom the information is processed. They have the right to know what information is held by the data user relating to themselves and to a copy of that information, a right to have inaccurate information corrected or erased, and a right to sue for compensation for loss or damage caused by the inaccuracy of personal data, or by its loss or unauthorised destruction or disclosure. More generally the individual has the right to complain to the Data Protection Registrar if he feels that the Act has not been complied with in some way as the Registrar has a duty to enforce the Act as a whole. A complaint may be based, for example, upon a failure by a data user to observe the *data protection principles* which are set out in the Act and which are central to its operation. The principles give a guide to good practice in the processing of personal data and are designed to safeguard the rights of data subjects. The Registrar has a number of powers available to him to secure compliance with the data protection principles.

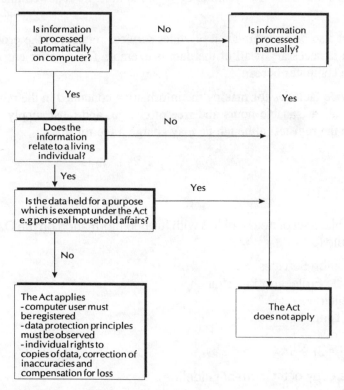

Figure 5.6 *Data Protection Act 1984: When does it apply?*

Registration

The Registrar maintains a registrar of data users and computer bureaux. Under the Act every data user who holds personal data is required to register unless all of the personal data which he holds is exempt. The information which is contained in the registration will include:

a. the name and address of the data user;

b. a description of the personal data to be held by him and the purposes for which they are to be held or used;

c. a description of the sources from which he intends or may wish to obtain the information contained in the data;

d. a description of any person to whom he intends to disclose the information;

e. the names of the countries outside the U.K. to which he may wish to transfer the data; and

f. the address for the receipt of requests from data subjects for access to the data.

Once the registration is made the data user must operate strictly within its terms. He will commit a criminal offence if he holds personal data of a type or for a purpose which is not specified in the registration, or if he obtains data from unregistered sources. Similarly if he discloses personal data to any person not described in the registration or transfers it to another country which has not been specified. The data user may alter the terms of the registration if this becomes necessary. This could occur, for example, if he finds that he wishes to disclose information to people or organisations which are not specified in the original registration. In any event the registration lasts only for three years after which is must be renewed and alterations can be made on renewal.

A computer bureau must also be registered if it provides services relating to the processing of personal data, although no registration is necessary if all of the data is exempt. The register entry will comprise only the name and address of the computer bureau.

The Registrar must provide facilities for making the information contained in the register available for public inspection by anyone at all reasonable hours and free of charge, and must supply a copy of the particulars contained in an entry on the register, although he may charge a fee for this.

Activity

If you would like a set of free booklets with further information on the Data Protection Act 1984, write to

Information Services
The Data Protection Registrar
Springfield House
Water Lane
Wilmslow
Cheshire SK9 5AX

and request a copy of the current guidelines.

The Data Protection Principles

The Act lays down eight Data Protection Principles which are intended to govern the way in which data users deal with personal data. Data users are required to observe all of the principles, but only the eighth principle, relating to security, applies to computer bureaux. The Data Protection Principles set out a framework of good practice which computer users must follow. They are as follows:

1.   The information to be contained in personal data shall be obtained, and personal data shall be processed, fairly and lawfully.

2.   Personal data shall be held only for one or more specified and lawful purposes.

3.   Personal data held for any purpose or purposes shall not be used or disclosed in any manner incompatible with that purpose or those purposes.

4.   Personal data held for any purpose or purposes shall be adequate, relevant, and not excessive in relation to that purpose or those purposes.

5.   Personal data shall be accurate, and where necessary, kept up to date.

6.   Personal data held for any purpose or purposes shall not be kept for longer than is necessary for that purpose or those purposes.

7.   An individual shall be entitled:

     (a) at reasonable intervals and without undue delay or expense

          (i) to be informed by any data user whether he holds personal data of which that individual is the subject; and

          (ii) to access to any such data held by a data user; and

     (b) where appropriate to have such data corrected or erased.

8.   Appropriate security measures shall be taken against unauthorised access to, or alteration, disclosure, or destruction of, personal data and against accidental loss or destruction of personal data.

The Registrar has power to consider any complaint that any principle has been contravened and a duty to do so if he thinks that the complaint raises a matter of substance and has been made without undue delay. Where he does consider a complaint he must notify the complainant of any action which he proposes to take. In order to enforce compliance with the Data Protection Principles, the Registrar can serve three types of notice:

An enforcement notice.

This notice will specify the principle which has been broken, the Registrar's grounds for believing this and the steps which must be taken in order to comply with the principle. The notice will give a time limit within which action must be taken. This will usually be at least 28 days, though in cases of urgency it can be as little as 7 days. Failure to comply with an enforcement notice is a criminal offence.

A de-registration notice.

This will be served where the Registrar is satisfied that an enforcement notice will not be effective to secure compliance with the principle or principles in question. The effect of a de-registration notice is to cancel the whole or a part of the data user's register entry. The effect of de-registration is that the data user will be committing a criminal offence if he continues to undertake the activities which were previously covered by the register entry before it was removed.

A transfer prohibition notice.

This has the effect of prohibiting the transfer of personal data to a place outside the United Kingdom and can be served where the Registrar is satisfied that a proposed transfer is likely to lead to a breach of any of the Data Protection Principles. Failure to comply with a transfer prohibition notice is a criminal offence.

There is a right of appeal to the Data Protection Tribunal against the issue of any of the notices described above. The Tribunal may allow an appeal completely or substitute another decision or notice on the grounds of an error in law or on the grounds that the Registrar ought to have exercised his discretion differently.

The Registrar has power to prosecute in the criminal courts where he considers that an offence has been committee under the Act. Where an offender is found guilty, a Magistrates Court may impose a fine not exceeding £2,000 whilst the Crown Court may impose a fine of any amount.

The Individual's right of access

If an individual wishes to know whether a particular data user holds information on computer about him, he must make a request in writing to the data user at the address given in the entry on the register. The individual is entitled to be informed by the data user whether he holds any such personal data and to be supplied with a copy of all of the information which comprises the personal data. The data user may charge a fee of up to £10 for dealing with the request. He has a duty to respond within 40 days of receiving it. However, he need not comply until the fee is paid, although the 40 day period starts to run as soon as the request is made. In certain circumstances the 40 day period does not begin until the data user receives further information from the individual. This includes any information he reasonably requires to satisfy himself as to the identity of the person making the request, any information reasonably required to enable him to locate the data, and/or any consent required from another person where this is necessary. Consent may be required where the nature of the data is such that the data user cannot disclose it without also disclosing information relating to another person who can be identified from the information.

In complying with a request, the data user must supply any data which was held by him at the time the request was received, although amendments or deletions which would normally have been made regardless of the request may still be made by the data user prior to supplying the information. If any of the information is not intelligible without explanation, the data subject must be given an explanation of the information, for example where it is in a coded form.

If the data user fails to reply to a request for access the individual may complain to the Registrar that there has been a breach of the seventh Data Protection Principle. The Registrar may then issue an enforcement notice requiring the data user to give access. If the data user does not comply with the notice he commits a criminal offence. Alternatively, the Registrar could issue a de-registration notice. Rather than complaining to the Registrar, the individual may apply to the court, which has power to order the data user to comply with the request for access and supply the information to the individual. The court will not use this power if it considers that in all the circumstances it would be unreasonable to do so, for example, because of the frequency with which the applicant has made requests for information to the data user.

Compensation for inaccuracy

Where an individual suffers damage due to the inaccuracy of data held by a data user, he is entitled to compensation from the data user for that damage and for any distress which he has suffered as a result. Data are inaccurate if they are incorrect or misleading as to any matter of fact. A statement of opinion cannot give rise to a claim for compensation for inaccuracy even where the individual does not agree with the opinion which is recorded about him. The Registrar does not have the power to award compensation and the individual must take action in the court. It will be a defence for the data user to show that all reasonable care was taken to ensure the accuracy of the data. It will also be a defence to show that the data accurately records information received or obtained from a third party where the data indicates the source of the information and also records any challenge which has been made by the data subject as to the accuracy of the information.

Compensation for loss or unauthorised disclosure

Where an individual has suffered damage because of a loss of personal data by a data user or a computer bureau he can claim compensation against them. It will be a defence to show that all reasonable care was taken to prevent the loss. Similarly if damage has been caused by the unauthorised destruction or disclosure of personal data or because someone has obtained unauthorised access to it, the individual can claim compensation. The defence that all reasonable care was taken also applies in such a case.

Correction or erasure of inaccurate entries

In an individual thinks that personal data held about him by a data user is inaccurate he may apply to the court for an order that the data be corrected or erased. The court also has power to order the erasure of data where the individual is entitled to compensation for unauthorised disclosure of the data or unauthorised access to it if it can be shown that there is a substantial risk of further unauthorised disclosure or access. The Registrar also has power to order the correction or erasure of inaccurate personal data.

Exemptions from the Act

Certain types of personal data are totally exempt from the workings of the Act. The computer user is not required to register, for example, nor is he required to give access to the data. Within this category are included personal data held for domestic or recreational purposes; and personal data held by a club and relating only to members of the club where the members are asked and have no objection to the data being held.

Other categories of personal data have partial exemption from the requirements of the Act. Disclosures made to people or organisations outside the terms of the data user's registration may be exempt, for example where they are made for the purpose of preventing or detecting crime, the assessment or collection of tax or in order to safeguard national security. Other exemptions have the effect of restricting or removing the data subject's right of access, for example, data held by the police for the purpose of crime prevention.

Procedure for Dispute Settlement Between Customers and Business

Here we shall examine the machinery which exists for enforcing consumer rights. While the High Court has an important role to play in hearing civil disputes concerning large sums of money the vast majority of civil legal actions which go to Court are dealt with at County Court level. Changes in the jurisdiction of the County Courts, have increased their workload by taking cases which previously would have been heard before the High Court.

Not all civil disputes however are resolved by means of court proceedings. Many cases are dealt with instead by arbitration. We will explore more thoroughly later in the chapter the nature of arbitration and its use in the context of enforcing consumer rights.

Sources of Legal Advice and Information

Many sources of legal advice and information are available to a consumer who has a legal problem. He may be able to research it himself by looking at law books in a library, but more usually he will seek outside help.

The Citizens Advice Bureau may be able to advise the consumer as to his rights and provide the information which he requires. In addition, there are a number of law centres which provide a similar, though more specialist, role in giving legal advice and acting on behalf of clients. Law centres tend to deal with legal problems arising in relation to social issues such as housing, immigration, consumer and employee rights. The consumer may consult a solicitor who will give advice as to his legal rights. Under the Legal Aid Scheme the consumer may be entitled to receive help with his legal problem. Depending upon his financial circumstances, all or part of the cost of legal help will be paid by the state. This can extend to representation before a court. In order to qualify for free legal aid the individual's resources must be very low, both in terms of capital and income. If he is not entitled to free legal aid because he has more than the minimum resources he may still get some help from the legal aid scheme but he will have to make a contribution towards his own costs. If the individual has capital assets or average income, however, he may be caught in the "middle income trap". This is described as a trap because he will be too well off to obtain legal aid but will not be sufficiently well off to be able to afford the costs of litigation himself. He may therefore have to decide not to take legal action in the courts, or to take legal action himself without the aid of a lawyer.

Suing in the County Court

Before an individual takes a decision to sue in the County Court, for example in relation to a consumer problem, there are a number of matters which he must consider carefully. Probably the most important factor will be that of cost, both in terms of money and in terms of the time and resources which must be invested in legal proceedings. Most of the plaintiff's costs will eventually be payable by the defendant if the plaintiff wins his case. However the plaintiff has a contract with his solicitor and is bound under that contract to pay the solicitors fees, and disbursements such as court fees, regardless of the outcome of the case. The plaintiff must therefore spend all of this money himself in the hope of later recovering it from the defendant. Even if the plaintiff is successful, he may not be able to obtain an order that the defendant pays all of his legal costs because a defendant can challenge the amount of a successful plaintiff's legal bill. This is done in a *taxation of costs* in which the court will require the defendant to pay only those costs which were reasonably and necessarily incurred by the plaintiff in the action. After a taxation, the plaintiff will usually have to pay some part of his own legal costs. These in effect are deducted from whatever damages he has recovered from the defendant.

Another important consideration, closely associated with the question of costs, is whether the defendant will actually be able to satisfy any judgment which is eventually made against him. If the defendant is a "man of straw", and has no resources, the plaintiff will be wasting his money by pursuing him in the courts. He may end up by having to pay all of his own legal costs and by getting them back from the defendant by instalments of one pound a month, or by not getting them back at all. For this reason it is essential that the financial circumstances of the potential defendant are investigated before proceedings are issued against him. There is no formal procedure for this type of investigation, so the plaintiff will simply have to conduct it in the best way that he can.

In making the decision to sue someone, the plaintiff must also be aware that the legal process is slow. It may take 1 to 4 years to obtain judgment against a defendant, depending on the complexity of the case and its particular circumstances. In extreme cases, litigants have suffered mental illness or depression as a result of involvement with litigation. There is recognised mental condition called litigation neurosis. Involvement in litigation over a long period of time is certainly a drain on the resources of the parties in terms of time, money and mental energy.

Publicity is another important factor. Proceedings before the courts are held in public and can be attended by anyone, including the press. Depending on the circumstances, the businessman may be inviting adverse publicity and a loss of goodwill by taking or defending legal proceedings. Involvement in legal action with an important customer can cause considerable damage to ongoing business relationships and business goodwill. This can work to the plaintiff's advantage in a consumer complaint as the business may conclude that it is better to settle the dispute without going to law.

In addition to these factors, it almost goes without saying that the plaintiff must have a sound legal basis for his claim and sufficient evidence to support it. This evidence may be documentary or may be provided by witnesses. In the case of the verbal evidence by witnesses, the credibility of the witnesses will be an important consideration. It may also be necessary to employ expert witnesses if the subject matter of the dispute is technical in nature, for example if it centres around a mechanical or electrical problem.

Negotiation, compromise and settlement

For one or more of the reasons given above, the parties to a dispute will usually try to reach a settlement without the necessity of taking legal proceedings. Negotiations will take place before legal proceedings are issued and will usually continue as an ongoing process right up to the date of the trial. If both parties are prepared to litigate, this is probably an indication that there is some merit in the case that each of them is arguing. If a compromise can be agreed this will probably result in the saving of costs, time and adverse publicity.

County Court Procedure

Assuming that the case is to be brought in the County Court, the plaintiff must decide which County Court to use. The claim must usually be brought in the district in which the defendant lives or carries on business or in the district in which the cause of action arose (for example where the contract was made).

The procedure for the conduct of the action is laid down in the County Court Rules. These are designed to ensure fairness between the parties. This is achieved by ensuring that the matter in dispute is understood by the parties and by the court, and that neither party is taken by surprise at the trial by the introduction of any new matter which ought to have been disclosed to him before the trial. The rules also give time limits within which procedural steps must be taken by each party. These are designed to ensure that there is no unnecessary delay in the conduct of the case.

Letter before action

The first step which must be taken by the plaintiff is to send a *letter before action* to the defendant. In it the plaintiff will state his claim, invite the defendant to comply with his demands within 7 days, and inform him that court proceedings will be taken if he fails to do so. A letter before action gives the defendant the opportunity to meet the plaintiff's claim without incurring legal costs, or to state any legitimate grounds of defence which are available to him, and which may give rise to negotiations for settlement of the claim. If the plaintiff does not send a letter before action, and the defendant meets his demands as soon as proceedings are issued, the plaintiff will be unable to recover costs from him.

Issuing a summons

Within a fortnight of sending a letter before action, if there is no positive response to it, the plaintiff may request the court to issue a summons against the defendant. A *default summons* is used whenever the plaintiff is claiming a fixed sum of money. A *fixed date summons* is used either when there is a claim for money which includes an element of damages to be assessed by the court, or a non-money remedy, such as an injunction, the possession of land or the recovery of goods. In this text we shall be examining the procedure which applies to a default summons, because this type of summons is most often used by the businessman. The procedure for a fixed date summons is broadly similar.

The plaintiff must file a request for the issue of a default summons, together with the summons itself at the County Court office. In addition he must provide two copies of the *particulars of claim*, one for the court and one for the defendant. In the particulars of claim the plaintiff must specify the legal basis of his claim and remedy which he seeks. He will also include a brief description of the material facts surrounding his claim. The particulars of the claim and summons will be served on the defendant by the court together with forms on which the defendant can either make an admission and a proposal for payment or put forward a defence and/or a counter-claim.

Judgment in default

If the defendant fails to respond within 14 days of receiving the summons the plaintiff may request the court to enter judgment against him. The plaintiff has in effect won his case by default, and can enforce the judgment against the defendant if he fails to pay.

Admission and offer of payment

On receiving the summons however the defendant may have decided to admit the claim in part or in full, and make an offer to pay the amount due either immediately or by instalments. If the defendant requests time to pay, he must provide the court with details of his financial circumstances and the exact terms of his proposals for payment. These will be forwarded by the court to the plaintiff, who will decide whether or not to accept the offer of payment. If he accepts, judgment will be entered in the terms of the agreement. If the plaintiff does not accept the defendant's proposals, the court will fix a date for a hearing before the district judge for a decision on the terms of payment. The decision of the district judge will be binding on both parties and judgment will be entered.

If the defendant fails to keep up payment, enforcement action may be taken against him by the plaintiff.

Defence

If the defendant believes he has a valid defence to the plaintiff's claim, he must file particulars of the defence in the County Court Office within 14 days of receiving the summons, in order to prevent judgment being entered against him in default.

If he feels that he has insufficient information about the plaintiff's claim to set out his defence in full or if he does not have time to prepare a full defence, but still wishes to defend the action, he may lodge a *holding defence* with the court within the time period and give *further and better particulars* of his defence at a later date when he is requested to do so by the plaintiff. A holding defence is simply a statement denying any indebtedness to the plaintiff.

Activity

Visit or write to your local County Court in order to obtain copies of the current free leaflets or booklet designed to help sue for small claims without the aid of a lawyer. Draw up particulars of claim based on the facts given in the assignment A Good Little Runner at the end of this chapter, for use by Mary Walsh in her claim against Tony Livingstone. Draw up a defence for Tony Livingstone.

Counter-claim

A counter-claim may be made by the defendant at the same time as he lodges his defence with the court. In a counter-claim he is making a separate claim for damages against the plaintiff, which will survive as a separate action if the original claim by the plaintiff is withdrawn. Where circumstances permit, a counter-claim should be made as it provides a useful bargaining tool in negotiations for settlement.

Further and better particulars

If either of the parties feels that he has insufficient information relating to the claim or defence of the other, he may, within prescribed time, request further and better particulars of the other party's claim or defence. The other party must then supply the information. The County Court Rules make provision for this so that each party may know the exact case which he has to answer, and neither may be taken by surprise at a late stage in the proceedings. In this way the process helps to narrow down the issues and highlight the points of difference between the parties.

Pre-trial review

Once the initial exchange of information about each party's side of the case has taken place, the court will fix a date for a pre-trial review. This will be held in private before the district judge. If the plaintiff fails to attend, the action may be struck out or discontinued on the order of the court. If the defendant does not attend the plaintiff may be able to obtain judgment if he can prove his case.

If both parties are present the district judge will seek to clarify the points at issue, if there is any doubt about them. He may also explore the possibility of a settlement at this stage. If the action is to go to trial, the district judge will give directions to the parties as to the things that they must do in order to prepare the case for trial. Directions given by the district judge at the pre-trial review may include orders that:

(i)   further and better particulars of the claim or the defence must be given;

(ii) each party prepare lists of the documents in their possession and exchanges them;

(iii) each party allow the other to inspect the listed documents, and take copies of them, a process known as *discovery of documents;*

(iv) the parties try to agree matters which are not disputed, to save the necessity and expense of proving them in court; and

(v)   the parties produce plans, photographs or experts reports, and try to agree on their contents.

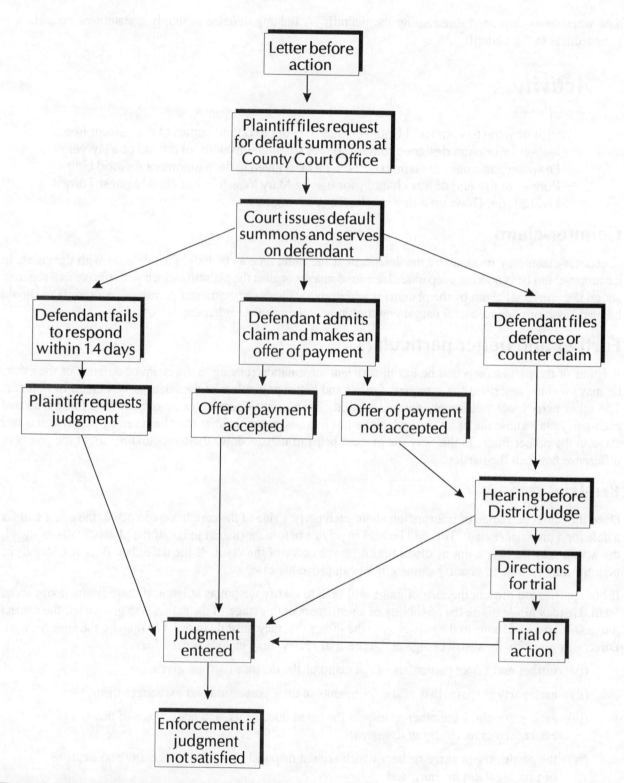

Figure 5.7 *Main Steps in a Default Action in the County Court*

Setting the case down for trial

When the directions given by the district judge at the pre trial review have been complied with, either party may apply to the court to fix a date for the trial. Once this has been fixed, the court will notify the parties, who must then complete their final preparations.

The trial

Many cases are settled on the doorstep of the courtroom before a trial takes place. This is because the pressure for settlement builds up to a peak when the parties are faced with the reality of a trial. They may be aware of some weakness in their case, or may doubt the ability of a key witness to appear credible and resolute in the face of cross examination. Even at this late stage considerable savings of costs can be made by settling the case.

The proceedings in a County Court trial are conducted in a formal manner. The plaintiff will have to present his evidence first, and any witnesses may be cross examined by the defence, or questioned by the judge. The plaintiff's lawyers can re-examine any of his witnesses, but must confine their questioning to matters already raised by them. Thus they could, for example, clarify any points which may have become confused in cross examination, or emphasise any important points which may have been obscured. Next it is the turn of the defence to present its evidence, and again there may be cross examination and re-examination.

Legal argument may then take place, followed by a summing up of each party's case. The judge will usually deliver judgment at the end of the trial, but may reserve judgment, particularly if there are difficult points of law to consider. If judgment is reserved the parties will have to attend court at a later date when judgment will be given.

Costs

As we noted above, the party who loses the case will have to pay the winner's costs, in addition to his own. He can however, challenge the amount of the other party's bill by applying to the court for a taxation of costs.

Appeal

An appeal can be made from a decision of the County Court to the Court of Appeal. The appeal may be on a question of law or a question of fact, and must be lodged within specified time limits. The costs involved in making an appeal will be very high and careful thought should be given before this step is taken.

Enforcement of a Judgment

If judgment is given against a defendant, payment is due immediately unless the court has made an order for payment by instalments or has otherwise postponed payment. If the judgment debtor does not make payment when it is due, steps can be taken to enforce the judgment. There are a number of alternative methods of enforcement, and it will be important to choose a method which will bear fruit having regard to the particular circumstances of the judgment debtor.

Oral examination

To assist in making an informed choice as to the method of enforcement, the party entitled to payment may make an application to the court for an order that the judgment debtor be orally examined before the court as to his means. The order may include provision for the production of books, accounts or other documents. The judgment debtor will be liable to imprisonment if he fails to attend. At the oral examination he will be cross examined on oath, as to his means and resources, by the judge and the applicant. It can be established, for example, whether he has any investments, bank accounts, savings or other assets such as a house or a car; or if he is working, the name and address of his employer and details of his salary and any other source of income. Armed with this information, a decision can be taken as to the most effective method of enforcement. The following are the principal methods.

Warrant of execution

A warrant of execution directs the County Court bailiff to seize any goods belonging to the judgment debtor, and to sell them to raise money to pay the creditor. It will be useful, at the oral examination, to establish what goods belong to the debtor and where they are located, in preparation for the issue of a warrant of execution.

Attachment of earnings

If it has been established that the judgment debtor has regular employment, the plaintiff can apply for an order under the Attachment of Earnings Act 1971. This is in effect a direction to the employer to deduct a specified sum from the debtor's wages each week, and pay it direct to the court, which will forward the money to the plaintiff.

Garnishee orders

If the plaintiff discovers, at the end of the oral examination, that the debtor is owed money by a third party, he may apply for a garnishee order. The effect of the order is to require the third party to pay the money direct to the plaintiff, or at least so much of it as will satisfy the judgment debt and costs. This type of order is particularly useful where, for example, the judgment debtor has money in a bank account or some other similar form of savings.

Charging order

The plaintiff can apply for a charging order on land held by the debtor or on any shares owned by him in a company. This gives him security for the judgment debt which can ultimately be enforced by the sale of the property in question.

Bankruptcy proceedings

A creditor will have grounds to petition for the bankruptcy of the debtor if a judgment debt of £750 or more remains outstanding after a warrant of execution has been issued but returned unsatisfied. In practice the threat of bankruptcy proceedings is a powerful stimulus to make a defaulting debtor find the money to pay the debt.

Arbitration

Arbitration is a means of resolving a dispute without recourse to the courts. An arbitrator is a person to whom both sides of the dispute put their case. He will consider the evidence and make a decision by applying ordinary rules of law to the facts before him. The decision of an arbitrator can be enforced in the courts, if necessary.

The legal framework within which arbitration operates is contained in the Arbitration Act 1950. This deals with matters such as the effect of arbitration agreements, awards, costs and enforcement. The Act does not lay down procedures for the conduct of arbitration, however, as these will vary according to the nature of the dispute and the way in which the parties wish it to be handled. In this respect, as we shall see, arbitration provides a more flexible method of resolving a dispute than proceedings in the ordinary courts.

Arbitration under codes of practice

The Director General of Fair Trading has a duty to encourage trade associations to promote voluntary codes of practice. The aim of these codes is the improvement of standards of service in particular sectors of business; and the laying down of methods for handling complaints about goods or services. Many codes set up low cost independent arbitration schemes for dealing with consumer complaints against traders who are members of the trade association which adopted the code. As we have seen, many professional associations also sponsor arbitration schemes as a substitute for litigation in relation to complaints against their members.

Activity

Find out further information about products and services covered by arbitration schemes by obtaining a copy of the free booklet "I am going to take it further!: Arbitration under Codes of Practice". This may be available from your public library, Citizens Advice Bureau, or local authority consumer protection unit. Alternatively it can be obtained directly from The Office of Fair Trading, Field House, Bream's Buildings, London EC4A 1PR.

Arbitration in the County Court

A claim for £1000 or less in the County Court, if defended, will automatically be referred to arbitration under the small claims procedure. Under this procedure the deterrent of being saddled with the opposing party's costs in the event of losing the case does not apply. The Court has only limited power to award costs, for example where the unreasonable conduct of one party causes expense to the other.

A County Court arbitration hearing usually takes place in private before an arbitrator without the formalities associated with a full trial. The arbitrator will usually be the County Court district judge but any other suitable person may be appointed if both parties agree. The procedure is designed to encourage people making small claims to handle their own cases without the assistance of a lawyer.

If the amount in dispute exceeds £1000, the matter can still be dealt with as an arbitration if both parties agree or if the court so orders on the application of one of the parties. It is possible to object to the use of arbitration, even for claims under £1000, in any of the following circumstances:

(a)   where the case involves a difficult question of law or an exceptionally complex question of fact;

(b)   where one of the parties is accused of fraud or deliberate dishonesty;

(c)   where the parties both agree that normal court proceedings shall apply;

(d)   where it would be unreasonable for the claim to be heard as an arbitration having regard to its subject matter or the interests of any other person likely to be affected, for example where the decision will, in practice, create a precedent which will be followed in a number of similar cases.

Where a dispute is dealt with by way of arbitration in the County Court, the hearing will usually be informal and strict rules of evidence will not apply. The arbitrator may adopt any method of proceeding which he considers to be convenient, so long as it affords a fair and equal opportunity to each party to present his case. The case could be dealt with by an exchange of documents for example rather than a hearing with the parties present in person.

Arbitration clauses in contracts

Many standard from contracts contain an arbitration clause. This is an agreement to submit any differences or disputes which may arise in relation to the contract to arbitration. An example of such a clause can be found in the standard form contract contained in Chapter 4. Condition 14 of the agreement gives the parties the power to choose arbitration as a means of resolving any dispute. Some standard form contracts contain conditions under which any dispute must be submitted to arbitration. This can be done by adopting the wording of an arbitration clause which was held to be valid in the case of *Scott v. Avery* 1856. Under such a clause the right of action in court only arises after an award has been made by an arbitrator.

Subsequent agreement to arbitration

Even where there is no arbitration clause in the contract, parties to a dispute can agree at any time to submit the dispute to arbitration. The agreement may be made after the dispute has arisen and any agreement to submit to arbitration operates as a binding contract.

An arbitration agreement comes into being where two or more persons agree that an existing or potential dispute between them shall be resolved in a legally binding way by one or more persons in a judicial manner. Under s. 32 of the Arbitration Act 1950 an arbitration agreement must be in writing. If an arbitrator is appointed under a verbal agreement he will usually invite the parties to enter into a written agreement, in order to bring the arbitration within the 1950 Act. The arbitration agreement may incorporate such matters as the method of appointment of the arbitrator and the procedural rules governing the conduct of the arbitration.

The unique features of arbitration

Where the parties have not laid out in advance any particular procedure, there is a large degree of flexibility in the way in which the arbitration can be concluded. With the agreement of the parties the arbitrator can adopt whatever procedure appears most appropriate. The case may be decided upon documentary evidence alone; or documents and written representations; or a site visit; or the examination of any goods which are at the centre of a dispute. Alternatively there could be a formal hearing of the case with expert witnesses and lawyers in attendance.

In addition to the flexibility of choosing an appropriate procedure, there is flexibility in relation to the location and time of any hearing. The arbitration can be heard at any place which the parties choose. This could, for example, be in a location near the site of the dispute, and take place at the weekend thereby avoiding the loss of working hours.

In a dispute involving matters of a technical nature, an appropriately qualified independent expert could be appointed as arbitrator. This may enable a swifter conclusion to be reached in the case.

Probably the single most important factor in the mind of a businessman who chooses to refer a dispute to arbitration is that the proceedings are totally private. Adverse publicity can therefore be avoided, and so can the public disclosure of confidential information or trade secrets. The advantage of privacy may be lost, however, if there is an appeal against the decision of the arbitrator.

Appeal against the decision of an arbitrator can be made on the grounds either that the proceedings were not conducted fairly, or that the decision contains an error of law. An arbitration award will only be set aside on grounds of unfairness if the arbitrator has failed to comply with the rules of natural justice. These are that he must be, and be seen to be, impartial and unbiased; and that each party to the dispute must be given a fair opportunity to present his own case and to answer the case put forward by his opponent.

One of the parties may suspect that the arbitrator has made an error of law in reaching his decision, but be unable to confirm that suspicion because the arbitrator has not given full reasons for his decision. In such a case that party can apply, under s.1 of the Arbitration Act 1979, to the High Court for an order requiring the arbitrator to give full reasons.

Arbitration is often a less expensive method of resolving business disputes than litigation in the ordinary courts. In some cases, however, where formal procedures are adopted, arbitration may actually be more expensive than litigation. One reason for this is that the cost of the actual hearing must be borne by the parties. This will include, for example, the arbitrator's fee, the cost of accommodation for the hearing, and of recording evidence. In most cases these costs are more than compensated for by the speed with which a case can be dealt with, the informality of procedures and the fact that the arbitrators award is final and cannot, except in the limited circumstances discussed above, be the subject of an appeal.

One of the disadvantages of arbitration is that an arbitrator, having reached a decision and made an award, in unable to enforce that award. In the event that the award is not complied with, it can only be enforced by taking action in the courts. The agreement to submit a claim to arbitration is a binding contract and failure to comply with an arbitrator's award is a breach of contract which can be the subject of proceedings in the County Court or the High Court. A simple procedure for enforcement is provided for in s.26 of the 1950 Act. Under this the award may be enforced in the same way as a court order with the permission of the High Court. This involves an application to the High Court for the enforcement of the arbitration award. If the court is satisfied that the award is valid it will enter judgment in favour of the successful party. The award can then be enforced in the same way as any other judgment of the court.

Unit Test Questions

1. In what ways are the rights of purchaser of goods different when he buys from a private seller as opposed to buying from a person selling in the course of business?

2. When is a sale of goods made by description?

3. What does the expression merchantable quality mean?

4. Where a buyer has made known to a seller a particular purpose for which he requires goods, in what circumstances will the seller not be liable where the goods supplied are not reasonably fit for that purpose?

5. What terms are implied in a contract for the sale of goods by sample?

6. In what circumstances does the Unfair Contract Terms Act 1977 allow a seller of goods to limit or exclude liability for breach of the implied terms relating to quality and description?

7. When will a buyer of goods deal as a consumer?

8. State three of the factors which will be taken into account by a court in deciding whether an exclusion clause is reasonable.

9. When and why will a statement indicating that the statutory rights of a consumer are not affected appear on the packaging of goods?

10. State two important differences between product liability claims in negligence and under Part 1 Consumer Protection Act 1987.

11. What types of damage can not be sued for in a product liability claim (a) in negligence and (b) under Part 1 Consumer Protection Act 1987?

12. What is the meaning and effect of the res ipsa loquitur rule?

13. When does the debtor under a consumer credit agreement have the right of cancellation?

14. State three factors which may be taken into account in determining whether a credit bargain is extortionate.

15. What is a debtor's liability on termination of a consumer credit agreement?

16. State three terms which are implied into a contract to supply services in the course of a business.

17. What are the differences between contractual negligence and third party negligence?

18. What is a package under the Package Travel Regulations 1992, and why is the definition important?

19. What information must be supplied to a consumer before a package holiday contract is concluded?

20. How have the Package Travel Regulations altered the liability of the tour operator for injury suffered by the consumer on holiday?

21. In what circumstances is it necessary to register under the Data Protection Act 1984?

22. What powers does the Data Protection Registrar have in order to enforce compliance with the Data Protection Principles?

23. What rights are given to data subjects under the Data Protection Act?

24. What are the main steps to be taken by the plaintiff and defendant in bringing a case before the County Court?

25. Briefly describe four methods of enforcing a judgment of the Count Court.

26 What are the principal advantages and disadvantages of arbitration over proceedings in the civil courts?

27. What factors ought to be taken into account before deciding to sue in the County Court?

Assignment   *A Good Little Runner*

You are a voluntary worker at your local citizens advice bureau. You work at the bureau on a part-time basis. Each month the organiser of the bureau arranges a case study meeting for all workers, in which one of them is asked to present a case study based upon an actual problem he or she has actually encountered in the bureau, and this month your turn has arrived to give the presentation. You have decided to tell the story of the sale of a motor vehicle, which you had to deal with earlier in the year. The case centred upon a Mr. Tony Livingstone. The facts were as follows:

Tony Livingstone is in full time employment as a clerk in a firm of turf accountants. His spare time activity is the acquisition of motor cars which he fixes up, runs around in for a while, and resells at a profit. He usually has two or three cars at any given time, and at the time in question had sold twelve vehicles through the classified columns of his local newspaper during the previous eighteen months, in each case giving the impression that he was selling the family car.

Livingstone bought a 1984 Ford Escort for £800 in February. The bodywork of the car was thin and rusty in places, and he repaired it using plaster filler and fibreglass patches. He repainted the car completely after smoothing down the repairs. He advertised the car for sale at £1,600, describing it as "a good little runner, in excellent condition for its age."

The advertisement was replied to by Mary Walsh. After a test drive and some negotiation she agreed to buy the escort for £1,450.

Mary became extremely dissatisfied with the car. Within a month of purchase the plaster filler and fibre glass patches started showing through the paintwork. More seriously, she discovered that the car was in fact two halves of different cars welded together, the front being part of a 1984 Escort and the rear part of a slightly older model. The mechanic in her local garage, whose examination of the car revealed this, told her that the car was unroadworthy because of it.

Mary responded by writing the following letter:

```
Dear Mr. Livingstone,

About the car you sold me five weeks ago. You said it was a good little runner.
Well I took it to the garage the other day and the mechanic told me it's total
rubbish - made up from bits of other cars! The rust is coming through and its quite
obvious you just bodged it up. You said it was your family car for years. You must
have known it had been in an accident or something. Anyway, I've been round to the
trading standards people at the council. They say you'll have to give me my money
back. And they're looking into it further. They've heard of you before and you
could get prosecuted. I'll be coming round to your house on Saturday morning to
bring the car back so you better have my money ready.
```

Mary Walsh

```
Mary Walsh.
```

Mary had not in fact been to the council. A friend had suggested that she should mention the trading standards department in her letter. When she arrived at Tony Livingston's house on the Saturday she was met with abuse and threats. In a distressed state she was interviewed by you later that day, when you advised her of the legal position.

Task

Prepare a handout for your fellow workers in which you clearly analyse for them the extent of Tony Livingstone's civil and criminal liability in respect of the sale of the Ford Escort. The handout will be given to them after you have given your presentation.

Index